Kiowa Ethnogeography

Kiowa Ethnogeography

WILLIAM C. MEADOWS

UNIVERSITY OF TEXAS PRESS 🐃 AUSTIN

Copyright © 2008 by the University of Texas Press
All rights reserved
Printed in the United States of America
First edition, 2008

Requests for permission to reproduce material from this work should be sent to:
    Permissions
    University of Texas Press
    P.O. Box 7819
    Austin, TX 78713-7819
    www.utexas.edu/utpress/about/bpermission.html

⊗ The paper used in this book meets the minimum requirements of
ANSI/NISO Z39.48-1992 (R1997) (Permanence of Paper).

Library of Congress Cataloging-in-Publication Data
Meadows, William C., 1966–
Kiowa ethnogeography / William C. Meadows. — 1st ed.
p. cm.
Includes bibliographical references and index.
ISBN 978-0-292-72160-9
ISBN 0-292-72160-9
1. Kiowa Indians—Social life and customs. 2. Names, Geographical—Social
aspects—Great Plains. 3. Cultural property—Great Plains. 4. Geographical
perception—978.004/97492. 5. Great Plains—Social life and customs. I. Title.
E99.K5M43 2008
978.004'97492—dc22
2008031022

*To the Kiowa people
for sharing their homeland with me.*

Contents

List of Maps

Pronunciation Guide

With the exception of quoted historical spellings, all Kiowa names and vocabulary have been standardized in the Parker P. McKenzie Kiowa Orthography. Because Kiowa is a tonal language, syllable pitch and length must be
marked for accuracy. The McKenzie orthography was developed by a Kiowa
who was intimately familiar with the subtleties of the Kiowa language,
and I find it to be the most accurate, thorough, consistent, and easy-to-use
orthography for writing Kiowa. The McKenzie orthography was designed
using the English alphabet so that it could be typed using a typewriter,
with diacritical marks added by hand. Today, computers and linguistic font
software programs allow both to be typewritten by computer.

Each Kiowa syllable can be pronounced in five possible ways. The McKenzie system uses five different diacritical marks in ten possible combinations to indicate pitch, length, and nasal quality. The following examples
use the letter *a* to demonstrate these diacritical marks. There are two ways
of marking pitch: á indicates a rising or short pitch (high) and à indicates
a descending or short pitch (low). Horizontal markings above letters indicate length, with ā̆ indicating a rising (long) or high pitch (long); horizontal
markings beneath letters mark a nasal pronunciation, a̰; and a circumflex
mark over a letter indicates a circumflexed or rising and falling pitch, â.
These five forms can be combined to produce ten possible pronunciations
of a syllable: á (high pitch short), à (low pitch short), ā̆ (high pitch long),
ā̀ (low pitch long), and â (circumflex). Each vowel can be also have a nasal
marking, such as a̰, indicating high pitch short, nasal, and so on. This IPA
alphabet can be downloaded as the SILmanuscriptreg font and created by
combining the Shift command (in Word 9.0 for Macintosh computers)
with the numbers 2, 3, 4, or 6, and an equals sign (=) without depressing
the Shift key to create the nasal mark.

Fourteen of the twenty-two consonants in the English alphabet (b, d, g, h, k, l, m, n, p, s, t, w, y, z) correspond to and are pronounced relatively the same as those in Kiowa. The remaining consonants in English (c, f, j, q, r, v, x) as they are pronounced in English have no direct correlation to Kiowa sounds. In addition, the consonants k, p, s, and t each have two additional variations, soft and plosive, in Kiowa for which English has no counterpart. These six consonants (c, f, j, q, v, x) were reassigned to represent other consonants in Kiowa, resulting in the following four clusters or related sounds:

f = a soft "p" sound
p = a regular "p" sound
v = a plosive "p" sound

ch = a soft aspirated "s" sound
s = a regular "s" sound
x = a plosive "s" sound, like an aspirated "ts"

j = a soft "t" sound, as in Jáifègàu
t = a regular "t" sound
th = a plosive "t" sound

c = a soft "k" sound
k = a regular k sound
q = a plosive "k" sound, like an aspirated "k"

Vowels—The six Kiowa vowels are much like their English counterparts except the Kiowa vowel a, which falls midway in sound between the *a* in "act" and the *a* in "arm." Unlike English vowels, which can have more than one pronunciation (*a* in the words "a," "arm," and "meat"), there is only one basic sound for each Kiowa vowel. There are six Kiowa vowels, each with a single pronunciation (in parentheses): e ("ay"), a ("ah"), au ("aw"), u ("ee"), o ("oh"), and u ("woo"). Kiowa has four diphthongs (syllables containing multiple vowels): ai ("ah-ee"), aui ("aw-ee"), oi ("oh-ee"), and ui ("woo-ee"), with the vowel i ("ee") making up the second element of the diphthong. Although Kiowa vowels and diphthongs are affected in varying frequency by nasalization, vowel quality or length, and pitch accent or accentuation, they do not veer from their respective sounds.

W and Y Sounds—U ("woo") occurs in Kiowa syllables only after the consonants g, k, c, and q, and in every occurrence the "w" sound always falls before the vowel u when voiced, but because it is a constant, and to reduce repetitive spelling, the "w" sound is retained in pronunciation but omitted in written Kiowa: thus, gu ("gwoo"), gui ("gwoo-ee"), ku ("kwoo"), kui ("kwoo-ee"), cu ("cwoo-ee"), cui ("cwoo-e"), qu ("qwoo"), and qui ("qwoo-ee").

When the consonants g, k, c, and q are the first letter in a syllable and are followed by the vowels a ("ah") and ai ("ah-ee"), these syllables are always pronounced as if a "y" were inserted between the consonant and the vowel. These are thus pronounced as follows: ga ("gyah"), gai ("gyah-ee"), ca ("cyah"), cai ("cyah-ee"), and so on. Because it is a constant, and to reduce repetitious spelling, the "y" sound is retained in pronunciation but omitted in written Kiowa. A few words, mostly of foreign origin, occur without the "y" sound; they are indicated by the presence of an apostrophe, as in C'aiwau ("Cai-wau," not "Cyah-ee-wau"), the Comanche pronunciation of Kiowa. For a complete account of the McKenzie orthography, see Meadows and McKenzie (2001).

Acknowledgments

Today, more than half of all Native Americans live in urban settings outside their tribal reservations or allotted communities. To understand how contemporary Kiowa relate to their geography and tribal community and how they experience the sense of a homeland, I interviewed a variety of Kiowa of different ages, religious focus, and residential settings. My consultants included individuals who had lived their entire life in the Kiowa community, or who were born in the Kiowa community but later moved to urban settings, or who were born outside the Kiowa community but returned to the community to live, or who were born in the Kiowa community, moved away for extended periods of time (mostly for jobs), and then returned.

I would like to acknowledge and thank several individuals. My late adopted uncle and Kiowa linguist, Parker P. McKenzie (1897–1999), provided many place names, information on Kiowa geographic forms and geography, and considerable linguistic assistance in this work, including help in translating Mooney's (1896, 1898) lists of Kiowa place names. All Kiowa lexicon is arranged in the McKenzie orthography (Meadows and McKenzie 2001) and has been checked for both grammatical and semantic accuracy. The names and associated histories we recorded and the trips we made together to Saddle Mountain, Elk Creek, Anadarko, the American Indian Exposition, Kiowa Ghost Dance sites, and elsewhere were memorable learning experiences. Atwater Onco took me on a tour of Saddle Mountain, Cutthroat Gap, Elk Creek, and the Hobart area in 1993. In 1993 and 2004, Dr. Jack Haley gave me thoroughly informative tours of his ranch and the Cutthroat Mountain site. Jake Ahtone, Fred Tsoodle, Christina Hunt Simmons, Delores Toyebo Harragarra, and Kenny Harragarra provided me with valuable information about Rainy Mountain Church, the second Kiowa Ghost Dance site located on Mrs. Harragarra's mother's allotment, and other named Kiowa sites. Vanessa Jennings showed me

many places around Redstone and Fort Cobb that held cultural and historical importance for both the Kiowa and Apache. Several other elders provided knowledge from their respective Kiowa communities, including Ger-
trude Yeahquo Hines (Meers), Ina Paddlety Chalepah (Buzzard Creek), Ina
Aunko Miller (Saddle Mountain), Gus Palmer, Sr. (Gawky Creek), Harry
Domebo (Stecker), Rev. Bob Pinezaddleby (Alden), Rev. David Paddlety
(Redstone), Atwater Onco and Ernestine Kauahquo Kauley (Hobart), and
George and Marjorie Tahbone (Mountain View). Anne Yeahquo showed me
her great-grandmother's allotment, Seven Sisters Creek, and other areas
around Meers. Anne Yeahquo, Dennis Zotigh, Al Bronaugh, Kent Sanmann, and other Kiowa graciously shared with me their views on the Kiowa
community and on living outside it.

Park manager Wanda Olszewski gave me an insightful tour of Hueco
Tanks and Comanche and Escape caves. Jim Coombs, associate professor of
library administration at Missouri State University, was most helpful with
the university's map collection and designed the maps for this work. I also
offer sincere thanks to Kent Sanmann, a Kiowa and fellow student while at
the University of Oklahoma. We collected and shared Kiowa place names
with one another and had a good time discussing the subject in the early
1990s. Finally, I would like to acknowledge Steven Schnell, whom Kent
Sanmann and I met at the University of Oklahoma just prior to his summer research on Kiowa geography in 1992. As the first in-depth studies
on Kiowa geography (Schnell 1994, 2000), his works have shaped and
stimulated my inquiries in numerous ways.

Because the Kiowa and Comanche shared a large territory and frequently interacted in a variety of activities, such as raiding parties, encampments, and Sun Dances, Daniel Gelo's work on Comanche place names
was especially helpful in providing data on a neighboring group for comparison with the Kiowa. Kelley and Francis and Keith Basso also stimulated my thinking concerning place names and how communities interact
with such locales. I also benefited from the exchange of ideas at the 2005
Plains Indian Museum Seminar (Native Land and the Peoples of the Great
Plains) at Cody, Wyoming. I offer sincere gratitude to Carl and Vanessa
Jennings, my adopted and host family, and to Delores Harragarra and her
son Kenny, who provided me with a home and much assistance during
the fieldwork for this project. Benjamin Kracht shared his copy of the 1935
Santa Fe Laboratory of Anthropology notes with me in 1989. Dr. Daniel
Gelo and Dr. Kracht read the manuscript thoroughly, and the queries, criti-
cisms, supplemental data, and suggestions they offered helped improve it.
Dr. Candace Greene of the Smithsonian Institution brought the Chaddle-
Kaungy-Ky map to my attention, assisted me in obtaining images of it,

and read and offered suggestions regarding Chapter 4. Linea Sundstrom enthusiastically shared her data on northern Plains Kiowa place names, which allowed me to check and supplement my own data. Delores Toyebo Harragarra read and commented on a draft of this manuscript. Kenny Harragarra accompanied me on trips through Oklahoma, Texas, and New Mexico, and read and commented on a draft of Chapter 4. A shorter version of this chapter was published in 2006 in the *Great Plains Quarterly;* I thank both Candace Greene and Kenny Harragarra for their thoughts on the material. Finally, I thank Theresa J. May, Lynne Chapman, and the University of Texas Press staff for their help with this work.

Having grown up in a rural community on a large farm, I have a strong sense of place and attachment to land and to particular geographic sites. I have always liked to be out on the land, and whereas many individuals look at land and ponder what it can be developed into, I consider what events have occurred there and hope that it remains as natural as possible. Although I have been blessed to know many special sites in Oklahoma, North America, and Asia, none will ever surpass my family farm in southern Indiana. Academia has taken me away from the area I consider my "homeland." Although I am able to visit periodically, the lack of daily interaction with this piece of land out of professional necessity is a constant personal struggle for me. And so I echo what Basso wrote: "I hope that those who thrive on attachments to places will find value in this account of how others do the same" (1996:xvi). Many of the views I discovered and that I describe in this work on the Kiowa parallel those I feel for my family's land and other areas in southern Indiana. If I can convey a sense of the history, respect, love, and responsibility that the Kiowa hold for their homeland to the reader, then I have succeeded in my endeavor.

Kiowa Ethnogeography

Introduction

This book explores the ethnogeography, or place names and the cultural and historical knowledge associated with them, of the Kiowa. Except for a few English versions and translations of Kiowa place names, most are un-known to non-Kiowa and even to many Kiowa. Studies of Oklahoma place names (Gould 1933; Shirk 1965) include only a few entries associated with the Kiowa, primarily those related to the post-allotment Anglo division of reservation lands in 1901 and the formation of towns and post offices. Only the names of a few mountains, streams, and historical sites are recorded. Reflecting on the mixture of Indian and non-Indian names in America, Gould (1933:14) wrote, "I found that Indian Territory names were chiefly of four kinds; namely Indian names, English translations of Indian names, English names and French names." Many existing Indian place names were determined more by Anglo land developments (counties, cities, post offices) or by the increasing prominence of the military, railroad, and cattle industries than by native associations.

The major work on Kiowa geography (Schell 1994) lists only a few of the better known Kiowa sites. U.S. Geological Survey 7.5-minute topographic maps, state gazetteers (DeLorme 1998a, 1998b, 1998c, 1998d), and other maps similarly show only a few of the best-known geographic locales of importance to the Kiowa, such as Medicine Lodge River, Rainy Mountain, and Saddle Mountain. These sites are unknown to most people outside southwestern Oklahoma, and even when local non-Indians are aware of the sites they often do not know the Kiowa's relationship to them. This body of knowledge is quickly disappearing in the Kiowa community. Although a few places are known by virtually all Kiowa, with the rapid decline of the Kiowa language even tribal elders know a limited number of Kiowa place names, the places themselves, and their history. Because place names are now more commonly heard in English translation than in Kiowa, efforts to preserve this genre of information are timely.

In gathering data for this book, I examined published sources and unpublished archival records, conducted fieldwork with Kiowa elders from 1989 to 2007, and made field trips to Oklahoma, Kansas, Texas, Wyoming, Colorado, and New Mexico. I have been able to find information on 427 place names for 444 locations, including 256 place names for 272 locations in the Kiowa language and 171 modern place names for 172 locations in English (six of which have counterparts in Kiowa) that were created by Kiowa or refer to them. I use these names throughout the book to demonstrate categories of place names and culturally and historically important locales and events.

In undertaking this work, I had several goals. An important one was to retrieve and preserve place names and their contexts for the Kiowa and others, and then consider what can be learned about Kiowa ethnogeography from place names. Thus, my study came to combine inventory, preservation, ethnography, anthropology, history, and linguistics. Many Indian place names are unique and speak directly to the circumstances of their naming: although there are numerous towns named Millersburg, Salem, or Washington, there is only one Anadarko, Gotebo, or Komalty. And although most Euroamerican place names are transplanted from earlier locales through commemorative naming and generally have little or no relation to their new address, Indian place names are more directly associated with the geography and human activities at the specific site (see Waterman n.d.-a in Thornton 1997:213–214).

This study also aims to preserve the core of this remaining body of knowledge. Kiowa elders are more secretive about favorite locations to gather wild plums or Indian perfume than they are about named places, and typically discussed named places freely. Today only the best-known named places are still known throughout the community, while many other locations that have been outside Kiowa control for several generations are no longer actively known. Nevertheless, even the older names of places no longer visited have entered the fabric of Kiowa society through oral history and written texts and have contributed to the Kiowa sense of a homeland. In pursuing this theme of ethnogeography throughout my work, I was concerned to learn from the Kiowa themselves how they viewed important locations in their history, and how those sites maintain a presence in their culture and demography. Geosacred sites in particular have become a source of contention in Indian–Anglo relations, yet they also offer a profound way to enter the Kiowa culture and an opportunity to grasp the nature of a living landscape as culture is practiced. These sites have shifted over time with the Kiowa's migrations over the centuries, and understanding the investment of a people in new landscapes seems critical to understanding broader themes of belonging to a particular society.

The five chapters of the book explore these various themes. Chapter 1 surveys the existing scholarship on American Indian or Native American ethnogeography, focusing on anthropological studies of American Indian, Plains Indian, and Kiowa ethnogeography.[1] The different classification schemes that have been applied to American Indian place names at one time or another generally tackle the linguistic forms of place names, or their grammatical meaning, and the concepts of intertribal land sharing, geography, and religion that are reified in place names. The data in this chapter range from the early 1700s to the present. Appendices at the end of the book list the place names discussed.

Chapter 2 takes up the geographic and historical content of Kiowa place names by looking at their relationship to personal names and to pictographic calendars, which name half-years according to significant events and are illustrated with symbolic drawings anchoring event to place. In this chapter I consider such prominent geographic and anthropological concepts as sacred geography (Walker 1988; Campbell and Foor 2004), cultural landscapes (Stoffle et al. 1997), and sacred islands (Sundstrom 2003). Using mainly eighteenth- and nineteenth-century data, my discussion concludes with a brief statistical analysis of the basis of Kiowa place names during this period.

Chapter 3 turns to the Kiowa concept of a homeland and how this concept has changed with migration from the northwestern to the southern plains, confinement of the Kiowa to the reservation (1867–1901), allotment (1901), and the subsequent growth of communities and outmigration for work. This chapter examines a wide range of topics and their role in the Kiowa relationship to land, including reservation and allotment experiences, Kiowa communities, the concept of an allotment as a home place, Indian towns, remaining traditional cultural forms (arbors, sweat lodges, tipis), modern sites of importance (homes, churches, cemeteries, schools, dance grounds), contemporary symbols of sovereignty (Indian Country, tribal offices, flags, license plates, gaming), the "invisible landscape," spiritual geography, and modern forms of art (painting, sculpture, literature).

Chapter 4 discusses Native American cartography as a specific written and drawn form of ethnogeography recorded by Indians themselves. In this chapter we look at a map drawn by Chaddle-kaung-ky or Black Goose, the only known existing Kiowa map, which dates to between 1893 and 1895. In pencil-drawn images on a square of muslin, the map shows the joint Kiowa, Comanche, and Apache (KCA) Reservation in Oklahoma Territory. More than 160 geographic locales are included, many with identifying labels in the form of pictographic images.

Chapter 5 considers contemporary Kiowa ethnogeography and its relationship to Kiowa culture and identity. From the discussion to this point, it is clear that despite migration and changes of residence, the Kiowa maintain a distinct sense of a homeland, now centered on dispersed allotted communities in southwest Oklahoma—the core area they still consider Kiowa Country. The Kiowa have also had a significant impact on the geography of southwestern Oklahoma and the surrounding southern plains from sites named by them or after them, although access to and protection of Native American religious sites may become an unavoidable issue in the future for the Kiowa. A quick comparison with Basso's work on the Cibecue Apache demonstrates similarities and differences in the ethnogeography of these two groups.

I have tried to take an emic (native or internal) view in the book, framing my discussions to present how Kiowa see and talk about their cultural geography. Some of the most poignant revelations about time and space came from my Kiowa consultants as we were casually driving around. I have also periodically reflected on how these issues relate to my personal experiences in both Kiowa and non-Indian communities as a means to help non-Indian readers relate to the Kiowa material presented here, as well as to stimulate their thoughts concerning their relationship to land, community, culture, and identity. I believe there is much to be learned from the Kiowa concerning this relationship.

All place names I collected in the course of my work, the basis for the name, the associated cultural historical significance, and geographic location data are listed by geographic form and in alphabetical order in the appendices. These lists show both old and new names and locations and show how the Kiowa concept of a homeland has shifted in both geographic basis and content. The place names also suggest the impact of Kiowa geography on large portions of the North American plains and modern America. While this collection by no means has every Kiowa place name, it does have the majority of those for which the Kiowa have had proper names in the Kiowa and English languages since the late 1800s.

Native American Ethnogeography and Research

NAMING PLACES is a cultural universal, a tool by which human groups identify, claim, and interact with their physical surroundings. Whether the name is linked to a base camp, a resource area, a historical event, a seasonal or annual migration, or a permanent residence, human groups use place names to distinguish and communicate about their physical surroundings. In turn, such communication promotes the more efficient organization of human activities. Because human activities are linked to geographic locales, much discourse among all peoples is spatially anchored by means of place names, which often appear in important narratives (Thornton 1997:220).

Places are named because they hold some degree of importance for a people. Thus, named places are part of a larger cultural and geographic landscape and are usually linked to stories, history, resources, or cultural activities. Whether we are mobile or sedentary, place names are also intimately linked to our sense of community, territory, and history—of what happened, where, and to whom. A sense of place, a sense of where one is from and where one belongs, is deeply linked to our connection to the past—to what happened in a specific place at a specific time in our personal history. As Keith Basso has written, "If place-making is a way of constructing the past, a venerable means of doing human history, it is also a way of constructing social traditions and, in the process, personal and social identities. We are, in a sense, the place-worlds we imagine" (1996:7).

Since the time of our earliest ancestors, human activities have become increasingly complex. Long before the emergence of written language systems and modern conceptions of history, place names served as enduring symbols and mnemonic devices that aided in planning future events and in remembering and imagining past events (Basso 1996:7). As demonstrated by the places we value—homes, local community sites, state and federal historical sites—and our economic pursuits, the importance of place in our visual, oral, and written traditions continues.

From the intimate relationship with their physical surroundings, Native American cultures have long possessed extensive knowledge of the areas they have traveled through and lived in. The history of a group's cultural-ecological relationship is reflected in the ethnogeographic toponyms or place names each group developed to give meaning to its physical surroundings. This detailed body of knowledge typically extended far beyond the group's home territory to include a vast area over which the group traveled, traded, conducted warfare, engaged in subsistence activities, or took up temporary residence. Indeed, many existing roads and travel routes in North and South America, as well as their modern place names, are based on older Indian and game trails (see Wilson 1919; Afable and Beeler 1997). When analyzed in their respective languages, place names offer a wealth of information on the culture, history, political relations, attitudes, and values of the people that created them and continue to use them.

Many place names reflect the cultural ecology of a particular region, emphasizing major geological forms, resource locales, and patterns of human land use—in other words, the ethnoecological history of a specific area. Often highly descriptive, names in this genre reflect detailed knowledge of an area and suggest how groups perceive, communicate, and make use of their surroundings. The clustering of place names in some areas points to the cultural importance those areas held for a population at particular times, especially for residential, subsistence, political, and ritual activities. Place names often figure significantly in a group's oral traditions and thus become a source of knowledge and instruction and a focus of ethnic identity. In turn, the antiquity of place names often reflects the ongoing cultural and spiritual importance of the named places through time (Afable and Beeler 1997:185–186).

The more important a geographic location is to a group of people, the more likely it is to be named. Place names suggest that certain locales are associated with knowledge deemed necessary to remember, and so aid in conveying knowledge from one person to another. Although oral accounts have to be recited from time to time to ensure their succession, they need not always be told in their entirety. Similar to Kelley and Francis's (1994:189–191) concept of compression, if oral accounts continue in a culture, condensed or abbreviated versions of a story typically develop over time. The degree of detail recited and the time of occurrence that continue in oral texts often diverge, leading to different versions and a melding of mythical and historical details. As a place name increases in impor-

6   KIOWA ETHNOGEOGRAPHY

tance, the mention of it alone can summon numerous associated meanings without further explanation. Some examples from the Euroamerican past are Bastogne, Gettysburg, Golgotha, and Rome, all of which activate much larger emotional and intellectual constructs. Place names encapsulate the knowledge of social groups and function as a shorthand by which these groups' experiences can be shared and disseminated. They also allow knowledge about a place to be conveyed without the repeated use of cumbersome and lengthy descriptions, and they neatly bridge gaps in space and time (Kelley and Francis 1994:49). Place names add an important component to the human linguistic trait of displacement, or the ability to talk about something in the past and/or future without oneself being present for the events discussed (Salzmann 1998:27). As Basso (1988:121) has noted for the Western Apache, place names may accomplish multiple important social actions simultaneously, such as producing a mental image of a particular geographic locale, evoking or referencing prior texts such as historical sagas, affirming the value and validity of ancestral wisdom, and so on. Some Apache place names may accomplish up to eight such functions simultaneously.

American Indian ethnogeography has its own taxonomy, and numerous categories exist. Gulliford (2000:70–91) identifies at least ten forms, including (1) religious sites associated with oral tradition and origin stories, such as locales associated with creation stories or clan migrations (the Choctaw Nanih Waiya or "The Hill of Origins"); (2) trails and pilgrimage routes (the Ute Trail in Colorado); (3) traditional areas for gathering resources such as acorns, fish, sage, mineral paints, or stone (Pipestone National Monument in Minnesota); (4) offering sites in the form of altars and shrines (Waconda Springs in Kansas); (5) vision quest and other individual-use sites (Bear Butte in South Dakota); (6) group ceremonial sites, including locations for dance, song, and sweat lodge ceremonies (Sun Dance sites); (7) ancestral habitation sites (Pueblo ruins, Plains Indian tipi rings, Northwest Coast clan house sites); (8) rock art of a ceremonial or historical nature (petroglyphs and pictographs); (9) burial sites, including individual, community, and massacre sites (the Marias River in Montana, Wounded Knee in South Dakota); and (10) observatories and calendar sites (Fajada Butte at Chaco Canyon in New Mexico, Medicine Wheel in Wyoming, Serpent Mound in Ohio).

Many American Indian cultures distinguish among types of places, often in relation to the presence or absence of human impact. Places in which evidence of human use has been minimal (no disturbance of form) include mountains, hills, bluffs, concavities, canyons, rock outcrops, formations of discolored stone or soil, streams, springs, concentrations of flora or fauna, mineral deposits, places where rocks and air produce echoes or sounds, and flat, open areas. Places where humans have left more lasting evidence of their activities include prehistoric ruins and village sites, rock art sites, territorial markers, battle sites, trails, trading posts, military forts, and religious sites such as Sun Dance encampments, cairns, burial sites, and vision quest sites. Some historic events, while not always leaving a visible impact, are deemed significant enough to merit a place name. Other sites, such as band encampment sites, graves, sweat lodges, settlers' homes, and hunting locales, may be so common that unless they are associated with a special event, they are not distinguished by name.

History of Place Name Research

ANTHROPOLOGICAL STUDIES

As we know from early European explorers' cartographic renderings of North America, aboriginal place names have long interested Euroamericans. Many of the earliest documentary sources are the written accounts of explorers and hand-drawn maps made by Native Americans and Europeans, some created from information provided by local native informants. Many current American toponyms for streams, lakes, parks, mountain ranges, cities, counties, and states come directly from the Native American populations that previously resided in the region, and may still reside there today. Yet place name studies exist for only a few North American regions, and they vary widely in research quality and in the number of associated tribes covered. Substantial place name studies in the Southwest, Arctic, and Subarctic have been undertaken over the past thirty years. Conversely, reliable works for the Northeast, Southeast, Plains, and Great Basin regions are relatively scarce, especially for some specific language groups, with extensive gaps in the knowledge base. Many county, state, and regional studies exist that often cut across geographic and linguistic borders (Afable and Beeler 1997:186–196).

Because place names form a distinct semantic domain in every language and are associated with rich bodies of geographic correlates and etymological histories, they have long been of interest to anthropologists (Basso 1996:76; Thornton 1997). Indian place names were important to early settlers, who frequently adopted translations of local tribal names as they familiarized themselves with the new lands they were attempting to settle. Many of these names continue, both as local folk names and as official place names in modern America. Schoolcraft's (1844) work on Iroquois place names and territory reflects the importance of this genre in American ethnology and anthropology from its earliest beginnings. Anthropological interest in native geography and place names was greatly stimulated by the work of Franz Boas, who studied physics and geography before shifting to ethnology. Early in his career, Boas expressed an interest in culture and environment, and he was instrumental in pioneering the study of cosmography, which he defined as a subfield of geography that was distinct from the physical sciences (Thornton 1997). Interested in applying geography to other fields of study, Boas (1887) argued for the preservation of a humanistic perspective while drawing analogies between physical and historical methods of inquiry. He also sought a dialectical approach that advocated the relationship between human thought and geographic phenomena as an ethnographic one (Thornton 1997:210–211). Impressed by the extensive geographic knowledge of the Baffin Island and Hudson Bay Eskimos, Boas (1901–1907) noted as early as 1900 that the investigation of geographic nomenclatures was one of the most promising ways to explore the "mental life" of Indian peoples. Eventually Boas incorporated ethnogeography and the study of place names in his approach to anthropology to reconstruct culture through an inductive method, by gathering systematic data on all aspects of a culture to arrive at the larger, more important patterns.

Edward Sapir, a student of Boas, recognized the value of understanding the relationship between language and environment as a means of exploring the geographic nomenclatures of cultures. Sapir (1912) similarly proposed that Indian vocabularies provided extensive insights into native conceptions of the natural world and what was considered significant in it. He argued that the physical environment is reflected in a group's language, but only insofar as it has been influenced by the group's social factors. He also maintained that of all of the dimensions of language, vocabulary, including place names, most reflected the "physical and social environment of its speakers." Like Boas, Sapir recognized that a group's place names marked not only the fauna and topographic features of the region but also "the interest of the people in such environmental features." His view of the relationship between environment and vocabulary remained relativistic, as he stated that "apart from the reflection of the environment in the vocabulary there is nothing in the language itself that can be shown to be directly associated with the environment" (Sapir 1912:227). Benjamin Whorf (Carroll 1956) and others later argued strongly that language shaped human views of the environment.

Other students of Boas took considerable interest in American Indian ethnogeography and place names, including Samuel Barrett, John P. Harrington, Alfred Kroeber, and Thomas Waterman. Harrington's 1916 work on Tewa place names is probably the most comprehensive account of the ethnogeography of any single American Indian group. Waterman's (1920, 1922, n.d.-a.) work on Pacific Coast groups from the Yurok in California to the Tlingit of Southeast Alaska, and on place naming in general, were also major contributions to the field. Waterman was aesthetically drawn to place names, attracted both by their descriptive or poetic quality and by their ability to relate the landscape to important aspects of culture such as food and resource acquisition, myth, the human body, and other conceptual categories. Waterman also noted several important patterns in place names. In particular, he noted that although Indians were prolific in their naming, they were also selective, naming only those aspects or things that were significant to them. For example, some groups might name certain aspects of a mountain or area but not the entire mountain or area itself. Waterman also noted the durability of place names, which often persisted despite migrations and linguistic changes. He brought rigor to the discipline, emphasizing the importance of recording the name, meaning, and precise location denoted by each place name, three key criteria that have remained the hallmarks of toponymic investigation. Place names are vulnerable to "folk etymologies," or post hoc descriptive explanations that seem credible but may or may not be accurate; a methodological approach helps sieve out later folk explanations. (Waterman may also have been the first anthropologist to develop a working typology of place names, such as descriptive names, names referring to food resources, and names referring to animals [Thornton 1997:213–217].)

Melville Jacobs's (1934) work on the Sahaptin-speaking groups of eastern Washington and Oregon led to recognition of the concept of a geographic text, a genre of oral history featuring an emphasis on the use of place names designed both to inform and to teach individuals cultural and historical information. Other students of Boas, such as Cora Du Bois and Frederica de Laguna, accorded place names and cosmology a significant place in their approaches to general ethnography. As Thornton (1997:217) notes, "These scholars saw indigenous geography and place names as key elements of culture that conveyed large amounts of information specific to that culture's language, environment, and world view" and incorporated them into their works as one of many methods to record ethnographic data.

Although focusing largely on word morphology, Boas's (1934, 1966) monographs on Kwakiutl geographic names, based on study of some 2,500 place names, supported his earlier belief that the study of place name systems could reveal much about the cognitive categories people use to organize and understand their environment. He also began to access the

KIOWA ETHNOGEOGRAPHY

structure of place names in relation to other aspects of Kwakiutl language, culture, and environment, concluding that "geographical terminology does not depend solely upon cultural interests, but is also influenced by linguistic structure" (Boas 1934:14). This assessment in turn served as a partial affirmation of the Sapir-Whorf or linguistic relativity hypothesis (Thornton 1997:211), that language determines worldview.

The development of American cultural geography and the idea of a cultural landscape as espoused by Carl Sauer, who taught at the University of California, Berkeley, from 1923 to 1975, greatly added to existing anthropological studies of American Indian geography. Dubbed "Berkeley cultural geography," the work of Sauer and his students included early studies on American Indian geography. Sauer and his students were also in frequent contact with Alfred Kroeber and Robert Lowie, both students of Boas and colleagues at Berkeley, who addressed geographic and environmental topics in their studies of American Indians. Thus, the approach to American Indian studies at Berkeley grew out of both geography and anthropology simultaneously (Rundstrom et al. 2000:87).

Since that time a body of work by students of Sauer and other geographers has gradually emerged (Rundstrom et al. 2000). After Boas, anthropological studies of place names and ethnogeography began to decrease just before World War II. Aside from a few articles in the 1950s, a notable report on Iroquois place names by Floyd Lounsbury in 1960, and de Laguna's 1972 monograph on the Tlingit, the number of anthropological studies on ethnogeography plummeted. As Basso (1996:43) observed, "The study of American Indian place-name systems has fallen on hard times. Once a viable component of anthropology in the United States, it has virtually ceased to exist, the inconspicuous victim of changing intellectual fashions and large amounts of ethnographic neglect." A. Irving Hallowell in the mid-1950s provided a link between the work of the Boasian historical-particularists and later scholars that focused on cognitive and symbolic studies of place names. Using the concept of a behavioral environment, Hallowell "emphasized the role of place names and other symbolic references to place as integral to how people experienced, interpreted, and acted on their environments" (Thornton 1997:218).

Although work on American Indian cultural geography has continued, in large part reflecting changes in the socioeconomic and political demography of Indians and the increasingly public discussion of ethnicity and sovereignty (Ross and Moore 1986; Fixico 2000), ethnogeography has traditionally not received as much interest. However, American Indian tribal ethnogeography has recently increased in importance, primarily because of legal cases involving tribal efforts to regain access to and protection for specific sites for religious use and historic preservation. The identification of specific geographic locales, their native toponyms, and a temporal association of distinct named locales and their cultural importance often lie at the center of contemporary legal disputes involving land. Consequently a related number of both academic and popular works have appeared.[1]

Stoffle et al. (1997) have explored the concept of traditional cultural properties and how to calculate the cultural significance of ecological and geographic forms. They also stress the importance of recognizing native views of cultural landscapes, rather than just individual components or sites within a landscape. Using a Paiute example, they demonstrated the need for state and federal land managers to recognize how many natives perceive the land and its resources as inseparable parts of culturally and geographically unique areas. As they explain, "Southern Paiute people tend to view cultural resources as being bound together in broad categories based on functional interdependency and proximity rather than being defined by inherent characteristics" (Stoffle et al. 1997:231). Kelley and Francis (1994:42) made a similar distinction between "piecemeal" and "holistic" accounts of how American Indians view culturally significant land bases. Following Kelley and Francis (1994), Stoffle et al. (1997) found the term *cultural landscapes* more useful than previously used terms (such as sacred geography, spiritual geography, sacred landscapes, or symbolic landscapes) for a number of legal and clarification purposes. In turn, they developed five major levels of cultural landscapes—in descending order of size, holy landscapes, storyscapes, regional landscapes, ecoscapes, and landmarks— which they use to support the conclusion that "American Indian cultural resources are better protected as cultural landscapes than as traditional cultural properties" (Stoffle et al. 1997:245).

Other works have focused on describing the relationship between specific tribes and the land, most of which have been on the Navajo (see, e.g., Watson 1964; Vanette and Tso 1988; Kelley and Francis 1994; Linford 2000), the Navajo-Hopi land dispute, the protection of religious and archaeological sites, resource development, the Navajo homeland (Jett 2001), and the dangers of commercial and residential development (Kelley and Francis 1994:50–60). Kelley and Francis collected 164 names of places deemed "significant" from eighty-one Navajo in thirteen chapters or districts. In another study, Kelley et al. (1991) reported 222 Navajo sacred places in the Hopi Partitioned Lands. Looking at the northeastern and southwestern portions of the 1882 reservation rather than the entire Navajo Reservation, Vanette and Tso (1988) recorded 689 sacred sites. Although several studies show considerable duplication in the listing of sacred sites, studies of Navajo ethnogeography differ primarily in scope rather than in content (Kelley and Francis 1994:81–84). Many more sacred sites on Navajo Reservation lands and in the surrounding region remain.

Two more recent works have focused on Indian place name research. Thornton (1997) has written a brief account of anthropological studies of Native American place naming, offering a number of useful observations and directions for future research. Afable and Beeler (1997) have contributed a section to the *Languages* volume of the *Handbook of North American Indians* that examines the range, characteristics, and anthropological and historical research and sources of North American Indian place names.

Although studies of place names and their geographic and historical associations have a long history in anthropology, rarely has the actual use of toponyms in everyday speech been investigated by linguists or ethnographers, or as a universal means of establishing a relationship to the physical environment. This often results from the view that proper names are solely agents of reference, used only to refer to or specify a place or object, which fails to investigate other linguistic and cultural uses of place names (Basso 1996:76).

A renewed interest in place names did not appear until the late 1980s (Basso 1996:156nn3–4; Thornton 1997:218–221). Julie Cruikshank (1981) and Eugene Hunn (1990) have shown how place names serve as clues to the natural and ethnoecological history of areas, including major ecological events and patterns of human land use, while Cruikshank (1990a, 1990b) has shown that place names are often used as important personal and cultural touchstones or mnemonic devices in autobiographical narratives. Concerning place name inventories, social groupings, and human cognition, Hunn (1994, 1996) has shifted from focusing on individual cultures to attempting to construct a basis for approaching place names as a distinct lexical domain, much as in earlier studies done on colors, animals, plants, and other subjects. His hypotheses relate to the motivations and constraints of human beings as namers of places, the importance of flora and fauna in place names, and the thesis that place name densities may have mathematical associations in use and memory retention (Thornton 1997).

In 1996, Basso critically examined the relationship among place names, cognition, and experience, demonstrating different functions of place names among the Cibecue Apache. Most Apache place names are structured as highly descriptive sentences that convey a rich imagery of a location and are linked to stories with a moral or lesson. Through reciting mythological, historical, and more recent stories, the Apache use place names to center stories with a lesson. Often these narratives include comment on the conduct of fellow tribesman, statements about themselves and the land, and descriptions of the relationship of a people to the environment, thus demonstrating more of a functional than a symbolic use. Like Waterman before him, Basso taxonomically classified Apache place names according to their linguistic and semantic references; some of his categories are descriptive, alluding to former activities, or referring to dangerous places. Although shortened forms of place names are used for everyday activities such as giving directions, making plans, and identifying places in a discussion, more formal names are used to interpret ancestral stories that apply directly to matters of urgent personal concern. Thus, place names are often used in stories as metaphors to indirectly communicate moral lessons (Basso 1996:90).

The Apache use of rich, descriptive place names stems from their use of land and their ability to convey large amounts of geographic information in concise form. As Thornton (1997:219) notes, particularly descriptive names become part of a culture's iconography. In the simplest expression of this iconography, places with names have attached to them stories with teachings. Eventually the association of knowledge with place names encompasses oral history, cultural and religious information, moral teachings, and geography. Thus Keith Basso's choice for his book title, "Wisdom Sits in Places."

Because Native American concepts of place and being are intimately linked through place names, which are used in a wide array of everyday activities, many no longer view names as linguistic artifacts but as cultural resources. Place names and the places they name are becoming an important part of land and resource management, both on and off reservations. There is increasing collaboration between scholars and Indians in identifying, mapping, and preserving such sites and their respective tribal names. The work of Kelley and Francis (1994) among the Navajo and of Thornton (1995a, 1995b, 1997) among the Tlingit serve as fruitful examples of this approach. As Thornton (1997:224–225) reports for the Glacier Bay Place Name Project among the Tlingit, "The process of documenting Tlingit place names in Glacier Bay and other areas has helped not only to reveal the multi-dimensional associations of the indigenous toponyms, but also to revitalize the native geography of Southeast Alaska and spawn other related projects." Winchell et al. (1994) have surveyed geographic research on Native Americans, while Rundstrom et al. (2000) have surveyed North American Indian and Inuit geographic research from 1990 to 2000.

Another rich source of information on American Indian place names is the literature on land claims. With the establishment of the Indian Claims Commission in 1946, anthropologists, historians, and geographers were hired to conduct research on Indian lands, place names, and their historical and religious relationships as documentary evidence for the courts. Historical documents and written tribal histories were used to establish and mitigate tribal land claims and helped lead to the development of ethnohistory in the United States. Data from these projects resulted in several tribal monographs and related ethnographic works (see Ross 1973; Sutton 1975; Sutton et al. 1985; DeMallie and Ewers 2001:40–41). Studies on intertribal views of Indian sacred geography (Nabokov and Loendorf 2004; Nabokov 2006) are also emerging.

Plains Indian Studies

Limited ethnogeographic research has been conducted on Plains Indians (Afable and Beeler 1997:186, 199) and even less on southern plains groups, with most works of a historical nature. Grinnell (1906) published a brief account of Cheyenne stream names and some of their origins, and an account of the Big Horn Medicine Wheel (1922). Toll's 1962 *Arapaho Names and Trails* is one of the most interesting firsthand accounts of Plains Indian ethnogeography. The work is based on a two-week pack trip Toll took in 1914 with three Arapaho men, two of whom had lived in the Estes Park and the Grand Lake region of north-central Colorado in pre-reservation times. In this way, Toll was able to acquire data while traveling through the actual area of inquiry.

Campbell and Field in 1968 identified several nineteenth-century Comanche raiding trails and crossings, and the general locations for others. However, their work was strictly ethnohistorical, based on travel accounts and historical maps, with no native place names or input from native informants. In 1972, Howard published a brief account of Yankton Dakota ethnogeography. Although most works in Native American ethnogeography have had a nominal or historical focus, other areas of inquiry exist. Parks and Wedel in 1985 examined Pawnee historical and sacred geography, linking unique geomorphological landforms categorized as animal lodges (where animals met and bestowed supernatural power on select Pawnee individuals) to Pawnee mythology and religious rituals. Concerning the protection of archaeological sites, status as sacred sites, and chronological and analytical studies, studies of Plains Indian rock art are increasing (see Keyser and Klassen 2001; Sundstrom 2003, 2004; Keyser 2004). Using historical and ethnographic resources, Gelo (2000) has identified and reconstructed a number of Comanche place names in the region of Oklahoma, New Mexico, and Texas. He shows that not only did the Comanche transplant place names from the north to new southern plains locations of a similar nature, they also helped condition Euroamerican responses to the landscape.

Afable and Beeler (1997) provide the most recent and comprehensive overview of Native American place name literature. In their contribution to the Smithsonian's *Handbook of North American Indians*, they discuss place name classifications (descriptive, locational, names referring to human activities at a site, names referring to history, mythology, or folklore, and other miscellaneous forms); the linguistic forms of place names (grammatical and lexical basis); and sources, both early and modern. Their work highlights some of the major concerns associated with the accuracy of written accounts. As they note (1997:189), many place name studies are highly unreliable because the writers were unfamiliar with the languages of naming, relied unduly on local tradition and folklore, sometimes adopted highly conjectural interpretations, and did not undertake a comparative linguistic analysis. The continued citation of such etymologies only further clouds the true basis and meaning of the names, and of naming in general.

Lounsbury in 1960 enumerated methods for understanding interpretations in the etymological study of place names. Ideally, analysis must include an accurate pronunciation of the name, the exact location referred to, and the meaning of the name. To adequately ascertain a name's composition and meaning, a researcher should know the source language's grammatical structure and, preferably, should have undertaken intensive, long-term work with fluent and knowledgeable speakers, and should be able to reconstruct the names from the historical record and from knowledge of the source language (see also Afable and Beeler 1997:189).

KIOWA GEOGRAPHIC LITERATURE

Although several works include Kiowa place names and geographic locales (see Nye 1937, 1962; Harrington 1939; Boyd 1981, 1983; Hickerson 1994), most of the data available are supplementary and descriptive, appearing in cultural and historical accounts and not the primary focus of study. James Mooney (1898:391–430) provided more than one hundred Kiowa place names, for many of which exact, corresponding locations were recorded. Rydjord (1968:310–324) briefly discussed Kiowa and Comanche place names in Kansas from archival and published sources but did not use a standard orthography, suggested little in the way of name formation, and did not attempt a synthesis of nominal, historical, or linguistic patterns. Kent Sanmann (1992), a Kiowa, produced a brief paper on Kiowa place names and geographic terms. Bright (2004) published a few place names used in English of Kiowa origin or association.

The first significant examination of Kiowa geography is Steven Schnell's (1993) master's thesis on the Kiowa homeland in Oklahoma, which was based on research conducted in the summer of 1992. Despite several small inaccuracies, most likely a result of limited time in the field, this work is to be commended. It effectively conveys many of the major geographic forms and current Kiowa views on geography, homeland, culture, and ethnicity. Schnell (2000) later published a shorter account of this work on the relationship between the Kiowa and their homeland in terms of physical imprint on the landscape, symbolic cultural constructs, and broader questions of group identity and community that are not reducible to individual features.

This work differs in major ways from prior work on Plains Indian and Kiowa geography. Although several topics discussed in this book, such as names of mountains, historical sites, arbors, churches, and cemeteries, were also addressed by Schnell (1993), the fieldwork I conducted in 1989–2007 led to significant differences. With more time in the field and greater input from informants, I was able to identify and define Kiowa geographic (lexical) categories and cultural forms while covering a wider range of place names across the plains, from which I was able to gather details on many discrete name references, such as salt and paint mines, Sun Dance sites, reservation communities, and historical sites such as Hueco Tanks. The relationship of Kiowa place names to personal names is addressed in this book, as is the relationship of Kiowa calendar entry names to geography. From this information I was able to conduct a statistical analysis of Kiowa calendar and place names. Throughout the book, I have also used a standardized orthography (Meadows and McKenzie 2001) for Kiowa lexicon and place names. The use of a standardized orthography to record and analyze Kiowa place names permits deeper linguistic insight into their semantic and linguistic content and a consequently greater understanding of Kiowa cultural geography. In a series of appendices I list the Kiowa names of all places recorded in this study, their precise geographic location, if known, and their associated cultural and historical importance to the Kiowa.

This work also provides a survey of American Indian ethnogeographic scholarship and how Kiowa geography relates to these classifications; a survey of American Indian cartographic literature and a detailed examination of the Kiowa map of Black Goose; and the recent literature on the concepts of sacred geography, related legal issues, and ecological islands. My investigations benefited from numerous discussions with a broad range of contemporary Kiowa consultants and from the field notes of James Mooney and Hugh L. Scott from the 1890s, and Alice Marriott and the Santa Fe Laboratory of Anthropology Field School from the 1930s.

The approach I have adopted in this book combines long-term cultural and ethnohistorical research with linguistic analysis and geography. Because ethnographers and ethnohistorians have paid little attention to geographic detail since Boas's time, an interdisciplinary approach that also incorporates geographic works is useful for two primary purposes. First, it underscores the growing overlap of the two fields and the benefit to be obtained from geographic studies, and second, it facilitates a better understanding of concepts such as sacred geography and geosacred sites.

Although the exact origins of the Kiowa before they took up residence in western Montana are unclear, Hickerson (1994) contends the Kiowa are descended from the Jumano. One Kiowa account (Meadows n.d.-a) supports a protohistoric migration from the Southwest to western Montana by at least some of the people who would later be recognized as the Kiowa, by around 1700 and before their subsequent migration to the southern plains. That the Kiowa gradually moved east from southwestern Montana and later into present-day western Oklahoma, Kansas, southeastern Colorado, and the Texas Panhandle between 1790 and 1830 is well documented (Mooney 1898). From this region the Kiowa continued to travel, explore, and raid throughout a large portion of western and southwestern North America.

In terms of the sheer extent of territory involved, the first three-quarters of the nineteenth century were a dynamic period for Kiowa culture. Some of the eldest Kiowa living in 1900 had been born in southeastern Wyoming. Throughout the mid-1800s, bands of Kiowa periodically traveled north to Montana to visit and trade with the Crow. Hunting, raiding, and revenge parties traversed vast regions of the Great Plains, the American Southwest, and Mexico, resulting in extensive knowledge of these areas. Kiowa elders state that the Kiowa had a great love of exploration and that many "war parties" were actually exploratory expeditions whose primary goal was to find out what was "over there," rather than solely a quest for scalps or horses. Both were often achieved simultaneously. Oscar Tsoodle described the journeys of his grandfather Tenadooah and his friend Big Bow (Palmer 2003:68):

> . . . Big Bow, and him, the old man, my grandfather, the two of them went exploring together. Like Daniel Boone. "We went around. They fed us. They treated us good. Those tribes we visited on our journeys. We just go. We just go for the heck of it. Those tribes welcomed us too. I prayed and him, he sang. That's what we did when we went out. They treated us good. . . . We were just travelers seeing what

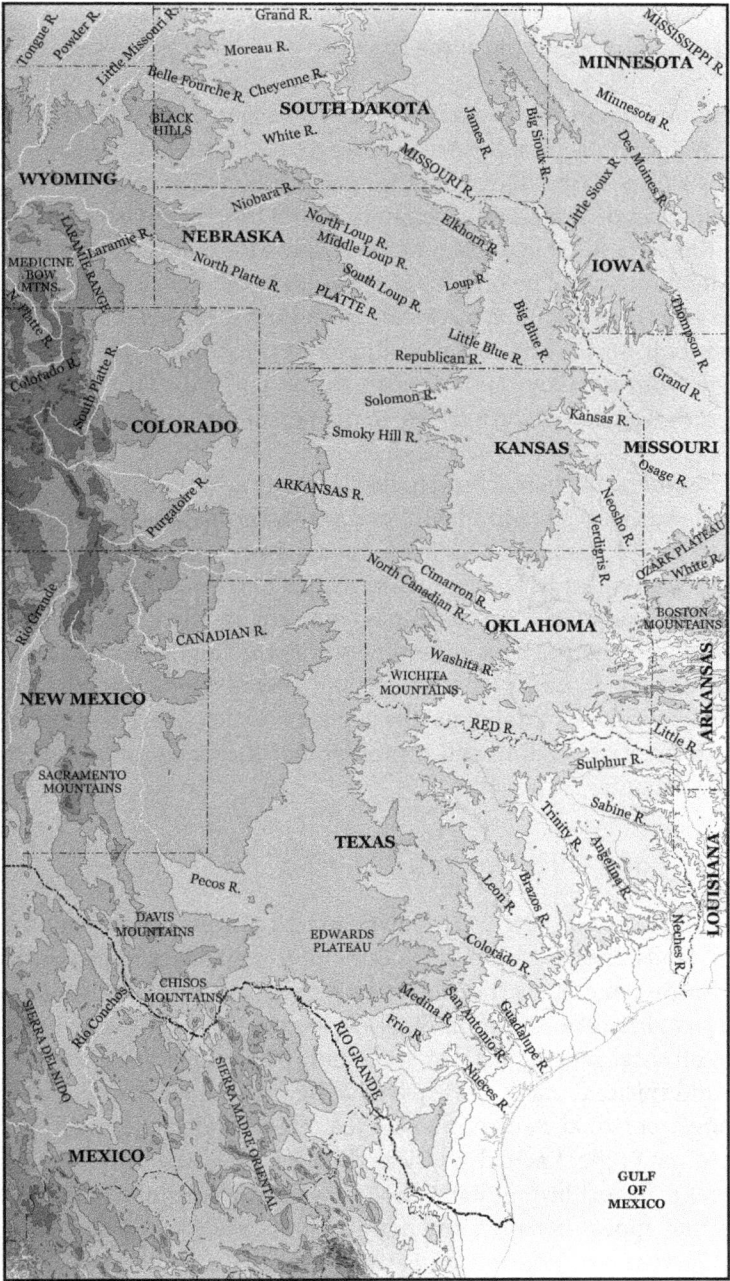

Map 1. Map of plains region showing major rivers, mountains, and noted locales. Map by Jim Coombs, maps librarian, Missouri State University.

there was to see in the land. . . ." Yeah, they were dàumsáumzèmà going around just looking at the land. . . .

Kiowa traditions report groups traveling as far as the Gulf of Mexico in Texas, Tamaulipas in tropical Mexico, and west to the Gulf of California in Sonora. Kiowa place names range from Montana and the Dakotas deep into the northern states of Mexico into Tamaulipas, and from the major streams of eastern Kansas and Oklahoma into the Rocky Mountains and parts of Arizona (Mooney 1898). The breadth of these extensive travels is reflected in the wide array of geographic place names and tribal names recorded by Mooney (1898:391–430) and by Kiowa linguist Parker McKenzie (n.d.-b), which range from the Sarci and Mandan in the north to the Carrizo of south Texas, to the southeastern tribes, to the Seri along the Sonoran Gulf of California.

With Euroamerican encroachment, the decimation of bison herds, final confinement to a reservation in 1875, allotment and homesteading in 1901, and the decline of Kiowa as a primary language, many native geographic lexical and place names have declined in use and are in danger of being lost. Currently, many place names are known only by the eldest generation, while younger generations often know only the English translations of a few tribal place names. Kiowa ethnogeography is rapidly contracting, concentrated now in a handful of northern plains locales and in the region around the former reservation and contemporary Kiowa communities in southwest Oklahoma.

LINGUISTIC FORM AND CONTENT

As Harkin (2000:64) notes, "Linguistic practices are intertwined with the physical landscape in ways that are difficult for outsiders to perceive." For many Native Americans the landscape provides an essential connection to the past, because—again in Harkin's words—"the landscape bears traces, both physical and linguistic of past events." The landscape also bears emotional and spiritual traces of the past that become known through oral history, songs, personal names, ghost encounters, and ritual practices. These traces may reflect actual physical changes, as in the origin of Up a Rock (Devil's Tower) or the Star Girls (Pleiades); or linguistic and cultural traces may appear in names and narratives, such as Place Where They Killed the Cheyenne or Prairie Dog Eating Creek, that serve to "inscribe meanings on the land." This breadth of origins reflects an indigenous and not solely an anthropological perspective. The diversity of place names also involves a complex combination of linguistic behavior, contemplation, physical experience, as well as cultural and historical continuity, and thus familiarity that forms a part of physical and cultural experience.

Harkin (2000:65) also notes that "History is a crucial element in this persistence of place-making." He uses the term "spatiotemporal" to describe the historical and cultural dependency on ethnogeography for several groups, the exact processes that reflect the Kiowa's shift in place and place names from the northern to the southern plains. Although a sense of attachment to an area is transferable (see Momaday 1969), it cannot replace firsthand experience, and thus the experience of place is primary, while talking about it is secondary. As Harkin alludes to, the ability to understand the attachment to place is inhibited when a physical landscape is viewed as an object rather than as an agent, as a place where things happen instead of a place that makes things happen, and when the temporal dimension of place is ignored. Objectification of place leads to a reconceptualization of it. However, all of us carry a sense of place with us, allowing us to recall memories of personal, family, or group history. In turn it is this history that "give[s] such places the power to act on us" (Harkin 2000:64–65).

Types of Place Names

Afable and Beeler (1997:190–191) have identified the main forms of North American Indian place names. Kiowa place names correlate with most of these forms, for which examples follow. The construction of Kiowa place names is similar to and just as complex as the grammatical content of other words, phrases, or sentences. Examples range from single unmodified nouns (Píhót, Peninsula; Soôldàum, Onion Flat), to complete phrases (Séttháidètháukàuimáimàufàcâundèvàu, Creek Where White Bear Brought the White Women). Place names with nouns (Pásángá, Plains Escarpment), verbs (Sépyáldá, Rainy Hill), affixes (Váuêl, Big River), or stems (Gúlváu, Red River) that express aspects of location such as position (Dóigàuváudáudéê, Place Where a River Is Positioned Deep Below), location (Váupfáhâl, River Confluence), orientation (Xóchéldéê, Where Standing/Positioned Rock Is), or direction (typically unspecified but inferable from context and common knowledge) are common in many languages (Afable and Beeler 1997:190). As these examples demonstrate, Kiowa place names frequently include more than one of these elements. Reflecting the grammatical structure of many Kiowa expressions, some Kiowa place names are adverbial forms rather than nouns (Qópgà, At or Toward the Mountains; Qóptháukáuidàumbè, Within the Mexican Country).

Many Kiowa place names include a noun or a component that identifies the type of topographical feature named, which can occur as an independent word. In Kiowa this occurs most regularly as terminal suffixes but occasionally as a prefix denoting a noun such as river, lake, spring, peninsula, mountain, hill, bluff or bluff recess, canyon or pass that forms the root of the place name, or other location indicators such as dé-ę̀, that imply "where" or "place at which" something occurred.

LOCAL AND DISTANT PLACE NAMES

In his interpretation of the range of Navajo geographic knowledge Carroll (1983:64) reported that "People have been told about significant locations in their own grazing areas by parents and kin but know only major locations in the surrounding region." Kelley and Francis (1994:44) offer similar findings from their work among the Navajo, noting that individual extended families become associated with particular homesteads, gravesites, and landmarks that in time become associated with a sense of belonging, family history, and use rights.

Prior to the reservation period, this trend was undoubtedly enhanced as Kiowa resided in their respective regionally based divisions, each made up of several fluctuating residence bands. Today this trend continues to some degree. While nearly all adult Kiowa know of Mount Scott, Medicine Bluff, Cutthroat Gap, and Rainy Mountain even if they have not visited them, only local residents are likely to know of places like Seven Sisters Creek or Paddlety's Pond. Consequently, I found different extents of place names between Redstone and Hobart Kiowa. Similar to information pertaining to family names, ceremonial organizations, and churches, when discussing geography, elder Kiowa often show respect for other communities by deferring to them and suggesting that you speak to someone from that community.

FORMAL AND INFORMAL PLACE NAMES

Another distinction of Kiowa place names involves proper or formal place names versus common descriptive designations or informal place names. Kelley and Francis (1996:49–50) describe this pattern among Navajo sacred place names: "We suggest that widely known places tend to have names, whereas places without names tend to be known and used only by a single person or family. The unnamed places, being in the family's customary land base, are near at hand, often within view . . . such sites tend to have common descriptive designations rather than proper names. . . ."

Whereas proper Kiowa place names such as Saddle Mountain are used, common descriptive designations are more frequently found in family or community contexts. On Vanessa Jennings's allotment they regularly use proper place names such as Mount Scott, Red Stone, and Paddlety's Pond to refer to these respective places and their surrounding areas, which are known to most Kiowa, as well as nondescript terms such as "the pond," "the cottonwoods," and "the old house" to refer to places on their own land. This trend is not limited to American Indians. On my own family land, we likewise have our proper (Frog Pond, Potato Patch Pond, Logan's Pond, Frank's Field) and commonplace names (the cave, the sand mound, the wildlife pond, the watermelon patch, the big wetland). Similar distinctions exist among many peoples in the selection of terms used to talk about locations. Unnamed sites tend to have common descriptive designations because they are the only such locale on a family's or small community's land and are contextually specific enough for the group talking about them. Descriptive names such as "the hill" or "the spring" were undoubtedly common in Kiowa communities, as many such locales of a similar nature existed in a variety of places.

NAME CLUSTERS

A single place name was sometimes given to two or more similar geographic locales, such as two similar hills. Names such as Red Mountain, Pecan Creek, Peninsula, and Onion Flat also indicate that proper place names were also commonly duplicated and suggest that either a respective local community used such locales or that existing place names were transplanted to new locales.

Name clusters based on a single name root with different geographic affixes in the form of a prefix or suffix that specified the type of geographic feature are common in place names among many American Indian cultures. Many Kiowa stream names expand on an existing name root, usually a hill, mountain, gap, or noted resource location, by simply adding a suffix such as -vàu (stream) or -tǫ̀ (spring) to denote the desired form, as in Kóyàldà (Dark Hill) and Kóyàldàvàu (Dark Hill River). Other Kiowa examples include Sépyáldá (Rainy Hill) and Sépyáldávàu (Rainy Hill Creek), Yîqòp (Two Mountains) and Yîqòpvàu (Two Mountains River), Ấjâun (Timber Gap) and Ấjâunvàu (Timber Gap Creek), Fàiqòp (Sun Mountain) and Fàiqòptǫ̀tép (Sun Mountain Spring), and Ấutǫ́thǫ́ivàu (Salt River) and Ấutǫ́thǫ́igàqùldéę̀ (Salt Place or Bed).

Place names may also extend across linguistic boundaries, especially in reference to sites that hold similar cultural and economic importance to multiple groups. Grinnell (1906) provides many identical meanings for Cheyenne stream names, as well as instances in which a place name was created by one tribe, then adopted through translation into neighboring groups, such as the Cheyenne adoption of the Kiowa and Comanche name for the Washita River. Several instances are noted among the Kiowa, Comanche, Apache, Cheyenne, Arapaho, and Lakota.

Some locales were similarly known by nearly all groups of a region. As reflected in the Kiowa names Sésèváu (Arrowhead River), the Arkansas River was know to many groups as Arrowhead River because of the abundance of prehistoric projectile points found at campsites along its course, and for some tribes possibly for the extensive outcroppings of Kay County chert further downstream in north-central Oklahoma. Parker McKenzie's grandfather Queton, born in 1849, told Parker of visiting known Indian campsites along the Arkansas River in the 1860s to scavenge prehistoric stone projectile points, which according to Queton the Kiowa had ceased making by this time.[2] Similarly, the South Platte was known as the Fat River to many groups, in reference to the multitude of bison in this area. These similarities were in large part due to the practice of intertribal sharing of regional territories. The more important a place is in the culture and geography of a group, the more significant, more well known, and more likely to be formally named it tends to be.

Intertribal Land Sharing

The concept of intertribal sharing of land is essential to understanding the political, social, and economic activities of historic Plains Indians. The sharing of territories, villages, multitribal encampments, resources, intertribal participation in social and religious activities, and mutual support in hunting and warfare was common among many Plains Indian cultures. Although these relationships fluctuated with varied circumstances, they nonetheless represent a widespread tradition of periodic sharing that may have been more common along tribal boundaries than in the center or heart of tribal lands. American Indian territorial systems and their uses in historic times have been studied from two approaches. Scholars have tended either to focus on the meanings that tribes attached to their lands and the beliefs through which they organized the use of that land as an expression of their political and economic systems or to examine the spatial patterns of occupation, particularly subsistence and demographic locales.

However, as Albers and Kay (1987:47) note, "In order to understand American Indian territoriality it is necessary to look at land-use from a regional rather than tribally-biased perspective, and to distinguish between ideological claims to and the actual use of a specific territory." Later, they continue (1987:72), "In general, when one begins to examine the ethnohistoric record from a regional rather than a tribally-biased perspective, it becomes apparent that joint cooperation and sharing of land among ethnically-diverse groups was not exceptional." In light of examples from the Great Lakes and the plains, it becomes apparent that the conventional model of tribal organization and territoriality inadequately accounts for the complexity of relationships that crosscut ethnic and geographic regions and boundaries. Albers's (1993) work on symbiosis, merger, and war in relation to plains economy and social organization further supports the importance and widespread nature of intertribal Plains Indian relations.

Intertribal sharing of land on the Great Plains often resulted from declines in natural resources such as bison or beaver and from continual land cessions, reducing native territories. Changing market conditions influenced not only where and how groups positioned themselves in relation to obtain strategic trade advantages but also how groups in a specific region interacted with one another in relation to resource acquisition, land use, and neighboring populations. Albers and Kay (1987:76) maintain that the effects of ecology and demography cannot be understood without recognizing "the social and historical circumstances in which native peoples jointly or separately utilized a given geographic space."

Kinship ties appear to have been as important as ethnic ancestry in the organization and distribution of Plains peoples and resources. Kinship became a predominant medium of integration that affected resource sharing, cooperation, food provisioning, political status, territorial defense, trade networks, and ceremonial activities. As Albers and Kay (1987:78) note, kinship was "the language of relationship" through which American Indians defined and established structural connections among themselves, and later with Anglos. In many contemporary American Indian communities, age, gender, and kinship are still key elements of social, political, and religious organization. Thus it may be more appropriate to examine certain aspects of American Indian social organization and territoriality using regional units of analysis—which reflect actual social organization and land use—rather than the traditional concept of tribe, which often introduces a biased concept in regard to the complexity of the ethnic identity of the groups using a given territory. Often boundaries claimed by a single tribe neither encompassed all of the tribe's members nor reflected the ethnic identity of everyone living within that region. Tribal lands changed over time with migration and expanded or contracted owing to many factors, among them climatic variation, trade, disease, symbiosis (mutually beneficial exchanges or agreements), merger, and war. Kinship relations were one means through which land use and the ethnic content of a given region could change peacefully. The role of kinship facilitates a more accurate understanding of the complexities of diffusion and the range of cultural institutions across ethnic boundaries and varied regional or tribal histories (Albers and Kay 1987:82).

As reflected in treaties, the failure to consider or recognize multiethnic rights to a given region, thereby leading to inaccurate assignment of jurisdictional boundaries based on the assumption of a single group's use, is a major problem in the jurisdictional rights of native peoples. Following the Indian Removal Act of 1830, the western half of Indian Territory was assigned by the U.S. government to the Chickasaw and Cherokee, even though the Kiowa, Plains Apache, Comanche, and Wichita were already living there. The multiethnic nature of indigenous social systems and land use patterns from prehistoric times to the reservation era (Albers and Kay 1987:80), and in modern times in regard to powwows, society dances, hand games, and some religious sites, must be recognized to more accurately understand these systems.

A Kiowa-Naishan Apache relationship has existed since at least these tribes' time on the northwestern plains. Although their relations were predominantly symbiotic, both groups remained separate in some respects and joined in others. The Kiowa and Apache used the resources of the same region and came together regularly in Sun Dance encampments, men's societies, and some raiding activities. This network expanded with an alliance with the Comanche in 1806, and again with a Kiowa-Comanche-Apache and Cheyenne-Arapaho alliance in 1840.

A comparison of Comanche ethnogeography (Gelo 2000) and the Kiowa data in this work discloses several similarities. The geographic nomenclature of both groups focuses on references to environmental conditions (geological forms, water sources, flora, fauna) and memorable human activities (trade, military activity). Both Kiowa and Comanche occasionally used the same place names for different features, a trait retained in the Euroamerican naming of places. The Comanche and Kiowa names for the Wichita Mountains, Mount Scott, Sugar Creek, Rainy Mountain, Trader's Creek, Double Mountain, the North Canadian–Beaver River, and probably several other locales are synonymous (Gelo 2000). Sometimes a descriptive name of a principal watercourse was applied to a tributary or to two completely unconnected streams. In both instances specificity was distinguishable in conversation by context (Gelo 2000:301). Many Kiowa and Comanche stream names refer to specific types of flora, usually a species of tree along the stream's course, such as walnut, cottonwood, or mesquite.

Noted hills and mountains often featured oasis-like areas that served as sources of water and wood and as base camps during traveling or raiding.

Although twin features in the form of landmarks such as two adjacent hills, mountains, or gaps are more common in Comanche ethnogeography, they are also found in Kiowa place names. Both the Kiowa and the Comanche responded to their regions as a fundamentally visual environment that elicited heightened observation and the differentiation at great distances of slight changes in the landscape signaling human or animal activity, natural resource concentrations, or shifts in the weather. Early military personnel noted the visual acuity of Plains peoples and their adeptness at seeing signals at great distances. The different means of sending signals—with horses, smoke, blankets, mirrors, or manual sign language—all related to the Indian adaptation to the plains as a visual environment (Gelo 2000:302–305).

Noting that several Comanche names for landmarks in Oklahoma and Texas resemble those found in Wyoming and Utah, Gelo (2000:272) suggests that "the Comanches transplanted a geographic scheme from their ancestral area." Although few Kiowa place names from the north are known, and there are no northern Kiowa-speaking populations for comparison, as with the Shoshone and Comanche, the similarity in syntax and semantic content of northern and southern plains place names, the multiple use of single place names, and the similarity in name and translation of several Kiowa place names with other tribes all suggest that the Kiowa may have done likewise.

Many modern American roads, cities, and landmarks bear the names given to the locales by local native cultures. In retrospect, an ongoing process of conditioning Euroamericans to Indian responses to the landscape has continued over several centuries, resulting in part in the initial travel routes and settlement patterns that constitute modern American geography. Just as the Comanche preconditioned later Anglo populations to certain geographic forms (Gelo 2000), so have the Kiowa. Some examples are the route of Oklahoma State Highway 58, which passes through the "Gap" in the Wichita Mountains, and the names of Rainy Mountain, Saddle Mountain, Jimmy Creek, Frizzie Head Creek, Stinking Creek, Two Hatchett and Buzzard creeks, among many other locales shared with other tribes. The subject of American Indian intertribal land use and ethnogeography warrants a major investigation of a regionally comparative nature.

Other place names reflect origins based on ethnic, tribal, or other group names that are specific to an area and a group residing in that region. Although this form may have once been common among the Kiowa, pre-reservation data are sparse. Place names referring to the territory of neighboring groups include forms such as Cûiqàvàu (Pawnee River), Íjàqóp (Ute Mountains), and Áthàukàuidàumgà (Timber or Forested Mexican Country). Pre-reservation Kiowa regional names for themselves are known only for northern and southern Kiowa, and more precisely with the formation of the Gúhàlĕcàuigù or Wild Mustang Kiowa in the late 1850s. After their final confinement to the reservation in 1875, however, new geographically based groups appeared by the 1880s and have continued, as Kiowa groups are now commonly referred to by their regional community names, such as Meers or Mount Scott, Redstone, Zóltǫ̀ (Stinking Creek), or Hobart Kiowa.

GEOGRAPHY AND RELIGION

Indigenous peoples who identify strongly with their surrounding physical environment tend to experience not only a strong sense of a homeland but also awareness of a spiritual landscape within that homeland. The intertribal shared use of religious or sacred sites, what I refer to as geosacred sites, was also common.[3] Gulliford (2000) provides an excellent discussion of Native American views concerning land, religion, and the contemporary issues of museums, repatriation, preservation of sacred sites, efforts to ensure religious freedom (with special concern for access to sacred sites and the necessary religious paraphernalia for conducting tribal religion practices), and tribal efforts to maintain their cultures.

Geographically, there are distinct differences between Anglo and Native American religions. As Gulliford (2000:67) writes,

> For traditional native peoples, the landscape includes not only the physical world or rocks, trees, mountains and plains but also the spirit world. Indigenous Native American worship depends on a detailed and particular sense of place that goes back in language and in stories for centuries, whereas Protestant Christianity has been evangelical, transportable, Bible-based, and not rooted to a particular landscape. Europeans abandoned their cemeteries and cathedrals as they set sail for America. They crossed the water and then crossed the continent and reconstituted their religious communities by building new churches. In contrast, Native Americans felt obligated to protect and defend the graves of their ancestors and the sacred locations where the Great Spirit resides and communicates with them. . . .

On the following pages he continues,

> For most tribes, a sacred place is one where the Great Creator or spirits, both good and evil, communicate with the living. Most

Anglo Americans consecrate a church as a sacred place, and it remains sacred as long as a congregation meets there. But when congregations outgrow a building, they may well sell it and purchase a new space to make holy. By contrast, what is important for traditional Indian religious believers is not the sacred space of a church or cathedral but rather a location made holy by the Great Creator, by ancient and enduring myth. By repeated rituals such as sun dances, or by the presence of spirits who dwell in deep canyons, on mountaintops, or in hidden caves. An entire landscape may be sacred because Indians migrated from place to place in search of food, on seasonal rounds that took them into the high country in the summer and to lower elevations in the winter. Sacred sites remain integral to tribal histories, religions, and identities.

Belden Lane (1988:11–12) identifies four criteria for sacred places: (1) A sacred place is not chosen; rather, it chooses. (2) Because the entire world is viewed as sacred, a sacred place is an ordinary place that is ritually made extraordinary by the activities that transpire there; the sacred place thus continues to be contacted by individuals, who in turn feed its power. (3) Sacred places can be trod on without being entered, and thus recognition of a sacred place is culturally determined, and its nature is not apparent to or characterized as such by all.[4] (4) The energy or impulse of sacred places is both centripetal and centrifugal, local and universal, all-encompassing.[5] As Forbes-Boyte (1999:28) notes in respect to Bear Butte in South Dakota, "The ritual centers are places where humans can come into contact with the spirit world. Bear Butte is one such place in Lakota cosmology."

One must be cautious not to romanticize Native American existence and demography as static. Many statements are accurate only when applied to a specific time period. In this light some part of Gulliford's statement is debatable. Archaeological, cultural, biological, linguistic, and geological data strongly support a series of Asian to North American migrations. Even in North America, both before and after contact, many tribes are known to have migrated to new areas, essentially leaving behind what was previously their traditional homeland, religious sites, and burial grounds.

As cultures change, both geographically and ideologically, their elements also change, including religion and memory, and thus what constitutes a homeland. Native peoples have used many sacred sites over millennia. As Campbell and Foor (2004:165) note, "each tribal-nation, as it migrated to the northwestern Plains, integrated 'institutions and life ways present among the more ancient residents,' including the recognition of certain geographical locations and cultural features as sacred sources of spiritual power." In accessing these recognizable special areas or sacred "portals" within their new residential region, they incorporated them into their own unique cultures and religious belief systems. Like other tribes, the Kiowa undoubtedly left behind many religious sites as they migrated to the central and southern plains.

Many tribes also adopted new religious traditions in both precontact (Southeastern Ceremonial Complex, Sun Dance) and post-contact (Peyote, Ghost Dance, Christianity) periods. That Euroamerican movements often appear to have spread faster and are better documented may lead to an inaccurate view of the processes of demographic change and associated concepts of ethnogeography. As the Kiowa data show, it is more logical and more accurate to look at a group's ethnogeography in terms of a series or succession of physical movements and associated cultural traditions that are at any one time focused primarily on one general region. Likewise, both the geographic range of residence and the associated ethnogeography of that region were constantly changing entities and associations. Nevertheless, whether one is examining the last 13,000 or 300 years of human existence, many of these distinctions regarding land and religion are real and are important for their respective communities.

For native peoples who continue to maintain indigenous or traditional religious practices, their needs often differ from those of non-Indians in terms of what constitutes freedom of religion. "In seeking and guarding access to sacred sites, American Indians need a guarantee of religious freedom for their ceremonies, festivals, medicinal plant gathering, and pilgrimages, which differ from Christian traditions" (Gulliford 2000:68). Often these rights and the access to religious sites and the natural materials necessary for conducting the religious practice have not been ensured and protected.[6] Many Native Americans exhibit a strong sense of respect and stewardship for the land in general, but especially for sacred sites. Often this entails a multifaceted obligation of physical care (maintenance and preservation of sacred locales), spiritual care (respect and conducting proper ritual procedures), and cultural responsibility in ensuring that both the site and the associated knowledge are passed on to succeeding generations of tribal members. But again, we must be careful not to overgeneralize or overromanticize this aspect of contemporary American Indian life.[7]

Native American sacred ethnogeography is thus defined, interacted with, maintained, and changed on native terms that often differ significantly from the constructs of other cultures. This requires non-Indians to acknowledge — even if they do not agree or fully understand — native views toward land and religious tradition. As former Hopi vice chairman Vernon

KIOWA ETHNOGEOGRAPHY

Masayesva said, "If an Indian says a rock contains the spirit of God, courts and judges must not dismiss this as a romantic description. Keep in mind, to a Catholic consecrated bread is no longer bread but the very physical body of Christ. . . . No court would challenge the Catholic belief in that regard, and no court should challenge as romantic overstatement that places or things contain the spirit of God either" (Gulliford 2000:91).

Although freedom of religion is a core concept of American law, it is not guaranteed to those who practice a land-based religion, such as Native Americans. Every year more areas are being destroyed through strip mining and development, as well as being physically altered and disrespected through designation as public lands where rock climbers, dirt bike and 4-wheeler enthusiasts, tourists, and New Age religious practitioners are increasingly inhibiting Native Americans from conducting religious practices at designated geographic locales. Perhaps even more problematic is the level of ignorance associated with the differential basis of many Native American religions. The documentary films *In the Light of Reverence* (Earth Island Institute 2001) and *The River Has Many Stories* (Idaho Power 2001) portrays the battles of the Hopi, Lakota, Wintu, and several Plateau tribes to protect the sacred geography of their traditional homelands. As former Western Cherokee chief Wilma Mankiller says in *In the Light of Reverence,* "The film clearly articulates some of the issues indigenous peoples all over the world face as they struggle to prevent their spiritual beliefs from being marginalized by people who believe spiritual places are structures built by men, not the Creator."

As Basso (1996) and Harkin (2000) demonstrate, many indigenous groups perceive the landscape as bearing traces of the activities of their ancestors. These traces are a significant means whereby subsequent generations interact with the landscape in present times, as well as reexperience the past. While physical forms of material culture may (as with petroglyphs and stone structures) or may not (as with totem poles or painted hide and wood) survive beyond the individuals that produced them, human traces on the landscape also survive in other nonmaterial contexts (Harkin 2000:51). As Basso has found among the Western Apache and Harkin has found among the Heiltsuk (Bella Bella), narrative and related linguistic practices such as assigning place names and personal names, joking, and I would add song and prayer, connect places with human actions. "Named features of landscape may thus serve as signs for moral values, shorthand for historical events and periods, and warrants for the present order of things" (Harkin 2000:51). In time, such relationships begin to function much like a dialogue between place and person or place and group. This relationship may serve as a means of maintaining continuity with the precontact past, an attempt either to hold on to an earlier way of life or to maintain some sense of continuity following processes that have altered or foreclosed much of that earlier way of life.

Even though history and archaeology show that associations with a homeland are historically relative and can change over time, those associations are nevertheless very real for the practitioners of a culture and religion at any given time. Although a longing for one's homeland is common among many peoples, for many Native Americans the relationship with their homeland is directly related to the quality of mental health. Matthiessen (1979:322) referenced a report written by the Navajo Area office that noted that Navajo facing relocation were

> "currently utilizing the mental health facilities of one of the IHS at a rate which is eight times greater than that of Navajos who will not be relocated." The Navajo describe themselves as inseparable from Big Mountain, a Navajo sacred site and the traditional home of Begochidi or One Who Created Man. As Kee Shey, a Navajo, described Big Mountain in Arizona, "The mountain is ours. . . . It is the place we go to pray for our livestocks [sic], and our medicine men go there to get herbs, and it is the place our women gather the medicine they use when they bear children. We need the mountain to live." (Matthiessen 1979:318–319)

Likewise, many Kiowa living outside southwestern Oklahoma frequently express a longing to return to "Kiowa Country."

Outsiders often have difficulty in viewing physical landscapes in the ways that Native Americans do: as physical forms bearing traces of their ancestors, and as forms intertwined with their concepts of the past, origins, language, oral history, personal conduct, and spiritual morals and direction. As Harkin (2000:53) shows, once an ethnographer learns to look beyond ethnography in terms of external categories of simply how places were used (resource area, village site, historical locale), the ongoing impact on human culture and behavior can be explored. "That is, places are not mere background for what I viewed as the important business of culture, but in a very real sense act upon persons, bringing them into line with the norms and values of a lifeworld" (Harkin 2000:53). Often this includes stories that serve to shape a person by place.

As land ownership, use, and development changed through time, this created problems in terms of Native Americans' access to land for cultural and religious practices. As Harkin (2000) has shown, non-Indians continue to enter, develop, and use places, then move on to other new areas that fit their perceptions "of landscape, a permanence that allows for no other claims on the landscape." I remember a discussion of a group of Anglo canoeing enthusiasts who had been taking trips together in Missouri for more than fifteen years. A large part of their talk reflected this ideology, as they noted that streams they had formerly enjoyed traversing now had too many people, polluted water, and too much trash (though they often picked up trash to clean up the streams), and that they needed to look for other, "better" areas. Harkin describes this phenomenon as "a cycle of penetration and colonization of ever-new territories, in a parodic replay of colonial history." Referencing Schama (1995:137), Harkin (2000:56) further explains that "The tourist sense of landscape shares much with the picturesque, but differs in significant ways. Most noticeably, the picturesque, especially in its colonialist version, values certain combinations of elements precisely because they have a Keatsian impermanence, and hark back to a nearly forgotten way of life."

It should not be surprising that a landscape promising beauty and access to a largely unaltered scene of nature for a tourist holds a much more complex meaning for the local indigenous people. As Harkin (2000:57) says of his Ahousat consultants and a hiking trail now used by Indians and non-Indians, "For the traditional Ahousat, on the other hand, this 'place making' as Basso (1996:7) calls it, is a means of constructing history. The trail is a trail into the past. Along the route are places commemorated in oral tradition, where events are inscribed on the landscape."

Because many geographic places in the Kiowa homeland are still known and prominently mentioned in many narratives, they remain active in the culture and exhibit power that both reflects, and today affects, demography, history, religion, cemeteries, and cultural events such as dances, for both past and present Kiowa. "What is more, these places continue to play a role in human affairs by virtue of their power, as points through which the ancestors continue to operate in the world" (Harkin 2000:58). It is at this point that Indian and non-Indian views on land use part ways, resulting in misunderstanding and conflict. Influenced by Townsend-Gault's (1994) work and reflecting the thesis of his article, Harkin (2000:60) writes, "Here, the sense of place as sacred and active provides a counterpoint to the idea of space as object and resource. Sacred space confronts scarred place."

In any community the land holds a greater degree of history and cultural association for its long-term inhabitants than it does for recent arrivals or tourists. As Parker McKenzie and I drove south down Highway 115 toward Saddle Mountain, the sheer number of historical accounts he recalled during the sixteen-mile drive was overwhelming. I had similar experiences with other trips with Atwater Once, Vanessa Jennings, and other Kiowa that made me reflect on the many unwritten accounts of activities I could recite along the rural roads, streams, and farms of my home area and of how the land spoke to me in my own terms in my "homeland." It made me think of the days driving through the countryside with my grandparents, the stories they told about the places we passed, and the activities we shared there: fishing, picnicking, skipping rocks in streams, looking for fossils and arrowheads. Often we must experience something elsewhere before we comprehend the full meaning and appreciation of it for ourselves and our own communities. From this vantage point, the physical and cultural forms of Kiowa ethnogeography, toward which this chapter has been steadily moving, are explored in Chapter 2.

CHAPTER 2

Kiowa Physical and Cultural Geography

KIOWA PLACE NAMES tend to be of two main kinds: names referencing geographic forms, or references to locations where cultural and historical events occurred. These types can be further divided into water- and land-based name forms (see Map 1).

Water-Based Name Forms

Throughout the late eighteenth century and the nineteenth century, the Kiowa used a variety of lexicon to distinguish different states and configurations of water. Because the Kiowa language specifies single, dual, and triplural forms of subjects, the letters *s*, *d*, and *t* are used in parentheses to distinguish these forms. Water forms include áusé (*s/d*) and áusέgàu (*t*, any small intermittent stream), dàumáuntǫ̀ (ocean), séchó (pond), séchóèl (lake), tǫ́tèp or tǫ́tèpgà (spring or seep), and váu (*s/d/t*, creek or river of any size). The terms áusé and áusέgàu are not common and appear in only one place name recorded in this study. The most common Kiowa geographic term relating to bodies of water is váu, a noun denoting any form of moving water and analogous to the singular and plural forms of the English "brook," "creek," "stream," and "river."

Although using one term for such a wide range of watercourses may seem confusing, an understanding of the Kiowa homeland sheds light on this pattern. Except on the Staked Plains, ponds and lakes were relatively rare on the southern plains prior to their construction in the twentieth century. In terms of size and volume, various rivers and creeks are also difficult to distinguish from the ground and during various dry or wet periods of the year (Sanmann 1992:3). Whereas Euroamericans distinguish creeks

"Bison Bull River": the Cimarron River, Cimarron County, Oklahoma.

and rivers on the basis of length, Kiowa did so on the basis of the continual presence or absence of water.

Regardless of size, streams with a dependable flow of water were essential to a subsistence strategy based primarily on the grazing of horses, the equestrian hunting of bison and other game, and frequent and long-distance equestrian-based travel for foraging, trading, and raiding. On the vast, semiarid, and relatively treeless rolling North American plains, streams provided an oasis-like ecosystem in the form of riparian forests. These narrow, timber-belted stream ecozones were a principal source of chert outcrops for stone tools and timber for fuel and various items of material culture, such as tipi poles and bows and arrows, as well as preferred camping areas with water, shade, shelter, collectible food sources, and pasture. Typical of Plains cultures, the Kiowa had an intimate relationship with riparian ecotones. Appendix C lists all the Kiowa place names for streams used in this book.

In much the same way that different forks of a stream may be known by different Anglo names, the major forks and tributaries of nearly every major stream in the Kiowa homeland had different names. The Kiowa often divided small and large streams into specific zones with different names.

"Trading Creek/River": Double Mountain Fork, Brazos River, Fisher County, Texas.

The Red River, which forms much of the modern Texas-Oklahoma border, provides a clear example of this naming tendency. The North Fork of the Red River in Texas and southwestern Oklahoma was known as Qópfévàu (Sand Mountain River), while the South or Prairie Dog Town Fork both above and below the North Fork was known as Févàuèl (Big or Great Sand River) from the prevalence of sand along its course.

Branches or forks of small streams might also have individual names. An example is Rainy Mountain Creek, in Kiowa County, Oklahoma. The western branch of the stream is known as Sépyáldávàu (Rainy Hill Creek), after nearby Sépyáldá, the northwestern tributary is known as Cháfîvàu (Prairie Dog Eating Creek), from a historic event in the 1870s, and the eastern branch is known as Xòdômvàu (Pebble Creek, modern-day Sugar Creek), from the prevalence of stones in the streambed. The lower portion of the main stream below the junction of these branches is called Chènváu (Boggy/Muddy Creek) because it is extremely deep-sided, muddy, and dif-ficult to cross. Appendix C lists similar examples for the Arkansas, Brazos, Canadian, Platte, and Red rivers, and for other rivers and creeks. Only a few Kiowa names for northern rivers have survived. Most of them are streams south of the Platte River, reflecting the more southern orientation of the

Kiowa homeland, as indicated by the place names recorded since the late 1800s.

The elder Kiowa whom I interviewed rarely talked about rivers in general but spoke of specific rivers by name. General characteristics of distant streams that one had not personally encountered could be understood in the context of the account being told. The size of local streams was common knowledge and did not require additional lexicon to the word vàu to differentiate size (Sanmann 1992:4). The same name was often used for more than one stream; some examples are Gúlvǎu (Red River), Jónáèvǎu (Pecan Creek), and Xóvàu (Rock River). Up to four streams were sometimes known by the same name, usually because of a similar size, geology, flora, or other characteristic. However, not all of these streams may have been known by the same name simultaneously or by all Kiowa, as they were sometimes well distant from one another. When two or more streams were known simultaneously by the same name, the speech context indicated which was meant. Just as Euroamericans sometimes differentiate big and little forks of a river, so did the Kiowa. In some instances two rivers with the same name root were distinguished by the addition of descriptive suffixes, as with Fóvǎu (Beaver River) Beaver Creek and Fóváusân (Little Beaver River) Little Beaver Creek east of Fort Sill in Comanche and Cotton counties of Oklahoma, and Vǎuêl (Big or Great River), the Rio Grande, and Vǎuêlsàn (Big Little River), the Pecos River.

The Kiowa term for ocean (dàumáuntǫ̀) is difficult to translate. James Mooney (1898:400) conjectured that the word meant "water surrounding the earth," but Parker McKenzie believed it indicated something more like "water reached after a long journey." The latter would correspond closely to the circumstances in which the Kiowa encountered the Gulf of Mexico, the Gulf of California, and possibly the Pacific Ocean during prolonged journeys of exploration and raiding. The term for ocean appears in several Kiowa Veteran's and War Mother's songs describing the travels of World War II veterans across the Atlantic and Pacific oceans (Meadows 1999:127–130).

The Kiowa term for springs, tǫ́tèp or tǫ́tèpgà, translates as "water coming out." This term may be used in the full form, as in Fàiqòptǫ́tèp (Sun Mountain Spring), but it is more common in the shortened form, as in Ǎuhį́tǫ̀ (Cedar Spring). The root word for water (tǫ́) may also be used to initiate a place name, as in Tǫ́bíndádàu (Boiling Water), Tǫ́kǫ́ (Black Water Pond/Lake), or Tǫ́dáuihyâ (Medicine or Mysterious Lake). Although less common than streams and springs, ponds and lakes were important water sources, especially on the Llano Estacado of Texas, which in some areas had no surface streams. These water sources were sometimes distin-

38

guished by size, as with Sénfólésécho (Water Lily Pond) and Séchóêl (Big Pond, i.e., Lake). In the case of Xógàzę̀mà (Shifting Stones), a lake was named from the effects of wave action on its shore rather than as a body of water. Kiowa and other tribes undoubtedly once had many more water-based place names for these vital oasis-like areas.

Knowledge of freshwater springs and basins was also essential for a highly mobile subsistence strategy that took the Kiowa through large areas with limited water sources. Although the water table in the Llano Estacado has fallen with significant lowering of the huge Ogallala Aquifer in the course of modern development, historical sources indicate that it was relatively well watered, with numerous springs, ponds, and lakes. James Mooney (1898) recorded several springs in the Staked Plains area of Texas and the area south of this. These water sources were often at well-known base camps used by tribes raiding into south Texas, New Mexico, and Mexico, such as Fàiqòptǫ́tèp (Sun Mountain Spring) and Xójôigáthà̀dàudéę̀ (Rock House in Which They Were Contained).

Water was crucial to crossing portions of the Llano Estacado (the Staked Plains) and other locales farther to the southwest. Laguna Sabinas (Cedar Lake) in northeast Gaines County, Texas, is one such example. Fenton (1981) provides an excellent account of the importance of dependable water sources in relation to travel, raiding, and trade activities on the Staked Plains. His account of Cedar Lake shows the ongoing importance of this site to Indians, Comancheros, soldiers, buffalo hunters, and finally cattle-men. As the largest salt (alkali) lake in the region (approximately six miles long by four miles wide), it was named for the stubby, twisted cedars that grew along its edge. Although the lake proper is brackish, it provided a year-round source of potable water. The lake is fed by several freshwater springs at the north end, some of which were once sizable perennial streams, but there were also several wells on the south end, some dug by Indians. Although several creeks and rivers on the northern Staked Plains provided well-known travel routes through the region, the southern Staked Plains was devoid of surface streams. Thus, Cedar Lake was an important water source along a route that ran through the southern Llano Estacado from the Colorado River to the Pecos River (Fenton 1981). This is probably Ā̀uhį́tǫ̀. Although many more trails have been recorded for the Comanche (Campbell and Field 1968; Gelo 2000), the Kiowa undoubtedly knew and used many of these same trails, especially since the Kiowa and Comanche often conducted joint raiding parties throughout the region.

Salt was also a precious commodity on the plains. In an interview with Alice Marriott in 1936, Mrs. Tanedooah reported four locales from which the Kiowa procured salt. While salt could be viewed as a mineral and thus

"Cedar Lake," Gaines County, Texas.

a land-based form, three of the Kiowa names for sources of salt are associated with nearby streams.

> There were only three or four places where you could get it. One place where we got salt was northwest of here (salt plains). We dug it out with pans and sacked it up and carried it home. There was no name for that place; we just described it. Sometimes we called it Adltodo—head wound. A man was killed there once getting salt. The Kiowa raided a Texas wagon-train and he was shot in the fight and died. They could see him lose his brains. We had a victory dance, but he died. Another place was Gudlp'a (Red River), where we found big lumps of salt, like rocks along the river banks. Another was Salt Creek—Atantaip'a—where there was more than anywhere else. White people got their salt at another place where we did on the big river—Aiyadldabep'a (South Canadian).[1]

These names clearly correlate with the following names and locales: (1) Áyàldàvàu (Timber Hill River) or Medicine Lodge Creek is a tributary of

KIOWA ETHNOGEOGRAPHY

the Salt Fork of the Arkansas in Kansas and Oklahoma. This area is part of the "salt plains" referred to by Mrs. Tanedooah and by George Hyde (1968:137, 282). (2) Áulthâudàu (Head Wound) is the salt plains in Alfalfa County, Oklahoma. (3) Gúlváu (Red River) is the South Canadian River in Oklahoma or the Big Wichita River near Wichita Falls in northern Texas. (4) Áutą́thą́ivàu (Salt River) probably refers to the southern branch of the South Canadian River in the Texas Panhandle near the border with New Mexico, where salt deposits occurred.

Hugh L. Scott recorded several "paint mines," or places where Kiowa recovered mineral paint for decorative and religious use. White paint was acquired in the middle of the road that went to Fort Sill just over the ridge, "where you can see Cheever's house," near the mouth of Rainy Mountain Creek, near Quanah Parker's home, and all over the plains of the Canadian and Cimarron rivers. Sources for red paint included a locale near Stumbling Bear's house on Timber Pass Creek, near the canyon of the Arkansas on the south side, and at "Big Red's" or Guo-laddle's home north of Mount Sheridan. Scott noted that although white paint was plentiful, sources for red paint were scarce. Sources for other colors included the head of Apache Creek near Carither's Mission (yellow pigment) and near Double Mountain in Texas (black pigment).[2]

Land-Based Name Forms

The Kiowa used a variety of terms to distinguish different types of landforms, especially those involving elevations and depressions. Hills and mountains were especially significant as landmarks for traveling. These landforms included áàutàun (a timber clearing), ábàulhàu (a forested knoll or hill), ákǫ̀dàu (a dark timber thicket, so thick that it shaded the side), ájǒbyǫ̂i (a circular opening in the timber, probably a meadow), àujáugà (an island), dáum (the Earth, land, ground, or a region of land), fádá (flat, grassy prairie), fédàum (sandy land), hîldà (a valley), jâun (any small canyon or depressed area), jòhâu (a concavity in a cliff, bluff, tree, etc.), káuikáuhótcà (a cave), pígáu (a hill, hillock, rise in the ground, or elongated hill), píhót (an area in a bend in the river), qáugáu (a precipice, bluff, or cliff), qóp (a mountain), sángá (an escarpment), xóchéldè (s/d) and xósáuldè (t, any conspicuous standing rock formation), xóhót (a canyon), and yáldá (a knoll, hill, or mound). Forms designating mountains, hills, and lands or regions are most common in Kiowa place names. A kį́ájôi (man-made breastworks) is a combination of earthen breastworks and fox holes constructed for defensive purposes. Appendix B lists all Kiowa place names for landforms used in this book.[3]

Mountains

The Kiowa term qóp generally corresponds to the English mountain, an elevated land mass higher and more rocky than a hill. Only a few Kiowa names of prominent mountains on the northern plains have survived, some of which are so prevalent that almost all tribes know them. At the time the Kiowa resided in Montana and Wyoming they undoubtedly had a much more extensive knowledge and nomenclature of mountains as they would have been practicing a more mountain-based subsistence strategy. Mooney (1898:155) stressed the continued importance of the mountains for the Kiowa:

> . . . it is worthy of note that in all their wanderings the Kiowa have never, for any long period, entirely abandoned the mountains. After making friends with the Crows, they established themselves in the Black Hills until driven out by the invading Dakota and Cheyenne, and now for seventy years or more they have had their main headquarters in the Wichita Mountains.

When the Kiowa migrated to the southern plains, mountains no longer seemed to hold as important a place in their ethnogeography, possibly because of geographic, functional, or subsistence changes. Although perhaps retaining symbolic importance, mountains are rare on the southern and central plains. Whereas areas like the Wichita Mountains provided important oasis- or island-like environments in the larger surrounding grass-dominated plains, mountains were fewer and smaller and contributed much less to the Kiowa subsistence strategy. In this ecozone, streams probably became more important than mountains, as reflected in the overwhelmingly greater number of streams and thus of stream names.

One indication of this change is that the Kiowa descriptions of mountains and rivers on the central and southern plains recorded by James Mooney and H. L. Scott indicate that mountains were used primarily as landmarks in travel. Many streams and other locations are described in terms of a number of days' journey or a direction from a certain mountain or hill. The Comanche similarly used hills and mountains as guides in traveling (Gelo 2000:291). Whether reflecting a loss of known place names over time or that the Kiowa only needed to name a limited number of mountains for their purposes, there are relatively few extant Kiowa names for individual mountains in the Wichita Range of southwestern Oklahoma, which, as the only significant mountain range in this region, has been a prominent part of their homeland since the early 1800s.

The plains remain a primarily visual environment, and these patterns reflect the larger Plains Indian tendency to conceptualize the region as such. The openness and the great distance that one can see often fool those unaccustomed to the region. Several accounts attest to the remarkable visual acuity of Plains Indians and their adeptness at seeing signals at great distances (Berlandier 1980; Dodge 1877; Clark 1885; Webb 1931). William P. Clark (1885:332) stated that "Indians are certainly remarkable for power and keenness of vision, which are inherited qualities, and they are greatly aided in detecting the presence of game by their intimate knowledge of the movements and habits of animals." In discussing Plains Indian communications, Webb (1931:73) noted that "On the Plains the eye far outruns the ear in its range." Colonel Richard Dodge (1877:368–369) similarly described the ability of Plains Indians to see and communicate at long distances:

> In communicating at long distances on the plains, their mode of telegraphing is . . . remarkable. Indian scouts are frequently employed by the United States Government, and are invaluable, indeed almost indispensable, to the success of important expeditions. The leader, or interpreter, is kept with the commander of the expedition, while the scouts disappear far in advance or on the flanks. Occasionally one shows himself, sometimes a mere speck on a distant ridge, and the interpreter will say at once what that scout wishes to communicate. . . .
>
> The only really wonderful thing about this telegraphing is the very great distance at which it can be read by the Indian. I have very good "plains eyes"; but while, even with an excellent field glass, I could scarcely make out that the distant speck was a horseman, the Indian by my side would tell me what the distant speck was saying.

Knowledge of principal landmarks and their distances from other landmarks was of great importance to the highly mobile western plains lifestyle. Plains Indians commonly used hills and mountains not only as guides in traveling but for reconnaissance as well. Even a moderately elevated hill could afford a view of several miles, allowing scouts or hunters to scan the surrounding region for animals or humans. Gelo (2000:291) discusses Comanche travel routes that consisted essentially of following a course periodically marked by mountains. Mooney recorded numerous such descriptions for Yíqòp (Two Mountains) or Double Mountain, a pair of six-hundred-foot-high hills in southwestern Stonewall County, Texas, and Two Buttes Hill, near the town of Two Buttes in Baca County,

"Double Mountain," Stonewall County, Texas.

Colorado. The latter is the most prominent land feature in the area where Kansas, Oklahoma, and Colorado meet. Visible for many miles, it is an important landmark in this region. Parker McKenzie, who grew up hearing of many of the raids and journeys undertaken by his grandfather Queton and others, stated that the main function of mountains for the Kiowa was in aiding navigation during travel. Sun Mountain (Guadalupe Peak) in Texas can be seen throughout much of southwestern Texas and New Mexico. Queton often told McKenzie, "You weren't a man until you had been to Sun Mountain."[4]

Numerous plains accounts attest to the use of hills by Indian scouts to signal the return of war parties, signal information back to others, detect pursuers and potential ambushes, and look for sources of food and water. While on patrol in New Mexico, Lt. E. H. Bergmann (Foster 1960:44) reported being intercepted by Comanche riders twelve miles outside their camp who proceeded to communicate the number and disposition of the troops back over that distance with mirrors, whereupon they obtained permission to bring the patrol to the village with a message of welcome. In this way, as Gelo (2000:302) notes, "Hills along a route . . . offered a measure

KIOWA ETHNOGEOGRAPHY

of control . . . in addition to serving as navigation marks." Prominent hills and mountains also frequently had concentrations of valuable resources such as timber, food and utility plants, and water sources in the form of springs.

Just as they subdivided major river systems into branches with distinct names, so too the Kiowa subdivided mountain ranges into distinctly named zones (this naming trait is common; Euroamericans similarly may have a single name for a large mountain range or river but assign different names to the smaller constitutent ranges or forks of the river). The Kiowa distinguished three separate zones of the Rocky Mountains. The mountains in Wyoming and western Montana were known as the Cáuiqòp (Kiowa Mountains), after the former home of the Kiowa.[5] The central Rocky Mountains of Colorado and New Mexico were called Ítàqòp (Ute Mountains), for the Ute of that region. The southern or Sierra Madre Range in New Mexico, Chihuahua, and Sonora was known as Qópétjàu (Great or Big Mountains), from the high peaks. The Kiowa also divided the Wichita Mountains into two separately named portions that were differentiated by the pass at present-day Cooperton, Oklahoma: the Tàugûiqòp (Apache Mountains) or eastern range of the mountains and the Thócútqòp (Wichita Mountains) or western range of the mountains around the present-day Quartz Mountains and Quartz Mountain State Park. This distinction is practically unknown among the Kiowa today.

HILLS

A yáldá (hill or knoll) is lower in elevation than a qóp and generally circular in shape. In contrast, a pígáu is an elongated hill or ridge. Kiowa conceptions of hills entail some degree of vegetation, including grass, in contrast to mountains, which usually exhibit more barren, rocky surfaces. Thàugúyàldà (Buck Antelope Antler's Hill), the Antelope Hills in western Oklahoma, Áyàldà (Timber Hill), on Medicine Lodge Creek in southern Kansas, and Chádàuyàldà (Prairie Dog Hill) west of Vernon, Texas, were all well-known hills.

Like mountains, prominent hills were some of the most noticeable landforms encountered on the open and relatively flat to rolling southern plains, especially in areas of low relief. Because they were easily ascended, they too, like the larger mountains, functioned primarily as landmarks in traveling and for reconnaissance. Bands and war parties had scouts ascend such elevations to ascertain whether they were being pursued or approached by others.

Major escarpments (sángá) were also noted geographic markers. The Llano Estacado or Staked Plains of Texas was a major geographic feature of the nineteenth-century Kiowa homeland and a primary area for bison and horses; numerous trails led from there into the southern and southwestern regions of present-day Texas, New Mexico, and Mexico. The Staked Plains were known as Fágà (Prairie or Open Field), from the adverb fágá ("out in the open field or prairie"). The western edge of this feature was known as Fásángá (Plains Escarpment) and, as today, marked the ecological border between the western Staked Plains and the beginning of the increasingly semidesert areas of eastern New Mexico.

Regions

The Kiowa term dáum can encompass Earth, land, or a specific region of land, or it can be used as a suffix to denote a specific type of land. In place names this term was generally used as a suffix in various forms of the adverb dáumgá ("on or at a point on the ground") to indicate the country or homeland of a specific population, as in Cáuidàumgà (Kiowa Country) or Câidàumgà (Comanche Country). Such distinctions were also later applied as nouns to various non-Indian populations as they became associated with specific regions, as in Qóptháukáuidàum (Mountain Mexican Country), or as adverbial expressions, as in Qóptháukáuidàumbè (Within the Mountain Mexican Country) or Qóptháukáuidàumgà (On/At Mountain Mexican Country). Several regional names were developed to specify the various groups of Anglo and Hispanic populations in the eastern United States, Texas, New Mexico, and the northern provinces of Mexico. Over time, place names relating to tribal homelands began shifting from an association with protohistoric and historic homelands to the area encompassing the Kiowa, Comanche, and Apache Reservation, and finally to post-reservation allotted communities.

The term dáum can also be used to describe particular landforms, as in fédàum (sandy land) or xódàum (rocky land). In southwestern Oklahoma, low-lying, flat, poorly drained land, often with a preponderance of wild onions and mesquite trees, is known as sôldàum (Onion Flat, lit. Onion Ground). The area between the Wichita Mountains, Rainy Mountain, and Hobart, Oklahoma, was known by this name. Originally used mainly for gathering wild onions and hunting deer and antelope, it was considered by many Kiowa to be of poor quality and unsuitable for taking allotments. Indians often selected allotments based more on the needs of the past and

"Onion Ground," Kiowa County, Oklahoma.

present—water, grass, and firewood—than on the needs of the future, such as good-quality soils for farming. There is thus a distinct demographic void with few allotments in this region of the old reservation, now Kiowa County. Anglo settlers cut down the mesquite, drained the soil, and turned this area into one of the most productive sections of farmland in the Kiowa area.

BLUFFS, RECESSES AND CONCAVITIES, CANYONS, AND PASSES

These landforms account for a significant group of geographic forms and place names. Qáugáu is the term for a bank, bluff, cliff, or precipice, as in the Kiowa personal name Qáuyâjè (Descending Over A Bank). The verbal adjective qãudãu when applied to a landmark means precipitous. A jòhâu (s/d/t) is a recess or concavity in a cliff, bluff, tree, or any vertical surface. This noun form is derived from jòhâu, a verbal adjective meaning to be recessed or concaved. The noun form jòhâu forms the basis of several Kiowa men's and women's names, including that of the well-known Jòhâu (Recess in a Bluff) and his son Jòhâusàn (Son of Recess in a Bluff, lit. Little Bluff Recess), the Kiowa tribal chief from 1833 to 1866. As explained by

Kiowa elders, a jòhâu exhibits a slight recess or concavity in its face or side and thus differs slightly from a qáugáu. This term would probably include any rockshelter or overhang, but not a true cave (káuikáuhótcà).

The Kiowa terms for bluff and concavity are often confused, and names containing the root jòhâu are often mistranslated as bluff in Kiowa personal names. One of the best illustrations of this geographic form is found in a Kiowa calendar drawn by Silverhorn. The winter 1893 entry marks the death of the latter Jòhâusàn, who died a short distance west of present-day Verden, Oklahoma, and has the image of a butte with a deep concavity in its face, reflecting this geographic form.[6] Hugh L. Scott recorded a site in the eastern edge of the Texas Panhandle called Medicine Butte. It is described as a high pointed butte on the north side of the Canadian River that "looms up high above the other—like a mountain with cut side—is [located] up the river it is called medicine butte (Tohausen's tipi)" and it is noted that it "can be seen from the top of the Antelope Hills." Scott recorded a story related to the site in the 1890s, probably from Isseo:

> There is a high pointed butte up on the Canadian that has a strong medicine. I knew an old man by the name of "Lean Old Man" [Táulqàptàu] who died when I was young, he was very sick, he went up and slept on that butte—and the medicine said to him, "Look at me. I see you lying there poor and sick. This is my medicine house. I live here—get up and go down by your lodge. I am going to take pity on you. You will attain old age."

Scott's name for the site, Medicine Butte, correlates with that recorded by Mooney (1898:398), Dáujóhâu, Medicine Bluff Concavity, the present-day Mount Rochester.[7] One of the best-known bluffs in Kiowa geography is Xóqáudáuhá (Medicine Bluff) on present-day Fort Sill Military Base in Comanche County, Oklahoma. The site is an awe-inspiring, sheer cliff that rises directly above the south side of Medicine Bluff Creek and was a frequent site for fasting and vision quests.

The term xóhót ("rocks crowding in") was used for any form of canyon. The largest canyon in the Texas Panhandle, Palo Duro, was called simply Xóhót. A pass or gap in a group of hills or mountains was known as a jâun. Gómgájâun (Wind Pass) is a canyon-like pass at the extreme head of the Double Mountain Fork of the Brazos River in Texas. The gap leading through the northeastern end of the Wichita Mountains northeast of present-day Meers, Oklahoma, is known as Ájâun (Timber Gap). This important pre-reservation route is now a portion of Oklahoma State Highway 58.

Formally Named Geographic Place Names

Stemming from Bright's (1958:174–175) work among the Karok, formal Native American names for geographic forms may be divided into several major types. In Afable and Beeler's (1997:189–190) classification, these are (1) descriptive names, (2) locational names, (3) names referring to human activities carried out at a site, and (4) names from history, mythology, or folklore. Distinctions between secular and sacred (or, perhaps more accurately, between greater and lesser sacred importance) may be added to characterize sites of reverence. All of these categories are found in Kiowa place names.

1. Descriptive Names

The largest group of Native American place names, these refer to a specific feature or characteristic of a given locale. Descriptively named sites may be named from (a) their physical configuration or appearance, (b) the seasonal or permanent presence of named animals, birds, insects, or fishes, (c) the resemblance of part of the site to a part of the human or animal body or other object, (d) the color of the site or its environment, or (e) a particular sound characteristic of the site. Many Kiowa place names are of the descriptive category, with attributes of flora, fauna, geology, weather, animals, or humans forming the basis of names of mountains, hills, streams, and springs. Corresponding Kiowa examples of this form include (a) Fàiqóp (Sun Mountain), named for the sun's reflections on the mountain's granite surface, and Fîyâujŏchéldè (House Upon the Summit) or Signal Mountain, named for a stone signaling house built on it by the army; (b) Cháfìvàu (Prairie Dog Eating Creek), based on the location of a prairie dog town, and Jónvàu (Fat River), based on the density of bison along this stream; (c) Sálkâuiqòp (Reticulum, Leaf Tripe, or Honeycomb Stomach Mountains), and Qópŏtágàu (Mountain That Is Lifting Its Chin), named for their resemblance to body parts; (d) Tháiqóp (White Mountain) and Gúlvâu (Red River), named for their color; and (e) Gómgájâun (Wind Pass/Canyon), probably named for the wind blowing through it.

2. Locational Names

These imply a contrast of location, orientation, or direction, such as up versus down, this side versus the other side, offshore versus onshore, or upriver versus downriver. Cardinal directions per se, though common in Euroamerican place names, appear infrequently in Indian place names

(French and French 1996:189). A few Kiowa place names of this form exist, such as Fíyâujóchéldè (House Upon the Summit), Xòaî (Rock That Grew Upwards), and Xóáutkáungà (At the End of the Stone [i.e., Mountains]).

Many Kiowa place names specify their association with hills or mountains. Names for locales not associated with hills and mountains were formed by adding the suffix dé-ę̀, an adverb denoting "at that point or place" or "there at." Place names in this genre include those based on both geographic and personal names, such as Xójôigáthàdàudéę̀ (Rock House in Which They Were Contained) and Dáuálkǫ̀gàiéhòldèę̀ (Place Where Black Kettle Was Killed).

3. Names Referring to Human Activities Carried Out at a Site

These may refer either to frequent or recurring activities or to the occurrence of man-made structures and culturally important artifacts of human activity (not flora or fauna) at a site. Place names of this type are common in Kiowa geography, with named sites including several well-known streams, Sun Dance sites, battle sites, forts, and trading posts. Some examples are named streams, such as Ǻgùntàvàu (Tipi Pole Cutting River) and Qáujóváu (Sun Dance Creek); trading posts, such as Xópáijó (Adobe House, lit. Rock Dust House); military forts, such as Ǻkǫ̀vàusòlę̀gàu or Ǻkǫ̀vàuyápfáhêgàu (Dark Timber River Soldier Place); and more recent cities, such as Jòáuidè (Many Tipis/Houses, Oklahoma City).

4. Place Names Derived from History, Mythology, or Folklore

These may be of obscure origin and require examination of oral traditions and ethnohistory to establish the context and meaning. Sites bearing names in this category include historical battle sites, such as Sáqàutjàuáàutàundèvàu (Creek Where the Cheyenne Were Annihilated), named after the defeat of forty-eight Cheyenne Bow String Society members by the Kiowa, Comanche, and Apache in 1837; Màunkàugúldévàu (Red Sleeve's Creek), named after a Comanche chief killed there in 1847; and Dáuálkǫ̀gàiéhòldèę̀ (The Place Where Black Kettle Was Killed), or the Washita Battle Site of 1868. One well-known historic locale is Xójôigáthàdàudéę̀ (Rock House in Which They Were Contained), whose name refers to a famous prolonged siege of Kiowa by Mexican troops in 1839 before the Kiowa were able to escape (Mooney 1898:302–305). Mythic and folklore origins are evident in site names such as Tǫ́dáuihyâ (Medicine or Mysterious Lake) and Jámátàunàváu (Star Girls Tree River). Xòaî (Rock That Grew Upwards) and the Jámátₐudàu (Star Girls), or the Pleiades constellation, would also belong to this category because of their mythological associations.

These four categories of place names and the basis of their composition are not discrete but overlapping. Thus, Kiowa place names may refer simultaneously to the physical characteristics of a site, its location, and activities undertaken at the site, or to a historical or mythic event.

Other Types of Place Names

Other types of American Indian place names include references to names of tribes, and names borrowed as loan words from Euroamerican languages (Afable and Beeler 1997:194). Both of these forms are common in Kiowa place names.

REFERENCES TO OTHER TRIBES

Kiowa place names referring to other tribes include land (Sáqàulgùljóhâu, Cheyenne Red Bluff Recess) and stream (Qáulvàu, Arikara River) forms. Tribal-oriented place names were also sometimes formed to note specific historical events, as in Qẚhífịvàu (Tonkawa Creek), named for an intertribal massacre of over 150 Tonkawa in 1862; Áthàuhâuigácàundèàusè (Stream Branch Where They Brought Back the Bonnet), named to commemorate a successful revenge raid on the Ute in 1869; and Sémhátvàu (Apache Creek), named for the Apache encampment during the reservation period. Such place names were also applied to non-Indian groups, as in Qóptháukáuiváu (Mexican Creek) and several locations and streams referring to Anglo trading posts and military forts in the 1800s.

LOAN WORDS

Names based on archaic or loan (introduced) words can be difficult to interpret and in time are subject to reinterpretation and folk etymology (Afable and Beeler 1997:194). Kiowa place names incorporating names from other cultures—mostly from the Comanche—are few and easily recognized. Fíbòyàldà is based on the Kiowa pronunciation of the Comanche term for a large horse and the Kiowa suffix for hill. Known as American Horse Hill, the name literally translates as Big Horse Hill and references a fight in which the Kiowa captured several American horses from Texans in the winter of 1841–1842, the largest they had seen at that point. Names borrowed from other tribes can be difficult to recognize, owing to altered pronunciation. Gúhàlĕvàu (Wild Horse/Mustang Creek, in reference to the Kwahadi of the Staked Plains), and Gúànàdèvàu (Quanah's Creek) reflect Kiowa pronunciations of Comanche names.

While place names based on Euroamerican loan words may have once been more common, especially those involving nearby non-Indian town names, they are no longer used. Kiowa place names borrowed from English include names such as Gúséjàn (Washington, D.C.), Ánádákò (Anadarko, Oklahoma), and Ócómsélę̀ (Oklahoma City, Oklahoma). Adverbial forms include Ézèncà (Inside or At the Agency) and Ézèyàu (In the Agency Area), the Kiowa pronunciations of "agency," and Láwtcá (At Lawton), in reference to Lawton, Oklahoma. These terms are usually known only by the eldest Kiowa and appear to have ceased being used around 1950 with the widespread acquisition of English and the use of English place names.

Some Indian place names have an obvious translation but an unclear interpretation.[8] The Kiowa name of the South Platte River is Jónváu, which literally translates as "Fat River" and is known as Fat or Greasy River by many Plains tribes. Although this translation might leave the impression that it was a very wide and expansive stream or one with a less than pure quality of water, the name refers to the abundance of bison there. Áulkáuijóhâu (Crazy Bluff/Concavity) does not clearly point to its etymology. Was some event of mental illness or insanity associated with the locale? Not at all: the name refers to an exuberant scalp dance held there in the winter of 1860–1861 to celebrate the acquisition of a Caddo scalp to avenge their killing of Bird Appearing earlier that year.[9] Áulthâudàu (Head Wound) references a Kiowa man who was shot in the head during an attack on a wagon train and later died, but the name is used for the salt plains in Alfalfa County, Oklahoma, where the Kiowa were gathering salt when the event occurred.[10]

Some Indian names of streams seem more appropriate than their English counterparts. Cannonball River in Kansas is more accurately described by the Kiowa name of Hạ̀uxòvàu (Iron Stone River), for the abundance of iron nodules in the vicinity. The river of the same name in North Dakota may have a similar etymological basis.

Kiowa Place Names and Personal Names

While the subject of ethnogeography commonly directs attention to physical locations and geographic forms, these forms also make up a significant genre of Kiowa personal names for both sexes. Four forms of Kiowa personal names linked to geographic place names have been identified:

(1) personalized place names, or places named after individuals, (2) geographic place names used as personal names, or people named after places, (3) people named after unspecified or generic geographic forms for which the full basis or associated history of the name form is needed, and (4) location-based names, or names based on events that occurred at specific locales.[11]

PERSONALIZED PLACE NAMES

Although the practice of naming places after persons is reported to be uncommon (Afable and Beeler 1997:190), several examples suggest that it was fairly common in mid- to late nineteenth-century Kiowa culture. Examples include streams, mountains, and other landforms. At least six pre-reservation streams named after individuals are known, including Cûiqòljévàu (Wolf Necklace's River), named after a Comanche of this name; Màunkàugúldévàu (Red Sleeve's Creek), named for a noted Comanche chief killed there in 1847; and Xólhę́dèvàu (No Arm's Creek), named after an Anglo trader. Jòhâudèhêmdèvàu (Creek Where Jòhâusàn Died) refers to the location where the Kiowa tribal chief died in 1866, while Sétthą́idètháukàuimáimàufâcâundèvàu (Creek Where White Bear Brought the White Women) was the site where White Bear exchanged a number of captive Anglo women. Qàunchèhâjévàu (Short Man's Creek) was named after a Kiowa man who lived near the head of this stream during the reservation period.

Land-based places named after individuals, such as mountains, simply had the term for mountain added, usually as a terminal suffix. Several individual-based place names developed with permanent residency in the reservation period. Gę́cį́nyíqòp (Long Horn Mountain) and Èàunhâfàuiqòp (Trailing the Enemy Mountain, now known as Unap Mountain) are both small mountains in Kiowa County, Oklahoma, named for the individuals who took their allotment near them. Other place names based on the proximity of individual allotments followed in the reservation period, such as Eagleheart Spring, Odlepaugh Springs, Catt Spring, Gawkey Creek, and Big Tree's Crossing, some of which may have once been used in Kiowa but all of which are now known only by their English name.

Names for locales not associated with hills and mountains were formed by adding the suffix dé-ę̀, an adverb denoting "at that point or place" or "there at." This genre of place names could include names based on both geographic and personal name forms, such as Xójôigáthàdàudéę̀ (Rock House in Which They Were Contained) and Dáuálkǫ̀gàiéhòldèę̀ (Place Where Black Kettle Was Killed).

"Sun Mountain": El Capitan and Guadalupe Peak, Guadalupe Mountains National Park, Culberson County, Texas.

Place Names as Personal Names

Geographic terms and proper place names also form the basis for several Kiowa personal names. Some personal names reflect proper place names of well-known geographic locations, such as Fàiqópjè (Sun Mountain or Guadalupe Peak), Gúlváu (Red River, the Canadian River), Váupfáhâl (Confluence, the Rio Grande-Pecos River juncture), Xɔ́gàzɛ̨mà (Shifting Stones, a Texas lake), and Váuêlsàn (Little Big River, the Pecos River). These names reference prominent streams, landforms, and base camps on raiding trails into New Mexico and Mexico and were probably given by male family members to commemorate travels and exploits in these regions. Other names such as Gúljóhâu (Red Bluff Recess) reflect births near landforms of the same name. Parker McKenzie was named Sépyàldà (Rainy Hill) after he was born in his great-grandmother's tipi during a grass payment encampment just north of Sépyáldá (now known as Rainy Mountain), southeast of Gotebo, Oklahoma. Delores Toyebo Harragarra was given the nickname Píhótcáimà (At the Bend or Peninsula in the River) as a child, from the location of her home in a bend of the Washita River. Titus Tappto was named Tàuqóp (Saddle Mountain) because his mother, Pearl Aunko, grew up near Saddle Mountain. Other Kiowa were given names from named locales, such as Váuêlsàn (Pecos River [lit. Little Big River]) and Yɪ́qòp (Two Mountains).

Many personal names referring to a specific geographic locale may be ambiguous in terms of the location referenced. In general, whether a place name is ambiguous or not depends largely on whether anyone living knows where the name refers. With confinement of the Kiowa to a reservation in the southwestern corner of Indian Territory in 1875, knowledge of the exact location referenced in many geographically based personal names decreased, as the Kiowa could no longer travel through much of their former homeland. As mobility decreased, so too did the ability to visit and remain familiar with the exact locales associated with the geographically based personal names.

In other cases, references to geographic forms are not obvious in the morphemes forming the name and require additional knowledge of Kiowa history and culture for clarity. The name Xɔ́ájɔ̀jàu (They Spoke To The Rock) refers to the Star Girls Story, in which children speak to a rock, instructing it to rise and save them from their pursuing sister turned bear. The name Xɔ́âitàlyɪ̀ (Rock That Grew Upwards Boy) also references this story and the geological formation now known as Devil's Tower in Wyoming.

Like personal names, Kiowa geographic names sometimes changed after significant events. Swiftwater River was renamed American Horse

"Confluence": the Pecos–Rio Grande junction, Val Verde County, Texas.

River after the Kiowa captured a large number of American horses there from some Texans (Mooney 1898:277). When the principal Kiowa tribal leader died in 1866, "Stream Where Jòhâusàn Died" became a byname for the Cimarron River. Mooney (1898:395) provides numerous examples of geographic locations for streams, trading posts, forts, and battlegrounds that were named for events occurring between the 1830s and the 1870s. Kiowa undoubtedly knew and had names for many of these locations. We will never fully know how many locations have been renamed as new events occurred in their vicinity.

KIOWA PERSONAL NAMES BASED ON UNSPECIFIED OR GENERIC GEOGRAPHIC FORMS

In addition to personalized place names and personal names based on geographic place names, personal names based on unspecified geographic terms form another body of Kiowa names. Kiowa personal names refer to a wide array of geographic forms, including islands, streams, lakes, hills, hillsides, ridges, mountains, mountain passes, bluffs or cliffs, bluff concavities, forest groves, and forest clearings.

Examples of male Kiowa names of this kind include Áujáujè (Island),

Háubápjè (Hillside/Slope), named by his sweethearts because his father used to stay with the Quahada Comanche on the Staked Plains of Texas, which have a border of sloping bluffs; Jâungùi (Outside a Mountain Pass), named after a scouting incident; Jòhâudè (Recess/Concavity in a Bluff) and Jòhâusàn (Little [i.e., Son of] Recess/Concavity in a Bluff); and Xóqàubóidè (Shining Cliff). Several Kiowa men's names contain the ensuing syllable for mountain, as in Qópfáhóldè (Killed Them at the Mountain) and Qóptáidè (Atop a Mountain).

Examples of female Kiowa names include Ábìhíl (Circular Timber Grove/Bend); Fàiqópjè (Sun Mountain), Guadalupe Mountain near El Paso, Texas, a favorite base for raids into Mexico because of numerous water springs; Píhótjè (Peninsula or Bend in the River); Tháijóhâu (White Bluff Recess/Concavity); Tháipímá (White Knoll); Tóqáudál (Round/Circular Lake); Vânétjè (Big Forest Clearing or Opening); Váugàgóp (Struck the Enemy in the River); Váugàhól (Killed Them in the River); Váugàjáuà (Pursuing Them Along a River); Váupfáhâl (Stream Confluence), the confluence of the Pecos River and the Rio Grande; Xógàzèmà (Shifting Rocks), in reference to waves hitting a lake shore; and Xóqàubóidè (Crystalline [Rock] Cliff).

Names referring to ridges and knolls appear in only a few Kiowa personal names. Two examples are Pídèà (Coming Along a Ridgetop) and Tháipímá (White Ridge or Knoll). The name Qópjóhâu (Mountain Bluff Recess) combines two geographic forms. Although based on known circumstances that occurred near or at specific landforms, and thus composed to commemorate an event and its associated locale, their precise location is not specified in the name form, and thus the geographic basis of many such names is now often unknown.

LOCATION-BASED PERSONAL NAMES

Many of the geographic locales on which personal names were based were last visited before the Kiowa were placed on a final reservation in 1875, and thus relate to a myriad of locations across the plains and portions of the Southwest. Some personal names were also not composed until many years later, and many of these locations are not directly conveyed in the syllables forming the name. That is, many Kiowa names lack syllables denoting geographic forms but reference actions that occurred at specific locations (some of which also have formal place names), and so reference the site by association. Many warfare-based names fall in this category because they are based on specific actions that occurred at specific locations. Two names illustrate this pattern. The personal name Étkàulésàu

(They Were Laid Side By Side) refers to the forty-eight Cheyenne Bow String Society members who were killed in 1837 by Kiowa, Comanche, and Apache and laid side by side beside a creek, which the Kiowa then named Sáqàutjàuáàutàundèvàu (Creek Where the Cheyenne Were Annihilated (Mooney 1898:271–272). Similarly, Èttáuhótjàu (They Are Being Starved) is a personal name originating from the Hueco Tanks siege near present-day El Paso, Texas, in 1839, which the Kiowa had named Xójôigáthàdàudéè̜ (Rock House in Which They Were Contained).

Although some personal names refer to specific, well-known locales, such as Guadalupe Peak, Rainy Mountain, and Devil's Tower, others (Qópfáhóljè, Killed Them at the Mountain; Váugàjáuà̜, Pursuing Them Along a River) refer to unidentified locales often known only in the oral history of particular families. Personal names and place names and their bases are often lost through the generations, especially among later generations confined to the reservation and unable to visit these dispersed locales. Like place names and songs, Kiowa personal names should also be viewed as compressed texts, with an extensive associated oral history that provides the context or basis of the name form needed to relate the full text, reference, and significance of a name. Although ancestral Kiowa names formed from geographic references continue to be passed down to later generations, other, newer Kiowa names refer to locations within the present-day Kiowa community of southwestern Oklahoma, which suggests this genre will continue among the Kiowa.[12]

KIOWA CALENDAR NAMES

Mooney's 1898 *Calendar History of the Kiowa* combines four separate calendars encompassing sixty years of collective Kiowa history, from the winter of 1832–1833 to the summer of 1892. Kiowa calendars were known as sá-cút ("year marks") and a calendar keeper as a sá-cút-jò-qì ("year marks keeper"). Two pictographic entries were made for each year, dividing the calendar equally into sixty winter and summer entries. During winter encampments, calendar keepers periodically recounted this body of tribal knowledge in chronological order. These historical recitations are said to have taken several nights to complete. Appendix E lists the names and translations of all Kiowa calendar entries recorded by Mooney. The pictographic images are full of references to individual persons and geographic locales. Summer entries depict a Sun Dance lodge, the central object of the most common pan-Kiowa religious ceremony. Winter entries are indicated by an upright black bar, thought to represent dead vegetation (Mooney 1898:143). Each entry has a pictographic drawing of the principal event above or beside it, often connected by a black line. Each year became associated by two names based on the principal event of each summer and winter, with the suffixes -qầu-jô (Sun Dance) for summer and -dè-sài (Winter in which, or Winter of) for winter. When no Sun Dance was held, no lodge was depicted, and an image of the primary subject was drawn between two winter entries and designated in name form with the suffix -fài-dà (Summer in which, or Summer of).

When the Sun Dance was nearly discontinued in the 1880s, some Kiowa calendars substituted the image of a tree in full foliage as the summer marker, and this image continued to appear in Kiowa calendars into the 1930s. Minor variations characterized some of the other Kiowa calendars (Mooney 1898:143–144). Because summer entries focused on Sun Dance sites, and some winter entries focused on geographic locations, calendar names can be viewed as combining historical and geographic place names. Two major patterns emerge: summer entries generally recorded the name or attribute associated with the Sun Dance of that year, while winter entries primarily recorded the deaths, whether natural or through warfare, of well-known men.

Summer entries tend to focus on three main aspects associated with annual Sun Dances: geographic descriptions of the area where a Sun Dance was held, streams or landmarks near the site of the Sun Dance, or an unusual activity that occurred during or shortly after the ceremony. Sun Dances named after descriptive names or local geography or flora include the summers of 1835, 1839, 1850, 1856, 1864, 1865, and 1885. Sun Dances named after stream or landmark names include the summers of 1836, 1840, 1854, 1859, 1863, 1873, 1874, 1876, and 1887. Several Sun Dances were named after unusual associated characteristics. Separated into semantic clusters these events included a variety of activities including: repeated Sun Dance ceremonies (1842, 1878), visits by members of other tribes (1844, 1883), unusual weather patterns (1851, 1853, 1855 1881), activities involving animals (1843), military society initiations (1846, 1848, 1867), warfare celebrations (1869), acquisition of trade goods (1866), religious events (1857, 1861, 1877), courting (1875), starvation (1879), Anglo military interference (1890), and in one case the death of a girl (1845). Four entries record major disease epidemics (summer 1849, winter 1839–1840, 1861–1862) and the Sun Dance immediately thereafter (summer 1862). One entry records a major astronomical event, the great meteor shower early on the morning of November 13, 1833 (winter 1833–1834), which became known throughout the plains.

Many winter and some summer entries have to do with warfare or related activities, such as battles, raids, and celebrations (winters of 1832–1833,

1837–1838, 1840–1841, 1846–1847, 1860–1861, 1879–1880; summers of 1837, 1838, 1868, 1869), funerary-based journeys (1870–1871), prison releases (winter of 1873–1874), and the deaths of individuals killed in fights (winters of 1834–1835, 1835–1836, 1836–1837, 1841–1842, 1844–1845, 1850–1851, 1858–1859, 1863–1864, 1866–1867, 1868–1869, and 1874–1875; summer of 1833), including noted Comanche (summer 1847) and Cheyenne (summer 1852) leaders. Other winter entries record the natural deaths of individuals (1835–1836, 1842–1843, 1859–1860), unusual events at camp locations (1877–1878), courting (1851–1852), intertribal incidents (1856–1857), hand games (1881–1882), weather and traveling conditions (1864–1865), false alarms (1869–1870), treaty locations (1867–1868), song-based phenomena (1862–1863), intertribal visits (1872–1873), and new religious forms (1890–1891).

According to Mooney's data, a large number of entries show no official name for that year. Twenty-five of sixty winters have no official name (1838–1839, 1843–1844, 1845–1846, 1847–1848, 1848–1849, 1849–1850, 1852–1853, 1853–1854, 1854–1855, 1855–1856, 1857–1858, 1871–1872, 1875–1876, 1876–1877, 1878–1879, 1880–1881, 1882–1883, 1883–1884, 1884–1885, 1885–1886, 1886–1887, 1887–1888, 1888–1889, 1889–1890, 1891–1892), and in the twelve years that a Sun Dance was not held (1834, 1841, 1860, 1872, 1880, 1882, 1884, 1886, 1888, 1889, 1891, 1892), no official name was created. Yet in 1885, a year when no Sun Dance was held, a name based on the impact of a severe drought was created. The sporadic nature of Sun Dances from 1872 on was largely the result of overwhelming pressure on traditional Kiowa lifeways in the form of Anglo encroachment, decimated bison herds, confinement to the reservation, and increasing Indian Agency pressure to forgo the ceremony. In both winter and summer entries, the lack of a formal name did not preclude drawing a pictograph to represent that period and the association of a wide body of historical knowledge.

Some calendar entries are known by more than one name (summers of 1837, 1867, 1870, 1877, and 1881; winters of 1862–1863 and 1867–1868). A review of the primary and alternate names for these entries shows the same general themes that run throughout the calendars. Alternative names are available for the summers of 1837 (warfare victory, warfare mourning), 1867 (a noted stolen horse, Dog Society initiations), 1870 (a post-dance activity [plant growth], harsh weather conditions), 1877 (a location-based name after an earlier medicine sacrifice, measles epidemic), 1881 (severe weather conditions, an individual's illness), and the winters of 1862–1863 (incidental echo from song, harsh winter conditions) and 1867–1868 (treaty encampment, a noted warrior's death). In each case the primary and alternative names fall into the same range of military, weather, disease, and incidental occurrences that characterize Kiowa pictographic calendar entries.

One noticeable aspect of Kiowa calendars is a concern with where things happened. As one scholar observed, Mooney could have called his book a calendar geography as much as a calendar history.[13] A geographic bent is most evident in the names of individual Sun Dances and their association with particular geographic locations, but it is also evident in the naming of battles, deaths, and other unusual events. This correlation of Sun Dances, their function-like place names, and the extensive historical data associated with each season creates a deep form of cultural text like that described by Kendall (1980) for Yuman personal names, and applies to my research on Kiowa personal names.[14] Thus, Kiowa personal and place names should both be viewed as cultural texts with multiple layers of meaning first accessed through the linguistic elements of the name.

COMPARISON OF KIOWA CALENDAR AND PERSONAL NAMES

The names of Kiowa calendar entries share several similarities with Kiowa personal names. Grammatically, calendar names are complex, compound linguistic compositions exhibiting a variety of grammatical forms—nouns, verbs, adverbs, adjectives, pronouns, combining forms, and standard recurring suffixes indicating summer, winter, or Sun Dance. Just as for personal names, different members of a tribe might know calendar entry names in slightly different forms. Calendar entry names also resemble personal names in their cultural emphasis and semantic content, with a high percentage related to martial activities, religious observances (mostly Sun Dances, but other events as well), and geographic place names, the exact basis of many Kiowa personal names. Thus, the formal names for specific calendar entries, and therefore years or seasons, served to commemorate significant historical events marking a particular year or season. Such events included warfare, epidemics, visits from distant tribal contingents, astrological events, treaty signings (usually referenced by location), intertribal activities, and unusual weather patterns. Because Kiowa personal names are generally based on a specific body of knowledge, they often serve as abbreviated texts in which the name summons up that knowledge. The prominent seasonal points recorded in Kiowa calendars also served as mnemonic devices to aid in the recollection of other events from a given season. Like Kiowa personal names, Kiowa calendar names serve as cultural and historical texts, and the understanding of each requires an in-depth knowledge of the associated oral history.

Geosacred Sites

Ethnogeography of a sacred nature is an important part of Native American naming systems. As Walker (1988:ii) has observed, "Sacred and cultural geography is a universal feature of indigenous religious practices across Native North America." Geomorphically unique landforms were often associated with supernatural power and the scenes of visitations from supernatural entities (gods, deities, spirits, culture heroes, or other sources of supernatural power) in the past or present. They were also places where humans might communicate with or acquire supernatural power. Unique, awe-inspiring geomorphic features might be found in mountains, buttes, bluffs, rock outcrops, erosion forms, lakes, craters, waterfalls, artesian springs, geysers, and other prominent land and water forms and were often chosen as sites for special prayers, offerings, fasting, and vision quests.

Native concepts of the sacred are typically cosmotheistic, seeing humans, animals, plants, the landscape, and natural phenomena as animated by spiritual power. As animated beings these forms are interrelated through reciprocal kinship and obligations. Through these bases of relationship to one another, spirit beings interact with one another, including human beings. These interactions involve the transfer of power, thus establishing a dialogue that requires ritual prescriptions of respect, moral acknowledgment, and ongoing reciprocity for efficacy. These complex relationships include and permeate the surrounding landscape. Because spirit beings are integrated into all aspects of life, social, cultural, and environmental, a cosmotheistic worldview encompasses the entire landscape as well as all conceptual levels and elements of that ecological system. This extensive and all-pervasive set of relationships is often expressed through the concept of sacred power, understood to suffuse the entire universe (Campbell and Foor 2004:164).

As Campbell and Foor (2004:174) note, major sacred sites of northwestern Plains Indians tend to be

> high or on dramatically up-thrusting landforms. It is here that symbolic linkages can be articulated, connecting the earth with innumerable aspects of the cosmos. These sites become primary cosmological and terrestrial anchor points, connecting all the spatial and temporal symbols in Native American religious life. Across the northwestern Plains, sacred sites comprise a constellation of fixed points on the landscape that, along with the star constellations and the seasonal progressions, serve to orient the physical and spiritual movements and activities.

That such geographically unique and often awe-inspiring sites could be recognized as sacred was brought home to me during a visit by a Native American friend, who spontaneously characterized two unique geographic forms in southern Indiana as "power places."[15] The sites were Pless Cave, on my family's property in Lawrence County, and Hemlock Bluffs, a steep shale cliff situated above a bend of Guthrie Creek in Jackson County.

Archaeological sites that predate the memory of living populations were often attributed to the work of spirits. Such forms were generally of stone, often the most durable source facilitating preservation for recognition, and included monuments such as the Medicine Wheel in Wyoming, effigies (especially those shaped like humans or animals), some tipi rings, and petroglyph sites. Many such sites became shrines where individuals or groups traveled to pray for longevity, good health, and luck in various undertakings, and leave offerings. These specially designated geographic religious locales may be classified as georeligious or geosacred sites.

Discussion of sacred geographic sites in Plains ethnographic and historical literature has long been sparse and often vague (Parks and Wedel 1985:167). However, the presence of geosacred sites among various Plains cultures suggests that the paucity of data reflects the greater attention paid by early explorers and scholars to a geography conducive to trade and military uses rather than social or religious uses. Sundstrom's (2003) recent work on northern Plains Indian sacred geography attests to the widespread presence and importance, past and present, of geosacred sites.

Just as Plains tribes had geographic ranges that demarcated the boundaries of their physical territory, they also had a set of geosacred sites that demarcated their religious territory. Religious territories could overlap, as in the case of a large mountain held sacred by many groups. At any time, the majority of a group's geosacred sites, like place names in general, fell within their existing homeland. But as territories changed over time, so too did the range and extent of their association with geosacred sites. Although many seminal geosacred sites associated with a group's creation or early history, such as Bear Butte, Devil's Tower, or Devil's Lake, remained fixed in the mythology and religion of tribes long after the group had left the region, geosacred sites of lesser importance were often replaced by others, and eventually forgotten. Both sites well known by the entire group and sites of a personal or individual nature, such as vision quest sites, could fall out of the cultural repertoire as people moved away and lost regular access to them. I refer to this process of losing knowledge of geographic locales and their names through an end of contact as disassociation.

Because Native Americans tend "to view cultural resources as being bound together in broad categories based on functional interdependency and proximity rather than being defined by inherent characteristics," Stoffle et al. (1997:231) prefer the term "cultural landscapes" to refer to Indian concepts of land. They have grouped cultural landscapes into five types: holy landscapes, storyscapes, regional landscapes, ecoscapes, and landmarks. Kiowa geography and place names show that the Kiowa named geographic sites in each of these categories, with several sites falling in more than one category.

Although the term "holy land" does not exactly fit American Indian views of ethnic origin lands and is a foreign introduction, many Indians have come to use it to convey Native American understandings of where their people originated and their perception of the land to non-Indians. A holy land is typically created by a supernatural entity that established an origin and a birthright between a group of people, however defined, and the region where they were created. This relationship generally continues even after a group has migrated elsewhere. A strong sense of the relationship created by the supernatural power and a bond with the area continue to be significant (Stoffle et al. 1997:234–235). Kiowa typically use the term Cáuidàumgà (Kiowa Country) to refer to their concept of a homeland, both of the past, on the northwest plains, and of the present, in southwestern Oklahoma. Although the exact site of Kiowa origins and early activities is unknown (emergence from a cottonwood log via their culture hero Séndé, Grandfather Snake and Grandmother Spider, the exploits of the Two Split-Boys, etc.), other sacred sites, such as Devil's Tower, Spear Lake, and the Black Hills, are known. The northwest plains continue to hold a prominent place in Kiowa concepts and discussions of origins, early culture and religion, and several personal names, and thus are accorded special respect by the Kiowa.

Storyscapes are holy areas named in Native American stories or songs. A storyscape becomes a cultural landscape more by cultural practice than by permanent residence or ecological range, and often is associated with events that happened in the distant past. These locales often physically represent what is conveyed in the story or song and, in accounts involving distance, encompass the land between and around the various places included in the account (Stoffle et al. 1997:235–236). Well-known Kiowa storyscapes include Devil's Tower, named in both a story and an associated song; Spear Lake, which one of the two Split-Boys walked into; battle sites such as Cutthroat Mountain, Hueco Tanks, and Palo Duro; and even the

Pleiades, where the Kiowa children became stars. I would add that story-scapes also include locales specified by personal names because names are associated with and serve as symbols for larger historical and cultural oral texts associated with their basis. The Kiowa woman's name Sétálmã (Bear That Chased) not only references the Devil's Tower story but is also associated with a song that describes the story's events. Several Kiowa personal names reference specific locales, battles, and other cultural-historical events.

Stoffle et al. (1997:236–237) define regional landscapes as components of Native American holy lands that are definable by geography and culture, by a distinct range of natural resources, by large size—usually hundreds or thousands of square miles—and a boundary edge created by a major geographic feature, such as a river basin, desert, canyon, or mountain range. Regional landscapes are the first level of cultural abstraction that corresponds with an ecosystem defined by its biotic (living) and abiotic (nonliving, including climate and social factors) characteristics. This relationship reflects and to some extent produces a recognizable and defined range of specific cultural adaptations that have been developed and incorporated into the cultural systems of that area (Stoffle et al. 1997:236–237). Since the 1700s the Kiowa have known several different regional landscapes, including the Rocky Mountains, the Black Hills, the Big Timbers, the Staked Plains, the Wichita Mountains, and the Chihuahuan Desert of southwestern Texas and Mexico.

Ecological landscapes or ecoscapes are areas within a larger regional landscape that mark a special relationship, often cultural or religious, between American Indian cultural landscapes and the natural ecosystems they encompass. Ecoscapes are defined by having an unusual, distinct, and recognizable local geography, an unusual or distinct cultural relationship to one or more native groups, and by having been named (Stoffle et al. 1997:237). Ecoscapes closely resemble the "sacred islands" or oasis-like areas of unique religious and ecological content discussed by Sundstrom (2003). For the Kiowa, such ecoscapes existed at Hueco Tanks, Palo Duro Canyon, and several lakes and springs on the Staked Plains of Texas. The area around Fàiqóp (Sun Mountain) in western Texas has several springs, perennial streams, and an unusual oasis-like plant community with plant groups that are otherwise unknown in this arid region of Texas and southern New Mexico.

Landmarks, the last of the five types of Native American cultural landscapes identified by Stoffle et al., are discrete physical entities within a cultural landscape that tend to be only a small part of the local geography but are topographically and culturally unique and easily defined in terms of physical boundaries and cultural importance. They are "easily identifiable places whose meaning is readily conveyed to others," places that draw intense cultural interest (Stoffle et al. 1997:237–238). Well-known Kiowa landmarks range from awe-inspiring physical forms (Devil's Tower or Medicine Bluff) to unique resource areas (Long Horn Mountain, a source of cedar), medicinal areas (Vomit Spring), and important landmarks (Rainy Mountain and Saddle Mountain). Hueco Tanks, Palo Duro, and Guadalupe Peak may also be considered landscapes because of their distinct identifiable form, ecoscapes for their surrounding oasis-like floral and faunal composition, and storyscapes for events and cultural practices that transpired there. Similarly, areas such as the Wichita Mountains and the Big Timbers have qualities of both regional landscapes and ecoscapes.

Sundstrom (2003) provides an excellent survey of the range and forms of sacred geography among northern Plains Indians. From historic Plains literature, she defines "inherently sacred landscape features" as both general kinds of places and as specific places that were regarded as sacred or mysterious. These included springs, round stones (often located far from water), lightning stones, fossils, fossil outcrops, caves, and cultural features such as rock art, ceremonial grounds, earthworks, some stone alignments and cairns, vision quest sites, commemorative stone circles, eagle-catching pits, horn stacks, and burial places and memorials (Sundstrom 2003:261–274).

Sundstrom (2003:275–284) also discusses what she defines as "sacred islands in the landscape" (buttes and mountain ranges; rivers, streams, and lakes; and divides, gaps, rocks, and unusual natural features) and "sites associated with sacred bundles and ceremony origins" (buttes, rivers and lakes, places associated with myths, and the sacred sites of others). Using Sundstrom's (2003) model, these geographic forms are defined, followed by Kiowa examples where applicable.

Many Plains tribes recognized springs, lakes, and rivers as places of power and the homes of underwater spirits or water monsters (Sundstrom 2003), and prayed and offered tobacco and other items at such locations to show respect to the spirits, as well as to ensure safe crossings, health, and longevity. The Kiowa often regarded such locales as areas where Zémáutqùné ("teeth-caught-rolled over and over") or underwater monsters dwelled. Some individuals became known for acquiring their medicine or power from water sources. Tónàuqúat (Rough Tailed, i.e., Snapping Turtle), a Kiowa man who doctored and practiced sorcery, acquired his power from underwater animals and entities. For some Kiowa, springs continued to have an importance with the introduction of Christianity through their use as baptism sites. Saddle Mountain Kiowa Indian Baptist

Church used at least three baptism sites along the same watercourse, including Odlepaugh Springs and Kokoom Pool. Harlan Hall (2000, 2002) describes the sacred nature of these sites in Kiowa Christianity.

Butte tops, pits, and cliffs containing round stones could also become sacred places. East of Meers, Oklahoma, many road cuts and hillsides yield round stones four to eight inches in diameter that Kiowa gather to use in sweat lodges. Although I have never heard references to this locale as sacred, its continued use as a source of sweat lodge stones is religiously oriented. Although many indigenous cultures do not share in the strong Western dichotomy of sacred versus secular, the Kiowa and other Native Americans do distinguish between locations of great sacred importance and those of lesser importance.

CAVES

Caves or caverns were often considered sacred because they represented a physical passage from the surface to the underworld, which was otherwise unavailable. Several Native American cultures, including the Kiowa, contain emergence stories that involve coming from the underworld to dwell on the surface of Earth. Nearly all northern Plains tribes hold beliefs that game animals lived underground and periodically emerged to replenish the herds (Sundstrom 2003:264). There are at least two scenarios in which caves might be considered sacred among the Kiowa. The Kiowa origin story describes the tribe's emergence from an underground location to the surface via a cottonwood log and the assistance of their culture hero Séndé. This locale was probably some sort of cave or cavern. Another Kiowa account attributes the disappearance of the bison in the late 1800s to their having gone underground on the north side of present-day Mount Scott in the Wichita Mountains (Marriott and Rachlin 1968:138–139).

ROCK ART

Plains literature has many references to the sacred nature of rock art sites. Rock art has been recorded as being used for divining the future, recording visions and historical events, as places where power could be obtained from spirits residing there, and as possible vision quest sites. In some instances clear distinctions between secular and sacred rock art appear likely (Sundstrom 2003:266–267). A large amount of rock art is found in lands inhabited by the Kiowa in the 1800s, from Montana to New Mexico and Texas.

Sundstrom (2004:141–149) and others (Sundstrom et al. 2001:18–21) have suggested that two anthropomorphic petroglyphs of upside-down heads on panel two at the Hulett South Site in Wyoming may be based on Kiowa Sun Dance imagery of the Taime figurine and shields, largely from the presence of round eyes, gridlike mouths, and what appear to be plumes or feathers extending from the heads of the images. The site is within view of Devil's Tower. At first considered to be the heads of decapitated enemies, similar to those depicted in Plains Indian pictographic writing, the gridded mouths are now thought to have a different meaning. Noting several similarities to the Kiowa and Crow Sun Dance effigies, Sundstrom and colleagues suggest the images resemble the face of the Kiowa Taime image, and may represent the upside-down faces on the Kiowa Taime shields. Although noting that some differences exist in terms of the absence of certain stylistic features found on the Kiowa Taime image, Sundstrom (2004:145) stresses the previously mentioned similarities. I am inclined to view the smaller of the Hulett images as a warfare image associated with an adjacent body and shield. They also report a large image and a similar pair of smaller images at the Medicine Creek Cave Site in Crook County, Wyoming. Although interesting, these appear stylistically different, and I do not see enough similarity to merit the analogy. Based on similar incising technique, Sundstrom (2004:144) attributes all three sets of drawings to a single artist. Although the images are from the prior region of Kiowa occupation, positive association is unclear, and at present no rock art images can be clearly linked to the Kiowa.

HUECO TANKS

The Hueco Tanks site has drawn considerable historical and ethnographic attention. The site is a unique formation of igneous rock hills between the Hueco and Franklin Mountain Ranges thirty-two miles northeast of El Paso, Texas. The formation consists of three large, irregular granite hills or domes, approximately one-half mile long and nearly as wide, that rise some 450 feet above the surrounding desert floor. The cluster of hills is located in the middle of a large, relatively flat basin-like area in a highly arid region that averages only eight inches of precipitation a year.[16] The site was formed some 34 million years ago when an upheaval of molten rock from Earth's interior penetrated a softer layer of sedimentary rock. The site takes its name from the presence of numerous *huecos* (hollows) in the rock and tanks (basins between the mountains). Vugs, or cavities caused by bubbles of gas, characteristic of many igneous rocks, are ubiquitous throughout the formation. As the softer layer of stone weathered away, the irregular, underlying mass of syenite porphyry (a low grade of granite) began to weather and was dented with countless huecos across its surface. Ranging in size from a quarter to a large basin size, the huecos catch and hold rainwater until it evaporates. Some huecos, shaded underneath formations, retain water much longer. The tanks are the areas between the mountains that catch rainwater. Because they too are shaded by much of the formations, evaporation is reduced, resulting in long-lasting bodies of water the size of small lakes. There are five major tanks at the formation. These basins, ranging in size from an orange to a large swimming pool, trap and hold large quantities of rainwater, making this site a virtual oasis in the surrounding dry and sandy Chihuahuan Desert. The moisture and soil conditions at the tanks support local desert grasses and plants, hackberries, wildflowers, ten species of ferns, the exotic datil yucca, which produces an edible banana-sized root, and remnants of an oak-juniper woodland (Arizona oak and one-seed juniper) that once characterized the area when the climate was cooler.

The irregular nature of the formation resulted in many piles of large rocks, overhanging cliffs, and crevices that provide natural shelters for human occupation. Smoke-blackened ceilings, mortar holes, rock art, and cultural debris indicate extensive human occupation, especially in shelters near the tanks.

Because the numerous natural rock basins caught and held runoff water during dry periods, the site was an important base camp for the local Mescalero Apache, and anyone traveling into western Texas and Mexico in historic times. Until wells and other sources were established around 1910, the tanks were the only reliable source of water in this area between the Pecos River and El Paso. In 1860 the tanks were capable of holding a year's supply of water. One tank reportedly holds 150,000 gallons of water, and some others more than 10,000 gallons. Because some of the tanks are shaded, algae do not grow in them, and the water remains potable year round.

Hueco Tanks is especially rich in prehistory. A Folsom projectile point found at the site indicates the presence of humans at least 10,000 years ago. More than 6,000 images of rock art, mostly pictographs but also some petroglyphs, have been found in nearly a hundred distinct sites in the various shelters, crevices, and caves at the tanks. Many of the abstract designs and hunting scenes, including animals and humans with shaman-like characteristics, are attributed to the Desert Archaic Culture (6000 BC–AD 450), whose hunters and gatherers resided in semisubterranean pithouses and produced many of the oldest paintings consisting of red and yellow zigzagging lines with simple figures.

Around AD 1000, agriculture, pottery vessels, and later aboveground adobe houses were added to the local hunting and gathering subsistence strategy, leading to the development of the Jornada Mogollon Culture, which dates to between AD 450 and 1400. A small village of pithouses dating to AD 1100–1200 was found just east of the natural opening formed by the three main outcrops of the formation and was partially excavated in the early 1970s. The Jornada Mogollon produced much of the rock art at Hueco Tanks and was followed by a brief settlement known as the Dona Ana phase, during which pithouses were replaced with multiroom adobe pueblos.

Of special significance are the more than 240 painted masks from this period that are stylistically similar to kachina masks. These pictographs represent the largest concentration of painted mask pictures in North America and are believed to represent a turning point in the syncretism of animistic images of the Desert Archaic with those of the Mesoamerican God of Rain Tlaloc, resulting in a new religious sphere. This body of masked deities includes figures of masked dancers that suggest a connection to the kachinas of present-day Puebloan cultures, in which masked dancers serve as intermediaries between the spirit and human worlds in rituals that combine ancestor worship rites aimed at inducing rain. Carbon from pictographs at the site dates to as early as AD 620. Because kachinas were believed to have originated in Arizona in the thirteenth century, these images indicate a far earlier influence of Mesoamerican religion and the origin of the kachina ritual in the region than previously believed. Early dates from the mask pictographs that resemble kachina masks suggest an earlier origin among the Mogollon peoples of western Texas and southern New Mexico. The importance of water is emphasized in several pictographs that depict clouds with falling rain and zigzags suggestive of lightning or lashing rain.

In historic times, the site lay along a heavily used trail that ran from a gap in the Hueco Mountains westward to the El Paso region. After AD 1500, several proto-historic and historic populations are known to have used the area, and inferably the site. These groups included the Mansos and Sumas, the Lipan and Mescalero Apache, the Tigua of Isleta Pueblo, probably the Jumano, and later the Comanche, Kiowa, and Naishan Apache. Later pictographs of snakes, dancers, handprints, rituals, Apache Nai'es or girls' coming of age/puberty ceremonies, men on horses, and at least one historical narrative are attributed to these and possibly other historical groups during this period. Because the numerous natural rock basins caught and held runoff water during dry periods, it was an important base camp for Plains groups raiding into western Texas and Mexico. In 1840 or 1841, J. H. Byrne, a member of Captain John Pope's survey crew (Pope 1855:53–54), made the following report:

About 14 years ago, the Apaches, having made a desperate foray upon the Mexicans, retreated with their plunder to these mountains. The Mexicans surprised and surrounded them, hemming them up in the rocky ravine forming the eastern Tank. Here an engagement took place, in which the Indians were totally defeated and nearly exterminated, only two or three escaping. It is said that upwards of one hundred of them were killed.

In 1854 John Russell Bartlett, chief of the American Boundary Commission, provided an account (Bartlett 1854:174) that alludes to the same locale, although some details differ:

The hills expand, forming an amphitheatre, which is celebrated from its being the place where the Apaches used formerly to hold their councils, and the scene of a contest between them and the Mexicans. The Indians had been committing some depredations and murders in the settlements, and, being pursued, were traced to the Waco Mountains. A party set off from El Paso, and surprised them in the narrow space or amphitheatre alluded to. The besieged retreated as far as possible; and finding no chance to escape, they built a wall across the entrance, which is about one hundred feet from one perpendicular mass of rock to the other. Here they were kept several days, when they were finally overcome, and all to the number of a hundred and fifty, put to death.

Although the reference to the "Waco Mountains" and its location near El Paso correlates with present-day Hueco Tanks, located in the Hueco Mountains, other aspects of this account are less clear.

James Mooney (1898:302–305) recorded a third account from the Kiowa. Although probably not in first person, as most of the participants would have been deceased by the time of his work in the 1890s, his consultants very likely heard it from the participants of the siege. In 1839 a group of around twenty Kiowa men planned to raid El Paso, but, perhaps finding it too heavily guarded, after staying only one night they abandoned the planned raid and began heading eastward. The Kiowa halted for the night "at a spring coming out of a cave . . . they describe it as a deep rock well with a large basin of water, and on one side of it a cave running under the rock from the water's edge." While resting there they were suddenly surrounded by a large force of Mexicans with Mescalero Apache scouts. After the Kiowa were driven into a cave and trapped, the Mexicans polluted the water by killing several of the Kiowa's horses and throwing them into the pool, and, apparently afraid to attack the Kiowa directly, simply waited in an attempt to starve them out from a lack of food and water. Realizing their plan, the Kiowa were soon limited to hastily grabbing drinks of water from the edge of the pool and cutting strips of putrefying flesh from the horses under cover of darkness. A Kiowa named Dagoi was shot in the leg in one such attempt. The dead horses soon made the water unfit for consumption. One of the Indian scouts is reported to have shouted encouragement to them in the Comanche language.

Growing desperate, the Kiowa began searching for a route of escape. Exploring the cave, "they found that it extended a considerable distance, and at the farther end was a hole opening to the surface." When a Kiowa thrust his head out of the hole he was seen by the soldiers, who quickly closed the hole. After ten days of suffering they resolved to make a desperate attempt. "The sides of the well were steep and difficult, but they had noticed a cedar growing from a crevice in the rock, the top of which reached nearly to the height of the cliff" (Mooney 1898:303). Forced to leave the wounded Dagoi behind, the party managed to ascend the cliff and escape, with only one man wounded by a Mexican firing wildly into the dark at a noise he heard. The Kiowa named the site Xójôigáthầdàudéẹ̀ (Rock House in Which They Were Contained).

Mooney (1898:302) accepted Pope's identification of the site as Hueco Tanks. Pope's description focused on the rocky ravine on the eastern formation. The valley in the middle of the eastern formation is known today as Mescalero Canyon. The attribution of this event to Comanche Cave seems to have come from W. W. Newcomb, Jr.'s research (Kirkland and Newcomb 1967). However, this assumption is beginning to be questioned. These accounts raise two possibilities: either a second and similar engagement involving a group of Apache occurred at Hueco Tanks within a year or two after the Kiowa engagement of 1839, or Bartlett and Pope reported information that confused the Apache and the Kiowa and that seems to have been greatly exaggerated, because the Kiowa party consisted of around twenty men, only two of whom were left behind.

One of the obvious problems is that the front of Comanche Cave does not fully resemble the descriptions in the Mooney and Bartlett accounts. While Comanche Cave has a large opening leading back to a tank, Escape Cave, a short distance to the south along the same side of the canyon, and with a ledge running along the west side to Comanche Cave, fits the description better. Another discrepancy concerns the Kiowa being surrounded at the site in 1839 by Mexican soldiers and Indian scouts, as Sonnichsen (1958:61–62) indicates that a military company at El Paso was not formed until the mid-1840s. Comparing the Bartlett, Byrne (Pope), and Mooney accounts with the Hueco Tanks Site, Jay Sharp (1987) has examined these discrepancies and offers a plausible explanation. Neither Bartlett nor Byrne provided a source for their information, which may have been obtained from Mexicans in El Paso or from the local mule drivers working on the survey crew.

In comparing Mooney's Kiowa account to the actual site at Hueco Tanks, Sharp (1987:87–88) ruled out Comanche Cave, located on the west wall of the amphitheater, as the site of the siege, as it contains no passage that extends a considerable distance with a hole opening to the surface. It matches neither Bartlett's nor the Kiowa's description of the mouth of the site. After rejecting another small cave on the west wall, Sharp found an area that matches the Kiowa account located near the end of the amphitheater with a rock well containing water, and an overhang or cave running under the rock from the water's edge on one side of it, just as the Kiowa account describes. This well was dry in 2007. The overhang continues into the far depths of the amphitheater and contains the mouths of several chambers. The distance between the two perpendicular masses of rock is about 100 feet, similar to Bartlett's account, which referred to the mouth and not the head of the amphitheater. Crawling into the chambers, Sharp found several holes that permitted an ascent, if perilous, to the top. He then discovered a narrow passage of about 200 feet that ran to the west and terminated as "a hole opening to the surface," as described in Mooney's account. This cave is now referred to as Escape Cave. Sharp reported that on reaching the surface, he had a view of the entire area, including where the Mexican force would have been camped around the cave. He believes that the siege occurred not in Comanche Cave, located approximately halfway down the west wall of the amphitheater, but in the caves at the very end of the amphitheater or canyon (Sharp 1987:86–88, 91), which is formed by the opening on the northwest side of the East Mountain (see Kirkland and Newcomb 1967:174). In visiting the site in 2007, I found only one entrance in Comanche Cave, and one exit showing daylight. Escape Cave has several openings along the narrow passage, some too high to reach and others accessible with a fifteen- to twenty-foot rope, terminating in a high opening at the end.

Scott recorded an account of the siege from the son of a nephew of Dohausan, who said he knew him well, in the 1890s:

> One time before the Osages cut the heads off the Kiowas, Tohausen was a young man and was down in Chihuahua with a big band of young men driving horses north. One day they were attacked by Mexican soldiers and all but 15 of them abandoned the horses and ran off. Tohausen remained behind with the others, all chiefs. They

got down in a place that had high walls of stone on both sides. It was at the head of a stream at the very head of which there was a cave with a spring in it. The soldiers surrounded them at once and killed 2 horses and one man. The others got back in the cave so they could not see them but the soldiers shot up the mouth of the cave and had them in a pocket with a cave in the upper end with straight walls and no timber. The next day the horse and the man swelled up very badly and they had nothing to swallow but water. Every now and then during the day the soldiers would fire a volley at the mouth of the cave and they would put wood on the edges of the walls during the day and make fires with it at night to see the mouth of the cave by.

One day they could hear wagons coming and a Mexican called down to them and they had a Mexican captive who understood Kiowa and told them they were near several forts and more soldiers were coming. Tohausen said, "Try hard men and we will all get out of here," and encouraged others. They were all chiefs and he knew them well. On the 9th day they had become emaciated and weak and the Mexicans began to throw rocks down on them and were going to cover over the mouth of the cave with stones and let them starve to death. Tohausen said, "I have decided to try and escape, bolt out. Which one of you will go first? If some of us lie dead on the prairie that is all right. Two or 3 will get away and carry the news to the Kiowa village, how we died fighting. Which one of you will go first?" No one answered him for a long time, then he said, "Nobody says he will go first so I will go first myself but I was going to go last." Then one man said he would go first. So they waited until dark and one at a time crept to the end of the wall at the mouth and were within a few feet of the soldiers.

Tohausen had made them all cut strings from their leggings to tie their bows to their wrists so they would not lose them if they should fall down in the rush. He then told them to go ahead and they made a bolt right into the midst of the soldiers, some of whom could not fire on account of their friends and the Kiowas got most of them through the middle of the soldiers in the darkness and stopped in a ravine close by. When Dohausen counted them he found three missing. They heard the soldiers galloping by looking for them and they kept quiet for a while then made off in a diagonal direction and escaped.[17]

Nye (1962:36–45) provides a fifth account from Hunting Horse and George Hunt that generally agrees with Mooney's account but provides more detail on some aspects. This account states that the Kiowa discovered their pursuers just prior to reaching the site, debated the choice of escape, had one man killed and another wounded, and were forced to take shelter in the formation. "At night Indians crawled from beneath their shelter to drink from a little pool of water in the rocks in the middle of the canyon." After an attempt to escape from a hole in the cave was thwarted, the Mexicans threw several rattlesnakes into the cave. Eventually the Kiowa "slipped silently out of the cave and ran single file down the gulch, keeping under its edge and hoping not to be seen." Dohausen pulled himself up the side of the arroyo by a cedar tree, then used his bow to help the others up. Dagoi was left here, and resigned himself to his situation; a few moments later the Mexicans shot him. The rest escaped, with Konate or Kone-au-beah (Black Tripe) being wounded, and hid in another nearby canyon until the next night. They proceeded to their base camp, where they had left spare horses and equipment with two young boys, then went to the summit of Sun Mountain, where Konate was left beside a spring in a cairn of rocks and branches to protect him.

Sharp (1987:88–90) also reports accounts from two Tigua men who

"Rock House In Which They Were Contained": Hueco Tanks, showing Comanche Cave at right center and Escape Cave at end of canyon, El Paso County, Texas.

were familiar with the site, the escape route, and a Tigua attack on a group of Apaches at Hueco Tanks. One of the men suggested that the Tigua may have been the scouts for the Mexicans, the other indicated that the scouts were Tigua, and described an account of the siege similar to Mooney's. Sharp (1987:90–91) surmised that Mooney's account was accurate except for the identity of the scouts, that no hostile Apaches were present at the 1839 fight, and that the Mexicans probably embellished their account of the identity (Apache instead of Kiowa) and number (100 or more rather than two) of Indians killed in the siege to pacify the El Paso community, which had long been clamoring for retribution for past Apache raids. Also, the addition of 700 troops to bolster the 100 dragoons at San Elizario did not occur until the 1840s, some time after this event (Sonnichsen 1973:61–62; Sharp 1987:84).

Of special significance has been the interpretation of a panel of rock art (Hueco Tanks Site 1) on the west side of the mouth of the Mescalero Canyon amphitheater that shows both Indians and Anglos. In 1939, Forrest Kirkland recorded this panel of images in watercolor as part of his study of Indian rock art in Texas (Kirkland and Newcomb 1967:176, Plate 124, 1-A). W. W. Newcomb, Jr. (Kirkland and Newcomb 1967) attributed the majority of the rock art to the Mescalero, and showed that most of the images reflected several southwestern influences, including the Pueblos. As Newcomb (1967:181) states, "That the Kiowas had any inclination to adorn the walls of their temporary prison is doubtful, and virtually all of the Indian paintings on the walls of Comanche Cave apparently should be attributed to the Mescaleros." Comparing the images in Hueco Tanks Site 1 to symbols in Indian sign language, rock art paintings, and military cryptography techniques, LaVan Martineau (1973) interpreted these images as depicting the 1839 Kiowa-Mexican Militia fight. However, his interpretations appear unreliable, for a number of ethnological and archaeological reasons.[18]

A Kiowa association with Plains rock art is difficult to make. That the Kiowa engaged in rock art during their time on the northwestern plains, in the eastern Great Basin, in the Southwest, and on the southern plains is likely but virtually impossible to prove. The Rocky Dell Site in Oldham County, Texas, contains historic images of mounted riders, bison hunting, and possibly longhorn cattle (Kirkland and Newcomb 1967:203–216). The Mujares, Brown's Camp, and Agua Piedra Creek sites contain images of men, horses, bison, longhorn cattle, and firearms. Although contemporary with historic southern Plains cultures, these images cannot be definitively associated with any particular group.

Following Martineau, Dewey Tsonetokoy, a Kiowa, has attempted to strengthen the connection between the Kiowa and the rock art at Hueco

Tanks Site 1.[19] His interpretation is that the Kiowa produced the rock art located there during this event and that it represents both the siege and Konate's ordeal.[20] Although his efforts have increased Kiowa awareness of the site, several factors bring into question whether the Kiowa made these images. Konate's wound and miraculous recovery did not happen in Hueco Tanks. He was wounded while escaping from the tank and was left by his comrades at Sun Mountain Spring, some seventy miles to the east on their escape route. Konate was later found by a Comanche raiding party and returned home, where he recovered (Mooney 1898:303–304). If the glyphs tell the entire account of the event, then who was there to finish the story? Already emaciated and shot through the leg, Dagoi was unable to escape, and was killed by the Mexicans in the gulch, within hearing of the other Kiowa. Dagoi could not have known the final result of the escape attempt or conveyed these in rock art. Furthermore, Hueco Tanks Site 1 is at least a quarter-mile from Escape Cave, and several of the panels are above the reach of a man standing on the ledge they are carved on (Kirkland and Newcomb 1967:202). There are also plenty of areas to produce rock art near Escape and Comanche caves. Although the Kiowa typically returned to gather the bones of warriors killed on journeys, there is no record of this or any related rock art, leaving only speculation.

Tsonetokoy also presents no real indication as to why these images should be considered Kiowa other than that because the Kiowa were once there they made them. Of the thirty-two petroglyphs in the panel, Tsonetokoy provides interpretation for only sixteen, some of which could easily be interpreted as other things (for example, no. 6 as a woman instead of a warrior who drank bad water and suffered cramps, no. 8 as a snake instead of a stream of water, and no. 31 as representing two escape attempts, an unclear interpretation). But, more important, there is no comparison with any other works in what is a sizable body of literature on Plains and Great Basin rock art. Archaeological and ethnological data relating to other groups that resided in the area is not addressed. I am unaware of any data directly linking the Kiowa to petroglyph making, including the region of southwestern Oklahoma where there are ample areas of red sandstone bluffs conducive to such works but relatively little rock art. Although pre-reservation Kiowa probably did produce petroglyphs, and although some of the Hueco Tanks glyphs clearly represent figures dressed in Mexican-style clothing, the Kiowa could not have made those images during the siege. Thus, while some of the glyphs may have been made by the Kiowa at other times, it is more likely that they were made by various peoples over different times and for a number of different spiritual or historical purposes. More important, as the battle seems to have occurred at the box end of the amphitheater rather than the mouth (Hueco Tanks Site 1), this panel has no direct association with the 1839 siege. Because Indians and non-Indians relied on springs for water, both were frequently drawn to these locales, sometimes resulting in skirmishes, as recorded in other accounts.[21] Early Spanish and Mexicans seem to have rarely visited the site, and although there are tales of battles taking place there, little documentation exists.

Mooney, Scott, and Nye indicate that the party escaped the cave, most likely following the ledge between Escape Cave and Comanche Cave until encountering the tree. Scott shows two drawings of the siege, a horseshoe-shaped canyon with a "c" at the end representing a cave and a second horseshoe with marks showing the Kiowa escaping on the upper left or west side near the canyon mouth, and a mark above them representing the Mexicans. Both are associated with these respective portions of the account. The Scott maps and the fact that the Kiowa had to sneak out at night to drink indicates that the siege was primarily in Escape Cave, which has a runoff channel that was dry in 2007, and not in Comanche Cave, which has a permanent water source. One tank periodically holds water that almost reaches Comanche Cave. While Tsonetokoy has demonstrated that escape from the caves with a rope is possible (Sharp 2005), only one account mentions the making of a rope (Nye 1963:39), which was not used in the cave, although both Scott and Nye, who used Scott's notes, mention the Kiowa cut strings from their leggings to tie their bows to their wrists before escaping.

While it is clear that the group reached Sun Mountain (Guadalupe Peak), it is less clear which spring Black Tripe was left at. Although Nye and Mooney both mention the Kiowa reaching the top of a mountain, it would have been very difficult to take Konate to the top, and park rangers report that no springs are currently known on the top of the formation. Several springs (Bone, Guadalupe, Pine, Upper Pine) exist around the base of Sun Mountain and farther up the Guadalupe Range. Many of these springs have been improved and altered through ranching and weathering and fluctuate in activity, so it is difficult to determine which spring was used. However, similar to other clusters of Kiowa place names, "Sun Mountain" and "Sun Mountain Spring" suggest that the spring is close by, perhaps Guadalupe Spring.

Following the Mexican War and the discovery of gold in California in 1848, several official expeditions were sent to find and open a road between the Austin–San Antonio area and El Paso. In 1849, Randolph Marcy and Robert Neighbors camped at the springs with their respective parties (Marcy 1849). The most reliable cistern in the site is Comanche Cave, which has a deep well under a rock inside the cave and various pictographs

KIOWA ETHNOGEOGRAPHY

attributed to the Tigua, Mescalero, and Kiowa (Mooney 1898:302–305; Gelo 2000:294). One trail led by John S. (Rip) Ford and Robert Neighbors passed by Hueco Tanks and was later developed as the Upper Road, a route that roughly parallels the present-day Texas–New Mexico border in Texas. In 1852, U.S. Boundary Commissioner John R. Bartlett visited the site while surveying the United States–Mexico boundary and copied several pictographs into his journals. In 1858 the Butterfield Overland Mail established a stagecoach stop along the north base of Hueco Tanks but abandoned it the next year in favor of a route to the south that offered better water and protection. Mescalero Apaches continued to use the tanks until at least the late 1870s (Thomas 1941:17; Sonnichsen 1958:48).

In 1898 the site passed into private hands. El Paso County obtained it in the mid-1960s and began using it as a county park. On June 12, 1969, the site was deeded to the Texas Parks and Wildlife Department, which, after obtaining an adjacent parcel of 121 acres, formed the present Hueco Tanks Historical Park in May 1970 (Fabry 1989). In 1998 the 860-acre park site was renamed Hueco Tanks State Historic Site. Today it offers a variety of recreational activities and is a popular site among rock climbers. Recently, the use of global positioning system technology, digital photography, and computer enhancement techniques has led to the discovery of many previously indiscernible sites bearing rock art, reemphasizing Hueco Tanks' importance as a sacred and historical place for several Native American tribes and strengthening the Park Service's concern to manage and protect the archaeological resources of the site. As an important desert crossroads for some 10,000 years, Hueco Tanks remains one of the richest sites of American Indian pictographs in Texas and one of the richest archaeological sites in North America.

Ceremonial Sites

Many Plains groups regarded places where ceremonies were held as sacred. These sites can often be identified from depressions in the ground, stone circles, or vegetational scars (Sundstrom 2003:267–268), or from remnants of former structures such as sweat lodges or Sun Dance lodges. For the Kiowa, this most frequently involved Sun Dance sites. Kiowa viewed these places, at least where Sun Dance structures were still visible, with passive avoidance—it was fine to travel or pass by such sites but one should never interfere with or physically alter the residual lodge. Occasionally the same general area or site was reused for multiple Sun Dances in the same year or for dances in subsequent years. The degree to which lodges deteriorated, and whether such deterioration had any effect on the decision to reuse a previous site, are unknown. Sundstrom (2003:267–268) lists several Plains Indian examples. For the Kiowa, the Medicine Lodge Creek area of south-central Kansas and the area between Belle Fourche, South Dakota, and Devil's Tower and Sundance, Wyoming, were particularly highly regarded as Sun Dance areas.

Hugh L. Scott recorded an account of a Kiowa religious site related to the acquisition of the bison hide for the center pole of the Sun Dance. The Bison Tree was a tree that grew through the bones of a bison that had been killed to obtain its hide for the Sun Dance center pole. It became a site where offerings were left.[22] Other types of offering sites, such as the tree associated with the Star Girls Ceremony (Mooney 1898:341), were probably once more common and reflect this type of geosacred site.

Another genre of cultural landform sometimes considered sacred was earthworks, such as burial mounds, effigy mounds, and sod effigies or intaglios. Although the Kiowa typically buried their dead in crevices, there is no known association with mound or intaglio construction. The Kiowa did occasionally erect defensive earthen breastworks for combat purposes. If outnumbered or forced to seek cover in open ground, many Plains groups dug defensive foxhole-like pits for cover. These enclosures are depicted in Kiowa and Lakota calendars (Mooney 1898:271–274). Kiowa refer to these hastily erected and defensive earthworks as kį́ájôi, and one Kiowa woman had this name. Parker McKenzie showed me the remnant of one such structure due north of his house in the Washita River bottom, on the west side of Rainy Mountain Creek and just above its confluence with the Washita. These earthworks were built when the Kiowa discovered Osage near their camp in 1833, prior to breaking camp and moving south. During his lifetime (1897–1999), McKenzie saw the site become almost unrecognizable through continual farming.[23] Another site that has yet to be specifically identified today but that would have been common knowledge to Kiowa in the pre-reservation period was the earthworks thrown up by the party of forty-eight Cheyenne Bow String Society members the Kiowa killed in 1837 in present-day Beckham County, Oklahoma. Kiowa calendars depict the Cheyenne inside the earthworks (Mooney 1898:271–272). Although probably not regarded by the Kiowa as inherently sacred, such locations would have been of great historical importance.

Other types of Kiowa cultural sites that may have once existed include Red Horse effigies, wood and clay statues of horses offered to tornados, and circles of rocks and wooden posts constructed to aid in forming impounding lines for game jumps or corrals. Religious rituals of imitative or sympathetic magic performed to ensure a successful hunt often accompanied the use of these structures. As plains archaeology supports, game drives and

KIOWA ETHNOGEOGRAPHY

corrals continued but were far more common before the Kiowa acquired horses.

FOSSIL EXPOSURES

Fossil exposures were another feature that Plains tribes often considered places of power, including both small outcrops of fossils such as ammonites and baculites (Sundstrom 2003:263) and the fossilized skeletons of dinosaurs and Pleistocene megafauna. Using information from oral and written historical sources, archaeology, paleontology, museum collections, and interviews with contemporary tribal elders, Adrienne Mayor (2005) has made a significant contribution toward understanding how American Indians perceived fossils before evolutionary theory developed. As Mayor (2005:14, 38) demonstrates, fossil finds of dinosaurs and Pleistocene megafauna are common along rivers, lakes, and marshes, leading many Native Americans to associate the large vertebrate fossils, teeth, and tusks found in these areas with horned water monsters; they also recognized some fossils as ancestral forms of the modern animals they were familiar with, and they used fossil bones for various religious and medicinal purposes. The cultural use of fossil bones, as Mayor (2005:92–93) reminds us, is a widespread practice known throughout Asia, Europe, North America, and Mexico.

Although fossil sites were more common on the northern and western plains and in the Great Basin, southern Plains tribes also knew of them. Having migrated through much of Wyoming, Colorado, Kansas, Oklahoma, and Texas, the Kiowa undoubtedly encountered the fossilized remains of prehistoric animals, as reflected in their term chóicàultǫ̀sègàu ("liquid-cattle-bones") for dinosaur bones and probably for Pleistocene megafauna as well. Elder Kiowa told Parker McKenzie that such bones were typically found near marshes and other water-bearing sites and eroding out of cliffs, hence the name. As McKenzie noted,

> Kiowa tradition supports the assumption the term originated from remains of prehistoric mammals of great size that they found protruding from eroded cliffs. Tradition also has it the tribe at some indefinite period of their wanderings passed through the so-called "dinosaur region" now known to be about the central portion of the plateau west of the eastern range of the Rockies.[24]

Although what the Kiowa thought of these remains and places or to what extent they had any special significance is unknown, the development of a distinct term for them suggests the Kiowa were well aware of them. By the early 1900s, the term chóicàul (s/d), chóicáutjáu (t), was being used for Old World elephants in circuses and fairs.[25] Another Kiowa elder used the following terms to refer to prehistoric creatures: Tsoy-Ghaul (woolly mammoth), Mahn-Pah-Hole (saber-toothed tiger), and Gope-Saw-Pole (cave men).[26] These terms are clearly chóicàul (dinosaurs, probably mammoth and mastodon, and later Old World elephants), mánpàuhól (furry-breasted, a term for African lions), and Qópsáupól (Mountain Owl, the Kiowa half-human Bigfoot and half-owl bogeyman reputed to carry bad children off). Whether the mánpàuhól was simply a later analogy applied to the saber-toothed tiger is unclear. However, the Kiowa spent considerable time in the western plains and plateau regions, where the remains of dinosaur and Pleistocene megafauna are common and well known to other tribes.

As Mayor (2005) demonstrates, specific fossil forms found in geological periods and geographic regions can sometimes be linked to tribal myths and stories about specific creatures. In some instances new paleontological data shed light on the probable basis for some of the creatures found in tribal legends and early history. In the hilly plains region from Kansas to the Dakotas and Montana, the fossilized remains of the mosasaur, a marine reptile resembling a colossal snake with a long, crocodilian-like head and teeth, are common. This creature may have been the model for the underwater monster common in the oral history and art of the region. Kiowa drawings of the giant horned Zẹ́máutqụ̀né closely resemble the skeletal remains of a mosasaur (Mayor 2005:191–192). Although the creature is popularly referred to as an underwater monster, the name literally means "teeth-caught-rolled over and over," in reference to how the creature killed its prey, similar to an alligator.

Small fossils conducive to transport were important components of medicine bundles and amulets among many tribes (Sundstrom 2003:263; Mayor 2005:166–167). Related to the Star Girls story and the formation of present-day Devil's Tower in northeastern Wyoming, Kiowa reported finding unusual clawlike forms at the base of the formation. Scott recorded two accounts of clawlike stones found at the base of the formation, one by Teybodal (ca. 1812–1899), the oldest living Kiowa at the time. In an interview with Jane Richardson in 1935, Kintadl (1844–1938) stated she had personally picked up "flints like bear claws" at the base of the formation.[27] Maurice Boyd's (1983:92–93) consultants also report that large ivory claws were found at the site.[28]

Adrienne Mayor suggests that two paleontological forms may explain the phenomenon of flintlike claws found at the base of Devil's Tower:

Quaternary alluvial deposits in the nearby Belle Fourche River, which are known to contain ivory mammoth tusks, and claw-shaped belemite fossils in the Sundance Formation (Mayor 2005:259). The Morrison Formation is exposed in the area around Devil's Tower and has yielded *Camarasaurus, Apatasaurus, Allosaurus, Stegosaurus,* and *Diplodocus* dinosaur fossils with very large talons. The fossils together with the vertical scratch-like marks of the formation could have led to conceptualization of a giant bear such as figures in the Bear Lodge story.

ARCHAEOLOGY (THE DOMEBO SITE)

The Kiowa have also contributed to the growth of Paleo-Indian archaeology, if indirectly. Mr. J. E. Patterson discovered portions of a mammoth skull, tusk, and vertebrae exposed along a deep arroyo-like spring-fed branch of Tonkawa Creek approximately three miles east of Stecker in Caddo County, Oklahoma. Adrian D. Anderson of the Museum of the Great Plains in Lawton, Oklahoma, reported the site in December 1961. A team of archaeologists, biologists, and geologists from the Museum of the Great Plains excavated the site, revealing a disarticulated mammoth skeleton. Although the bones had no cut marks, placement of several of the bones and artifacts suggests that the animal had been butchered. The mid-section of a Clovis point was found near two articulated vertebrae during the initial reconnaissance of the site. A complete Clovis point was found in situ in an area of disarticulated ribs and vertebrae, while a second complete Clovis point was found in situ near a pair of articulated vertebrae. Three small waste flakes were found in the bone bed, suggesting that someone either made or resharpened tools at the site after the animal was killed. In the adjacent gravel bed immediately downstream from the bone bed, a third complete Clovis point of fine-grained quartzite, a flake scraper, and a worked flake were found. All of the artifacts except the fluted point found downstream were made of Edwards Plateau chert from central Texas. The bones were too poorly preserved to show any butchering marks (Leonhardy 1966:16–20; Haynes 2002:61–62).

Located on the Domebo allotment, this branch of Tonkawa Creek was named Domebo Branch. The site was named the Domebo Mammoth Kill Site and recorded as site 34CD50. Dome-bo is the agency spelling of the Kiowa personal name Jó-bâu (Eagle Bone Whistle), who became known as Charley Domebo. In Kiowa, this term is used for an eagle bone whistle, wooden flute, whistle, or any type of horn instrument, including a bugle. (The similarity of the name Domebo to the later Disney character Domebo and the finding of the mammoth in 1961 are purely coincidental.) Thus, a Kiowa name is now associated with one of the more important Paleo-Indian sites in the southern plains. Domebo is one of the better dated Clovis-age deposits in North America, and numerous paleoecological studies have been conducted on it. Paleoecological data indicate that the surrounding area was then a part of a large "humid woodland" that dominated the river valleys, while grasslands covered the surrounding uplands. Compared to today, more moderate winters, fewer and shorter periods of subfreezing temperatures, and cooler summers were characteristic of the region. Evidence from pollen, snails, vertebrate faunal remains, stratigraphy, and radiocarbon dating of fossil bone through accelerator mass spectronomy have made the site an important reference locality for studies of the Clovis culture, Paleo-Indian mammoth hunting, Plains culture history, and southern Plains Pleistocene to Holocene paleoenvironments (Hoffman 1998:215; Haynes 2002:61–62).[29]

STONE ALIGNMENTS AND CAIRNS

Stone alignments and cairns are other geographic features considered sacred by many Plains tribes. The great Medicine Wheel in the Bighorn Mountains is the best-known site of this type and probably the most controversial. Today, nearly every Plains tribe claims some connection to this alignment. Of the Kiowa elders I spoke with, only one stated that the Kiowa had a connection to this site. Although one elder Kiowa woman claimed to know such a story, she refused to share it with other Kiowa elders and me at a meeting one evening, leading the others to doubt her claim. In any event, the Medicine Wheel does not appear in Kiowa mythology, early history, or recorded stories, and there is no known Kiowa name for the site.[30] Not all cairns had religious significance, as formations as trail markers and residue from clearing areas of stone are known. However, because many contemporary tribes associate them with markers of burials, visions quest sites, and pilgrimages, they must be viewed with respect (Sundstrom 2003:269–271).

While cairns are more common on the northern plains, it is likely they also existed along trails through Texas and Mexico. Gelo (2000:306–307) mentions the Comanche custom of leaving tally marks on the ground on a high spot or in nearby timber, as well as the use of sticks stuck in the ground leaning in the direction a party was moving. Other Comanche practices involved the use of "turning trees," or markers made by tying down a sapling to point in the direction of water off a path, or the planting of saplings with split trunks around a water hole. In time, these trees grew in their altered shapes and continued to serve as markers. Another Comanche practice recorded in several counties involved the carving and painting of hunt scenes, animal figures, geometric designs, tallies, and combat scenes on trees, similar to pictographs and petrogylphs on rocks (Jackson 1938; Gelo 2000). Owing to their larger population and closer proximity to the Spanish and Mexicans, more historical frontier documents exist for the Comanche than for the Kiowa. However, because the Kiowa shared much of the same territory with the Comanche and frequently participated with them in encampments, war parties, and in attending Kiowa Sun Dances, the Kiowa undoubtedly knew of if not practiced some of these methods, and in turn probably once had place names for some of the Texas and Mexico locales that Gelo (2000) provides Comanche names for. This is also supported by the presence of other recorded Kiowa place names throughout this same region. Like tipi rings, cairns, trail markers, turning trees, tree decorations, and other communicative forms are susceptible to degradation from weather, agricultural practices, cattle grazing, and development. Many more of these features undoubtedly once existed. Corwin (1958:143, 146) recorded and photographed the placement of a large stone between two trees by Hunting Horse, a Kiowa, in front of the tipi where his son Albert Horse was born in 1886. This occurred on Frizzie Head Creek, south of the present-day Meers-Saddle Mountain Road.[31]

Vision Quest Sites

Vision quest sites are typically classified as sacred. As Sundstrom (2003:271) notes, "A vision quest could take place anywhere that was secluded and considered a place of spiritual power. . . . Places traditionally used for vision quests were considered sacred as sources of spiritual power. Vision seekers used these places repeatedly." Some of the best-known vision quest sites were Bear Butte in South Dakota and Devil's Tower in Wyoming, both of which the Kiowa maintain claims to. After the Kiowa migrated to the southern Plains, the Wichita Mountains provided a spiritual resource frequently invoked by Kiowa medicine men and healers seeking power. As was common with most Plains cultures, awe-inspiring and secluded locations were sought out for the fasting, prayer, and meditation associated with vision quests. Kiowa sometimes built rock cairns at such sites. In 1935, Mrs. Hunting Horse described Kiowa vision quest sites to Alice Marriott:

> The man made a bed of sagebrush on which he lay, wrapped in a
> robe. If rocks were available, a shelter wall might be constructed, but

the piling of rocks or building of a wall was not a ritual part of the quest.[32]

Residual cairns are still visible on the south side of Medicine Bluffs on Fort Sill Military Base and could be considered as an unusual natural feature (Sundstrom 2003:279).

Marriott recorded the following from Atah concerning vision quests:

> Anyone who seeks visions goes out alone and a spirit comes and speaks to him and tells him just how to do and that's where they get their medicine. If the spirit tells them to go back to their camps, they have failed. Others see visions and hear voices speak. Two young men went to Cutthroat Gap and stayed within earshot of each other. They made sage beds and lay down to stay for four days and nights. On the fourth day the voice spoke and told them to go to their camp; that spirit wouldn't give them any blessing. By that time they were worn with fasting. What else it said is unknown, but they probably did see something. After that they weren't lively the way they were before. It seemed there was something in their lives that bothered them. They probably saw some visions, but they did not receive power. She never heard of anyone's going to Cutthroat Gap after the men [were] refused power there. Apparently, they were the first to go there. There were no special places that were known as giving extra strong power. Each man went to a place that seemed to him promising.[33]

Marriott (1968:155) lists four locations where Kiowa frequently sought supernatural power: the north slope of Mount Scott (also the site where Lone Wolf was buried in 1879), the dip between the two peaks of Saddle Mountain, a group of mineral springs south of Carnegie that went dry in the 1930s, and a large artesian spring that later supplied water for the Hobart swimming pool. Marriott recorded a fifth locale in Frank Given's vision quest site on the west side of Mount Sheridan:

> When he went to get power he went on the side of Mount Sheridan where O.M.H. [Old Man Horse] went. His uncle was sick and no one could cure him. He stayed and at first it seemed that nothing would happen. At last, on the fourth night, a big mountain boomer came. He saw it coming toward him. He seemed to fall asleep but he still saw it. It did not speak but blew its breath and he felt words come into his heart. He told why he was there, and the thing told him the

uncle would recover and live through the summer but would die in fall. He had always prayed to sun and daylight and the mountain boomer told him to pray to Maindetak'oyk'i [Máidéthâukàuiqî], the White Man above. He says this part of it was a dream; he actually saw the lizard, but it could not have spoken. He doesn't know whether it were the animal or a spirit. He was to pray: White Man Above have mercy on my uncle that he may recover. No one understood the prayer, but an Apache man who was there said it was a true prayer. He told them it was an unfavorable dream, but not just what he had dreamed. It came true. The uncle had hemorrhage in the fall, and died.[34]

Medicine Bluffs was another well-known vision quest site. Such sites were believed to be places where good spirits resided and were regarded as power places. Parker McKenzie showed me a location just off Highway 9 on the cap rock between Gotebo and Hobart, Oklahoma, where White Bear is reported to have undertaken a vision quest after his release from prison in October 1873. This is Tháiyàldà (White Hill). According to Sangko, "Power could be sought only on a hill. T'at'ohak'o(p) — One hill-medicine mountain. Here was a favorite place to go for power, the spirit always granted what was asked. It was tender-hearted. Mesa to the west."[35] The name is probably Dáujóhâuqòp (Medicine Bluff Concavity Mountain). As Sangko lived near Mountain View, this probably refers to the butte near Kiowa Flat School, two miles west of Mountain View. Born in 1881, Bert Geikaunmah attempted a vision quest as a young man, but was unsuccessful. In the 1990s two young Kiowa men undertook fasts and vision quests on Rainy Mountain but were unsuccessful. Undoubtedly there are many more vision quest sites we will never know of.

OTHER LOCALES; BURIAL SITES

Other types of Plains Indian geosacred sites include commemorative stone circles, eagle hunting pits, and horn stacks. Some tribes constructed circles of stones at village sites to commemorate the dead. I know of no Kiowa instances of this practice. These sites could easily be confused with residual tipi rings and could also be easily altered through herding and agricultural practices. Eagle trapping pits and related features are regarded as sacred because they were associated with highly ritualized activities, including prayer vigils, self-torture, and elaborate ceremonies. Although the Kiowa did hunt eagles, no identifiable pit structures of this form can be associated with the Kiowa. Hugh L. Scott recorded that the Kiowa used sites on the plains and several sites near the head of the Arkansas River to trap eagles.[36] Horns and antler stacks have been found throughout the northern plains, but whether these were viewed as sacred or not is unclear (Sundstrom 2003:273).

One of the most common and perhaps obvious types of sacred sites is a burial place and a memorial site. Locations where the dead were laid to rest were regarded as sacred and were associated with specific types of ritual behavior (Sundstrom 2003:274)—practically a human universal. Kiowa buried their dead across the plains, and even after they entered the reservation a wide number of locales were used for interments. Because the Kiowa preferred burial in crevices and ravines rather than in graves dug in earth, mountains were a favorite location for burials. Many Kiowa around Hobart, Oklahoma, were interred on Támchéqòp (Burial Mountain). I recorded other burial sites along the north range of the Wichita Mountains. Such sites are commonly found when beads wash out of interments in crevices higher up. Following the establishment of Christian churches and allotment in 1901, formal cemeteries were begun in Kiowa communities. The respect accorded the deceased has continued through the use of the modern-day cemeteries for Kiowa, Comanche, and Apache, where families periodically visit to pray for the dead, care for the graves, or leave offerings such as feathers, tobacco, seashells, and toys. This adaptation to cemetery burials has also entailed the relocation of the burials of White Bear from Huntsville Prison in Texas and Big Bow from Elk Creek Cemetery near Hobart, Oklahoma, to Chieftain Knoll in the Fort Sill Military Base cemetery. Here white marble military style tombstones mark these and other notable southern plains leaders of the 1870s, and of scouts such as Iseeo and Hunting Horse. Respect for the deceased has also evolved to include modern markers such as the monument marker for Cutthroat Gap on State Highway 54 south of Cooperton, Oklahoma, the Kiowa veterans' memorial at the Kiowa Tribal Offices in Carnegie, Oklahoma, and the numerous bronze busts at the National Indian Hall of Fame in Anadarko, an attraction started by non-Indians. Just north of Lawton the state of Oklahoma has placed a sign along the H. E. Bailey Turnpike marking Sitting Bear Creek, the small branch on the Fort Sill Army Post that Sitting Bear indicated he would not go past and where he was killed while being taken in chains to Texas in 1871.

Common to many American Indian groups, and increasing with pan-Indian insistence on respect for and protection of the land, references to all land as sacred or holy are common. As one Kiowa man commented, "God put us here. This is our holy land." In other instances specific sites may be regarded as sacred.

Sacred Islands

Sundstrom (2003:275–284) defines certain geographic forms as "sacred islands in the landscape" and "sites associated with sacred bundles and ceremony origins." These include buttes and mountain ranges, rivers, streams, and lakes, divides, gaps, and rocks, and unusual natural features for the former, and buttes, rivers and lakes, places associated with myths, and the sacred sites of others for the latter.

THE WICHITA MOUNTAINS

Rising out of the relatively flat but rolling plains, the Wichita Mountains are visible throughout much of southwestern Oklahoma. Stretching some seventy miles across, these mountains are named for the Wichita Indians, a number of autonomous but culturally similar tribes of which the Wichita proper were a smaller component, who had villages along the range. These mountains are located along part of a large geological fracture zone and formed around six hundred million years ago when pressure in the Earth's interior forced magma to the surface. Bubbling up through sedimentary layers deposited by ancient rivers and seas, the magma hardened into black igneous gabbro. One hundred million years later molton lava forced its way upward through the cracks and vents of the overlying gabbro, depositing a layer of distinctive red granite, which dominates the range today. Extensive erosion has since worn down the former sharp peaks of the range into many rounded formations and boulders (Morgan 1973; Wichita Mountains 1997).

The Wichita Mountains are the only significant mountain range in this region of the plains and are geographically and ecologically unique in that they represent a mountain enclave in the center of the southern Great Plains. This "island" marks the transition between the tallgrass prairie to the east and the shortgrass country to the west and has a variety of ecotones, including mixed grass prairies, scrub oak forests, intermittent and permanent streams, and rock-crowned mountains. These mountains also have relict stands of the Cross Timbers biota that once ran from central Kansas into north-central Texas. Covering much of central Oklahoma, it marked the shift from the Great Plains to the eastern woodlands (Wichita Mountains 1997).

Since the late 1700s, the Wichita Mountains have been an important area for the Kiowa. By the early 1800s some portions of the tribe had established their primary residency in this region. Several of the mountains in the range rise above 2,000 feet in elevation, with Mount Pinochet, the tallest formation in the range, at 2,476 feet. Much of the range rises some 1,100 feet above the surrounding area and creates a marked contrast to the predominantly gypsum and brick red sandstone of the surrounding region. On clear days, Mount Scott is visible from my host family's home near Redstone, forty-three miles to the northeast and along the northern border of the old reservation. As Mooney (1898:155) noted, these mountains may have a special significance associated with the earlier mountainous Kiowa homeland.

In earlier times these mountains served as a protective barrier to the south and as a retreat area from northern hostilities, and as a base from which Kiowa bands traveled for raiding or bison hunting to the south, west, and north. Elk, deer, antelope, turkeys, wild plums, and other food sources were common throughout the Wichita Range. Today 806 plant, 240 bird, 64 reptile and amphibian, 50 mammal, and 36 species of fish are found in the refuge. The mountains also provided a spiritual refuge, with several vision quest sites known here.

The Wichita Mountains figure prominently in tribal, family, and individual oral traditions. One account states that Mount Scott is the site of a cave that opened up in the late 1880s, exposing a lush green habitat into which the last of the bison herds disappeared; the cave then closed forever. This occurred on the north face of Mount Scott (Marriott and Rachlin 1968:138–139). In addition to Fort Sill, a large portion of the mountains is now in the Wichita Mountains Wildlife Refuge, with an interpretive center showcasing the local ecology. It is also the home of the largest bison herd in the area, and on this account attracts many visitors. As Harlan Hall (Toncacut 2000:38) has written:

> At times, I am afforded the opportunity of returning to KIOWA Country—the land of my rearing. I always try to take my family out to see the buffalo herd on the Wichita Mountains Wildlife Refuge.
>
> I love to look at the herd bull's eyes looking at me. My grandfathers always told me that if you do that, it means he wants to talk KIOWA to you. KIOWAS and buffaloes have lived together many centuries.

The Wichita Mountains are a prime example of the kinds of changes in land ownership, native access to land for cultural and religious purposes, and modern use and development that have emerged through time. Kiowa views on the contemporary refuge are highly varied. Although virtually every Kiowa I spoke with appreciated the refuge as a nature habitat and recognized that tourism is good for the local economy, its continued cultural importance is more varied. Access is not a major issue, as much of the Fort Sill army base, including Medicine Bluff, is open to the public. Vision quests are no longer actively practiced, and other religious activities such as sweat lodges and Native American Church meetings can be held virtually anywhere and do not require refuge access. While some Kiowa still see the refuge as a somewhat pristine remnant of their traditional homeland and visit certain areas to pray, gather herbs, and reminisce about the past, others view it simply as a tourist attraction that has been out of Indian hands for a long time. As one Kiowa woman said,

> I don't have those kinds [religious] of feelings for it. However, I feel sympathy for them since that is where the buffalo herd was returned to after being decimated almost into nothing. I feel sympathy. That is a pitiful way to describe what it feels like. But I guess it is the way that I feel for a child that I know has been deliberately mistreated and unloved. . . . Well, it does not rate with Devil's Tower. However, it is a good place to go and camp. It is good to see the buffalo and longhorns, and the prairie dogs. The tourism is good for the local economy. __ says that he really feels like a tourist when we go up there. I think it has been out of Indian hands for so long that I feel it is truly a refuge park. It has an excellent visitor's center. It is fun to watch the buffalo and longhorn auction. The eagles have returned. It is good.[37]

Originally the Kiowa referred to only a small portion of the range as the Wichita Mountains. Parker McKenzie stated that his generation associated this term with the mountains west of the break at present-day Cooperton, Oklahoma and not with the eastern range of the mountains.[38] Documentary evidence provides an even more precise designation. As Mooney (1898:267) noted, "The mountains immediately about the site of the village visited by the dragoons are still known to the Kiowa as Do'gúat Kóp, 'Wichita Mountains,' the name not being applied by them to the more eastern portion of the range." The Black Goose Map contains the label "Original Wichita Mountains" at the small cluster of mountains on the north side of the North Fork of the Red River where the historic Wichita village was in 1834.[39] This would include Stewart Mountain, Soldiers Peak, Devil's Canyon, and probably adjacent King Mountain. For numerous historical and spiritual reasons, the contemporary Wichita Mountain Range remains one of the most prominent symbols of the Kiowa homeland.

"Medicine Bluff," Comanche County, Oklahoma.

MEDICINE BLUFF

The best-known Kiowa geosacred site in the Wichita Mountains is Xóqáudáuhá (Medicine Bluff), a prominent bluff located on the south side of and overlooking Medicine Bluff Creek, on the present-day Fort Sill Military Base. Scott reports that the Comanche used Medicine Bluff and the point of Mount Sheridan for vision questing.[40] Rock cairns on top of the site and the Kiowa name for it suggest that they used it in a similar fashion, which Kiowa elders affirm. Elder Kiowa told Scott that the first time they saw the bluff they were astonished at seeing a mountain split in two and half of it gone, as there was nothing like it anywhere they had been.[41] The noted Kiowa doctor Tónàuqàut (Snapping Turtle, lit. Rough Tailed) renewed his underwater animal medicine and doctored individuals in Medicine Bluff Creek (Nye 1962:259).

LONG HORN MOUNTAIN

Another geosacred site that has remained particularly important to contemporary Kiowa is Gúcị̃nyíqòp (Long Horn Mountain), southwest of

Mountain View, in Kiowa County, Oklahoma. Because the cedars on this mountain are said to be sweeter than any other in the area, this mountain has become a preferred site for gathering cedar sprigs to dry and use for cedaring ceremonies—prayers and blessings using burning cedar as incense. Cedar incense is commonly used in cleansing and blessing a new home, as a blessing after nightmares, ghost encounters, or funerals, in Peyote and naming ceremonies, prior to a marriage, by dance societies prior to ceremonials, or just for receiving a blessing. As Ernestine Kauahquo Kauley recounted,

> That's where we get our cedar. We use only the cedar from there. It's something we've known since we were born. You know, that if you're going to burn cedar in the house, we burn Long Horn Mountain cedar. It's very medicinally powerful. It has a more-cedary smell.[42]

Many Kiowa go to great effort to gather their cedar from this mountain, and a host of offerings, including feathers, tobacco bundles, cloth strips, coins, food, and other items, have been placed on the mountain. One Kiowa man told me of an offering of food he once saw placed on top of the mountain that consisted of an open carton of chocolate milk and a Hershey's chocolate bar laid beside it with the wrapping peeled back.[43] From on top, much of the Wichita Mountains can be seen, including Mount Scott, Mount Sheridan, Saddle Mountain, Rainy Mountain, and other named locales. In addition to cedar trees at the base and on the sides of the mountain, there are substantial groves of cedars on the mountaintop. On one peak I observed a rock cairn shaped like an elongated horseshoe with an opening to the west.

CUTTHROAT MOUNTAIN

The first summer entry in the Kiowa pictographic calendars dates to the summer of 1833 and records Ém qóltàdèfài (The Summer That They Cut Off Their Heads), the Osage massacre of a Kiowa camp. By the 1830s the Kiowa were firmly established in what is now southwestern Oklahoma. Expanding Anglo population pressures from the east and the removal of woodlands and southeastern Indian tribes to Indian Territory by the U.S. government resulted in subsequent ripples of intrusion into the Prairie and eastern Plains tribes. With increasing Anglo settlement in Missouri, the Osage were already residing in portions of northeastern Indian Territory, and were expanding their hunting and raiding territories westward.

In the spring of 1833 the Kiowa were camped just west of the mouth of

Rainy Mountain Creek in the bend of the Washita River just northeast of present-day Mountain View, Oklahoma. Most of the adult warriors had left on a journey against the Ute, leaving only a few warriors with the women, children, and elders of the camp. Finding no buffalo, the camp moved to the location later known as Eagle Heart's, south of present-day Carnegie, and then to Apache Creek, where Carither's Presbyterian Mission (also known as Cache Creek Mission), six miles southwest of Apache, later stood. One morning some young Kiowa men went to the Keechai Hills in the vicinity of present-day southern Grady County, Oklahoma, in search of bison, and discovered a bison that had been killed, with a broken Osage arrow lying beside it. One account reports that some young men out looking for their horses found a bison with an Osage arrow in it, while other reports state some of the Kiowa came upon the Osage and, after exchanging fire, separated, with one Osage wounded and one Kiowa killed. (It is possible that more than one Kiowa party was out and that both events occurred.) Upon hearing the news, the camp brought in their horses and stood guard all night. The next day they broke into three or four distinct groups and left the area. According to Taybodle's account, he and his father were in one group that went south of Mount Scott, another group containing Tohausan headed back to the site at the mouth of Rainy Mountain Creek, while the third containing the tribal head chief Island went in behind Saddle Mountain through the gap and stopped at the head of a spring now known as Jackson's Spring. This site is just northwest of a low hill located on the north side of the Wichita Mountains along what is now Boggy Hollow Creek, a branch of the East Fork of Otter Creek, and about one-half mile southwest of Grace Mountain in Comanche County, Oklahoma. The geographic importance of this area is that it contains a narrow natural gap or pass through the mountains.

The Osage tracked this group of Kiowa to their new camp. One account states that two Kiowa girls walked up to a pool near their camp to get a drink just before dark. When they bent over the pool of water they saw the reflections of two Osage men peering down at them from the cliff above. Frightened, they returned to the camp and reported what they saw. Unfortunately the other Kiowa dismissed it as Kiowa boys trying to scare the girls.

The next morning, while most in the camp were still asleep, a young man went out to look for his ponies when he sighted the approaching Osage, who began pursuing him and firing at him. When he ran back to the camp, calling out that the Osage were coming, only a few of the women were awake in the camp. Upon hearing the news, Island awakened the camp to the cry of "To the rocks! To the rocks!" With too few warriors to make a defensive stand, what followed was largely the massacre of an overrun and underdefended camp in a surprised and panic-stricken flight.

Jack Haley, who has lived and worked on the ranch that encompasses the site his entire life, has met and visited with many elder Kiowa about the site over the years. According to the accounts he was given, when the Kiowa fled, they went in two directions. Those who went up the small rocky hill directly south of the encampment were surrounded, overrun, and killed. Those that ran toward the east, where a rocky hill and plateau leads to larger hills behind it, survived. Despite considerable heroism on the part of several men and women, the Osage killed five Kiowa men and a large number of women and children. As was their custom, the Osage decapitated the victims. As the Kiowa had recently traded for many brass buckets from the Pawnee, the Osage placed each head in a bucket in the camp, burned the camp, and proceeded back east along the northern edge of the mountains. According to Taybodle's account, the heads were found in a circle to the left of the pass at the foot of a little rocky hill on the west side of the range. Following this tragedy the small knoll to the south and east of the camp over which the Kiowa fled was named Qóltàqòp (Cutthroat Mountain, implying Neck Severing or Beheading Mountain). Aside from the severe casualties inflicted, the Osage captured two of the three Táimé medicines, killing the bundle-keeper's wife as she tried to untie the case they were stored in from the tipi pole they were secured to. The Sun Dance was not held for two years until the bundle was returned from the Osage, with whom peace was made through the efforts of the U.S. dragoons at Fort Gibson.[44]

The massacre site was just east of the To-Gei-Ah allotment and is now part of the Jim Haley Ranch. During the Rainy Mountain Church Centennial Celebration, a visit to the site was included on June 4, 1993, as part of the "Grand Historical Tour of the Kiowa People" (RMKIBC 1993:3). On January 20, 1995, the Kiowa and Oklahoma Historical Societies dedicated The Historical Marker For the Site of the Cut Throat Gap Massacre of 1833, along State Highway 54, 2.5 miles south of Cooperton, Oklahoma. Although Mr. Haley is very accommodating to visitors, many Kiowa have not had the opportunity to visit the site because of its remote location and the physical difficulty of access. The site represents the most severe Kiowa defeat in warfare known. Some Kiowa attach a sacred quality to the site, which remains one of the most important landmarks in Kiowa history. As one elder explained, "People go to Cutthroat to mourn, to remember. Some call it a pilgrimage, to renew themselves with what happened there in the past." Mr. Haley has known many of the Kiowa who have visited the site. In his youth he remembers a family of Kiowa from which one member

"Cutthroat Mountain," Comanche County, Oklahoma.

always came the evening before Easter, climbed the high ridge east of the site, and remained there singing through the night. In the morning they were always gone.

In 1994, I visited the site with Atwater Onco and gained a greater understanding of and appreciation for the geography of the area and what occurred there. I revisited the site in 2004, during which visit Mr. Haley provided a thoroughly informative tour of the site, passing on much of the detailed information he had learned from elder Kiowa during his lifetime. A small granite marker commemorating those killed at the site in 1833 was erected on the small ridge to the east of the actual site by a private group of Kiowa. The site itself is now largely overgrown with cedar trees. Mr. Haley hopes to leave the site to the Kiowa tribe. Signage is an important visible marker that directly relates to who controls the history of an area. The recent implementation of signs bearing Indian names and history is an important symbolic step in the reclamation of Indian cultural and historical knowledge and recognition of their associated sites across the landscape. Similar changes are occurring across the nation.

Addressing a group of Kiowa at Cutthroat Gap, tribal elder Atwater Onco gave a moving account of the events that transpired at the site, stressing

KIOWA ETHNOGEOGRAPHY

the spiritual significance of the site in both the opening and closing of his account:

> You are entering a very sacred place of the Kiowa people. Remember that. Very, very sacred place of the Kiowa people. According to the white man['s] history this happened in 1833, Kiowas had no history about dates. About that time, 1833, according to the research there was about two thousand Kiowas living. They were getting a war party ready. A young war party was going to the warpath with the Utes, cause Utes was our worst enemy of the Kiowas. The hunting party went out and they found a slain buffalo, so the Kiowa hunters went up there and there was an arrow in the buffalo and they pulled the arrow out and they looked at it and said it's a Osage. They knew all weapons of the enemies then. Osages were enemies. They said it's an Osage arrow so they went back to camp and they said that the Osages were in this area. We better prepare to defend ourselves because at that time the Osages had rifles that they got from traders up east and they had long saber knives. Kiowas the only thing we had was our lances, tomahawks, hatchets, bow and arrows. So they knew that the Osages were a dangerous enemy, so they start preparing where they was all camped. They keep waiting for the Osages to attack but they never did, so after a few days, maybe a week, they decided that the Osages was not going to attack so the war party went out the young men, the warriors. Ok, the group that stayed, the chief was there with that group and his name is Aundaytay interpreted Island Man. One morning a little boy, a Kiowa boy, went out to check on his family horses early in the morning. As he approach a hilltop he noticed the Osages, they had shaven heads, so he run back to the encampment here. And he said he spotted the Osages. Everybody better get ready and get out of here, defense, nothing but old men here, old chiefs, women, children, old ladies, so the only ones over here, noncombatants.
>
> The Osages probably knew that, so they swept down on them from the east and they caught them all in this area here, and when they kill a Kiowa they cut their head off. There was nothing but non-combatants here. If the man warriors were here they couldn't have done that. They attacked the village, started killing little kids, little boy, little girl, old women, old men, start killing them, slaughter them. They're trying to get away, Kiowas trying to get away. Climb up that way probably that area, probably even in this area. They were so powerful and so bad that the man that handled the Taime for the

Sun Dance he got scared, and he left his medicine bundle, his wife went over there and got the medicine bundle off the tipi, and as she was getting it down they killed her.

Another war chief, so bad, that he left his war shield, course he's an old warrior, but you still not supposed to do that, he left his war shield. They were screaming and hollering and everything I'm sure in this area but there was some bravery among the Kiowas even though they're old they're brave. They fought for the young ones, the old people so that they could escape. One chief, Tai-aun, he grabbed a hold of his baby wrapped him up in a blanket, carried him with his teeth, would stop and shoot arrows at the Osages. His wife was running by him was handing him his arrows to shoot at the Osages. One little Kiowa boy fought the Osages. One woman fought the Osages to put a protection for the little ones, noncombatants. One visiting Pawnee he fought the Osages so that women and children could escape. The Osages killed 150 of us, mostly little kids, old people, noncombatants. They kill 150 of us and to make it worse, right in the middle of encampment wherever there was, Kiowas have their buckets they use to cook their meat in. They had their buckets sitting in a straight line here. They had a 150 heads of Kiowas, girls, boys, old people, young girls, all in a row there to show them that they've done something brave by killing noncombatants. What the Kiowas don't like, at that time we were at war with other tribes, the white people, that was a way of life at that time. But it was not a way of life where you go in there and kill little children, old women, and old men. And then display their heads in a bucket. When the war party returned they've seen what happened to their kinfolks here, they were mad. Right away they form a war party and they start chasing the Osages but they were gone, were out of the territory. Audaytay, Island Man, they take away his chieftainship, can't be a chief and not protect your people although they're young, old, whatever, your job is protecting. They took his chieftainship away they made Dohausen chief, Hunting Horse my friend there, tell me, used to come here. A lot of Kiowa used to come here and mourn. It's not a good feeling for me to be here, too sacred, too holy. Hunting Horse said somewhere in this area they dug a mass grave and buried 150 bodies and their heads in the grave. I'll say this in closing. We're Kiowas, we're brave, put up with a lot of things, them days cause that's what we're trained for, battle. But when they seen what happened even the warriors wept. You don't see warriors weep. Kiowa chiefs what they seen, they wept.

But I want you all to know that this is a sacred ground. Whenever you're up here, remember that. The older Kiowas like me still don't like it. We don't like it.[45]

The spiritual and historical significance of the site was apparent as the emotion welled up in his voice. Although Qóltàqòp actually means Cutthroat (i.e., Beheading) Mountain, Kiowa refer to the locale in English by the names Cutthroat Mountain for the hill and Cutthroat Gap for the general area and the pass leading to the area. Nearby Cutthroat Lake and probably Time O-Day Spring (a mispronunciation and reference to the Táimé Bundle being captured) are named for the site.

Rainy Mountain

The hill now known as Rainy Mountain is probably the best-known place name in Kiowa culture owing to being the site of many pre-reservation Kiowa activities, frequent encampments, and a major Indian boarding school, the subject of a book by noted Kiowa author N. Scott Momaday (1969), and the location of nearby Rainy Mountain Kiowa Indian Baptist Church, which began in 1893. Known as Sépyáldá, the name actually means Rainy Hill or Knoll, because it is said to have always rained whenever Kiowa camped near this vicinity. The hill is located approximately six miles south-southeast of Gotebo, in Kiowa County, Oklahoma. It is a small, round-topped limestone knoll that on close inspection is littered with many small rocks cropping up between the vegetation. Because it is limestone it is geologically a part of the limestone-based Slick Hills and not the granite-based Wichita Mountains proper. If it were located among the larger formations of the Slick Hills or Wichita Mountains, which merge in this area of southwestern Oklahoma, it would be inconsequential. However, its isolated location some nine miles north of the main range makes it a highly noticeable and unique geographic feature as the northwest marker that one is approaching the Wichita Mountains.

The site has come to symbolize many things for various Kiowa. The area around the northwest end of the Wichita Mountains, including this hill, became an early center of Kiowa activity when they reached the southern plains. In the 1880s several large Kiowa encampments were held here for distributing grass leasing payments. Kiowa elders state that the Kiowa, then camped in the area between present-day Gotebo and Hobart, received the Óhòmò (Omaha) Society and dance from the Cheyenne near this area in the summer of 1884.[46]

Rainy Mountain was also the site of Rainy Mountain Indian School from

"Rainy Mountain," Kiowa County, Oklahoma.

1893 to 1920. Originally the school was planned to be built along Sugar Creek near Saddle Mountain. The Kiowa near Saddle Mountain at the time were against anything "white" being constructed in their vicinity, and when workers arrived with lumber to begin building the government school, they were met by Pape-dome and a group of mounted Kiowa men bearing rifles, who drove them away (Crawford 1915:55). Had the school been built elsewhere, a significant historical component of the Rainy Mountain community would have never developed.

After the school was built on the eastern side of Rainy Mountain, many Kiowa families moved and camped on the eastern side of the school to be near their children. Elders recall Corwin Boake's trading posts, the first of which was located just south of the county road and on the extreme northeastern edge of the Rainy Mountain Indian School Grounds. This store was replaced by the second, also built along the southern edge of the same county road but a mile due east of the school. The remnants of this store are still standing and in fair condition. Boake's stores were a major source for groceries, dry goods, and other supplies.[47]

Rainy Mountain held a special significance for one Kiowa, who was born

KIOWA ETHNOGEOGRAPHY

in his great-grandmother's tipi just north of this hill on a small bend on the southern side of Rainy Mountain Creek. This site is visible from the county bridge over the creek just north of the mountain. Born during a Kiowa encampment for a grass lease payment on or around November 15, 1897, this boy was subsequently named Sépyàldà. He would later receive the Anglo name of Parker Paul McKenzie. In 1991, I visited the site with McKenzie to photograph and map his birthplace. On that day and others he recounted stories and personal memories of the school, its campus, curriculum, and faculty, the athletic teams, games, forms of student punishment, and how they avoided getting caught speaking Kiowa by the teachers. On one visit to the school in 1994, Ben Kracht and I were surprised to see two local ranchers loading stone from the wall of the old boy's dormitory. When I asked them what they were taking the stone for, they said they needed it to fill in the potholes along the driveway on their ranch.

Although only a few building remnants are still standing, memories of the school site remain strong in the Kiowa community. Kiowa author N. Scott Momaday (1969) has eloquently written about the nostalgia and the feelings the hill evokes for him and how he relates portions of his personal, family, and tribal history and beliefs to the site. Already important to the Kiowa, Momaday's book introduced the site to a wider audience outside the Kiowa community and remains a staple in Native American literature classes around the country. Clyde Ellis (1996) provides a historical account of the school and its relation to the larger policies of forced assimilation during the period of 1893 to 1920.

Built in 1893 and taking its name from the nearby hill some three and a half miles away, the Rainy Mountain Kiowa Indian Baptist Church has been a hallmark and a principal hub of Kiowa Christian activity for a sizable segment of the western half of the Kiowa community. Numerous elders attended both the school and the church, and some have described the various services, camp meetings, and Christmas encampments they attended there. Parker McKenzie put together a list of the first 338 church members from January 22, 1893, to April 8, 1928, listing their names as recorded in church records, Bureau of Indian Affairs records, and their Kiowa names in the McKenzie orthography.[48] In 1939, stone from the Rainy Mountain Indian School buildings was used to build a new dining hall for the church that still stands today, having been being rebuilt after a fire in 1982. While educational and economic opportunities have reinvigorated the mobility of the Kiowa, the area around the mountain and church is still a special place that seems to call the Kiowa back to the area. As Clydia Nahwooksy described in the Rainy Mountain Church Centennial Booklet (RMKIBC 1993:2),

Rainy Mountain, a mystical name that seems to sing in the heart and mind. Rainy Mountain Kiowa Indian Baptist Church, a place name that continues strong through generations of families. It attracts the far traveling descendants of Kiowa church members home again just as it weekly welcomes its regular church goers from as far away as fifty miles distant.

One hundred years ago an early Kiowa convert said, "it is my prayer that no matter how far we travel, we will always come home again to this beautiful place that God has given for our use." It appears that prayer is answered over and over again, and possibly more strongly during this Centennial period than ever before.

Kiowa commonly visit the old Rainy Mountain School grounds, and those that are able frequently hike to the top of the mountain, which offers a grand view in all directions.

Rainy Mountain is featured on two of the ten murals in the Kiowa Tribal Museum in Carnegie. These murals provide a sweeping depiction of Kiowa history, from the tribe's origins and early myths through their triumphs on the Plains, the assault on their traditional culture, and their current status. Parker Boyiddle, Sherman Chaddlesone, and Mirac Creepingbear each painted three murals. In one of Chaddlesone's paintings, titled *Kiowas, Comanches, and Cheyennes Fight the U.S. Cavalry*, Rainy Mountain forms the backdrop of a large encampment of tipis on the eastern side of the mountain, below the ledger-style depictions of Indians and cavalry fighting. Collaboratively painted by the three artists, the last mural is entitled *The Kiowa Today*. The central scene of this mural is of a modern paved highway bordered on each side by crop fields, fences, and a power line extending into the horizon toward the base of Rainy Mountain. Above the horizon are depictions of the Kiowa Black Legs Society and women in buckskin and victory dresses dancing in front of the society lodge, the six Kiowa Gourd Clan war trophies, and the imprint of two painted human hands.[49]

Rainy Mountain is incorporated into the Kiowa tribal logo created by Roland Whitehorse. The logo depicts a mounted warrior carrying a bow and arrows and a shield with Rainy Mountain on it. As Whitehorse (Boyd 1983:304–305) explained, "The shield depicts the sacred Rainy Mountain in Oklahoma, the ancient Kiowa burial ground at the end of the great tribal journey." With a large population, many allotments nearby, the church, school (once the site of annuity payments), and trading post, the area was a hub of pre-reservation activities and has been analogized by some Kiowa as the "Early Kiowa Capital." The church cemeteries (the original cemetery southwest of the church and the new cemetery northeast of the church) are the final resting place for many Kiowa, together forming one of the largest Kiowa tribal cemeteries.

Rainy Mountain has come to represent a sense of a permanent homeland for a once highly nomadic people. It symbolizes the final stopping point of the Kiowa migration from the northland. Most Kiowa do not attribute their relocation as a response to military pressure from the Lakota and Cheyenne, increased access to horses, changes in bison migration, and assignment to a reservation that included Rainy Mountain but to "a long term journey that, from the start, had a purpose, a final destination. After much movement, they found a spiritual center for their activity in the Wichita Mountains, where they could bury their dead, and return for generations. The base of this mountain, symbolically at least, marks the spot where the Kiowa realized that their southward journey was complete" (Schnell 2000:169). As Kiowa author Gus Palmer, Jr. (2003:64) writes, "Kiowas know and love the geography around them. Sépyáldá (Rainy Mountain) is a point of reference for Kiowas for all times. . . . It is the place where Kiowas ended up in their long migrations across the Plains. There are hundreds of other such geographical locations on the Plains from Montana to Mexico, but Sépyáldá is the granddaddy of them all, so to speak."

THE MEDICINE LODGE TREATY

In October 1867, the Kiowa, Comanche, Plains Apache, Cheyenne, and Arapaho signed the Medicine Lodge Treaty along Medicine Lodge River, a tributary of the Salt Fork of the Arkansas in south-central Kansas named for the site of several Sun Dances. The treaty required these tribes to retire to assigned reservations, cease raiding Anglo settlers, and allow railroads to be built through the region. In return, the Indians were to receive protection from encroaching white bison hunters and, despite the Indians' protests, to be provided with schools, churches, farming implements, and instruction in adapting to an Anglo lifestyle. Although rations were not specified in the treaty, they were implied and believed necessary to draw Indians away from their traditional lifestyles (Nye 1937:45–46). Although the Kiowa and other tribes continued to travel, hunt, and raid far outside their reservations, increasing pressure from the military, white settlement, and decreasing game supplies forced them onto their respective reservations in the southwestern part of present-day Oklahoma by 1875. After 1867, Medicine Lodge took on a new importance as the location where the Kiowa traditional life began to change radically and quickly.

In 1926 the newly formed Medicine Lodge Indian Peace Council Treaty

Memorial Association invited Kiowa elder I-See-O to identify the exact spot of the 1867 Medicine Lodge Treaty. Iseeo, who was 18 years old at the time of the signing, located the site approximately one-third of a mile south of Medicine Lodge, just below the confluence of the Medicine Lodge River and Elm Creek. George and Lilian Hunt were elected to the board of officers and directors. The local Lions Club enabled 250 Kiowa, Comanche, Apache, Cheyenne, and Arapaho to camp, establishing the "Indian Village" at the first Indian Peace Treaty Pageant held on October 12–14, 1927. Contingents of Kiowa and other tribes have regularly attended the event, being hired to perform dances in the village encampment. Some Kiowa like the event for the economic opportunity it presents, others feel it is exploitative and complain of the declining organizational role that Indians have in the event and that the majority of the profits go to non-Indians. Nevertheless, the event continues to emphasize the importance of the treaty, which forced the Kiowa and other southern plains tribes onto a smaller reservation in Indian Territory. Today, the Indian Peace Treaty Pageant is held every third year on the last weekend of September. It features Indian dances, an Indian village, parades, a carnival, rodeo, craft shows, street dances, night shows, food sales, and other events (Medicine Lodge 1994).

PALO DURO CANYON

If Devil's Tower represents the beginning of the Kiowa migration across the plains, Palo Duro Canyon represents the end of their pre-reservation-era journey and lifeways (Schnell 1994:80). There are two Palo Duro creeks in the Texas Panhandle, one on the extreme northern border and the other south of Amarillo. The latter is the main northern tributary of the Prairie Dog Town fork of the Red River. The canyon's name, Palo Duro (Hard Wood) is derived form the abundance of juniper trees in the canyon. The Kiowa call Palo Duro Canyon Xóhót (Canyon, lit. Rocks Crowding In).

Approximately 120 miles long and 600–800 feet deep, it is the second largest canyon in the United States and had only one natural entrance into it. In the last armed act of resistance to forced reservation life, a group of Kiowa and other tribes attacked the Kiowa Agency at Anadarko on August 21 and 22, 1874. Over half of the tribe fled up the Washita River and onto the Staked Plains of Texas. Enduring miserable rainy weather, Kiowa, Cheyenne, and Comanche sought shelter in Palo Duro Canyon. Although the canyon had only one access trail, Colonel Randall MacKenzie's troops found and attacked the encampment on September 28, 1874. The battle was more of an economic than a combat victory. Although only

"Canyon" and "Big Sand River": Palo Duro Canyon and Prairie Dog Town fork of the Red River, showing the entrance into Palo Duro Canyon, Randall and Armstrong counties, Texas. Photo courtesy of Kenny Harragarra.

four Indians were killed, the cavalry captured and destroyed their villages, personal property, and nearly 1,400 horses, 1,100 of which were shot (Nye 1937:206–234). The loss of their horses, tipis, food, clothing, and supplies and the approaching winter forced most to retreat and surrender at Fort Sill over the next few months. The loss of their horses signaled not only a symbolic defeat in the loss of the basis of their wealth but their final military surrender and the end of their pre-reservation way of life.

Much of the canyon and battle site was owned by the RA Ranch (led by Charles Goodnight) from 1876 to 1890. Goodnight and Charles Loving blazed the Goodnight-Loving Trail from north Texas up the Pecos River and through New Mexico into Colorado. By 1886, Goodnight and John Chisum were driving thousands of cattle into New Mexico annually. In 1934 the state of Texas acquired a deeded parcel of 16,402 acres in Randall and Armstrong counties, which opened as Palo Duro State Park on July 4, 1934. Recently the adjacent 2,036-acre Canoncita Ranch was purchased and added to the park. Because this parcel included much of the Indian encampment, it is an important addition to the park. At present, archaeological surveys have located two of the three main Indian encampments associated with the 1874 fight (Palo Duro Canyon 2004).

The importance of Palo Duro Canyon in Kiowa history is largely seen in retrospect. Kiowa calendars (Mooney 1898:145) hardly mention the outbreak and pursuit of 1874, now dubbed by historians the Red River War. The canyon is now a Texas State Park and figures prominently in the exhibits of the Panhandle-Plains Historical Museum in nearby Canyon, Texas, and in the history of this region. The heightened significance of the canyon to the Kiowa and Texans is largely a post-1874 development, and the canyon is now accorded a symbolic status associated with representing the military defeat and the end of the classic plains life for the Kiowa. Many Kiowa tribal members, including group trips, visit the canyon to connect with their past, and several Kiowa still maintain family accounts of the attack and flight from the site and express feelings of pride in their tribe's resistance to subjugation. In the canyon, a layer of yellow clay outcrops some twelve feet above the floor. One Kiowa artist uses this clay for painting the traditional buckskin clothing she makes.

Anglo Locales of Significance

In native ethnogeography research, the focus is often on the place names and locales of sites that were of aboriginal significance or are considered "traditional." Culture contact situations invariably produce an exchange of information and activity regarding place names and the use of important locales. That context leads to changes in the use of land and the formation of new place names.

As Anglos entered the plains, they became aware of significant streams, travel routes, resource sites, and areas of unique geography. As Anglos became more established, Kiowa began to form new place names to signify sites associated with Anglo residence and activities, including streams (Xólhę̌dèvàu or No Arm's Creek), trading posts (Xópą́jǒ or Adobe House), and military sites (Tànyáldáyápfàhêcà or At Bare/Bald Hill Soldier Place). Appendices B and C list examples of these types of names. Although most such names appeared during the mid- to late 1800s, they became seminal locales for the Kiowa since the late pre-reservation period.

FORT SILL

For the Kiowa, Fort Sill and its associated history are inseparably intertwined. General Philip Sheridan founded Fort Sill in 1869 during his winter campaign to subjugate the southern plains tribes. Permanent buildings appeared in 1870 (Nye 1937:99–105). Reflecting the high number of adverbial phrases in the Kiowa language, the Kiowa called Fort Sill Xóqáudáuhágà (At Medicine Bluff), an abbreviation of Xóqáudáuhágà-yápfàhêgàuqúldéê (Where the Soldiers Stay at Medicine Bluff, lit. Rock Cliff Medicine at Soldiers Collective Place They Are). In terms of physical preservation and visual elements the post is perhaps the richest and most historically concentrated locale on the southern plains, especially for the Indian tribes in the surrounding region. The post was the site of most military-Indian interaction after 1869. Although the surrounding military base now serves as a field artillery training center, most of the old post has been preserved as a tourist attraction near Lawton, Oklahoma. Other notable features include Chieftain Knoll in the post cemetery, the Fort Sill Museum Archives, which contain a wealth of documentary records and material culture of the southern Plains tribes, the Old Post Guardhouse Museum, and the new Fort Sill Museum, currently under construction.

THE OLD POST GUARDHOUSE

Finished in 1873 and now often called the "Geronimo Guardhouse," this structure was used to hold the Kiowa leaders Sitting Bear, White Bear, and Big Tree, the noted Apache leader Geronimo, and others in the mid- to late 1800s. The guardhouse is now a museum containing various displays on the Fort Sill cavalry and the southern Plains tribes. Inside, one cannot help but notice the signs of a prison on the basement level. Thick, smooth, worn hardwood doors, small individual rooms, small barred windows on the doors and along the walls at ground level, dim lighting, well-worn stone steps and floor, the smell of the dark, slightly cool, and well-worn wood and stone all clearly convey a feeling of confinement and age.

THE OLD STONE CORRAL

The stone corral is another eminent symbol of the final military subjugation of the Kiowa, Comanche, and Naishan Apache that is also open to visitors. The corral was built in the summer of 1870 to stop repeated Kiowa and Comanche raids on the post's horse and mule herds, and replaced a wooden post structure. After the Palo Duro fight in September 1874, the remaining Indians were forced to retreat with their fellow tribesmen along the Wichita Mountains to Fort Sill. Surrendering from September 1874 through June 2, 1875, each band was driven into the stone corral, where they were deprived of their weapons, shields, and most of their possessions. Initially, most of their horses were taken out and shot, and some of their possessions were burned. The remaining horses were auctioned off. The well-known war leaders were placed in cells on the north side of the basement of the guardhouse. Women and children were placed in a detention camp east of the post on a flat along Cache Creek. Some 103 warriors were placed in an unfinished stone icehouse consisting of only a floor and walls at the base of the hill east of the post. They lived in pup tents, and meat was thrown over the walls once a day to feed the prisoners (Nye 1937:229–230).

Some Kiowa and Comanche elders retain family stories from their grandparents or great-grandparents who were confined there.[50] An elder Kiowa man described how they "threw meat over the walls to feed them like animals." The corral is a painful reminder of forced military subjugation and the end of the nomadic pre-reservation-era lifestyle. As Hall (Toncacut 2000:40) notes, "The stone post corral still stands at Fort Sill, Oklahoma today; the actual site and a monument to Kiowa men, women and children who were physically held there under arms. A people finally subdued."

The 7th Calvary–Indian Baseball Game

Another important activity at Fort Sill is baseball, first played in Indian Territory at Fort Sill during January–March 1869 between Col. George A. Custer's 7th U.S. Cavalry and the 19th Kansas Volunteer Cavalry. Soldiers often played baseball and competed for prizes provided by the post trader during July 4 celebrations. Fort Sill was unique among frontier army posts in having all-Indian teams as well. Quickly becoming popular, games soon developed between the cavalry soldiers and an all-Indian team of scouts in Troop-L, which served from 1892 to 1897. In 2003 this event was revived with the holding of a "Vintage 19th Century Baseball" game between the "Fort Sill Indians" and the "Fort Sill Cannonballers," using period uniforms, equipment, and rules (Faces of Fort Sill 2004). The all-Indian team won the annual games from 2003 through 2005, the soldiers in 2006. These vintage baseball games reflect the bicultural history that Fort Sill continues to preserve and commemorate.

Analysis

During this study I was able to collect a total of 256 place names for 272 locales for which names in the Kiowa language exist, and 171 names of modern places bearing names in English or anglicized forms of Kiowa that were either named by the Kiowa or that reflect Kiowa identity or activities.

Classified by geographic forms, these place names are divided into the major categories used by the Kiowa in the pre-reservation and reservation periods (see Appendix F). These range from the northern plains to locales in Mexico and the Southwest. These data are from two types of primary sources: the ethnographic field notes and publications of James Mooney between 1892 and 1921 and the field notes of Hugh L. Scott in the 1890s, and my own fieldwork since 1989. While the context of Mooney's compilation of Kiowa place names is unclear, I suspect most were incidental acquisitions obtained while he recorded data on the Kiowa calendars. Because the data ranged from historical recollections of the northland to the present-day reservation in southwestern Indian Territory, now Oklahoma, he clearly included a large and spatially well-balanced sample. In my own fieldwork I sought to record all known Kiowa place names. Although many place names have been lost through time owing to Kiowa confinement to southwestern Oklahoma, I believe this combination represents as thorough as possible and a well-balanced compilation of place names for analysis.

Language study is important for identifying and understanding the native user's point of view. As Salzman (1998:101) notes, an understanding of semantics is "helpful to ethnographers, who strive to understand what members of the societies they study consider culturally important and how different aspects of culture appear to relate to one another." Kiowa place names focus on one or more physical or cultural traits in associa-

TABLE 1. MAJOR CATEGORIES AND NUMBERS OF KIOWA PLACE NAMES

CATEGORY	NAMES	SITES
Mountains	34	37
Hills, ridges,	12	14
Bluffs and concavities	11	13
Other land locales	39	42
Recent locales	08	08
Subtotal	*104*	*114*
Streams	126	132
Stream crossings	1	1
Springs	18	18
Subtotal	*145*	*151*
Astrology	7	7
Modern English names	171	172
Total	*427*	*444*

tion with a geographic form such as a mountain or stream. Componential analysis is a technique applied to a set of terms or lexicon that belong to a highly patterned and well-defined cultural domain, such as color terms, disease names, types of drinks, or kin terms, that, when analyzed according to their components, disclose the semantic basis that makes a group of related terms distinct from one another. This method is useful for revealing the psychological reality of a group as reflected in the content and organization of the folk taxonomy used by its members (Salzmann 1998:59). As Salzmann (1998:61) explains, "to discover the underlying semantic differences among the terms of domains from other cultures helps anthropologists determine what is culturally significant in those societies and how their members structure their experience linguistically." Although it is well known that Plains Indian ethnogeography is structured around a primarily visual landscape, little work has been done in this area.

Using a limited degree of component analysis, I examined the place names of each category to determine their primary basis for named categorization—that is, what the place was named for. Although many place names have more than one semantic component in their makeup, for example Dáu-ál-kǫ-gài-é-hòl-dè-ę̀ (The Place Where Black Kettle Was Killed) could be categorized as person-killed (warfare context)-location, the larger categorization of warfare event is the principal context of the place name. Thus, physical traits were clustered in categories such as flora, fauna, resource location, color, shape, size, position, location, motion, soil, and weather, while cultural traits were clustered into categories such as individual or group location (residence or territory), warfare event, civil conflict, death from old age, religion, architectural structure, trade, and the ransoming of captives. These clusters largely distinguish between naturally occurring phenomena and human activity.

Analysis of the 256 place names recorded in the Kiowa language shows several trends. (1) These place names include 104 names for 115 land-based locales, 144 names for 151 water-based locales, and 7 names for 7 astrological locales. (2) As most place names refer to geographic or human characteristics, Kiowa place names are based on one of three forms: forms denoting naturally occurring physical traits, such as flora, fauna, mineral, or geography (134); forms denoting human activities, such as tribal or individual residence, dwellings, warfare, disease, and houses (78); and forms denoting a combination of naturally occurring physical traits and human activities (27). (3) With the exception of Devil's Tower, the Black Hills, and Medicine Lake, no known Kiowa place names relate to the early mythical era. All other names are of natural phenomena or post-1700 cultural events. (4) Place names were often repeated for a similar location or, especially for northern plains sites, perhaps as a replacement for previously named and disassociated sites—sites no longer in the tribe's range and thus no longer commonly encountered. Overall, the Kiowa data support the major analytical discoveries associated with anthropological studies of place naming over the last century (Thornton 1997:221–222).

The Kiowa Homeland

IN GEOGRAPHY, the body of literature attempting to define what is meant by "homeland" is considerable (Nostrand 1980, 1992, 1993; Carlson 1990; Nostrand and Estaville 1993, 2001:xiii–xxiii; Schnell 1994:2–8, 2000:155–157, 2001). Although several scholars have provided discussions hinting at the concept of a homeland, it was not until Richard Nostrand's extensive work on Hispanic communities that the idea emerged as an analytical tool in geography (Schnell 1994:5). As Nostrand (1992:214) writes,

> The concept of a "homeland" although abstract and elusive has at least three basic elements: a people, a place, and identity with place. The people must have lived in a place long enough to have adjusted to its natural environment and to have left their impress in the form of a cultural landscape. And from their interactions with the natural and cultural totality of the place they must have developed an identity with the land—emotional feelings of attachment, desire to possess, even compulsions to defend. . . .

Nostrand and Estaville (2001:xviii) later suggest a combination of "people, place, bonding with place, control of place, and time" as the essential components in the construct of homeland. As they (2001:xxiii) conclude:

> Homelands, then, account for those human values that are rooted in place:
>
>> a love for one's birthplace and home;
>> an emotional attachment to the land of one's people;

a sense of belonging to a special area;

a loyalty that is defined by geographical parameters;

a strength that comes from territoriality; and

a feeling of wholeness and restoration when returning to one's
homeland.

Most scholars agree that a homeland involves the conscious emotional bonding of a group with a particular area of land, with an explicit focus on group identity and attachments that reinforce that identity on both personal and group levels. Thus, a people, a place, a sense of place, the control of a place, and a temporal period in which bonding between a people and an area occurs are integral elements. Various factors have been suggested to support the existence of a homeland, including demographic strength, the presence of toponyms, historical sites and shrines, anecdotal evidence, political heritage, voluntary associations, ethnic festivals, and museums. Differences in language, names, kinship systems, social organization, folklore, and other cultural aspects also serve to reinforce a people's distinctiveness. Clearly, these and many other factors are involved in the various ways in which people create cultural and psychological constructs of a homeland out of geographic and cultural territories (Schnell 1998:7–8). Schnell (1994:8) cautions against too rigid a definition for homeland, which could negate full recognition of the complexities and uniqueness of the attachments of ethnic groups to geographic locales.

Two other factors also merit attention. First, a homeland is far more than an empirically observable area of land, but the concept, like the concept of a culture area, is a useful ideological cultural construct, a conceptual tool for discussing a specific region. Second, Plains and for that matter most Indian homelands are not always mutually exclusive but often overlap and are frequently shared by multiple distinct ethnic groups, both in the pre-reservation period and today. Obviously, such relationships may change over any given time period examined. The overlapping and shared territories of the Cheyenne and Lakota, Cheyenne and Arapaho, Iroquois, and the Kiowa, Comanche, and Apache are but a few examples. Numerous georeligious sites such as Waconda Spring (Parks and Wedel 1985), Devil's Tower, Bear Butte, the Black Hills, and Medicine Bluff were used by different tribal groups, most of which still identify these sites as part of their historical and geosacred homeland. Like most North American Indians, contemporary Kiowa are a minority population in their own homeland in southwestern Oklahoma. Although several urban and rural concentrations of Kiowa remain, few or no members now live in some areas of great cultural significance, such as Saddle Mountain and Rainy Mountain. Never-

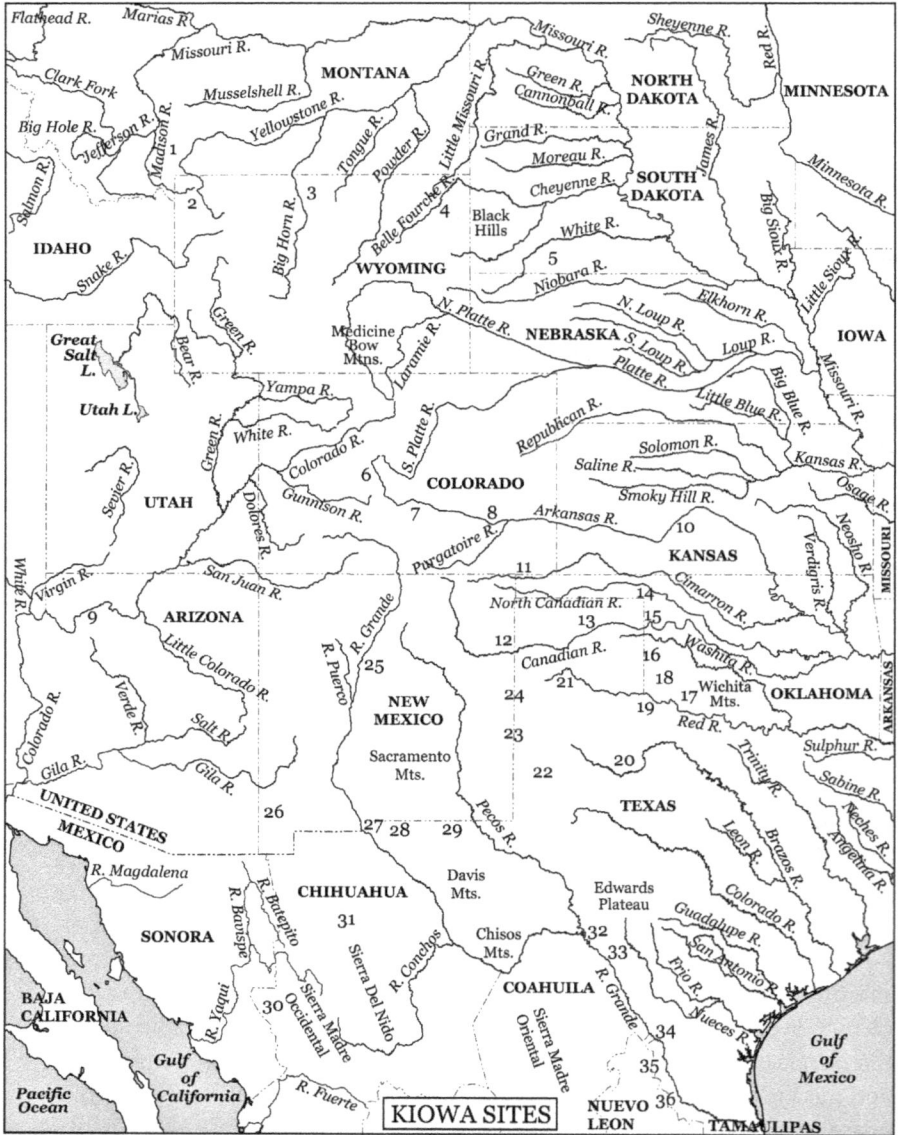

Map 2. Map of plains region showing noted Kiowa locales with place names. Key: 1. Kiowa Mts. 2. Yellowstone. 3. Big Horn Medicine Wheel. 4. Devil's Tower. 5. The Bad Lands. 6. Pike's Peak– Central Rocky Mts. 7. Big Timbers. 8. Bent's Fort. 9. Cataract and Colorado Canyons. 10. Santa Fe Trail. 11. Cimarron River. 12. Salt Place/Bed. 13. Adobe Walls. 14. Wolf Creek Fight (1838). 15. Antelope Hills. 16. Cheyenne Bow String Society Fight (1837). 17. Ft. Sill. 18. Quartz Mts. 19. Medicine Mounds. 20. Double Mt. 21. Palo Duro Canyon. 22. Cedar Lake. 23. Blackwater Draw. 24. Llano Estacado Escarpment. 25. Mountain Mexican Country. 26. Rock Mountain Mexican Country (Silver City). 27. El Paso. 28. Hueco Tanks. 29. Guadalupe Peak. 30. Sierra Madre Mts. 31. Santa Rosa Mts. 32. Rio Grande–Pecos River Confluence. 33. Ft. Clark. 34. Ft. McIntosh. 35. Salado River. 36. Forested/ Timbered Mexican Country. Map by Jim Coombs, maps librarian, Missouri State University.

theless, their emotional ties to their home region are an important part of their cultural ethos and identity. In light of these factors, I have chosen to use a broad definition of homeland, as nearly all of these aspects apply to the Kiowa historical experience.

While *homeland* often brings to mind a contiguous intact land area of temporal longevity, the dynamic events that occurred from roughly 1680 to 1890 produced a large-scale geographic reorganization for many North American cultures, especially in the plains region. Considerable migration and one or more reestablishments of a focal residential area were typical for many cultures, including the Kiowa. As John Harrington (1939) demonstrated, while relocation of the Kiowa to new areas did not totally abolish prior concepts of a homeland as applied to sites of prior habitation, such movements and the transfer of the focus of a homeland to new areas definitely occurred, resulting in geographic disassociation. Although many Kiowa still express some affinity for the northwestern plains, it is largely an amorphous and differentially valued association that pales in comparison with the sense of place, belonging, history, and ethnic identity expressed in relation to the present homeland in southwestern Oklahoma. Yet some northern locales still hold considerable importance in Kiowa culture and history (see Map 2).

As one middle-aged Kiowa man who grew up outside Oklahoma explained,

> Kiowa country originally extended from the headwaters of the Yellowstone to the Black Hills and from Southern Alberta to Northern Colorado. However, Kiowa explorers have been into (depending on the time period), Sarcee tribal history [territory], Old Mexico, and Navajo country. Our oral history includes: Kiowa Pass in the Montana Rocky Mountains, Devils Tower, and the Wyoming Medicine Wheel. . . .[1]

Clearly, more than one tribal group occupied these areas at any given time.

Origins and Early History

Accounts of Kiowa origins are limited (Mooney 1898:152–153, 238–239; Parsons 1929:xvi–xviii). Parsons (1929:xvi–xviii) noted that the Kiowa lack a real origin story. "Sendeh" (Séndé, or One Who Is Nose Mucous), a common figure who is an uncle to all, is described as the first person in the world, the human prototype, and although he can change himself into many forms, he is in the form of a human and not a coyote. Although there are brief and obscure references to a great flood and the origin of Spider Old Woman, there is little that resembles an origin story proper (Mooney 1898:238–239; Parsons 1929:9). Boyd (1983:2–14) reports that Saynday is "from the Great Mystery," suggesting the Supreme Creator or God, and brings out ants from a hollow log that become the Kiowa people. Additional accounts describe a flood, the survival of Grand Mother Spider and Snake Man (also known as Stoney Road), a cycle of Grandmother Spider stories, the Son of the Sun, his transformation into the two Half-Boys, their series of adventures, the making of the Ten Medicines, and one Half-Boy walking off into Spear Lake in present-day Wyoming while the other divides himself into ten portions, which are placed in each of the ten medicine bundles.

Kiowa origins state that with the beckoning of their culture hero Séndé they emerged from the underworld through a cottonwood log or tree (á-hị̀, "real or original tree") until a pregnant woman became stuck in the hole, preventing any more from exiting.[2] This stage of their emergence is said to explain why the Kiowa have always been relatively small in number. Although the location of this occurrence is unknown, the range of the eastern cottonwood (*Populus deltoides*), which is native to the front range of the Rockies eastward, may give a clue to the geographic range when this account developed, or perhaps a modification after moving into the zone of this species. Since at least the late 1800s, Kiowa memories of the northland are clear and fixed, but the number of fixed place names is limited (Mooney 1898; Harrington 1939). The earliest remembered homeland is in the region of Cáuiqòp (the Kiowa Mountains) in western Montana near the headwaters of the Yellowstone and Missouri rivers, where the struggle for survival was said to be difficult. While the tribe occupied this region, a quarrel between two leaders over the distribution of a slain antelope resulted in the division of the tribe into two separate entities. The group that departed, henceforth known as the Àuzáthạ̀uhyòp (Those Who Went Away [Disgruntled] On Account Of The Udder), became lost to the remainder of the Kiowa. Although some Kiowa still allege a Kiowa-speaking group north of their old homeland, they remain an enigma, and no anthropological or linguistic work has ever confirmed their presence. If they survived, it is likely that they merged with a larger population.

The earliest known specific locale in Kiowa tradition is Spear Lake, in Wyoming, which is associated with several seminal elements of Kiowa origins. Accounts from this region explain their relationship with the Sun, Grandma Spider, the origin of the two Záidétàlyî (Split or Half-Boys) and the departure of one into Spear Lake and the ritual division of the other

(Mooney 1898:239). Sundstrom (2005) believes Spear Lake may be Lake DeSmet.

When Sherman Chaddlesone, Parker Boyiddle, and Mirac Creepingbear were commissioned in the winter of 1986 to paint the ten murals in the Kiowa Tribal Museum, Creepingbear undertook the three murals depicting the early Kiowa history before their southern migration onto the plains. Sherman Chaddlesone was approached by Scott Tonemah, who related an account linking the Kiowa to the Yellowstone Park area, or Tǫsáldàu (Heated Water). In the story, people of various tribes are called together to decide who will live in a certain unpopulated area. In a barren area of bare dirt, rocks, and active geysers, the people are challenged to jump blindly into a cauldron of boiling water. After most are scared away, the Kiowa protagonist Kǫ́uhę̀ (No Name) completes the challenge and, thanks to his faith in God, when he emerges from the cauldron, the area is transformed into a lush landscape that becomes the Kiowa homeland. The Kiowa remained in this area until No Name died and was buried near the cauldron. The Kiowa then began to drift from the area. No Name's act of faith also led to the Kiowa becoming paramount or preeminent among all peoples and remaining closest to the heart of God. One Kiowa identified the specific locale or cauldron described in the story as the Dragon's Mouth, next to Mud Volcano, north of Yellowstone Lake (Nabokov and Loendorf 2004:67, 71–75). Although known by various names, this account is supported by similar versions recorded by Hugh L. Scott in the 1890s and by Parsons (1929:15) in 1927.[3]

Mooney (1898:160) noted that the Kiowa had origin stories associated with both Devil's Tower and the Black Hills. Devil's Tower or Xòâi (Rock That Grew Upwards) in northeastern Wyoming is the most prominent landmark in the Kiowa physical geography of the northern plains. Many Plains tribes, including the Kiowa, have oral traditions of its formation (Stone 1982), including the well-known Kiowa story of the children who were playing Bear (Sétyáiàum, or Bear Play) when one of their siblings turned into a bear, began chasing them, and tried to eat them. After several events the children were about to be overtaken when a stone instructed them to run around it four times, climb on it, and instruct it to grow. As the rock rose upward, the bear attempted to reach the children by repeatedly lunging against the monolith, sliding down the side each time and leaving deep scratches. The children were saved, and after being instructed to shoot an arrow seven times into the sky, they were transported with each shot and became the constellation Pleiades. Although versions differ as to the sex of the seven children and their sibling-turned-bear, the bear's names in the Kiowa story (Sétálmã, or Bear That Chased, and Mátàunyàul, or Wild, i.e., Rabid Girl) are both feminine compositions and were both later bestowed on female Kiowa.[4]

Locales of this type would be considered unusual natural features (Sundstrom 2003:279). Beyond explaining the origin of this formation of intrusive igneous phonolite porphyry, the story provides many other metaphorical explanations relating to the inherent lessons of stories. For the Kiowa, these include supernatural protection, rebirth, emergence onto the plains, and the change from a pedestrian, dog-and-travois-based hunting culture to an equestrian, horse-and-bison-based culture (Schnell 1994:77). The protection offered from the bear is symbolic and significant in lieu of its ambiguous status in Kiowa culture, as elements of both evil destruction and power and strength are found in Kiowa oral history and belief. Although Kiowa in the late 1800s describe a pervasive taboo against eating or possessing any portion of a bear, the use of bear claws, fur, and bear-based personal names suggests that this taboo against using any physical part of a bear may have applied to only some individuals or may have been a late development, much like that associated with the owl. Much like Eastern Cherokee beliefs, the Devil's Tower story links humans and bears in a transformational basis implying that any subsequent consumption of bears would be akin to cannibalism. In addition, celestial and earthly realms are linked through ethnonomy, a feature usually analyzed separately by non-Indians.

A series of four mountains is also associated with the origin of Devil's Tower. Harrington (1939:168) states that "four places were named from four intestinal tract organs of the old buffalo who sacrificed himself to aid the escape, each of these organs when thrown backward by the fleeing ones becoming a terrain of similar shape or qualities to those of the organ and bearing the organ's name as a permanent placename." Although bison have four stomachs, the organs named by Delos K. Lonewolf (Harrington 1939:168) appear to refer to other organs, not solely the stomach. Although it is unclear whether they are in order of their occurrence in the narrative, these four organs are (1) sál-kâui (reticulum or leaf tripe, honeycomb stomach), (2) áu-kàui (honeycomb portion of the tripe, lit. wrinkled), (3) bím-sàl (hairlike part of the tripe), and (4) chól-fá-káui or qá-gòp-bím-kàui (lit. brain sack). Based on Lonewolf's account, the corresponding four mountains would be Sálkâuiqòp (Reticulum or Leaf Tripe [Honeycomb Stomach]) Mountain), Áukàuiqòp (Honeycomb Tripe, lit. Wrinkled Mountain), Bímsàlqòp (Tripe Hair Mountain), and Chólfákáuiqòp or Qágòpbímkàuiqòp (Brain Sack Mountain).

The Kiowa obtained the core elements of their religion (the Ten Medi-

"Rock That Grew Upwards": Devil's Tower, Wyoming.

cine Bundles, the Ṭáimé bundle, and the Sun Dance) while in the north. As Mary Buffalo told Alice Marriott, "They had the Taime when they came south. They also had the Ten Grandmothers, no one knows where they came from, or when."[5] In 1936, George Poolaw explained to Alice Marriott how the Ṭáimé Keeper took the bundle on a vision quest near Devil's Tower that resulted in the origin of the Ṭáimé shields, which figured prominently in Kiowa warfare and the Sun Dance.

> Taime Shields are not as old as the Taime. A certain man invented these shields and made seven for the Taime. Taime ki—Taime Shields. The man who had the Taime was the one who made the shields to protect it. During a war a man who had one of these shields could not be killed. He had a vision of a sacred thing and knew what to do. The Taime told him how to make the shields. This old man that owned the Taime took it upon a mountain and fasted four days and four nights and saw the vision. The Taime told him he would live a long time, if he made the shields. He was a young man when he had the vision. Devil's Tower, Wyoming is near the place.[6]

Today Devil's Tower is the most important northern plains locale that the Kiowa retain a name for and is often associated with a pre-horse "golden era." The story contains clear lessons and morals in the references to the consequences of forcing others to do things they do not want to, the power of faith, God's mercy, and the power of right over wrong. Contingents from the Kiowa Elders' Center make regular trips to the site, and many Kiowa have photographs of visits to the site.[7] While some Kiowa speculate on the origins of the Medicine Wheel near present-day Lovell, Wyoming, which tribe or tribes constructed it is unknown. Many tribes agree that it resembles the outline of a Sun Dance lodge. By the mid-1700s, the Kiowa began to move eastward out of the mountains and into the region of the Black Hills (Xók̖ǫ̀qòp, or Black Rocks Mountains), by which time they had acquired horses and entered the classic horse culture era. The Black Hills region was an important area for hunting and spiritual activities, and figured prominently in many early stories. In the 1890s, Iseeo described to Hugh L. Scott how the Kiowa used to visit the Crow along the Ice Sticking Down River or Hard Ice River (Missouri River), named for the sections of ice that stuck down under the water as the river ice broke up in the spring thaw. Kiowa accounts note that the Crow frequently braved hopping from one ice mass to the next to retrieve bison that had drowned and were floating down the river.[8]

As the Naishan Dene or Plains Apache (Kiowa-Apache) are reported to have met and allied with the Kiowa while on the northwestern plains, their origins may shed light on those of the Kiowa. McAllister (1935:6–7) reported the home of the Apache to be in the region around the Black Hills in South Dakota and Wyoming. In this area the Apache maintain that they hunted near *Castiził* (Bear Hill), and that they obtained the Four Quartz Rocks Bundle, one of their original three tribal medicine bundles, from a lake known as *Kutijje* (Medicine Water). McAllister (1965:215) later notes that "Medicine Water . . . is thought to be located in the Black Hills of South Dakota in a region known as Bear Mountain or Black Rock." These are probably Bear Butte and Bear Butte Lake. Although Bear Mountain could refer to either Bear Lodge (Devil's Tower) or Bear Butte, the latter is located near the Black Hills. As the Kiowa, Plains Apache, Cheyenne, Arapaho, and others have similar stories for this area, it is difficult to determine whether a single legend has diffused from group to group or whether some or all of these groups were at one time in the same vicinity (McAllister 1935:7) and had similar beliefs or experiences, especially in relation to Bear Butte. Sundstrom (2004:142, 148) lists Sundance Mountain as a site of Kiowa and other tribal summer ceremonies and states that although the Kiowa do not specifically refer to Bear Butte as a preferred site for Sun Dances, it was and still is one of their most important holy places. My older Kiowa informants have no name for the location and do not discuss it as a site of significance.

Places such as Devil's Tower, Spear Lake, the Black Hills, and the Medicine Wheel serve as prominent physical markers and the focus of important protohistoric cultural events. However, the lengthy temporal distance from this area is now several generations beyond firsthand pre-reservation experience and has relegated them to a largely quasi-historical and mythological context. With the exception of Devil's Tower, those sites most frequently spoken of as important to contemporary Kiowa are on the southern plains and within the geographic and historical range of documented personal knowledge and experience. As noted in Chapter 2, many Kiowa personal names are based on formally named geographic sites or less well-known locales or generic geographic forms, including those in mythological accounts.

Throughout the 1700s, Kiowa expanded their range southward, often in conflict with several other tribes. From 1727 to 1800, thirty-five Kiowa are reported to have been baptized and six buried in New Mexico, presumably captives. In 1800, the Kiowa began looking to New Mexico for a connection with the Spanish. In the first half of 1806 the Kiowa and Naishan Apache made peace with the Comanche and thereafter regularly visited Santa Fe for treaty ceremonies, gifts, and trade (John 1985:381–394).

Social Organization and Communities

SOCIAL ORGANIZATION

Because people organize themselves into distinct communities that become associated with particular locales, social organization provides another source of place names through ethnonyms. Whether communicated through group names or through cultural association with a specific region, names often serve as markers of cultural and physical geography. In the mid-1800s the Kiowa were divided into six recognized and formally named divisions: (1) Cáuigú (Kiowa), (2) Kį́èt (Big Shield, or Big Shields Kį́bį̀dàu), also known as the Káugàbį̀dàu (Big Hides/Robes), (3) Kǫ́tályóp or Kǫ́tályôi (Black Boys), also known as Séndèiyòi (Sainday's Children), (4) Qáutjáu (Biters, lit. Arikaras), and (5) Qógûi (Elks). A sixth band, the Kútjáu (Emerging/Coming Out [rapidly]), was exterminated by the Sioux around 1780, while still residing on the northern plains. The Naishan Apache tribe constituted a bandlike but autonomous component at the Kiowa Sun Dance. Clark (1885:230) and Mooney (1898:228–229) recorded these divisional names, the latter from his reconstruction of the 1867 Kiowa Sun Dance.

Beyond coming together for Sun Dances and the shared use of regional subsistence and residence areas throughout the year, divisional groupings held little significance. On a daily basis the multiple jòfàujógàu or jódáu (camp or residence bands) constituting each division were more important. Kiowa bands were composed of smaller families and individuals associated with one or more core extended families, generally containing the jòfàujóqî (camp or residence band leader). Band size fluctuated seasonally and according to the wealth, prestige, family size, and leadership abilities of the camp leader. Hawaiian kinship terminology and bilateral descent permitted close kin ties on both sides of an individual's family. Sororal polygyny (marriage of a man to sisters), levirate (the remarriage of a widow to her deceased husband's brother), and arranged marriages extended and strengthened sibling bonds. Postmarital locality varied, and although patrilocality predominated, a significant portion chose short-term matrilocality (Mishkin 1940; Richardson 1940; Levy 1959; Meadows 1999:35–36).

In the pre-reservation era a regionally based nominal distinction was made between the northern (Thóqą̀hyòp or Thóqą̀hyòi Northerners, lit. Cold People) and southern (Sálqą̄hyóp or Sálqą̄hyói Southerners, lit. Hot People) divisions and bands. This system was changing by the 1850s, as reflected in the formation of the Gúhàlècàuigù (Wild Mustang Kiowa or Gúhàlè Kiowa) from their increasing proximity to the Kwahadi Comanche and wild horse herds of this region.[9] Further changes resulted from the formation of pro-peace and pro-war bands in the late 1860s, as reflected in their proximity to and degree of interaction with Fort Sill in the early 1870s. Though restructured to some degree, Kiowa bands were largely free to move about within the reservation from 1875 through 1900. Although distance from the tribal agency where annuities were issued every two weeks was a factor, encampments existed throughout the reservation.

Kiowa tribal censuses from the late 1800s reflect some aspects of the social organization of the time. The Kiowa population ranged from 1,070 people in 1874–1875 to 1,037 people in 1895. Although fairly accurate census counts appear to have been made throughout this period, a complete enumeration by name was not done until 1884 or 1885. Earlier censuses reflect this and are of one of two basic forms. The 1878 census lists thirty-three male band chiefs, with the number of people in their band listed beside their name. In this census, the thirty-three leaders each had eighteen to fifty-five people in their band, for a total population of 1,120. The 1880 census lists 491 adults, most of them males. The names of band chiefs are underlined, with the word "chief" in parentheses following their name. After each adult name are columns indicating the number of people associated with that person, mostly women and children.

Most commonly called "beef bands," these groups were small enclaves of Kiowa residing in a camp under a principal male bandleader that periodically came to the agency as a band to receive annuities. Initially annuities were determined by band size and given to the band chief, who in turn administered the redistribution among his own band. Indian agents desiring to break up old allegiances to prominent older chiefs and their influence later began distributing annuities to the heads of households, thereby bypassing and refusing to acknowledge the social status and position of the so-called beef band chiefs.

RESERVATION COMMUNITIES

Although many Kiowa were already residing in fairly permanent camps prior to allotment, the assignment of specific parcels of land (usually 160 acres) to individuals, and the sale of remaining lands to the public in 1901, firmly established eleven distinct demographic concentrations of Kiowa that have continued in varying degrees to the present. The Kiowa soon developed names for these communities, many prior to allotment, as they were based on preexisting camp areas, geographic features, and later allotment clusters. These camp names were formed from the combination of a geographic place name and the suffix jó-dàu (encampment or band).[10]

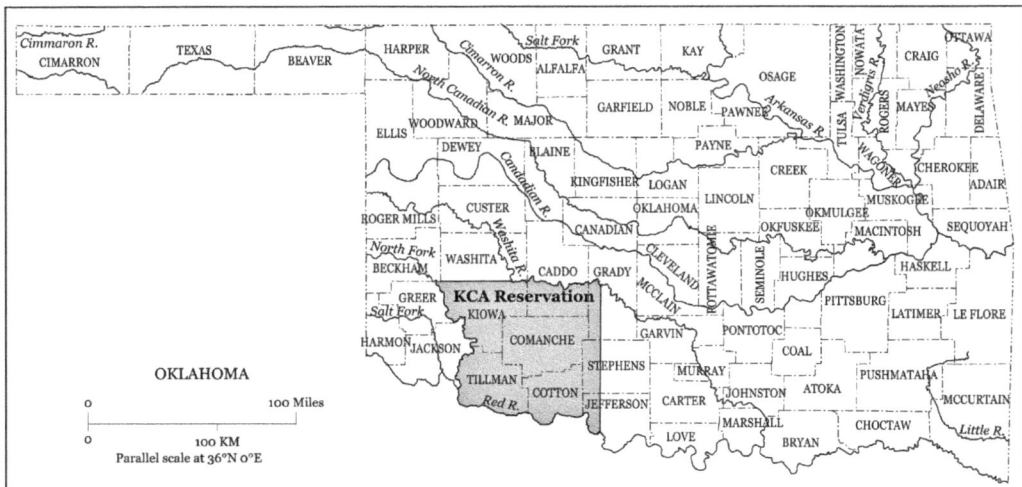

Map 3. Map of Oklahoma counties showing Kiowa, Comanche, and Apache Reservation. Map by Jim Coombs, maps librarian, Missouri State University.

The reorganization of the Kiowa band system into war and peace bands and allegiances to various bandleaders in the 1870s contributed to the formation of reservation communities extending east to west from what are now the modern-day towns of Verden to Hobart, Oklahoma, in the north and from Meers to Saddle Mountain in the south. Geographically this region is largely bordered by the Washita River to the north and the northern edge of the Wichita Mountains to the south and is located in present-day Caddo, Kiowa, and Comanche counties of Oklahoma.

These Kiowa communities included Verden, Anadarko, Hog Creek, Stecker, Meers, Red Stone, Carnegie, Zodletone (Zóltǫ̀) or Stinking Creek, Mountain View, Saddle Mountain, Hobart, and Lone Wolf, around which individuals later took allotments. Of the Kiowa names for these eleven communities, seven are named after streams, two after mountains, one after a series of stone bluffs, and one after a timbered grove. These communities include the following:

Ákàulèjódàu—Timber Grove Camp, in and around Verden, Caddo County.
Ą̀ucùvàujódàu—Sidedish Creek Camp, along Elk Creek, south of Hobart, Kiowa County.
Àuhívàujòdàu—Cedar Creek Camp, southeast of Carnegie, Caddo County.
Chènváujòdàu—Mud Creek Camp (lit. Boggy or Mirey Creek Camp), along Rainy Mountain Creek and Mountain View, Kiowa County.

Qópêljǒdàu—Big Mountain Camp, north of Mount Scott and near
Meers in Comanche County.

Sétchéyòvàujǒdàu—Hog Creek Camp, lower Hog Creek west of
Anadarko, in Caddo County.

Sólèvàujǒdàu—Soldier Creek Camp, along Cache Creek, near Fort Sill
in southern Caddo and Comanche counties, probably including
Kiowa south of Alden along the upper Cache Creek.

Tàuqòpjódàu—Saddle Mountain Camp, around Saddle Mountain, in
Kiowa and Comanche counties.

Xòdômvàujǒdàu—Pebble Creek (lit. Stone or Rocky Bottom Creek)
along Sugar Creek, south of Sedan, in Kiowa County. This creek
was later called Sugar Creek and the Kiowa community along its
course was called Fénhàvàujǒdàu (Sugar Creek Camp). It is unclear
whether Kiowa or Anglos introduced the name Sugar Creek.
However, when Kiowa renamed a location it was usually in relation
to a historical event of significance occurring there, and not a
change in descriptive terminology.

Xǒgúljǒdàu—Red Stone Camp, southwest of Washita, Caddo County.

Zóltòvàujǒdàu—Vomit Creek Camp, along Stinking Creek west of
Carnegie, Kiowa County.

A twelfth community, Cúnjǒdàu (Dance Camp), was later named for
the families around the second Kiowa Ghost Dance site on the allotments
of Taup-ko-ba, Ba-chin-ma, Kah-gem, and Sa-maun-ty from 1894 to 1917,
approximately 1.25 miles upstream from where Stinking Creek joins the
Washita River northwest of Carnegie in Kiowa County. Although some
Kiowa resided permanently in this locale, the Ghost Dance camp was a
seasonal and annual aggregation. This area was also sometimes known as
Samone, from the nearby Samone school and cemetery.[11]

These communities had begun to camp in definite locations by the summer of 1882, only seven years after final confinement to the reservation. Corwin's (1975:154) list of ten communities includes Mount Scott, Sugar Creek,
Saddle Mountain, Hog Creek, Red Stone, Elk Creek, Rainy Mountain, Stinking Creek, Samone Camp, and Cedar Creek People.[12] These names all correlate with the prior named Kiowa reservation communities, with Samone
Camp People being the Kiowa near the second Ghost Dance grounds.

The Post-allotment Community

The process of forced allotment in 1901 was devastating to the Kiowa. In
addition to having their reservation broken up and non-Indians forced on

them as neighbors to facilitate assimilating them, only 17 percent of their original reservation as designated by the Medicine Lodge Treaty remained by 1906 (Levy 2001:918). Kiowa efforts at farming met with little success. Land quality varied significantly from one area to another, and some older men refused to perform what they saw as the work of women and agricultural tribes, which limited agricultural potential. Overall, Kiowa farming equipment and practices were outdated compared with those of the neighboring Euroamericans, and most of those who were successful at farming and ranching had their efforts halted by the ecological and economic changes of the Great Depression and the Dust Bowl of the 1920s and 1930s.

Moreover, a 160-acre parcel of land proved insufficient to support the majority of better supplied and better trained Euroamerican farming families, let alone less financed and less equipped Indian families. Much of the land proved better for ranching than for cultivation; however the checkerboard nature of the post-allotment community and the lack of large contiguous areas undermined attempts at ranching. Consequently, most Indians began leasing their parcels to non-Indian farmers and ranchers who had the equipment and the capital to work several such parcels successfully. In time, this became the most practical way for many Indians to earn income from their lands, and the practice continues to the present. To complicate matters, additional fragmentation of existing allotments through fractionalized inheritance and an increasing tribal population with a diminishing land base have resulted in most individuals owning parcels too small to be economically viable, or numerous heirs owning a single parcel. Twenty to thirty owners of a 160-acre quarter section are not uncommon. These parcels are too small to provide all owners with a place of residence, too small to be economically viable for individual Indians to work, and produce only small to minuscule amounts of money to their owners through leasing. Today I know of only two older Kiowa who actively ranch and farm.

Although many individuals originally resided on or near their allotment, some did not, and extended families and some community-style encampments continued, especially during the warmer months in large traditional brush arbors. Based on these reservation and post-reservation clusters, individuals and families began to come together in units of social organization that became the named communities of the reservation era, alignments that were clearly distinct from those of the older generation. Although some modern Kiowa still claim descent from and affiliation with a pre-reservation tribal division, these claims are highly varied in terms of consistency in tracing and claiming such descent, often combining male

and female lines. As Parker McKenzie, born in 1897, said, "My generation thinks in terms of reservation communities, Hobart, Rainy Mountain Creek, Hog Creek, Redstone, and so on, rather than the traditional
Kiowa bands. My grandparents were more associated with those distinctions."[13] As this statement reflects, reservation communities named after
geographic locales rather than pre-reservation named divisions or bands
became the standard by which people began identifying their residence,
community, and in turn themselves. The emergence of post-allotment
Anglo-founded towns, the use of English in schools, and the gradual move
of Kiowa to these towns produced more recent community names, such as
Anadarko, Carnegie, Hobart, Meers, and Mountain View. Today the names
used to refer to Kiowa communities are a mix of Kiowa, English, and English translations of Kiowa, as in the names of Zodletone, Hobart, and Red
Stone.

While allotment was designed to break up reservations geographically
and to destroy traditional residence and economic patterns, it often failed
in its larger goal of forcing the assimilation of Indian peoples. Despite radi-
cal and traumatic changes, allotted communities tended to become new
cultural homelands by providing permanent places where native identities
were reformulated and passed on. In time these communities became centers for awareness and hope (Hoxie 1979:3; Schnell 2000:173).

Many Kiowa maintain a strong sense of community, continuing to identify themselves with a specific community, as in "Rainy Mountain People"
or "Redstone People." In doing so they communicate not only a geographic
location but a consanguineal and social connection to a specific community, based on a set number of resident families dating back to the reservation period (1875–1901) and in some instances to earlier divisions. As
Grobsmith (1981) has shown for the Rosebud Lakota, marked differences
between contemporary Indian communities, even on the same reservation, are largely due to the different histories they have experienced. This is
typical of many reservations with so-called "traditional" and "progressive"
communities. Although this contrast is oversimplified, and a wide range
of cultural and religious foci can be found in each community, there are
usually communities that reflect these contrasts on a general level. Just as
Grobsmith (1981) contrasts Antelope and Spring Creek on the Rosebud
Reservation, some Kiowa contrast Meers, associated with higher rates of
Christianity, church activities, and education, with Carnegie, where more
individuals are associated with older activities such as dancing, traditional
doctoring, the Ten Medicine Bundles, and Peyote. Based on assumptions
of less education, higher unemployment, and more dependence on government programs, some Kiowa refer to the Carnegie Kiowa as the "Hang

Around the Fort Bunch." While there is historically validity to these asser-
tions, the contrast is less today as more individuals in Meers are involved
in powwows and society dances and more people in the Carnegie area are
pursuing higher education.

Beyond collectively shared Indian and tribal heritage, identification
with specific community and kin ties places a person within other levels
or contexts of Kiowa social and tribal history. To some degree the increasing amount of mobility and intermarriage (intra- and intertribal and non-
Indian) has began to alter these associations between particular areas and
families. Yet these associations can remain even after an entire family has
relocated away from its family allotment and community. That Kiowa communities still consider themselves distinct from others is an important
marker of social and community identity. As one Kiowa man in his forties who grew up outside Oklahoma noted, "My relatives in the Hobart
Community have a unique Kiowa subculture apart from the Kiowa tribe
proper."[14]

Place names signify more than just the geographic locale people are
associated with. Kiowa distinctly associate geographic locales with Kiowa
residential communities (i.e., reservation communities) through family
names that represent extended kinship units. This pattern typically refers
to the first generation of Kiowa to have surnames, and thus the adult and
older allotees. The connection between named places, the surrounding
area, and the Kiowa of that area is unconsciously inseparable. In other
words, when the Kiowa talk about a specific geographic locale or area, they
often speak in terms of the families of that community. In conversations
with Atwater Onco about the Hobart area, he regularly listed the names
of the early Kiowa families from that region. When elders spoke of Rainy
Mountain, they spent more time talking about the school, church, local
families, and the community history of that area than about the actual
mountain itself. Similar responses, during both field interviews and phone
conversations, were encountered among members of various Kiowa communities. In compiling a list of Kiowa students who attended Carlisle
Indian School during an interview, Parker McKenzie recited from memory the name of each student, his or her community, and an extensive list
of family surnames for each respective reservation-era community.[15]

With final entrance onto the reservation in 1875 and allotments in 1901,
sedentism increased, and the Kiowa intensified their familiarity with specific areas of the former reservation. These areas became the recognized
Kiowa communities of the early twentieth century, which continue to the
present. Thus, families are linked both to the geographic area they came
from and to an association with other families of that area. It was also dur-

ing this same period that Indian surnames came into use, mostly for purposes of managing allotments, bank accounts, tribal censuses, and other
agency records. This led to clearer associations between specific families
and geographic areas. These associations play a seminal part in past and
present Kiowa concepts of their homeland and family histories. Dating
back to the late 1800s, these communities are inseparably associated with
where specific Kiowa families came from and in many instances still
reside.

This tendency to associate specific geographic areas with specific lin-
eages was demonstrated by Atwater Onco, who recalled,

> Like Qópêl ["Big Mountain," i.e., Mount Scott], I know the people
> from there. Qópêl, you're thinking about all the Sahmaunts, the
> Quoetones, Yeahquos, the Rowells, you think about even Daddy's
> [Onco's family], Tsatighs. Oh there's a lot of people, Aunko, Bofpiah,
> Hunting Horse, there's just a lot of people in that area you're think-
> ing about. . . . Gotebo area your thinking about Spotted Horse and
> Tahbonemahs. . . . Stecker, you think of all the Domebos, Kotays. . . .
> First thing you say Sétchéyòvàu [Hog Creek] you think of the Wares,
> there's a million of them (laughs).[16]

The duration of this form of family-area association continues even
after entire families have moved from the area. A good example is Saddle
Mountain, a small Kiowa community that once included several influential
Kiowa and played a seminal role in the beginning of Christian practices
among the Kiowa. Although several Kiowa allotments near Saddle Mountain remain, few Kiowa presently live in the area, most having relocated
to other locales. Yet everyone knows that the Kokoom family is a "Saddle
Mountain family." Likewise, the names of Dautobi, Doyeto, Kauahquo,
Kauyedauty, Kiowa Bill, Komalty, Lone Wolf, Mausanap, and Spotted Bird
are immediately recognized as "Hobart Kiowa." Even with increased mobility and urban relocation, these associations are reflected by Kiowa who
continue to live in these areas and by the predominance of specific family
names associated with specific tribal cemeteries and named locales.

The name Rainy Mountain is a good example. The name references not
only the hill but also the adjacent Indian boarding school and the Kiowa
encampment to the east of the school, Boake's Trading Posts, the Rainy
Mountain Kiowa Indian Baptist Church and Cemetery, numerous allotments along Rainy Mountain Creek, and myriad personal, family, and
community experiences. A brief description of two other communities
further illustrates this pattern.

REDSTONE

Just southwest of Washita, along the southern side of the Washita River in Caddo County, the Redstone area is named for a long series of high and steep red sandstone bluffs. Although it was not a significant pre-reservation area, many Kiowa began residing there after the agency moved from Fort Sill to Anadarko in 1878. This area provided closer proximity to the government ration distribution held every two weeks at Anadarko. Eventually a sizable number of Kiowa took allotments in this area, and the Redstone Baptist Church and Cemetery were established in the local community in 1896. Redstone was one of the most traditional communities in terms of continuing dancing and has been the core area of Ohoma Society membership and ceremonies since the 1920s. Family names such as Bert, Emhoola, Keahbone, Konad, Mopope, Oheltoint, Paddelty, Paudlety, Tsalote, Turkey, and White Horse are known as "Redstone Kiowa" or "Red Stone People." As Dorothy Whitehorse DeLaune reflected, "I grew up in this area where we call it Red Stone Valley. And it's the Mopopes, the Palmers, the Geikaun-mahs, the Emhoolas, Paddletys, White Horses, this was our valley."[17]

SADDLE MOUNTAIN

Saddle Mountain, Oklahoma, is located on the northern edge of the Wichita Mountains, 15.5 miles south and two miles east of Mountain View in the southeastern corner of Kiowa County. Named for nearby Saddle Mountain 1.5 miles to the southeast in adjacent Comanche County, the name was also given to the town, creek, and the Saddle Mountain Baptist Mission Church (1903–1962), Mission House, and Cemetery. Missionary Isabel Crawford (1915, 1998) describes the emergence of the community and church at the turn of the nineteenth century. A local store served as a trading center for the community until it closed in the 1940s. In 1963 the church was purchased by Herbert Woesner and was moved to his property, known today as Eagle Park in Cache, Oklahoma, where Indian congregations continue to use it. In 1993–1994, descendants of the original Saddle Mountain Church members, including members of the Tongkeamha and other families, reopened a small Southern Baptist church in a trailer beside the cemetery.

Ina Aunko Miller described what growing up in the Saddle Mountain community was like in the 1920s and 1930s:

> Oh it was fun. We all visit one another. And sometimes those farmers would lose a cow you know and they'd tell my dad that it

broke a leg or something. They'd tell him right away and he'd go butcher and then we had a big arbor outside, tables you know, and beds, those Indian beds, and we'd just, we all went to that Saddle Mountain Church you know. It was a good life over there. There wasn't like no drinking or drugs or nothing like that. It was mostly church. We went to camp meetings and visit one another. All of us kids played together. In the summertime they had Bible School for us kids you know. Our pastor was named Perry Jackson. He really taught everybody well you know, and he taught us a lot of things that we didn't know. And then Christmas, all of the Indians they would camp—cold as it is—they'd camp, and it would be real nice, real warm, and us kids would just play around. We had a good time around Saddle Mountain. Then we had a store where we could go buy groceries, stuff we need, or sometimes some of them would come to Carnegie or Mountain View to buy their groceries. It was a real good clean life.[18]

Because of the poor quality of the soil in this region and the absence of any businesses, few Kiowa now live in the Saddle Mountain community.

Kiowa camp northwest of Saddle Mountain, confederated Kiowa, Comanche, and Apache Reservation, ca. 1890s. Photograph by James Mooney. Courtesy Smithsonian Institution (no. 062727.00).

Yet despite migration from the community, Saddle Mountain still holds a strong symbolic link for the Kiowa tribe and for families that came from there. Those who grew up there still retain the association with the community and consider themselves Saddle Mountain Kiowa. Likewise, family names such as Aitsan, Geimausaddle, Kokoom, Odlepaugh, Tonemah, and others are still referred to by other Kiowa as Saddle Mountain Kiowa, even if the family members have never themselves lived there. Origins and association generally outlast residence. As Schnell (2000:174–175) notes, areas of psychological importance to the Kiowa do not necessarily coincide with modern demographic concentrations.

In fieldwork with the adjacent Apache and Comanche, I have noticed a similar form of talking about geographic locales, reservation communities, and families, as in the distinctions made between "Boone Apaches" and "Fort Cobb" or "Washita Apaches" (see Meadows 1999:189–190, 232). Kent Sanmann (1992:1) raised the question of whether non-Indians, especially rural whites, think of geographic features and locales in this way. From my experiences in my home area, in some areas of rural southern Indiana people do associate certain creeks, hollows, ridges, and demographic vicinities with one or more particular families, and these names still appear on U.S. Geological Survey maps and are still well known among local residents. In my home area of Lawrence County, Indiana, many people know that the Bartletts came from Bartlettsville, although they are now scattered over a larger portion of the county. Yet local individuals also know that many Clarks, Deckards, Donicas, Hearths, Kinsers, Meadows, Ramsays, Sowders, Todds, and other families came from this same area. Likewise my home county contains many other place names of small towns, townships, creeks, ridges, and hollows named after families whose descendants may or may not still reside in that locale.

From my experiences in Indiana, this pattern was clearly stronger in the past, before mobility increased, people moved from farms to the cities, and many family farms were sold, all resulting in the gradual breakdown of extended kinship ties. These factors have produced a situation whereby this pattern is rapidly changing, including even the formal renaming of long-known roads for permanent 911 addresses on a first-come, first-served basis. Although the association of communities and specific families continues, it is strongest among the eldest generation and families who have lived in the same area for multiple generations. A stronger and more contemporary analogy to allotted communities can probably be made for the Amish or Mennonite communities in adjacent counties of southern Indiana, where large concentrations of close kindred have settled in a checkerboard pattern, intermarried, and remained close together in the midst of a much larger non-Amish population, in some cases for well over one hundred years.[19]

INDIAN TOWNS

Oklahoma towns originated by non-Indians, located near Indian communities, and containing a large Indian population are often called "Indian towns" by local Indians. This categorization is largely based on a high degree of Indian residence and activities. Non-Indians often outnumber Indians, and ongoing racial tensions may exist. Along Highway 9 on the northern edge of the old reservation are several of these small towns. Although Anadarko evolved from the Indian Agency established there in 1878, most of these towns originated as border settlements where non-Indians awaited a land rush from the sales of remaining unallotted lands within the reservation or were soon established along the railroads shortly after allotment. Of these towns, Anadarko, Carnegie, Mountain View, and Hobart are most commonly referred to as Kiowa towns. The construction of railroad lines through these towns and substantial agricultural production ensured their early survival and later growth.

Just as many small non-Indian towns have come and gone, so have other small locales in Indian communities. While one rarely hears about Kiowa from Alden, a small crossroad south and east of Carnegie that now bears only a church, it is common to hear about Kiowa from Carnegie, Meers, and Anadarko. Consequently, as more and more Indians began to reside in these locales, town names became a source of community identification. Names such as "Carnegie Kiowa" or "Hobart People" reference both the Indians living in town and those living on surrounding rural allotted lands. However, the demography of these towns is much more varied than that of traditional allotted communities, as people whose families originally came from one Kiowa community may move to or chose to reside in other towns. A friend of mine grew up in the Stecker community, joined the army, worked a career in the Indian Health Service in Oklahoma City, retired, and moved to Mountain View, then moved back to Oklahoma City. Yet because of his origins, he is still considered a Stecker Kiowa. One family that has lived out of state for many years and in which the last two generations of this family were born and raised out of state is still considered Hobart Kiowa, because that's where the family originally came from. Because many Indian towns are of more recent origin and include a diverse assortment of relocated residents, this form of regional designation is not always associated as strongly with specific family surnames, as the earlier geographically based and named reservation-era residence communities are.

MEERS

Meers was originally a small boomtown on the northern edge of the Wichita Mountains that was founded on rumors of gold in the area (Hale 1981). Today Meers consists of only a couple of tourist-oriented businesses and a rustically decorated and popular hamburger restaurant where one can order a "Meers burger." Located at the intersection leading to the northeast end of the Wichita Mountains Wildlife Refuge, it is on the only north-south road through the central portion of the Wichita Mountains and a high-traffic area. The Mount Scott Kiowa Methodist Church and the Mount Scott Kiowa Cemetery are located 4.0 and 4.5 miles east of Meers, respectively. A small Kiowa community still resides around Meers, and the phrases "Meers People" or "Meers Kiowa" are still commonly used to refer to families residing or originating in this area. In contrast is Fort Cobb, located on the north bank of the Washita River and outside the Kiowa, Comanche, and Apache (KCA) Reservation. Although it has a significant Indian population (Kiowa, Comanche, Apache, Caddo), only one Indian store (Ahtone's Trading Post, now closed) has been active since the early 1990s, and no major Indian activities are conducted there. Thus, Fort Cobb is generally not regarded as an Indian town.

ANADARKO

The Indian presence and its relationship to current place names are most evident in Anadarko, Oklahoma, the self-proclaimed "Indian Capital of the World." Anadarko is derived from the Caddo town name of Nadarko in eastern Texas and is usually translated as referring to wild honey. The Kiowa are one of seven tribes located around Anadarko through the old reservation system. Indian people regard Anadarko as a generic or pan-Indian town for several reasons. Located just north of the town across the Washita River are the Bureau of Indian Affairs (BIA) Regional Office that serves the tribes of Oklahoma and Texas, the intertribal BIA Riverside Indian School, the Wichita Tribal Headquarters, and the Delaware Tribal Headquarters and Casino. Just south of the river is the Kiowa Area Office, which serves the seven tribes under the Kiowa Agency (Kiowa, Comanche, Naishan Apache, Wichita, Caddo, Delaware, Fort Sill Apache). The Kiowa Housing Authority and the Apache Tribal Headquarters and Apache Housing Authority are located along the southeast side of Anadarko.

Tourism is a large part of the local economy and is apparent from various banners and Indian motifs throughout the town. A brief drive around Anadarko elicits a wide array of Indian derived place and business names.

While many of these businesses focus upon Indian history, crafts, and tourism, such as: McKee's Indian Store, the Southern Plains Indian Museum, the National Hall of Fame for Famous American Indians, the Oklahoma Indian Arts and Crafts Co-Operative, and Indian City U.S.A.; others do not, such as Warrior Mart (a Texaco, now Shell station), The Redskin Theater (movie theater), and the Indian City Lanes (bowling alley). Other Anadarko businesses are tribal specific in name as with Kiowa Tribe Head Start, Apache Tribe of Oklahoma Smoke Shop, Apache Tribe of Oklahoma Tribal Trading Post, and Delaware Tribal Games. Churches include the Indian Capital Baptist Church and Faith Indian Baptist Church. At Hog Creek, a few miles west of Anadarko, the Oklahoma Indian Missionary Conference United Methodist Church Western District Center and the Oklahoma Indian United Methodist Western District Center Campground are located just north of Ware's Chapel.

While some of these advertisements contain beautiful works of art by local Indian artists such as the large mural paintings by Huzo Paddlety at the Gallery of Art and at Trader's Store, others are generic, stereotypical, and less than tasteful non-Indian productions. The Redskin Theatre has long been a well-known movie theater in Anadarko. Kiowa indicate that it has been there so long that it is simply a part of the town, and they do not see it as racist or offensive. A host of tourist-oriented businesses exist on the east side of the small town of 5,000. The Department of the Interior's Southern Plains Indian Museum contains an excellent permanent display of Southern Plains Indian material culture, a rotating exhibit featuring the work of contemporary Indian artists, a painting exhibit in the newly added Rosemary Ellison Gallery, and the adjacent Oklahoma Indian Arts and Crafts Cooperative that sells contemporary Indian-made art forms. The National Hall of Fame for Famous American Indians contains an open-air walking tour of bronze busts of famous Native Americans and a selection of books on Oklahoma Indians for sale. Although slated for closing in 2007 due to government cutbacks, the efforts of local tribes, Indian artists, and others have motivated the government to continue supporting the institution. Situated in the old train station, the Anadarko Philomathic Pioneer Museum contains exhibits of the history of Anadarko and the local Indian tribes. Two miles south of Anadarko is Indian City U.S.A., which opened on June 26, 1955. Although essentially a tourist trap, Indian City U.S.A. offers a craft and supply shop, an indoor museum, an outdoor museum containing replicas of Plains Indian dwellings and culture, and during the summer months live song and dance performances by local Indians.

Since 1934 the weeklong American Indian Exposition is held every August at the Caddo County Fairgrounds in Anadarko, drawing Indians and

"Now Playing: *White Chicks*." Redskin Theater, Anadarko, Oklahoma.

non-Indians from great distances. Commonly called "The Indian Fair," a week of family encampments, an Indian princess contest, a guest native celebrity who is awarded the title of "Indian of the Year," Indian themed pageants featuring tribal dance performances, parades through downtown Anadarko on Monday and Saturday mornings, Indian dance competitions, a hand game tournament, an Indian art contest, art and food sales, greyhound dog racing, and a commercial carnival with rides and games comprise the main fair events. Several Indian stores (featuring Indian art and art supplies), art and jewelry galleries, and pawnshops are also found in Anadarko. Employment and school opportunities with the Bureau of Indian Affairs Regional Office, the Kiowa Area Office, and Riverside Indian School have attracted many Indians from all of the local tribes as well as from other states. These factors have created a very diversified Indian population in Anadarko and while Carnegie is the center of Kiowa Indian activities, Anadarko is a major hub of intertribal activity for both specific tribal and intertribal pan-Indian activities. From these diverse factors, it is easy to see why the town popularly bills itself as "The Indian Capital of the World."

Other Indian-derived names can be found both in non-tribally specific names in nearby towns such as: Indian Nations Photo Supply (Chickasha), Roberts Indian Crafts and Supplies (Verden), the Boone Apache High School Warriors (Apache), and several street names in numerous towns; and tribal-specific businesses in surrounding towns such as A-kau-ley Smoke Shop (Verden), Comanche Nation Games (Lawton), and Comanche Nations Smokeshop (Elgin). The Caddo-Kiowa Vocational Center (Fort Cobb) provides vocational training for both Indians and non-Indians.

A few small towns were named after individual Kiowa. Most of these were a part of a large wave of post office/mercantile stores that sprang up overnight following allotment in the attempt to start towns and provide goods to new settlers for their farmsteads across the recently opened reservation (Shirk 1965:xi-xiii). Gotebo and Komalty were named for minor Kiowa band chiefs who took their allotments in these areas when the Rock Island Railroad was built through the Kiowa community. Lone Wolf was likewise named for the Kiowa tribal leader who took his allotment nearby (Gould 1933:101). Like Komalty and Lone Wolf, the former hamlet of Ahpeahtone, named to commemorate the Kiowa tribal leader, is now only an unincorporated crossroads. Similar post-allotment (1901) post office-hamlets such as Eschita, Quanah, and Koonkazachey were named for neighboring Comanche and Apache leaders (Shirk 1965). Located six miles southeast of Gotebo, Tokio was derived from the Kiowa name of Jó-cyôi (long building or house), the term they used to describe the 125-foot

Komalty town sign, Kiowa County, Oklahoma.

long store located there that housed a post office. Other locales like Rainy, named for the Rainy Mountain Church and Mission, and Saddle Mountain, named for the Saddle Mountain Indian Mission, were by-products of Kiowa names (Shirk 1965:174, 185, 207).

On May 23, 1903, a great flood swept through the Rainy Mountain Creek area. The family of Jasper Briles lived south of the Rainy Mountain Church Cemetery. As the water rose that night, Briles and his oldest son Roy managed to reach a tree. His wife Hattie, his other son Marvin, and their home were swept away. Early the next morning Gotebo, the Anglo pronunciation of his enrolled name of Kau-ta-bone, heard their cries for help and rescued Briles and his son. To honor and commemorate the rescue, the nearby small town of Gotebo, Indian Territory, was formed and incorporated in 1904. Later that same year the adjacent town of Harrison was annexed to Gotebo. Oklahoma would become a state in 1907 (KCHS 1976:219–220; RMKIBC 1993). Once an important trading center, Gotebo now contains only private homes and a few stores, most of which are agriculturally oriented, as most of the old downtown is boarded up. Although only a few Kiowa reside around Gotebo, the town continues to bear a distinctive Kiowa name. In terms of Indian population, these communities

KIOWA ETHNOGEOGRAPHY

are no longer significant as Indian towns, and except for Gotebo they are unincorporated. Only a few Kiowa remain in the rural areas surrounding these locales, and even fewer reside in these towns.

Several other place names that originated during this period are the direct result of an Indian presence in the region in relation to the military and Indian Agency presence that was required to achieve U.S. governmental policies, including confinement to the reservation and allotments. Place names such as Fort Cobb, Fort Sill, and Fort Supply in Oklahoma and Fort Elliott in Texas all stem from the perceived need to monitor and manage the Indian presence during the late 1800s. The small towns of Randlett, Stecker, and Randlett Park in Anadarko all bear the surnames of Indian agents. Mount Scott was named after Lieutenant-General Winfield Scott (Gould 1933:34; Shirk 1965:145). Kiogree was the name given to a post office located near the boundary of Kiowa and Greer counties (Gould 1933:91–92).

While allotment was intended to make Indians into self-sufficient farmers and to facilitate their assimilation into a middle-class, literate, capitalist, and Christian lifestyle, it made many of them poor and landless. The effects of allotment changed little until the Second World War, when opportunities for military service and wartime civilian work offered many Indians a chance to leave their economically impoverished communities. When many jobs ended after the war, however, many people returned to Indian communities, where conditions had not dramatically improved. Some Indian veterans used the G.I. bill to obtain vocational and college training. Other Indians chose to participate in the economic opportunities of the government-sponsored relocation programs of the 1950s to areas such as Chicago, Dallas–Fort Worth, Denver, Los Angeles, and Minneapolis. Since the 1950s some Kiowa have continued to move to larger urban areas in Oklahoma (Lawton, Oklahoma City, Tulsa, Norman) and elsewhere to find work. During this time other significant social and cultural changes were emerging. With increases in education, job skills, off-reservation experience, and interactions with members of other tribes, there was a resurgence in Indian ethnic identity, pride, and interest in civil, political, and legal rights. Since the 1960s these developments have led to a major refreshing of many forms of Kiowa culture, both inside and outside the southwestern Oklahoma Kiowa community.

Today approximately half of all enrolled Kiowa live outside the former reservation area. Yet what has not changed for most is their attachment to their home and tribal community of southwestern Oklahoma. Many Kiowa living away from the community regularly return for visits, family reunions (often held on family allotments), society ceremonials, weddings, funerals, church activities, powwows, the American Indian Exposition, and other events. Despite the current legal ownership of a limited amount of land, allotted land and the surrounding region making up the former reservation remain the basis for the Kiowa sense of a homeland. In various ways, it has remained the core of their social, religious, family, and historical community. Similar population densities and attachments to reservation and allotted lands are found in the demographic patterns of other Native American tribes (see Grobsmith 2001).

Remaining Visible Cultural Forms

Many observable native elements add to the texture and richness of Kiowa geography and the Kiowa sense of a homeland. Whether traditionally Kiowa, introduced by Euroamericans, or Kiowa innovations of Anglo creations, these elements exhibit a Kiowa quality distinct from that of non-Indians and in some aspects from that of neighboring tribes. Although less common today, aboriginal forms of architecture still appear in the Kiowa community in the form of willow arbors for shade, circular arbors around dance grounds, sweat lodges, tipis, and at one home a góm-só-á (a windbreak, often made of saplings or blood weeds) around a tipi. Some of these forms, such as arbors, may be replaced yearly. Others, such as sweat lodges, may last years before needing replacement. Still others, such as dance grounds, may remain in use for decades. As is true of Plains Indian views on many forms of material culture, the symbolism and use of these forms are typically of greater importance than the nature or physical structure and durability of the actual physical structures. Arbors and benches come and go, but the activities that occur at a family arbor or dance ground, the traditions associated with that locale, and the memory and continuation of these traditions are more important. In many instances, knowledge and meaning are valued more than physically tangible forms of material culture.

ARBORS

Brush arbors are known as thó-pòt, a term later applied to canvas arbors and house porches. Common into the 1950s, brush arbors or "Indian shade" were used as a source of protection against the blistering Oklahoma summer sun. Kiowa typically construct arbors with a layer of willow branches on top of a roof of saplings supported by wooden corner posts. Arbors were left up year-round. Each spring new willows were cut and placed on the top of the structure. Wetting the ground beneath them kept the dust down, while wetting the willow branches released cool air underneath, leading to the appellation "Indian air conditioning." Many families used to live almost exclusively in arbors during the summer months, and middle-aged and older Kiowa still reminisce about the carefree days and long summers of their youth spent around the family brush arbor (see Momaday 1976:6–8). These shaded and well-ventilated structures also provided a communal setting where people gathered to work, cook, eat, socialize, and sleep in a chô-chén-á (an improvised bed of poles and reed mats, later of boards).

Ernestine Kauahquo Kauley described the use of arbors among her family near Hobart, Oklahoma:

> It was probably the '50s [1950s] when we still had them, when we still built them around our homes. I remember we used to sleep outside and weren't afraid of anything. But you can't do that now, and feel safe. Yeah, under the arbor, what do they call it? We were very extended families. You know we all stayed together. We didn't live together but sometimes houses were in clusters together. You know we lived out here and there was probably about four houses there that the families lived in. So we always had an extended family. We all met for meals in that one arbor. All the women cooked together and we all met there and ate our meals.[20]

With increased access to electricity and air conditioning through the Rural Area Electric program, the use of arbors in the Kiowa area declined after 1947. Although an individual or family today occasionally erects an arbor beside the home during the summer for working outside or visiting, they are now rare. Although canvas shades, tents, and dining flys are more common now, arbors are still used at multiday Indian encampments and at the American Indian Exposition. Large circular arbors are still built for the annual ceremonial dances of the Kiowa Gourd Clan, the Kiowa Tia-Piah Society of Carnegie, the Apache Blackfeet Society, and the Wichita Tribal Powwow. Arbors are particularly symbolic as they provide a physical and social link between the communal gatherings at the Sun Dance and Sun Dance Lodge and the dance arbors of past and modern tribal gatherings.

Arbors are also constructed out of modern materials such as wood, canvas, and sheet metal, their function being more important than the materials used to construct them. The Momaday family home east of Mountain View has a permanent arbor of wood, with screened-in sides and modern roofing. Before community activity buildings became common, some arbors had sides added to them to form small permanent buildings for cultural activities. Such buildings were used in the 1950s through the

1970s as settings for hand games. Their continued use is both a statement of modern identity and a recognition of the past, allowing the Kiowa to continue one aspect of their ancestral culture even if now mainly for special events. Although practicality has declined, the symbolic importance of arbors has increased in modern times (Schnell 1994:43, 2000:161).

SWEAT LODGES

Sweat lodges, known as sál-cú-gàu (heat striking) or tép-gàu (emerging), are still occasionally found throughout the Kiowa community. A few families have a permanent sweat lodge site where they leave the frame of the structure (usually of willow branches) intact, covering it with tarps and blankets prior to use. Sweat lodges are used for regular bathing, prayer, and for ritual purification before social and religious activities. I have seen sweat lodges used before Peyote ceremonies, naming ceremonies, a marriage, and a hand game tournament, and I have participated in several sweat lodge events, including one held to offer prayers for an older man undergoing heart surgery. Offerings of small bundles of tobacco were tied to the top of the lodge and left after the ceremony. He soon recovered. For Kiowa following a more conservative or traditional lifestyle, sweat lodges remain a direct link to their religious, spiritual, and ritual heritage.

TIPIS

Kiowa call the tipi jó-hį̀ (real or original house/dwelling). As the typical form of western plains housing, the tipi is one of the most pervasive symbols of Plains Indian culture. Although a few Kiowa elders and families continued using tipis into the early 1900s and a few elders continued using them into the 1950s, modern houses have long since become the norm. With the decimation of bison herds on the southern plains by the late 1870s, canvas replaced hide in tipi construction as a lightweight and portable mode of dwelling for a still somewhat mobile society.

Group-oriented camp life was a major part of Kiowa life into the early 1900s. Mooney (1911) provides a description of Kiowa camp life and his work among the Kiowa in the 1890s. Large extended family camps in summer arbors were common up to the Second World War. Although no longer used as homes, tipis remain a principal symbolic link to the Kiowa past and are still used in several ritual contexts, primarily tribal encampments at ceremonials for the Black Legs, Gourd Clan, Ohomah Lodge, and Kiowa Tia-Piah Society and for Native American Church meetings on private allotments. Some families set up tipis and arbors for the annual American

Indian Exposition in Anadarko. However, recent changes in Kiowa camping practices have become apparent, as the number of camps at these ceremonials continually decreases. Some families set up wall tents or modern camping tents rather than tipis. For some families it is still considered important to set up a camp, even if they are not staying at the encampment, because of what the camp represents. Some families erect tipis at an encampment but use them only during daytime activities and for meals, returning home each evening. However, there are also practical reasons for continuing to set up a camp each year. Tipis and tents allow a convenient location for dancers to dress and undress, while tables, chairs, and a dining fly provide shade and a comfortable place to watch the proceedings, visit, and eat. If an individual or family does not set up a camp each year, another family may try to take over the spot, which usually results in arguments between families. At the American Indian Exposition, several elders have pointed out that the camps used to fill the entire fairgrounds, with different tribes clustering in their respective areas. Elders recall that the encampment used to extend southward to the edge of Highway 9, where the Southern Plains Indian Museum now is, and express concerns about the overall decline in family camps at Kiowa encampments.

In 1992, Gabriel Morgan's family erected sixteen tipis, many of them painted, in a circular fashion for his wedding. A few families have painted tipis, the symbols of which are usually directly linked to the experiences of the owner or some aspect of family history. The Museum of the Southern Plains in Anadarko used to set up a red, white, and blue tipi every year in conjunction with July 4 celebrations. Unfortunately, this tipi was partially burned by an Indian youth in 2002.[21] Every August, the museum also erects several other painted tipis from its collection before and during the American Indian Exposition. These include replicas of historical tipis, such as the Kiowa Battle Picture Tipi, the Medicine Tipi of the Naishan Apache medicine man Daveko, and more recent forms (see Ellison 1973). Although not original to their tribal descent, the family of Vanessa Morgan (now Jennings) built an Eastern Plains-style earth lodge at their home in the 1980s. Over the years, many community meals, Ohomah Lodge meetings, singing practices, and other cultural activities have been held in this structure.

Although architecture is only one genre of what many Kiowa still uphold as an archetype of what is considered traditional, it remains highly symbolic of the past. Most forms are now used only a few times a year for special events, but they represent a direct link to the architecture and pre-reservation life of their ancestors that many Kiowa still view as a golden age.

Allotments as Home Places

A major part of the Kiowa concept of a homeland is an association of belonging in a particular region. After communities, families are often associated with extended kin groups and allotments. Although individual land ownership was originally a foreign idea to Native Americans and served as a major source of misunderstanding and conflict during Euroamerican expansion, this changed dramatically with forced entry onto reservations, and even more so for the Kiowa with allotment in 1901. Kiowa residence in present-day southwestern Oklahoma dates back to at least the late 1700s and intensified with final confinement to a reservation in 1875, and the further loss of land through allotment and sales since 1901. Indians can still apply for a fee patent or title to their land and sell it if they wish. While some Kiowa have chosen to sell their allotments out of economic necessity, many have kept their land in trust status for the few benefits it does provide. Today, land ownership at a tribal, family, and individual level is a reality for the Kiowa. Allotments reinforce this connection by serving as "home places," residential foci for extended families that strongly link individuals to particular geographic regions and community histories. All allotted land remaining in trust status is managed through the Bureau of Indian Affairs.

Designed to help Indians retain a land base for the future, trust status land has both positive and negative aspects. Native people retain residence, inheritance, and use rights and tax-free status on that parcel and any income produced on that land. However, because the U.S. government holds the legal title to trust status land, an individual cannot use his or her land as collateral for loans. Agricultural leases must be approved and supervised by the BIA, and federal laws apply to that parcel of land. Like most tribes, the Kiowa population has increased even as its land base has slowly decreased. Most allotments are now owned by many heirs and are fractionalized to the point that they cannot provide adequate income through leasing to non-Indians or through farming or ranching by Indians themselves. Fractionalized inheritance of remaining trust status land often produces a situation in which one to a few dozen individuals hold equal shares to a parcel of allotted land of 160 acres or less. Because the consent of all heirs is required for building, development, or leasing, this scenario often leads to frustration and the virtual impossibility of acquiring consent from all heirs. In turn, many individuals are discouraged from living on some parcels and are led to move off Indian land if economically possible. This has contributed to a drain of the Indian population from rural to urban areas, whether local, as with Kiowa moving to Anadarko, Hobart, or

Lawton, or to more distant locales, such as Oklahoma City or Dallas–Fort Worth. Yet allotments continue to hold tremendous cultural, historical, social, and psychological importance to the Kiowa.

Many allotments have at least a few acres set aside for one or more heirs to have a home, the rest often being leased to non-Indians. Some allotments contain clusters of multiple homes representing a large extended family. Although Kiowa may or may not reside on a family allotment, these locales remain important because they always provide a family home or "home place" to return to. Even in cases where individuals no longer live on the land, allotments provide a valuable form of psychological security and support as a symbolic home. For others, allotments are important as a physical vestige of Kiowa land that is still theirs—indeed, allotted land that remains in trust status is land that has technically never been out of Indian ownership, and thus a powerful symbol of survival. Whether a home remains on an allotment or not, it is the parcel of land, the family connection, and their associated memories that are most significant to Kiowa.[22]

Kiowa often gather at family allotments for weekend visits, vacations, and annual family reunions. In 1995 I attended the Tonemah family reunion at the home and allotment of Alice Apekaum near Meers. Anne Yeahquo described what her great-grandmother Alice Apekaum's allotment means to her as a Kiowa:

> I can't begin to tell you the importance of my great-grandma's place. For me, a fairly young, contemporary, Kiowa Indian woman, it fills me with pride and admiration that that allotment is still intact, for the most part. My grandma was married three times, two Indians and one white man. It's amazing that it's still intact and we still have it within our family. I think that says a lot about our family. It's kinda unreal that it's lasted this long without being ripped up. . . . It's very important to me. I only wish I had the means to restore it like it used to be. It was such a pretty place when I was little. . . . It's just the places from my childhood that are special to me. I guess I cope with it [living away from the home area] by trying to get back to those places whenever I go home to visit. And I visit them in my mind whenever I want or need to.[23]

Other Kiowa hold annual family reunions on family allotments, in Kiowa churches, and in city parks, and reunions are regularly announced in the local newspapers.

Individuals frequently speak fondly of their childhood experiences spent on family allotments or "home places." Because much oral history is family or kin oriented, allotments or home places also form an important reference in Kiowa storytelling. Kiowa author Gus Palmer, Jr. (2003:64) describes Oscar Tsoodle, a respected tribal elder and relative, telling a story at Palmer's family home in 1998:

> Uncle Oscar gestured about with his hands as he talked. I thought, He's doing this in order to more clearly imagine the ground around us, where my grandfather had built his house and now where my mother's house stood. It was as if he needed to establish common ground before he could really talk about things. He wanted familiarity of terrain. He was using the home place as a reference point in order to come to terms with present time and his own recollection of events right here long ago.

Today, allotments continue to link large extended families, many of which now live in widely dispersed contexts, back to a common area. Typically referred to by the name of the original allottee, allotments also constitute a principal form of place name in most Indian communities. Many individuals still refer to specific allotments and parcels of land by the name of the original allottee, such as the "Botone" or "Paddlety" allotment, decades after the death of that individual, and in some instances even when the land is no longer Indian owned. In Kiowa, allotments are typically spoken of by the name of the allottee and the suffix -jè-dàum (his/her [possessive]-land) or in "Botonejèdàum" (Botone's land). Allotments represent the geographic focus of their immediate ancestors, including the original allottees—many of whom made the transition from the nomadic prereservation lifestyle to the reservation—those of the reservation period, and those of the post-allotment era. These individuals are especially regarded in high esteem and viewed as the link to the past or traditional Kiowa life. Through a geographic and genealogical focus of recent family origins, economic links of leasing shares, and as a safeguard and cultural anchor of Kiowa history, kinship, and traditions, allotments or home places hold a special attachment and a deep symbolism for contemporary Kiowa. Allotments offer an important quality of familiarity, security, and a sense of knowing they still have a place to return to. Schnell (2000:171) discusses the "psychological restorative power of the homeland" as the single key aspect of a homeland, noting that "[p]eriodically returning to southwestern Oklahoma provides a means of restoring and sustaining a separate Kiowa identity." Kiowa often refer to this as "recharging their batteries."

For many Kiowa, the parts of Kiowa Country that mean the most to them are those most directly related to their personal and family history.

When I asked Anne Yeahquo, a member of a Kiowa family from the Meers area, what areas of Kiowa Country mean the most to her and why, she responded,

> Mount Scott, my great-grandma's house, Mount Scott Church and
> Cemetery . . . Jimmy Creek Spring, which you can only get to on
> foot. My dad's land, where all his sisters live. I have good memories
> of all those places, even the cemeteries. I guess that's why they mean
> so much.[24]

Vanessa Jennings described her relationship with her grandmother and continuing to live on her grandmother's forty acres of allotted land, which she inherited.

> My artwork provides a life for me. A way to take care of my camp, my
> giveaways, to take care of Ohomah. My children, I have tried to raise
> them as if my grandmother were there, teaching them. I can walk
> on some of the same paths she walked on, stretch hides in the same
> area she stretched hides. It is a direct physical contact between my
> grandmother and whoever comes after me.[25]

Throughout the twentieth century, many American Indians were forced to leave their home communities in search of economic opportunities. Although a gradual outmigration of Native American population has existed since the First World War, many more left during and after the Second World War. Indians who have left reservations and allotted communities for military service, employment, or relocation programs often express a longing for their families, communities, and native lands. As Iverson (1998:111) says of Indian peoples during the 1940s and 1950s,

> Whether in field or factory, Indian employees generally had to
> combat overwhelming homesickness. They were accustomed to
> seeing members of their extended family on a daily or at least
> frequent basis. Native workers also missed the sight of traditional
> landmarks—the mountains or mesas, the creeks or lakes—that had
> offered a sense of place. They longed for others who spoke their
> particular tribal language or who listened to the same kind of music
> or told the same kind of jokes.

Many Indian people, although unable to visit or experience family or community places on a daily basis, developed patterns of returning home to visit as often as possible. These visits were often made to coincide with major tribal ceremonials, dances, homecomings, or other special Native American Church and Christian Church activities. The draw of and the importance that allotments and Indian communities still hold for native peoples are perhaps best evident in the postretirement demography of tribal elders, many of whom return from off-reservation careers to live on allotted land or elsewhere in the home community.

Modern Forms of Geographic Locales

When Native American ethnogeography is discussed, non-Indians often concentrate on geographic locales on a geological basis and their associated place names, especially those relating to older forms such as rivers, mountains, or states. However, this view generally excludes ethnogeography associated with reservations and post-allotment periods, and thus the majority of landforms that are most pertinent and familiar to contemporary Native Americans, who often speak of recent place names more frequently than they mention earlier pre-reservation place names.

Because ethnogeography changes with relocation to new regions and new subsistence strategies and lifestyles, this should not be surprising. Throughout the twentieth century, cultural revival, the reestablishment of sovereignty, and a conscious effort to affirm ethnic identity have been major developments in Indian communities. These events have resulted in new genres of ethnogeorahic forms and place names. Although often containing both Indian and non-Indian aspects, these syncretic forms clearly exhibit distinct Indian themes. Modern markers of Kiowa ethnicity and community include contemporary Indian homes, churches, cemeteries, schools, tribal offices, tribal license plates, dance grounds, hand game sites, Native American Church meeting sites, gaming centers, mailboxes, and signs.

MODERN HOUSES

Permanent houses first appeared on the KCA Reservation in the fall of 1877, when government leaders built houses for ten of the most prominent Indian leaders, among them the Kiowa leaders Stumbling Bear, Heidsick, Gunsadalte (Having Horns, also known as Bao or Cat), and Sun Boy, near the Meers Gap area north of Mount Scott, and the Apache leaders White Man and Taha.[26] These houses were rarely used for residence. By 1886, only nine Kiowa families were living in houses, most of which were later abandoned or rented to Anglos, the Kiowa preferring to live in their tipis

Mailboxes of Jack Yellowhair family (*above*) and Carl and Vanessa Jennings family (*left*) showing mixture of Kiowa and English personal and family names, near Fort Cobb, Caddo County, Oklahoma.

(Mooney 1898:342–343). Aimed at increasing assimilation and adaptation to permanent residences, the government in 1892 built sixty additional houses with money from the KCA grazing leases (Mooney 1898:364). Only a few of these structures still stand. Most are in poor condition, such as the homes of Big Tree and Apache John. Although modern Kiowa have not attempted to preserve these structures, many view them as historical sites and as representations of some of the earliest traces left by their ancestors on the reservation.

The houses of prominent leaders were often the hub of reservation and early post-reservation social and ritual gatherings such as dances, Peyote meetings, and Christmas encampments. During the 1970s the Department of Housing and Urban Development (HUD) undertook a program of building low-income housing for many Indians. Because each tribal government was allowed to select a house style that suited its needs, it is often easy to distinguish Indian homes from those of non-Indians. Consequently, there are many houses of the exact same size and style in the Kiowa community, the most common of which are those built in the 1970s. Kiowa generally refer to these houses as "Indian homes." Elders often joke about this house form and in giving directions will often say something like, "After you turn left there, it's the third Indian home on the right." More recently built homes reflect greater variation in style.

CHRISTIAN CHURCHES

After a lengthy period of appointing military personnel as Indian agents, President Grant placed control of Indian agencies with religious groups. Under the direction of Indian agents Laurie Tatum and James Haworth, Anglo Quaker missionaries began introducing Christianity among the Kiowa in 1869. Tatum served as agent from May 1869 to March 31, 1873; Haworth served from April 1, 1873, to March 31, 1878. The U.S. government consciously used the Quakers to further assimilation of the Plains tribes (Hagan 1990:58). Despite their efforts, Kiowa raiding continued until the Kiowa were finally forced onto a reservation in 1874–1875. In April 1878, the government replaced the peace-oriented and pacifistic Quakers with a series of more stronghanded agents. Because no Quaker mission churches were established, their influence is virtually absent today in the Kiowa landscape.

Methodists began work among the Kiowa in the late 1870s, becoming a major religious influence in 1887 when J. J. Methvin came to Anadarko and established a church soon thereafter. In the fall of 1890 Methvin opened the Methvin Methodist Institute, just south of Anadarko. Methvin succeeded in teaching white values and the English language to many converts, several of whom became Kiowa ministers and religious leaders who furthered Christianity among the Kiowa, such as Andres Martinez. The establishment of a Methodist Mission church at Mount Scott in the 1890s continued as an outgrowth of Methvin's work in Anadarko and his recruitment of Kiowa converts around Mount Scott. The following spring missionaries from the Catholic Indian Missions established St. Patrick's Mission on the west side of Anadarko, opening a mission school on November 25, 1892. Although the school closed in the early 1960s and the last buildings were torn down in the 1990s, the church remains active (Kracht 1989:912–929; Ellis 2002:29–37).

Baptists began missionary work among the Kiowa in the late 1880s. At the invitation of Lone Wolf, missionaries were sent to the Kiowa camp on Elk Creek in 1892, south of present-day Hobart, Oklahoma. Baptist churches at Rainy Mountain and Elk Creek were started in 1893. This led to other Baptist churches at Redstone, beginning first as a home church at the residence of Paddlety and later becoming an official mission church in 1896, and at Saddle Mountain in 1896, where the first permanent church was built in 1903.[27] Missionary Isabel Crawford (1915, 1998) provides an early history of the Saddle Mountain Baptist Church. Beloved by the Kiowa community, Crawford (1865–1961) is still spoken of affectionately among the Kiowa and is buried in the Saddle Mountain Cemetery. Eighty acres of land and a five-acre plot for a cemetery were given to the Baptists at Rainy Mountain and Elk Creek (RMKIBC 1993:8).

Efforts by other Christian sects met with little success among the Kiowa. By 1900, nineteen churches were active on the KCA Reservation (Ellis 2002:30). Today the majority of Christian Kiowa are Baptist or Methodist, with a smaller number of Catholics affiliated with St. Patrick's Mission and small numbers of Pentecostals at the White Church. Several of the original Kiowa churches remain active, including some of the original Indian mission Baptist (Rainy Mountain, Elk Creek, Redstone, Saddle Mountain) and Methodist (Mount Scott, Cedar Creek, Botone) churches. Although Christian missionaries sought to promote assimilation and self-sufficiency among the Kiowa, they incorporated these Anglo institutions quite differently in their respective communities. Mission churches became major centers for communal and tribal activities and continue as such for many families. These churches continue to draw a primarily Indian congregation and thus serve to reinforce rather than replace Indian identity. Although some Kiowa choose to attend other, primarily Euroamerican churches, many prefer the older mission churches, which contain the majority of Kiowa Christian participation. While some Kiowa express feelings of nonacceptance in non-Indian churches, the manner in which Indian churches allow them to practice a brand of Christianity that is uniquely tied to families, communities, and a shared Kiowa ethnicity is perhaps more important. A sense of shared kinship, community, history, and Kiowa hymns is a major part of this. This development is similar to the experiences of Second World War and Korean War Kiowa veterans, who, feeling somewhat unwelcome and culturally unfulfilled in Veterans of Foreign Wars and American Legion posts, soon revived some of their traditional military societies to honor veterans and express themselves in more culturally familiar ways (Meadows 1999:396–397). The depth of these community experiences is visible in how the Kiowa talk about Christianity, their churches and church histories, Kiowa church hymns, and at church functions (see RMKIBC 1993).[28]

Although Kiowa church sermons were originally translated from English to Kiowa and later were delivered in Kiowa by Kiowa ministers, all are now in English. However, the regular singing of Kiowa church hymns and the constitution of the congregation, fellowship, and history of these churches were clearly modeled along primarily Kiowa lines, as reflected in the membership lists of these churches and their associated cemeteries. Kiowa Christianity is still a relatively young tradition, as the last children and grandchildren of some of the original converts are today's elders. Although a few Kiowa Christian hymns were reportedly translated from English, most, including the original hymns, were made by the first generation of Kiowa Christians. Their descendants composed other Kiowa Christian church hymns. Many elders still know who composed particular hymns and which church they originated in. These songs are cherished in the community and, for those still fluent in the language, have embedded in them deeper levels of family, community, and spiritual meaning. But this brevity of historical existence does not diminish the importance that these churches hold for certain families in these communities. While churches have often been presented as arbiters of cultural change and loss in Indian communities, they are perhaps better understood as a new cultural form that provided a solid cultural focus for much of their surrounding communities. While never totally assimilating the Kiowa, churches resulted in the unification and tying of significant numbers of Kiowa to specific areas, church activities, and communities. Since the 1890s the concept of Christian Kiowa communities and cultural histories must be recognized and understood.

For many Kiowa these churches have been the center of their religious, social, and cultural world for several generations and are a fundamental part of their ethnicity.[29] When I asked Delores Toyebo Harragarra how she

Botone Methodist Church, between Fort Cobb and Carnegie, Caddo County, Oklahoma.

felt about Rainy Mountain Church and what it means to her, her answer echoed the importance of Rainy Mountain as a center of Kiowa Christian tradition.

> Well that's just the roots of my Christian heritage, it's the beginning of it. And so therefore it's important to me that it's still there. Whereas some of the other communities no longer have their churches and so it's important to me that way. That God blessed us with missionaries who were willing to live with us and spend their lives with us. And they came at a time when the Kiowas were searching, they were lost. I mean as far as the ways go, I'm not talking on the spiritual religious Christian sense at this point. But see, they didn't have their Sun Dance, they didn't have anything. And so this came along and they embraced it and they never left it. And they all had experiences as real Kiowas. They all went on the warpath. They all knew the real Kiowa ways, they were real Kiowas and they were adults. They were mature men and women. They were not children when they embraced the Christian faith. And so that tells

me a lot cause they've been through a lot. They've participated in Kiowa religious ways, participated in Kiowa ways, and then this new message came and they embraced it, so that tells me a lot. You know it had something for them and they never left it. They never walked away and they've been blessed by it. And our Kiowa people have been blessed because of the Christian faith. I really believe that. And now we don't walk as close and so I think we're missing the blessing.

We don't walk as close as the older Christians did. In fact they call it, you know[,] the Jesus Road. And so we don't follow as [close], because of a lot of reasons. One is communication, one is transportation, one is other activities that they didn't have in those days. And one thing that I consider fortunate as far as Kiowa Christianity goes is that the first Christian missionary encouraged Gotebo to compose a song. She wanted the Kiowas to sing a carol in their own language. She didn't attempt to teach them an English tune or anything. She apparently observed that they were musical people who had many songs because she worked in their camps. And so, anyway, I just think that God has been good to us in that way. And so today we have many, many Kiowa Christian songs that are our own. They're based on our own tunes, in our own way. They are not based on [English] Christian [hymns], there are several but, for the most part they are our own, our own way of singing. And she was very wise and I think that God was good to us in that way that the missionary encouraged Gotebo to sing in his own language and so he did. That's the first hymn. And so I consider, you know you ask me about Rainy Mountain[,] that's what it means to me. That he, God, was very good to send those missionaries to us.[30]

Her answer resembles that of other Christian Kiowa, offering multifaceted reflections that link tribal and family history, community, Christianity, church, the recognition of blessings, and song.

I feel fortunate to have been able to attend Rainy Mountain Church for services, dinners, funerals, family reunions, and other activities. Regardless of the congregation size, a strong sense of Kiowa community, history, and fellowship permeates the activities there. Although Rainy Mountain represents different things to people, in many ways it has come to symbolize the center of the southern homeland and to signify contemporary Kiowa Country.

Integrally associated with Indian Christian churches are their baptismal areas, in which generations of Kiowa have been inducted into Christianity. Harlan Hall (Hall 2000:211) reflected on the significance of the baptistries used at Saddle Mountain Kiowa Indian Baptist Church from 1893 to 1963:

> On the northern side of where the church then stood, is a small waterfall that stays dry most of the time. Below the falls, perhaps fifty yards, is the first Baptistry used by the original charter members of the church, and, others later. It is beautifully carved in the rock, and, standing above it looking down, which we did many times it could have been an open sepulcher. That is what it resembles, yet today; as you view it and ignore the small tree, bushes, and other wildstuffs that now partially shroud its location. When GOD, THE FATHER, spilled all of those rocks out of HIS pockets, and to form the foothill that is about it, HE must have paused, using HIS LOVELY FINGERS, to make this especially for Cauigu, for HE knew that there would come a day that these children of HIS would be learning more about HIM, and that they would have need for a place to baptize their new Christianity converts. And that is exactly what it was used for: over time, there was a second, third, and fourth Baptistry, all of them nearby. The second one, which flowed from a foothill side spring, was later named Odle Paugh Springs. The writer of this article was baptized there at the age of fourteen. I am of the positive opinion that this is one of the most hallowed of all Cauigu sites, even including the renowned battlefields, where a people held their own at a former time.[31]

The original Saddle Mountain Baptism Pool, Odlepaugh Springs, and Kokoom Pool were all used for baptisms at Saddle Mountain Kiowa Indian Baptist Church, all along the same stream course.[32]

Although many Kiowa have moved from family allotments to urban areas, most of these early churches remain in rural areas, where large numbers of allotments were taken. Often requiring many miles to drive to for services, their rural locations may be seen as impractical. Yet even as people have moved away from areas served by rural churches, the geographic and cultural significance of churches as the places where their ancestors took up the "Jesus Road" and gained hope in a time of great cultural upheaval has increased. This significance is reflected in the long trips made by individuals for regular services or for special events such as Easter and Christmas, and in the large number of Kiowa who continue to be buried in church cemeteries.

In recent decades many Kiowa Christian churches have experienced a declining membership. Kiowa elders attribute the causes to increasing social and contest powwows, society dances, the Native American Church, non-Indian activities and popular culture, increased mobility and residential distance, the strictness of existing church doctrines, which fail to attract and hold widespread youth participation, and other factors. Most likely several factors apply in each case. This trend worries elder Kiowa, who are cognizant of the greater participation of their grandparents' generation and the diminished participation of contemporary youth. Nevertheless, churches remain a focal point in the Kiowa community, and although their initial effort at assimilation may not have been entirely effective, they have been paramount in the biculturalism of several generations of Kiowa and have contributed to a sense of community and homeland for their congregations. These attachments to tribe and community are sometimes transferable in a modified form, as some Kiowa have started small church congregations in urban areas such as Norman and Oklahoma City. In the 1990s I attended several Methodist services in Norman, Oklahoma, with a group of Kiowa from around Meers. Beyond shared layers of meaning as Christians and Methodists, this congregation exhibited a strong sense of Kiowa and extended family relations. Some Kiowa also participate in district-, state-, and national-level Indian church conferences and events, which provide another forum for fellowship and the display of Kiowa Christian values and practices.

CEMETERIES

Closely linked to Kiowa Indian churches are church cemeteries. Kiowa cemeteries are one of the oldest and most visible links to one's ancestors in the Kiowa community. As mission churches became established across the KCA Reservation in the 1890s, they began constructing mission cemeteries. Although a few stones date to as early as 1900–1907, most of the earlier stones that are still legible are from the 1910s and 1920s owing to the nature of the stone used in early grave markers. The joint KCA Business Committee owned and supervised all KCA cemeteries until the three tribes formed separate governments between 1966 and 1972. However, they have maintained a joint Land Use Committee that oversees all tribal cemeteries. Fifty-gallon-barrel trash cans with the letters "KCA" painted on them are at each cemetery. Although some cemeteries contain members of more than one tribe, their location to allotted communities and the names on the headstones quickly demonstrate that most are associated with members of a particular tribe and community.

This clustering reflects the geographic and historical sense of individual community orientation derived from early reservation-period bands, as well as the association of communities with specific churches, which generally sought to convert members of a particular tribe or from a discrete area. The major Kiowa cemeteries are Cedar Creek (southeast of Carnegie), Elk Creek (south of Hobart), Mount Scott (east of Meers), Rainy Mountain (southwest of Mountain View), Redstone (west of Anadarko), Saddle Mountain (north of that mountain), Samone (west of Carnegie), Ware's Chapel (west of Hog Creek), and Stecker (behind the old Methodist Church). With the exception of Mount Scott and Stecker, the names of all of these communities originated in traditional Kiowa geographic and personal names. Smaller family cemeteries also emerged, such as those of the Anquoe, Satepauhoodle, Tanedooah, Tanehaddle, Togamote, and Two Hatchet families. A few Kiowa are also buried in the Cache Creek Indian Cemetery, the primary cemetery for the Plains Apache and some Comanche west of Apache, Oklahoma.

Urban cemeteries began only after the opening of the reservation to non-Indian settlement in 1901. Since the mid-1940s small numbers of Kiowa have been buried in the Anadarko, Carnegie, Fort Cobb, Gotebo, Hobart, and Lawton city cemeteries. Reflecting the evolution of Kiowa naming practices, older gravestones typically bear the single names of individuals, the oldest often in the hyphenated agency style of assigned spelling, such as Gap-Kau-Go, as surnames were not formally implemented until around the allotment era. Hyphenated agency spellings of individual Kiowa names are also found on military-style white stone markers for those Kiowa who served as Indian scouts in the 1890s. Later post-allotment graves typically bear English-given names and agency-spelled family surnames, including white stone military gravestones with unhyphenated names for Kiowa veterans since the First World War. Burial in KCA cemeteries is free for tribal members. Although some Kiowa choose to be buried outside of the Kiowa community, most are buried in these cemeteries alongside their ancestors, families, and friends. The cemeteries thus contain the majority of all Kiowa since the 1890s.

Another significant cemetery for the Kiowa is known as Chieftain Knoll, in the Fort Sill post cemetery. Begun in 1869, this was the only Anglo cemetery in southwestern Indian Territory until Indian mission cemeteries were started in the 1880s. At Chieftain Knoll are buried many of the last chiefs and revered leaders of the Kiowa and neighboring tribes from the treaty period of the 1860s and 1870s, including Sitting Bear, Kicking Bird, Stumbling Bear, and the Comanche leader Quanah Parker. With the permission of the Texas legislature, Satanta's or White Bear's remains were removed from the Huntsville Penitentiary in Texas, where he died in 1878, and reinterred at Chieftain Knoll in 1963. Similarly, Big Bow's remains

Gravestone of Tayboodle (Thépòl—Packing a Quarter of Meat) showing Indian Agency spelling (Tauboodle) of Kiowa name. Saddle Mountain Cemetery, Kiowa County, Oklahoma.

were moved from the Elk Creek Cemetery to Chieftain Knoll in 1964.[33] The inscriptions on the stones include each leader's name, tribe, and whether he was a signer of the Little Arkansas or Medicine Lodge treaties. A few stones of U.S. Army Indian scouts such as Big Bow, Iseeo, and Hunting Horse, who became well known during the reservation period, are also at this locale. Although some early chiefs were buried there against the wishes of their families, Chieftain Knoll has become a part of the Kiowa homeland and a source of pride for many of these leaders' descendants.

Kiowa author Harlan Hall writes of Kiowa cemeteries as "Sacred Kiowa places." Although modern cemeteries are known and local, countless others exist across the plains from earlier periods of Kiowa history that will never be known. As Hall (Tocakut 2000:71) notes, "There are today, many Kiowa Indian cemeteries. There are also an unknown number of private family plots, and even older than all of these, many very old burial grounds. No one is left to tell us where, and to be sure, KIOWAS veritably rolled across the land in a bygone day. Burials of old could have been at places on the big plains." As a contemporary, sedentary form, modern cemeteries represent important physical and spiritual markers of Kiowa social organization and community history, and are undeniably a prominent modern form of geo-sacred site.

Schools

Like churches and cemeteries, the earliest schools were missionary schools, some smaller and of brief duration, others larger and of longer duration. Government-run schools followed in the early reservation period. As assimilation-oriented institutions, these schools were designed to instill Euroamerican values and practices aimed at replacing traditional Indian customs and culture. At Rainy Mountain, which operated from 1893 to 1920, only remnants of the lower walls and foundation of the boys' dorm and the brick academic building remain. Attended primarily by Comanche, Fort Sill Indian School continued until it was closed in 1980. The buildings of this school are old but largely intact and are periodically used for dances and other tribal activities. In the 1980s the Comanche Nation planned to transform the school into an Indian community college, first as a vocational program and eventually as a four-year college. However, they opened the Comanche Nation College in Lawton in 2002.

Just north of Anadarko and beside the Anadarko Area BIA Office, Riverside Indian School continues as the oldest continually operating Indian school in the United States. Many elder Kiowa attended Riverside, where they received a formal education and met many fellow students from other tribes, leading to many intertribal friendships and marriages. Today Riverside averages around 650 Indian students from all over the country, with many Indian educators and alumni as staff. The school offers courses in mainstream subjects, Indian culture, and some languages, and has active Indian and sports programs.[34]

DANCE GROUNDS AND HAND GAME SITES

Ceremonial dances and powwows are some of the most common and visible forms of contemporary Indian culture. In pre-reservation times, most Kiowa dancing was performed at the men's and women's military society dances, parades, and initiations prior to each Sun Dance. Although Kiowa Sun Dance sites were named for geographic locations or an event occurring around that time, only a few were used repeatedly. Because military society dances occurred only at Sun Dances and the Omaha Dance and powwow were not yet acquired, the concept of named dance grounds was traditionally limited to Sun Dance sites and not to the annual society dances that accompanied them. With the end of warfare, Plains Indian men's and women's societies quickly declined during the reservation period.

Following the end of the Kiowa Sun Dance in 1890, surviving dances and new types of dances such as the Ghost Dance and the Omaha Society Dance began to be held in new contexts and locales. These dances were often linked to specific communities, and none ever fully succeeded in integrating the entire tribal population as the Sun Dance had. Although ceremonial in some aspects, Omaha Society Dances and powwows and their associated dance grounds were primarily social, honorific, and commemorative martial-oriented activities, in contrast to the religious focus of the Sun Dance and Ghost Dance. Despite cultural suppression, the Kiowa have maintained one or more dance societies since the late 1880s. The Kiowa acquired the Omaha or War Dance in 1884, resulting in an increasingly popularized version of this society song and dance style that, with the influences of Indians hired to dance at fairs and carnivals, contributed to the development of the modern powwow by the 1920s. Although the primary Kiowa Ghost Dance, held in 1890 and 1894–1917, was linked to two specific sites between present-day Carnegie and Mountain View, Oklahoma, other smaller dances are reported near Fort Cobb, Hatchetville, and south of Hobart.[35]

The revival of the Black Legs (1912–1927) and Jáifègàu societies (1912–1938) enabled older warrior society song and dance traditions to be passed on to younger generations. Since the 1930s, several factors helped to reinvigorate and continue the growth of Kiowa dancing. These include the emergence of the Fancy Dance among the Kiowa in 1917, Indian dancing at Dietrich's Lake in the 1910s and 1920s, the Craterville Fair (1924–1933), the artistic influences of the Kiowa Five since 1926, the American Indian Exposition, which began in 1934, the general cessation of government opposition to dancing and other cultural forms after the 1934 Indian Reorganization Act, and the burgeoning powwow of the 1930s and 1940s.[36] During the Second World War, honor dances for outgoing and incoming servicemen were commonplace from 1941 through 1946, and again for Korean War veterans from 1950 through 1954. The revival of the Kiowa Gourd Clan in 1957 and the Kiowa Black Legs in 1958 and the ongoing Kiowa Ohoma Society continued traditional Kiowa dances emphasizing martial, ceremonial, and ethnic identity and maintenance. Although many powwows maintained tribally distinct aspects, the growth of pan-Indianism in the 1950 and 1960s reestablished Indian pride and ethnic identity on an intertribal level never before seen, with numerous Kiowa serving as prominent singers and dancers on the Indian powwow circuit. These factors contributed to the revival of Indian dancing among the Kiowa (Meadows 1999).

Throughout this period, many locations became identified as dance grounds, some briefly, others intermittently, and others to the present. Besides the lengthy Ghost Dance encampment (1894–1917) west of present-day Carnegie, no dance grounds appear to have been named before the 1910s and 1920s, when dances began to be repeatedly held on the allotments of Lonebear, Eagleheart, Frizzlehead, Kiowa Bill, Whitefox, and Whitehorse. Over the decades the focus of Kiowa dances has shifted. Some early Ohoma Society Dances were held near Rainy Mountain in the late 1800s. Dances for First World War veterans were held at various locales, including the allotments of Ahpeahtone and White Fox near Carnegie and in the Meers community. In the 1920s, the Jáifègàu, Black Legs, and Ohoma Dances were centered on the communities of Carnegie, Stecker, and Redstone, respectively. Dances are no longer held around Rainy Mountain and have been relatively rare around Hobart since the 1920s, with the exception of dances for returning Second World War veterans, an occasional honor dance for an individual, and a recent annual fall powwow. Whereas dances used to be held in nearly every Kiowa community, most now are held near the towns of Anadarko, Apache, and Carnegie, Oklahoma. However, elders are still familiar with many of the older rural dance grounds and can easily point them out, such as Konad's near Washita, Jack Sankadota's near Stecker, Whitehorse's and Mopope Hill west of the Apache Wye, Frizzlehead's on Cache Creek, Eagleheart's and Kiowa Jim Tongkeamah's south of Carnegie, Cornbread Tanedooah's east of Carnegie, and White Fox's northwest of Carnegie.

Some dance grounds are known by name alone. Parker McKenzie lived near the site of the first Ghost Dance and the Harragarras live beside the second Kiowa Ghost Dance site. Remains of this encampment, scattered across the field, include broken dishes, glass, buttons, marbles, and other utilitarian items. Lone Bear's southeast of Carnegie was the site of Gourd Dances in the 1920s and has been used by the Kiowa Warrior Descendants organization since the early 1970s. Whitehorse's near Redstone was the site of many Ohomah Dances from the 1920s through the 1970s. During July celebrations, the annual Kiowa Gourd Clan ceremonials are held in the Carnegie City Park, the Carnegie Tia-Piah Society at Chieftain Park south of Carnegie, and the Tia-Piah Society of Oklahoma at Nelson Bigbow's near Lawton. The annual May and October Black Legs ceremonials (now held only in May) and Ohomah Lodge ceremonials in July are now held at the Indian City USA Campground south of Anadarko. Other well-known dance grounds are found in neighboring tribal communities, including Redbone's (Naishan Apache), Whitewolf's (Comanche), Mithlo's (Fort Sill Apache), Wichita Park (Wichita), and Murrow's (Caddo).[37]

Today, the annual encampments of the Kiowa Gourd Clan, Tia-Piah Society, Black Legs, and the Ohomah Lodge represent the largest and most traditional Kiowa dance societies. Many individuals regularly travel from distant locales, such as Washington, D.C., California, and New York, to attend these ceremonials. One year an elder Kiowa man who had been diagnosed with terminal cancer was determined to travel from New Mexico to Oklahoma to dance one last time at the fall Black Legs ceremonial. He received his wish, passing away later that fall.

The Kiowa Gourd Clan ceremonial is the largest gathering in contemporary Kiowa culture, bringing together the greatest number of Kiowa families for a single event. Whereas the ten tribal medicine bundles were brought together during the Sun Dance, today a contingent of Gourd Clan officers, members, and relatives make an annual pilgrimage-like visit to pray at the Kiowa Medicine Bundles each spring after the first thunder. Although not directly associated with celebrating the Fourth of July, Kiowa have begun to stress both Kiowa traditions and American citizenship in how they speak of the event. The three-day ceremonial and social dances held each July 2–4 also coincide with many individuals being able to get time off work to attend.

In many ways, the annual Kiowa Gourd Clan celebration is replete with symbols of the old Sun Dance and Jáifègàu Military Society ceremonies, and analogies between past and present activities are commonly made. The dance is held at approximately the same time of year that the Sun Dance once was and continues the use of a large circular shade arbor, which is indirectly similar to the building of the Sun Dance arbor by the societies in the past. Brush, Gourd, Rabbit, War, and social dances all relate to social activities held before the annual Sun Dance. Since the revival of the Gourd Clan in 1957, many families have maintained individual camping locations at the annual encampment, which periodically changes with deaths and the establishment of new camps. Although they are similar to assigned camping units during the Sun Dance era, I have found no correlation between these arrangements and any earlier band formations, and little evidence of relationships to later reservation communities. Camp selection is based more on kinship, friendship, size and prominence of one's family, and availability than on community residence. And although communal hunts are a thing of the past, society members distribute daily rations of food each morning. Similar to individually sponsored feasts in the past, pledges of money and beef fund the meals for the encampment.

Atwater Onco, who often served as emcee for the Kiowa Gourd Clan, analogized the contemporary encampment to the old Sun Dance, emphasizing the society's maintenance of Kiowa ethnicity and the Jáifègàu name:

> Its not a Sun Dance. . . . But this summer gathering over there, it goes to show that we're still trying to get the Kiowas together once a year, to be Kiowas, to live like Kiowas, to fellowship and go around and visit, and just have a great time like Kiowas. That's why we have the Kiowa Gourd Clan. It's strictly Kiowa. A lot of Kiowa talking. It's strictly Kiowa, singers, everything, dancers, you've got to be Kiowa to dance there. . . . At least once a year we keep it Kiowa and show other people that it is a Kiowa dance. That's the reason of it, the Jáifè.[38]

Some individuals describe the annual visit to the ten medicine bundles and the summer trip to the Gourd Clan celebrations as a homecoming, pilgrimage, and spiritual connection similar to the old Sun Dance, as a journey to a shrine or sacred place. Many Kiowa living outside the tribal homeland of southwestern Oklahoma view their trips to Carnegie in this way. As the largest arena for bringing Kiowa families together, it is clearly a time of renewal, celebration, and a reaffirmation of Kiowa ethnic identity.[39]

Many Kiowa set up tipis and wall tents around the circular dance arena in the center. Each day a morning devotional, flag-raising ceremony, and the redistribution of rations to each camp from previous donations are held. At 10 a.m. the leader of the Rabbits Society calls for the children to gather in the arena for the Rabbit Dances. After quickly cleaning up the dance grounds of all debris with trash bags, the children are led in a parade around the inside of the arena and then dance to songs sung for them. Finally they are rewarded with treats and invited to eat lunch sponsored at a family's camp.

Reminiscent of the brush dragging in the construction of past Sun Dance arbors and of the brush carried and shaken by female supporters of Sun Dancers, a series of Brush Dragging songs is sung in the late morning. Around 1 p.m., several family and society war trophies are placed on red painted poles in the center of the arena. The afternoon program begins with a processional, followed by an all-Gourd Dance program interspersed with rest breaks and specials during which initiations, naming ceremonies, speeches, giveaways, pledges for the next annual, and the honoring of individuals are held. The program focuses on Kiowa and society traditions, history, rituals, and protocol. Oral history accounts are told in individual family camps and publicly by the emcees during the ceremonials. Although non-Indian attendance is permitted, participation in the dancing and singing is not, thereby reinforcing Kiowa ethnicity. Dancing generally concludes around 5:30 p.m.

After an evening prayer, people return to their camp for supper. In the tradition of Kiowa hospitality, visitors are invited to eat at various Kiowa camps, an invitation that should never be refused. Today most meals differ little from mainstream American family cookouts and dinners. In some camps it is not unusual to see twenty-five to fifty people sharing a meal. Oscar Tsoodle explained the tradition of redistributing rations and of having open camps at the Kiowa Gourd Clan:

> That's the reason why our camps are open to anybody. Just like ours, she [his wife] cooks and put up a big long table there. Anybody can come there and eat, breakfast, dinner, supper, just enjoy. . . . That's our Indian way, we just welcome anyone. I have a lot of visitors and non-Indians come to visit. . . . That's the reason that whenever you come down to Fourth of July you just go to anybody's camp and you're welcome. You're welcome. That's the reason we give out rations and then we tell them, "Feed your visitors, feed your friends. . . ." Fellowship and eating together that's what it is, and we do that.[40]

After supper, dancing resumes around 7 p.m. with the Kiowa Flag Song and a single-file processional parade. After a final session of fast-paced Gourd Dance songs and a set of Buffalo Dance songs, an intertribal program of war and social dancing follows. Despite the fission of the original

Brush Dance. Kiowa Gourd Clan Ceremonials, Carnegie Park, Carnegie, Oklahoma.

Gourd Clan into four dance societies, Kiowa still refer to the Kiowa Gourd Clan as the "granddaddy of them all."

Just as the Kiowa Gourd Clan has become a hallmark of Kiowa ethnic identity and tradition, the Kiowa Black Legs ceremonials in May and October enact a series of rituals associated with traditional concepts of warrior status. Requiring Kiowa tribal enrollment and veteran status for membership, and including Scalp, Victory, War Mothers, and Black Legs society songs (many with martial lyrics) and dances (some of which reenact the joy of veterans returning home or combat and include the recounting of a war deed by a combat veteran), this ceremonial focuses on traditional forms of honoring veterans and represents the core of past and contemporary Kiowa martial heritage. The annual Ohomah Lodge ceremonial in July focuses on the heritage of the War Dance and its legacy as the only Kiowa society that never stopped dancing during the era of government suppression in the early 1900s. The encampments of these societies contain many of the same cultural practices and connections to past and present Kiowa concepts of generosity, hospitality, recognition of status, redistribution of food and wealth through giveaways, commitment to one's kinfolk, and a strong

Kiowa Black Legs Society Initiation Dance. Indian City U.S.A. Campground, Caddo County, Oklahoma.

desire to hear the songs of each society and to participate in or watch the associated dancing.

An integral part of these ceremonies involves remembering and honoring one's ancestors. Vanessa Jennings stated that she tries to live her life as if her grandparents were right beside her, that is, to their level of traditions and expectations. She described how she remembers her grandmother, the late Jeanette Berry Mopope, during the Scalp and Victory dances at the Kiowa Black Legs ceremonials:

> Yes, I think about her. I can hear her lulu. She's with me all of the time, but most especially during the Scalp Dance and the Victory Dance, you know she's the one I watch to keep in step with. You know I may not be able to match her strength for strength and courage for courage you know, but I'll sure make an effort to attempt to match her. She was really something. Yeah, she's there with me.[41]

Other large dance gatherings include annual powwows and descendants' group meetings. Focusing on singing, dancing, and feasting, pow-

166   KIOWA ETHNOGEOGRAPHY

wows are held for a wide variety of purposes, including celebrating an organization's existence, honoring someone for a particular achievement, or as a benefit dance to raise funds for a cause. Descendant gatherings may be dance (descendant's powwow) or non-dance oriented (family reunion) and generally involve a sizable group of people linked to one another through a particular ancestor. At these events, relatives gather to visit, socialize, sing and dance, hold naming or cedaring ceremonies, play various games, perform religious rituals, eat, commemorate ancestors, and share family history, traditions, and fellowship. With multigenerational family participation at these activities, it is easy to understand why these locations are important in Kiowa culture.

Elders also recall favorite locales where hand games used to be held, usually on individual allotments, such as Maunkaugul's, Haumpy's, Dupoint's, Cornbread Tenedooah's, and Whitefox's during the annual Armistice Day encampments, all near Carnegie, and Major Pewenofkit's (an Apache) between Carnegie and Fort Cobb. Other noted hand game locales are "Billy Goat Hill" and the "Astrodome," a small dome-shaped hand game building of the Apaches, both near Boone, Oklahoma. When Jack Yellowhair's family had a new home built in 1972, they cleared out the old house and turned it into a hand game building which they named "Shady Front," from a row of cedar trees that shaded the front side of the house. This site was used for several years until a tornado destroyed the house in the 1980s.[42] Elders also recall old Native American or Christian Church camp meeting sites, each with its own rich history and importance.

These cultural and religious activities provide Kiowa with another range of connections to the land, that of an association of specific activities at specific locales. Reflecting the importance of focused activity locales such as dance grounds and churches, various Kiowa have commented that they are "singing where our ancestors sang," "worshiping where they worshipped," or that they are still "dancing where they danced." The attachment to focused activity locations and the Kiowa emphasis on respect for and remembrance of elders and what they provided form an important part of cultural identity in the Kiowa community.

Symbols of Sovereignty

Although federally recognized Indian tribes have limited sovereignty, they continue to expand the range of that status in its political, economic, and legal aspects. Consequently, geographic indicators and place names reflecting these developments are increasingly appearing in tribal communities.

As the hub of tribal activity, tribal governmental complexes are major markers of ethnic identity and political sovereignty. When first entering the Kiowa tribal complex on the west side of Carnegie, Oklahoma, one is met with a painted wooden sign that reminds visitors they are now in "Indian Country" and that certain federal laws apply to this parcel of ground. The "Kiowa Housing Authority" sign in Anadarko identifies another tribal government office and program. Increased sovereignty has allowed the development and expansion of tribal gaming centers throughout Indian Country. For several years a large sign reading "Kiowa Tribal Gaming Center" was visible as one entered Carnegie from the east. Although Kiowa gaming operations have been intermittent, two Kiowa gaming casinos are currently under construction along I-44 near the Red River in southern Oklahoma. Similar markers of tribal identity and sovereignty are found in the government offices, gas stations, and gaming centers of neighboring tribes. Across the countryside, one occasionally sees a "smoke shop," a kind of Indian 7-Eleven or tribally run tobacco and convenience store on trust status land that can legally implement tribally determined taxes and offer discounts. These places all relate to legal concepts associated with the term Indian Country.

The term Indian Country has become one of the most important terms in Indian communities, especially from a legal standpoint. Originally this expression was used as a vernacular term among Anglo-Americans to describe all unorganized territory populated by "savage" Indians (Deloria and Lytle 1983). Later, the term was applied to commonly held reservations and other individual Indian lands held in trust by the U.S. government, lands subject to different laws than adjacent non-Indian lands. Following confinement to reservations and subsequent allotments, the term was essentially applied as a strict legal definition of these remaining lands. Reinforcing its military origins, the term was again used to refer to territory held by the enemy during the Vietnam War. More recently, a fourth vernacular use of Indian Country has emerged that refers to reservations, privately owned Indian land, and to any and all regions across the country that have substantial rural Indian populations. While Indians typically use this term in reference to rural communities, most often Indian areas in the western United States, they do not extend it to urban areas.[43] Wilkins (2002:337) defines Indian Country in the following way:

> Broadly, it is country within which Indian laws and customs and
> federal laws relating to Indians are generally applicable. But it is

also defined as all the land under the supervision and protection of the U.S. government that has been set aside primarily for the use of Indians. This includes all Indian reservations and any other areas (e.g., all other Indian communities, including the various Pueblos and Indian lands in Oklahoma, and individual allotments still held in trust by the federal government) under federal jurisdiction and designated for Indian use. And according to some courts, it also includes privately held non-Indian lands within the boundaries of Indian reservations, rights of way (including federal and state highways), and any additional lands tribes acquire.

Schnell (1994:31) writes, "This archipelago of rural centers of Indian culture, both of reservation and non-reservation peoples, is as much a psychological region as it is a physical place. Indian Country is where one can feel comfortable as part of an Indian community." For Indian people this designation can exist even in allotted communities where the majority of the surrounding land and population is non-Indian. Whether on large reservations or dispersed allotments, Indian people are well informed through person-to-person interaction, or the "moccasin telegraph," and virtually every form of modern communication, including cell phones, e-mail, faxes, flyers to announce cultural events, local and tribal newspapers, and radio programs such as the Saturday morning *Indians for Indians Hour* broadcast from Anadarko, Oklahoma.

Originating in pre-reservation intertribal exchanges (trade, Sun Dances, military society dances, Calumet ceremonies) via spoken and sign language, cultural exchanges only accelerated with increased intertribal proximity and the introduction of boarding schools during the reservation period. Further interaction occurs and much news is still spread today through personal contact via intertribal visiting, intermarriage, interaction through BIA jobs, boarding schools such as Riverside or Haskell, and attendance at intertribal cultural and religious activities such as church services, dance societies, powwows, hand games, and softball leagues.

For the Kiowa, these exchanges and links in Indian Country are most frequent and visible with other neighboring Plains tribes with which they share a lengthy history (Comanche, Apache, Cheyenne), with the Crow of Montana, through a lengthy friendship and the exchange of annual visits and hand games, and with the Pueblo and Navajo of the Southwest, through intermarriage (Schnell 1994:33). Kiowa and Pueblo exchanges date back to the 1700s, and Kiowa and Navajo warfare continued until the reservation period. Exchanges with the Pueblos continued in the reservation period during 1872–1873 and 1880–1881 (Mooney 1898:336, 347), and with the Kiowa sending a Baptist missionary to the Pueblo in 1903 (RMKIBC 1993:9). Artistic exchanges increased with Kiowa participation in intertribal dances at Gallup, New Mexico, and through the invention of the Oklahoma style of Indian painting in 1926. This style later diffused to the Southwest, where it was first taught in 1932 at the Studio in Santa Fe, and after 1935 with the formation of an art department at Bacone College in Muscogee, Oklahoma. As most of the students attending both schools were Indians from Oklahoma, New Mexico, and Arizona, this artistic style spread quickly. The inauguration of the Institute of American Indian Arts in 1962 on the site of Dorothy Dunn's Studio also allowed Indians of many tribes to interact and study together for extended periods, and the institute became the principal wellspring for Indian artists and intertribal artistic exchange (Feest 1992:98–101; Berlo and Phillips 1998:215–225).

TRIBAL FLAGS, LICENSE PLATES, AND CASINOS

With the resurgence and strengthening of tribal governments, many tribes have adopted tribal flags as a symbol of sovereignty and ethnic identity. The late Roland Whitehorse designed the Kiowa tribal emblem, which consists of a circular logo depicting a Plains-style warrior riding a horse, surrounded by a ring of ten overlapping black-and-white golden eagle tail feathers. At the base of the logo and overlapping the row of eagle feathers is a small circle divided into a green half on the left and a yellow half on the right, containing the silhouette of a bison bull's head. The legend KIOWA TRIBE OF OKLAHOMA in bold black letters on a pale blue background is positioned around the outside edge of the logo.

The warrior rides an Appaloosa horse, a breed developed by Plateau tribes of Montana and Idaho and near the earlier homeland of the Kiowa. The horse has a painted lightning bolt on his front leg, representing Ohoma Society traditions and the voice of thunder heard each spring. A similar lightning bolt held in the talons of an eagle represents the Great Drum formerly used by the Ohoma Society, which holds a major purification ceremony each spring after the first thunder and in which Whitehorse was a member. The ten eagle feathers are said to represent the well-known Ten Medicines — a set of ten hereditary religious bundles, or, according to some, the ten sash owners of the Qóichégàu Society.[44] The warrior wears a red Spanish- or Mexican-style military officer's cape, a red headband, and a bone breastplate. While Kiowa ledger book drawings indicate that several such capes were once owned by the tribe, this cape represents the contemporary Kiowa Black Leg Society, which wears red capes in commemoration of one family's ancestor, Young Mustang Colt, who captured one in a fight with Mexican soldiers. Whitehorse was also a member of this society, and his father used to borrow this cape to wear in parades in the early twentieth century (Meadows 1991).

The mounted warrior carries a shield depicting Rainy Mountain, the symbolic end of the Kiowa's great tribal journey and an area of long historical importance. Healy (1997:75) reports that the recurring circular patterns in the sky, feathers, and shield motifs symbolize the sun and moon, which were important components of the Kiowa Sun Dance, Feather (Ghost) Dance, and Peyote or Native American Church. This design now serves as the official emblem on the Kiowa tribal flag, license plates, signs, stationery, clothing, and a variety of other tribal items.

The development of tribal license plates is another major and perhaps most visible marker of tribal identity and sovereignty. In 1974, the Red Lake Chippewa filed suit and successfully won the right to issue their own license plates and vehicle registrations. Since then many tribes have begun to exercise this right as part of tribal sovereignty. The Kiowa offer their own tribal vehicle tags to any enrolled member of the Kiowa Tribe over the age of sixteen and possessing a valid Oklahoma driver's license, insurance verification, and a signed and notarized vehicle title in the applicant's name. The Kiowa Tax Commission sells license tags for automobiles, motorcycles, trailers, veterans (with proof of a DD-214 form), out-of-state students, and disabled individuals (with a disabled placard or a tribal application filled out and signed by a physician) at half price.[45] At a price significantly lower than the state charges, any Kiowa member residing within Oklahoma may buy a tribal license tag, with proceeds from the sales going into an account supporting tribal activities. In addition to providing a service for tribal members at reduced costs, this activity continues to aggravate the Oklahoma Tax Commission, which typically opposes sovereign tribal licensing. Aside from their political and financial impacts, Kiowa license plates are an important and conspicuous symbol of tribal identity. With the increase in Indian pride and ethnic identity, license plates are another way of demonstrating the continuation of Indian culture and communities, both as ethnic groups and as semi-sovereign nations.

The evolution of Indian license plates has tended to follow that of non-Indian society in that the number of personalized plates is increasing, with family names such as "BOINTY" or "TSOODLE," individual Kiowa names such as "KOY-E-MAH (Kiowa [Woman]) or "AKEEMAH" (Plum Blossom [Woman]), labels such as "WARPONY," nicknames, and veterans' plates such as "VET-1" or "VET-34" becoming increasingly popular. In June 2006 the Kiowa tribe began offering tags to former tribal princesses with the words "Kiowa Tribal Princess" on top, the year of the ostensible princess's

Kiowa Amusement Center, Carnegie, Oklahoma.

reign at the bottom, and the tribal seal with the tag number written on each side of the tribal seal in the center.[46] Some tribes are examining the possibility of multitribal tags or the sale of tags to any Indian living in Indian Country. While distinct Indian surnames have long been used on mailboxes, many individuals are also using Anglicized spellings of their personal or family Kiowa names in their e-mail addresses.

Following the growth of tribal sovereignty, the Kiowa Casino Red River opened in May 2007 just off I-44 in Cotton County, Oklahoma. This venture not only provides an important visual marker of tribal identity and sovereignty, it is strengthening Kiowa economic developments, which have tended to lag behind those of many other Oklahoma tribes.

The Invisible Landscape

Anyone who spends a period of time in a community will become familiar with many geographic locales that hold tremendous significance, memories, and attachment for people in that community. After spending much time in the Kiowa community, I sometimes find that some Kiowa expect me to know certain things, such as where people live and geographic

locales. Although most people think of geography in terms of visibly per-
ceptible forms, many events have transpired that leave no visible signs on
the landscape but that nevertheless are of tremendous cultural and historical importance. While some locales of significance are visible, named,
well known, and marked as historic sites, most have none of these qualities and are invisible to an outsider. Thus, paralleling every community's
visible landscape is its invisible landscape, sites where important events
have transpired without leaving a physical sign. The invisible landscape is
significant in Kiowa ethnogeography because of the history and meaning
associated with the events that occurred there.

Schnell (1994:82–84) briefly introduces the concept of an invisible
landscape, and touches on the idea that the connection between a people
and a landscape exists primarily in the significance attached to places in
the landscape and the passing of this significance as a form of cultural
knowledge from generation to generation. "Even material features on the
landscape rely on less visible cultural ideas for their continuity" (Schnell
1994:82). Because most historical and personal experiences associated
with specific geographic places are not recorded, one could argue that invisible landscapes far outweigh the visible landscape in cultural importance. It is this body of knowledge of unrecorded events, transmitted in the
form of oral history, stories, and symbolism, that informs how the Kiowa
perceive, remember, and talk about geographic sites and that gives meaning and significance to these locales for the Kiowa. That the Kiowa have
many such invisible sites speaks to the pervasive nature and importance
of this landscape and to the role of oral history in Kiowa culture.

From a drive with Poetomah (Mrs. Tsatoke), Marriott (1945:287) vividly
describes how Kiowa relate to their physical surroundings in terms of
geography and oral history:

> She took the back road, down through Cutthroat Gap and around
> Saddle Mountain. It was longer than the highway, but it was pretty.
> Grandmother showed her places as they went along.
>
> That big bend there, by the river, Buffalo River. That's where they
> held the Sun dance the year I was born. That little butte over there.
> That's where the three boys froze to death, the time they ran away
> from the government school. See where that hole is, where the
> ground kind of dips down? That's where the old trading post stood.
> It burned down, the Year They Ran Away to Texas.
>
> On and on. Every little dip, every bend and curve—the spring
> where they stopped to drink and water the radiator, even the beds
> of water cress below it—had their histories and their names. It was

all alive, this country; people walked across it that Leah could not see, but Spear Woman could. She did not call their names, for they were dead, but she told to whom they were related, and how that made them kin to her and to Leah. Some places were happy; there had been Sun Dances and ceremonies. Other places were unhappy; people had died there, and been mourned. . . . On and on.

Some of my trips with contemporary Kiowa elders were similar. During a visit with Parker McKenzie in 1991, he mentioned that he wished he knew where the grave of Taybodle was, his great-grandmother's brother. I replied that I knew where it was, at Saddle Mountain Cemetery, and that I would take him. Soon after I drove him to see it. From the time we crossed Rainy Mountain Creek just east of Mountain View, Parker began to recall various stories of historical events he had either witnessed or been told of. The fact that elders reminisce while driving along is not unusual, but the sheer quantity of accounts that McKenzie told me during the sixteen-mile drive was astounding. These ranged from where individuals' allotments were to the house where noted Kiowa author N. Scott Momaday spent his summers as a child in the Kiowa community, to campsites, to where Big Tree, Gotebo, and Saingko played a joke on an overanxious group of non-Indians who had gathered to watch them butcher a beef. Hardly a half-mile passed by that he did not point out a location and recite an event that occurred there. On another trip to Elk Creek Cemetery, he showed me a vision quest site of White Bear and other unmarked and little-known historical places.

I had a similar experience in 1993 with Atwater Onco on a trip to Cutthroat Gap, Hobart, and the Elk Creek Cemetery. In the Redstone–Fort Cobb area Vanessa Jennings showed me numerous sites and told me of their associated history for both Kiowa and Apache. That this form of oral historical geography is so common reflects the close cultural and historical association of the Kiowa with their community and its homeland. While such extensive and detailed histories can also be found in Anglo communities, they are quickly decreasing, owing to the increased mobility and relocation of younger generations, who have not experienced the same historical depth and intimacy with a single homeland area. Because most of this knowledge is still oral history, it is always one generation away from being potentially lost, especially for Kiowa living outside the home community. As Schnell (1994:83) writes, "The symbolic nature of the Kiowa homeland is largely invisible to outsiders, and this invisibility makes it fragile." For these places and traditions to continue to have meaning for the Kiowa, they must be passed on, for traditions without cultural association and meaning are often quick to disappear. These traditions are linked to how Kiowa culture is still passed on, largely through oral accounts as stories that reference how and why they are relevant to the Kiowa, and in spontaneous rather than formally organized settings.

SPIRITUAL GEOGRAPHY

Another form of invisible landscape that is very real to the Kiowa is the spiritual landscape of ghosts. Although Kracht (1989, 1997, in press) and Gelo (1986) have briefly discussed topics in this genre, particularly haunted areas and ghosts as whirlwinds, dust devils, and owls associated with individuals getting "twisted" (pópqûngà—facial or Bell's palsy, or in euphemism—chòicúngà) by spirits of the dead via owls or seeing actual ghosts, it has not been fully addressed, and I only briefly touch on the subject here. A belief in the presence of ghosts and in ghost encounters is still fairly prevalent among the Kiowa today. On several occasions I have witnessed cedaring ceremonies of individuals and homes after ghost encounters or nightmares. As a member of one family was near death one evening, another member coming to the house saw a large group of people of varied ages in the field a short distance from the house. The family realized that it was their ancestors waiting for her. During my time around Redstone, many Kiowa mentioned that the area was prone to ghost sightings. While visiting J. J. Methvin Church with two students, we ran into an elder Kiowa woman whom I had not seen for several years. She asked one of my students where we were staying. When they replied just west of Redstone, the woman got a look of surprise and said, "Oh my, that area has got more kómjós [ghosts] than about any area among the Kiowa." One evening in 2004 three elder Kiowa women told a series of ghost stories, including several that involved the allotment we were on and the surrounding Kiowa community of Redstone. During the conversation one of the women stated, "This whole land is alive, a lot of things have happened around here, and sometimes you hear things." Another of the women explained that when ghosts were heard singing, talking, or visiting, they were not there to scare you, so one should not be afraid. She explained that it made her feel good to hear them, and said, "You just let them go on their way." She later added that "You don't question these things, they just are."[47]

Although I had heard many ghost stories over the years, this visit reminded me how much Kiowa consider past activities part of the contemporary landscape. These traces in the landscape were not so much physical—although ghost encounters can be both visual and auditory physical events—as they were spiritual. One individual stated that many activities had been held on her land in the past and many people had been there, and therefore I should not be alarmed if I saw or heard things, as these entities were just going about their business. Elder Kiowa understand both physical and metaphysical geography as a normal part of the landscape and of life, and although people may burn cedar to protect themselves from ghosts and other entities, they do not become overly excited about them. Thus, two well-developed genres of spiritual geography relating to ghosts or supernatural forms exist among the Kiowa, knowledge that a wide array of prior activities have occurred across the landscape in general and knowledge that specific activities have occurred at specific locales.

SIGNAGE

Throughout Caddo, Kiowa, and Comanche counties, the majority of existing historical markers erected by the state of Oklahoma commemorate military posts, schools, and other agencies of assimilation (ODTR 1992:28–31; Schnell 1994:83). Only in 1995 was an official state marker erected to recognize the site of Cut Throat Gap, 2.5 miles west of the actual site on Oklahoma State Highway 54, south of Cooperton.[48] By the 1980s many Oklahoma counties with large Indian communities exhibited disparity in the maintenance of county roads in areas of high Indian population versus non-Indian population. After this issue was brought to attention, a national program called the Indian Reservation Roads Program, which secured funds from the Federal Highway Administration, was funded in the late 1980s to improve rural roads in areas of high Indian population and use. Further maintenance was to be monitored by the local, county, and state highway departments. The Oklahoma Department of Transportation also sought to identify important locales in Indian communities and to mark them with road signs similar to those in non-Indian communities. By the mid-1990s several official highway signs bearing the English translations of Kiowa names for several creeks and bridges had been erected, such as Two Hatchett, Seven Sisters, and Rainy Mountain creeks, and Sitapatah and Luther Sahmaunt bridges.[49] After years of political pressure, on April 25, 2005, the Comanche County Commissioners in Oklahoma voted to change the name of Squaw Creek, which runs through the county seat of Lawton, to Numu Creek, the Comanche name for themselves. This change is not only politically significant but also aids in the preservation of the Comanche language.[50]

Signage is an important means of marking one's presence within a specific region. Signage in both English and tribal languages is increasing in many Indian communities throughout the country. In marking these

Millie Durgan Marker showing common style of Oklahoma State Historical Society Marker. Marker is located east of Mountain View, Kiowa County, Oklahoma.

sites, the increase in official signs and historical markers will help, but not ensure, the survival of the knowledge associated with these sites. Just as with named historical road signs in non-Indian communities, the cultural and symbolic basis of these Kiowa place names depends on the continuation and maintenance of family and tribal history and ethnic identity. The invisible landscape is essentially the assignment of cultural meaning to a landscape that has not yet been marked. While some sites are known by nearly everyone, there are far more other locations with Kiowa and/or English place names that are largely unknown outside individual Kiowa communities or the tribe. Swimming holes such as "The Big Hole" and "Red Cliff" near Saddle Mountain (Tokacut 2000:147) and Soldier Creek near Redstone are examples of this form. Yet the fact that many such "invisible" or unmarked places are still known and still hold cultural significance for the Kiowa speaks to the resiliency of their oral traditions, to the extent of an invisible landscape throughout Kiowa Country, and not just to the physical longevity of geographic forms.

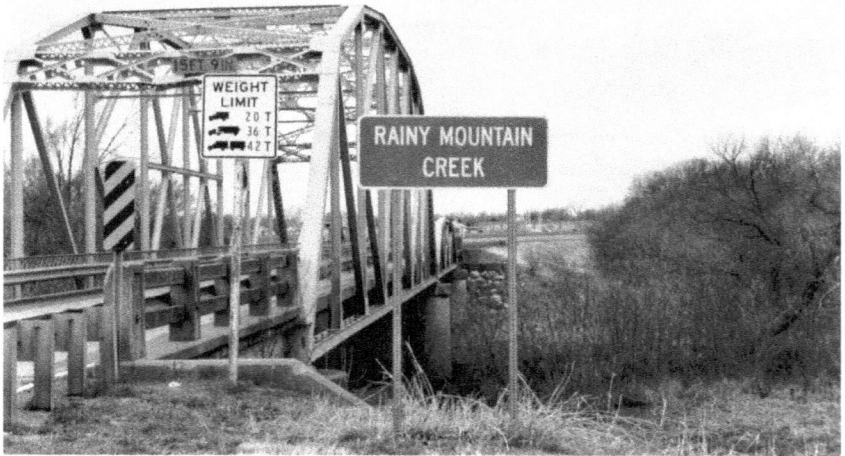

Two Hatchett Creek sign east of Fort Cobb, Caddo County, Oklahoma; Rainy Mountain Creek sign east of Mountain View, Kiowa County, Oklahoma.

Art

For many Native Americans, art is a major form of expression of tribal culture, ethnic identity, and homeland. Throughout Kiowa Country various artistic works have become enduring fixtures in the community. These include paintings by Kiowa Five artists such as Stephen Mopope and Monroe Tsatoke. Paintings by Mopope can be found in the Anadarko Public

Library, the Anadarko Post Office, the Southern Plains Indian Museum, the Philomathic Museum, and the Indian City Museum, while several of Tsatoke's paintings are in the Oklahoma Historical Society in Oklahoma City. Other paintings are found in the Kiowa Tribal Museum at Carnegie, the Southern Plains Indian, Indian City, and Anadarko Philomathic Pioneer museums around Anadarko, and on building walls in Anadarko.

In the Kiowa Tribal Museum in Carnegie are ten murals depicting the history of the Kiowa. Sherman Chaddlesone, Parker Boyiddle, and Mirac Creepingbear each painted three murals, and all three collaborated on the tenth, entitled *The Kiowa Today* (Denton and Maudlin 1987). The murals were commissioned by the Kiowa tribal leaders in 1984, who gave the three artists the task of conveying "What it was, and is, to be Kiowa." Drawing on the strengths of each artist, these vibrant works capture the history, culture, and changes the Kiowa have experienced from their origins to the present day. Figuring prominently in the murals are several impressive geographic settings inhabited by the Kiowa, including Spear Lake and Devil's Tower in Wyoming, the Rocky Mountains, and Rainy Mountain and portions of the Wichita Mountains in Oklahoma.

On the north side of the Gallery of Art in Anadarko, Huzo Paddlety painted a 120-foot-long mural entitled *Transcending the Plains* that depicts the history of the Kiowa. Ten faces represent the Kiowa "Ko'ett Senko" (Qóichégàu). At the end of the mural is a large fancy dancer painted by Robert Redbird (Gallery of Art 2003). Paddlety painted another mural on the side of Trader's Steakhouse just west of Anadarko, as did Darwin Tsoodle in 2006. Huzo Paddlety, Jeff Yellowhair, Cruz McDaniels, Darwin Tsoodle, and other Kiowa artists are continuing the rich tradition of Kiowa painting.

The National Hall of Fame For Famous American Indians contains busts of notable Indians from across the country, including several of the most famous Kiowa leaders from the mid- to late 1800s. Roland Whitehorse, Sherman Chaddlesone, Ted Creepingbear, Ace Yellowhair, and Allie Chaddlesone have also produced numerous sculptures.

LITERATURE

In addition to a long history of influential dancers, singers, bead workers, painters, and sculptors, the work of N. Scott Momaday stands out as a seminal influence on Native American literature. Momaday is probably the most discussed and analyzed Native American writer to date. Trimble (1973), Schubnell (1985), Roemer (1988), Woodard (1989), Velie (1991), Schnell (1994:85–92), and Scarberry-Garcia (1996) have provided

Tohausan Statue, National Hall of Fame for Famous American Indians, Anadarko, Oklahoma.

extensive discussions of Momaday's literary work. Many authors point to Momaday's uncanny ability to describe the Kiowa landscape in a manner that is both accurate and meaningful for the Kiowa themselves. In novels both imaginative and reflective of personal history, Momaday writes of his experiences and the interconnected symbolism of his Kiowa heritage in southwestern Oklahoma. His writings often feature the family house and arbor, which still stand just east of Mountain View, Oklahoma. More impressive than his use of historical references is, according to many Kiowa, his ability to accurately depict Kiowa ideas and values. Author of several fictional, autobiographical, and poetic works, Momaday won the Pulitzer Prize in 1969 for his book *House Made of Dawn*. That summer he was honored with induction into the Kiowa Gourd Clan and was presented with a gourd rattle and an eagle feather fan.

A number of rich cultural and ethnogeographic themes pervade Momaday's work: the ability of the natural world to continuously generate healing powers, the bestowal of blessings on people and the land, the strength of the bond between people and their cultural and geographic homelands, the ties that connect an individual to place, the ways in which individuals reaffirm their connections to the land, a sense of wholeness in conjunction with the cyclical nature of life, and the profundity of human relationships with specific landscapes (Scarberry-Garcia 1996:472). In discussing the lengthy relationship of humans to land in North America and the reciprocal investment of humans into landscape and place into human experience, Momaday (1976a) also helped raise awareness of the multifaceted and indivisible native idea of land as sacred. As Momaday (1976a:14, 18) said, "I believe that . . . there grew up in the mind of man an idea of land as sacred," and "[i]n the natural order man invests himself in the landscape and at the same time incorporates the landscape into his own most fundamental experience. This trust is sacred."

Momaday was born February 27, 1943, in Lawton, Oklahoma. That August, Kiowa George Poolaw (Pohdlohk) held him in his arms near Rainy Mountain Creek, where he named him Xóâitàlyî (Rock That Grew Upwards Boy), after the Kiowa name for Devil's Tower in Wyoming. As Momaday later recognized, the naming linked his spirit to that physical locale (Momaday 1976b). Shortly thereafter, Momaday's family took him to Wyoming to visit and make physical contact with the site, which is frequently referenced and repeatedly honored in Kiowa mythology. "Momaday's bond to Tsoai, the place for which he was named, forms the basis for his identity, and the Kiowa story of the bear/children incident that took place there becomes the central story that Momaday retells in all of his major works"

(Scarberry-Garcia 1996:468). The presence of a bear figure and its healing powers is also a frequent theme in Momaday's work.

Momaday has spent most of his life in the Southwest. Between 1936 and 1943, his parents lived on the Navajo Reservation in Arizona. In 1943 they moved to Jemez Pueblo in New Mexico. He finished high school at a military academy in Virginia, then attended college in New Mexico and California. The greater part of Momaday's residence in Oklahoma occurred during summers at his grandparents' home, and it is to this landscape of his youth that Momaday frequently turns for inspiration in his works, which manifest a unique ability to convey the subtle colors, shapes, smells, and seasons of the physical landscape of southwestern Oklahoma. It is this evocation of land, place, and identity that is so stimulating in Momaday's work. Perhaps due to the combination of his Kiowa ancestry, his upbringing in the Southwest, and his overall affinity for the land, Momaday's Kiowa-based writings serve as a bridge to help him retain his sense of identity and link to the Kiowa in southwestern Oklahoma. This unique plains-oriented outlook has made Momaday a premier voice in American Indian literature. As Scarberry-Garcia (1996:475) notes, "we have come to expect exquisite descriptions of landscape, especially of landforms as seen by a Plains man from a distance. The clean, exhilarating prose that distinguishes Momaday's writing may ennoble us because it allows us to take a fresh look at the world, at the time of creation, when everything is bursting with original, transformative energy."

By the 1970s, Momaday's work had appeared in nearly every major anthology on American Indian literature. As Scarberry-Garcia (1996:471) writes of *The Way to Rainy Mountain*, "Of all of Momaday's works, it most forthrightly articulates the land ethic that has made him famous as a philosopher of environmental issues," and "Momaday's trademark style of precisely describing the minutest details of animal life and the lay of the land, in 'elevated' formal diction, has earned him the respect of a wide and diverse audience. . . . Momaday's love of the land, expressed through his love of language, becomes one of the highest values of his life" (Scarberry-Garcia 1996:472–473).

Momaday's works are significant because, while they focus on a distinctly Kiowa mode of perception, thought, and experience that repeatedly references geographic sites of importance, they readily elicit among the Kiowa vivid comparable memories of personal experiences they and their families have had. Topics such as spending summers in the family arbor, traveling about the Kiowa community, storytelling, community interaction, and respect and admiration for tribal elders and the former Kiowa way of life are common. Combining place, myth, history, and personal experiences, Momaday's works capture many of the essential elements of what it means to be a Kiowa because these elements are interrelated and combined through the shared geographic, social, and historical Kiowa community (Schnell 1994:88–91). As Schnell (1994:85) writes,

> the most important aspect of a homeland is its ability to instill a sense of identity in a people, and this ability is not reducible to a handful of mapable features. The Kiowa homeland is much more than a clustering of tipis, arbors, and churches. It is a place where individual strands of meaning . . . are combined and subsumed as part of a greater web of Kiowa identity

Furthermore, it is these "synthesizing forces which give the entire region a vitality for the Kiowa people, making it the home of Kiowa identity."

Despite Momaday's winning the Pulitzer Prize with *House Made of Dawn,* putting the contemporary Kiowa homeland and Kiowa geography on the map with *The Way To Rainy Mountain,* and enjoying a successful academic career, his status in the community is debated. While his accomplishments are acknowledged, skeptics point out that he has lived most of his life outside the community, has never returned permanently, and doesn't speak Kiowa, which Momaday readily acknowledges himself (Woodard 1989). However, his regular visits for the Gourd Clan ceremonials and Rainy Mountain Church services and his recent efforts to develop a cultural and historical center match if not exceed the efforts of some Kiowa residing outside the home community and thus reflect the importance of the Kiowa homeland to Kiowa living outside it.

That Momaday can repeatedly return to this homeland and write in such an emotionally moving way speaks to his ability to mentally transport one's concept of a homeland to other locales. This style also shows his ability to record and convey this sense of homeland to modern and future generations, for which the vitality of the traditional Kiowa language is close to passing. Although some cultural practices are clearly fading and some elders fear that Kiowa culture is dying out, the renewed emphasis on Indian ethnicity will facilitate the maintenance of some body of Indian cultural forms. These cultural forms in turn will undoubtedly provide the means for maintaining a distinct Indian and Kiowa identity in the future. It is a reciprocal relationship. Because only a few Kiowa today are fluent speakers, many tribal members leave the home community for jobs, and more and more Kiowa are being raised outside the homeland, the significance of Momaday's works is likely to increase with time (Schnell 1994:91).

As Shanley (1998:138) notes of Native American authors such as N. Scott Momaday, D'Arcy McNickle, James Welch, Leslie Marmom Silko, Ray Young Bear, Louise Erdrich, Simon Ortiz, and others, "Many of the writings by American Indians make place, particularly homeland, a primary theme, something more than setting." This attachment to homeland is also appearing in other genres of Native American writing (see Velie 1991), including recent works by Kiowa authors that, while concerned with other, often nonfiction, topics, draw on geographic locales, historical experience, and cultural traditions associated with the Kiowa community of southwestern Oklahoma. As more Kiowa publish works focusing on their experiences in the Kiowa community, as individuals and in collaboration with scholars (Hall 1995, 2002; Hail 2000; Meadows and McKenzie 2001; Jennings 2002; Lassiter et al. 2002; Palmer 2003; Meadows and Harragarra 2007), newly discovered genres of Kiowa cultural meaning and experience are becoming available for others to examine and relate to.

Black Goose's Map of the Kiowa, Comanche, and Apache Reservation in Oklahoma Territory

PLAINS INDIAN CULTURES have left numerous forms of native paintings and drawings executed on clothing, robes, tipis and tipi liners, shields and shield covers, calendars, ledger books, religious and historical drawings, maps, and other forms that scholars may study. Although two-dimensional renderings by women tended toward abstract and geometric designs, those by men were more naturalistic, showing humans, animals, and occasionally flora and fauna in profile. Some ledger art by men was set against cartographic backgrounds depicting hills, mountains, streams, and timber groves, as well as man-made features such as trails, roads, buildings, and wagons. Although somewhat rare, these forms increased in later ledger art, especially in some Kiowa and Cheyenne works at Fort Marion.[1] And although renderings of flora in hide paintings are extremely rare, Silverhorn sometimes drew trees and hills in calendars and scenes of the Sun Dance that he created (Merrill et al. 1997:92, 207, 209). Native drawings of geographic features are distinguished from other types of drawings by their attention to territory rather than individual features such as a hill or a river.

Many excellent works in a growing body of literature on Native American cartography have appeared over the past twenty-five years.[2] Although no precontact artifacts have been reliably identified as maps, their early presence leads scholars to believe that they existed prior to Anglo contact, and while several hundred references to their presence exist, the number of extant maps and the body of literature on them is relatively small in comparison (Lewis 1998:14). Native maps are recorded for every major region of North America. Although most extant native maps date to the nineteenth century, Lewis (1980) provides examples ranging from 1540 to 1869. De Vorsey (1978) and Harley (1992) demonstrate that nearly every major North American explorer from Columbus to the late nineteenth-century explorers used cartographic information or maps obtained from Native Americans. These documents have numerous uses for anthropologists, archaeologists, historians, and geographers (Lewis 1980:18). American Indians drew maps for a variety of purposes: to illustrate and enhance oral accounts of noteworthy events; for astronomy and religion (Pawnee); to record travel routes, villages, and related information; as messages to report successful hunting (Passamaquoddy); to leave travel directions for others (Upper Mississippi Valley, Great Lakes); to serve as mnemonic devices in recounting migration routes and tribal and religious histories (Southern Ojibway); as evidence in land disputes with neighboring tribes (Iowa); to instruct outgoing war parties heading into new or distant areas (Comanche); for legal defense of territory (Lewis ed. 1998:94–96); to record intercolonial competition; and in land use projects (Inuit) (De Vorsey 1978; Lewis 1979, 1980; Lewis ed. 1998:19–22, 96).

Indian-made maps also often reflect the current political situation between Indian nations and between Indian and non-Indian groups (De Vorsey 1978:75–76; Brody 1982). Early white trappers, traders, explorers, and military personnel regularly sought information on interior lands from their present locales, travel routes, and inhabitants, and commonly noted the accuracy of native-drawn maps. As geographic works produced by natives familiar with these areas, such maps held obvious value in terms of competition in the fur trade. In the nineteenth century, soldiers, missionaries, scientists, and government officials began replacing fur traders as scholars and collectors of Indian cartography (Lewis 1980).

Previous publications on Indian maps often limited their scope to examples from Plains Indians.[3] Ewers (1977, 1997a, 1997b) discussed the value of using native drawings and maps in studying Plains cultures. Whereas several maps credited to northern Plains groups exist, there are few examples from southern Plains groups, especially the Kiowa, Comanche, and Plains Apache.[4]

Edwin Denig (1930:605), a trader along the upper Missouri River from the 1830s to the 1850s, noted the tendency of older Indians to illustrate their oral accounts of travels, combat, and other events by "drawing maps on the ground, on bark with charcoal, or on paper if they can get it." Native maps were inscribed, painted, modeled, and carved in or on skin, bone, stone, wood, living trees, mats, birch bark scrolls kept in medicine bundles, and possibly in rock art. Maps were often made of more ephemeral materials, including soil, silt, snow, wood ash, sticks, stones, corn kernels, or combinations of these materials, indicating they were intended only for immediate use for instruction and not for long-term reference. Natives were usually concerned with the information itself rather than with the maps as artifacts or with preserving them. Thus, native-drawn maps were "transitory illustrations for the oral documents" and "pictures of experience" more than cartographic records of finite geography (Warhus 1997:3).

Most extant maps made by Indians were created in response to the request of a European (Warhus 1997:58; Harley 1992). The concept of making a map as an item of material culture to preserve information and periodically reuse it was rare except for migrational and religious oriented maps. Consequently, there was little native emphasis on preserving maps, and because non-Indians were concerned more with information than with the maps themselves, most tended to transfer the information to maps of their own style, thereby making transcripts rather than preserving the originals (Lewis 1979:29, 32). Thus, most early maps were collected for use, while later maps were collected out of ethnographic and academic curiosity. Although Europeans have described Indian maps and their use since the early 1500s, a scholarly interest did not develop until the late 1700s. In America this interest was most prevalent from 1819 to 1911, then, after a lengthy hiatus, resumed after 1970. In addition, Lewis believes that not all types of Indian maps have yet been recognized (Lewis ed. 1998:11, 35–64).

Native maps were also used to familiarize members of a party with the principal landmarks of distant territory before a raid or warfare venture. Several accounts of ephemeral maps are recorded, including Comanche and Naishan Dene (Kiowa-Apache) examples. Dodge (1882:552–553) recorded one such account in the 1850s from Pedro Espinosa, a Mexican scout and guide who had been captured by the Comanche around 1820 at around the age of nine and lived nineteen years among them:

> When the youngsters wished to go on a raid into a country unknown
> to them, it was customary for the older men to assemble the boys for
> instruction days before the time that was fixed for starting.
>   All being seated in a circle, a bundle of sticks was produced,
> marked with notches to represent the days. Commencing with
> the stick with one notch, an old man drew on the ground with his
> finger, a rude map illustrating the journey of the first day. The rivers,
> streams, hills, valleys, ravines, hidden waterholes, were all indicated
> with reference to prominent and carefully described landmarks.
> When this was thoroughly understood, the stick representing the
> next day's march was illustrated in the same way, and so on to the
> end.

Espinosa told Dodge of a party of young men and boys, the oldest not over the age of nineteen, and none of whom had ever been to Mexico, making a raid from Brady's Creek in Texas as far as the city of Monterrey, Mexico, a trip of approximately 1,000 miles, solely from the information represented on the sticks, which they had committed to memory. In 1820, a Kiowa-Apache in what is now southeastern Colorado drew a map of a saline deposit in the sand for geologist Edwin James (1822–1823:80–81). Lieutenant Amiel Weeks Whipple (1855, 1856) reports that similar maps were drawn by Yuma, Paiute, and Tigua Indians during his survey for a potential railroad route to the Pacific.[5] These and other examples suggest the widespread presence and use of such maps.

Ewers (1977, 1997b) identified several basic characteristics of Plains Indian maps that are typical of most nonprofessional maps in general. They were drawn to a scale based on travel per day and not solely on linear distance; they included what the cartographer considered important to the subject at hand and thus did not show every geographic detail; and they reflected the visual nature of plains geography, with mountains indicated for purposes of bearing taking and orientation, and not all formations represented.[6] Although referencing rock art, Lewis (1984:92) similarly noted some of the most salient characteristics of maps drawn by preliterate peoples that also apply to other forms of maps: "Such maps are always constructed topologically; that is they do not conserve true distance or true direction. Likewise, they never consistently represent the relative physical magnitudes of topographical features; culturally significant but topographically inconspicuous features are prominently presented and vice versa." Thus, virtually all Indian maps are based on topological (with little concern for precise geometric depictions of distance, area, or shape) rather than Euclidian (precise geometrical) principles (Lewis 1980:15). As with most Plains Indian picture writing, the events portrayed were considered far more important than the physical environs (Warhus 1997:186).[7]

Although scholars often emphasize the topological nature of Indian maps and their lack of precise accuracy when compared with modern maps, there are exceptions.[8] Lewis (1979:29) noted that "The cartographic component . . . along the route, was perfectly intelligible to those with a knowledge of the area but variable scale, stereotyped representations of features and disregard for direction resulted in patterns quite unlike those on a modern topographic map." Firsthand experience was valued more than a map and symbols, and Indian maps generally lacked a framing or border mechanism found on European maps (Belyea 1998:141–142, 148). Belyea (1992) notes that Amerindian maps, as is typical of most informally drawn maps, are best understood as just that—maps drawn by and intended for use by Indians familiar with the ecological and cultural makeup of a given region—and should not be construed in terms of western European cartographic conventions. Like all cartography, Indian mapping often did not represent geographical knowledge in absolute terms, but was instead conventional and culture specific (Rhonda 1987; see also Belyea 1992:267; Wood 1992). As Warhus (1997:35) writes, "Distance, direction, and orientation were part of traditional knowledge. They were part of one's 'mental map,' and a graphic system was not needed to express them." Scholars who miss this point miss the larger cultural and political significance of Indian maps.

Many early accounts noted that Plains Indian maps often contained an enormous spatial range of geographic knowledge held by individuals in these cultures (Ewers 1977, 1997b:186). Chief Ackomokki (Blackfoot) drew a map encompassing an area larger than 200,000 square miles for trader Peter Fidler in 1800–1801 (Warhus 1997:2). Big Eagle's (Comanche) 1839 map spanned nearly the entire southern plains and northern Mexican territory (Ewers 1997b:186). Despite some directional inaccuracy of streams, the 1825 map drawn by Gero-Schunu-Wy-Ha (Oto) covered approximately a third of a million square miles of the northern and central plains. The "I. Taylor 1801" or "Indian Chart Rocky Mountains" map of 1801 depicts the lakes and rivers from Hudson Bay west to the Canadian Rockies and from Lake Athabasca south to the Great Plains of Alberta, Saskatchewan, and the Dakotas—an area of more than one million square miles (Lewis 1984:99–100, 103–104). Mooney's 1898 list of Kiowa place names indicated a broad knowledge of geography, ranging from Montana and the Dakotas well into Mexico and from the Rockies to the major streams of the eastern plains.[9]

Ewers (1977) notes two primary discrepancies in Plains Indian maps: the orientation of watercourses and mountain masses often is not correct, and Indian maps tended to become less accurate with increasing distance from the maker's home. Although these shortcomings are typical of nonprofessional maps in general, such maps were nevertheless extremely useful for an individual or party traveling in a distant region. With no need for absolute direction and scale, shapes and patterns of features could be distorted to some degree (Lewis 1984:104).

Black Goose

Chál-kǫ́-gái (Black Goose) was born in 1844 to Audle-ko-ety (Ául-kǫ́-ét-jè or Big Black Hair) and Pau-gei-to (Vǎu-gà-jǎu-ą̀ or Pursuing Them Along a River) and was enrolled at the Kiowa-Comanche-Apache Agency as Chaddle-kaung-ky. Sometime in the late 1800s he acquired the given name of John. He was a full brother to Black Turtle, Mam-me-da-ty, who received the name Cûi-fá-gàui or Lone Wolf in 1874, Ho-va-kah, and Ta-ne-quoot. They made up a large and influential Kiowa family from the western part of the Kiowa, Comanche, and Apache (KCA) Reservation. Black Goose was of the last generation of Kiowa to fully experience the pre-reservation equestrian lifestyle. Although he was first listed in the 1881 tribal census as Chaddle-kaunky or Black Crane (KTC 1881:333), Black Goose appears to be the correct translation of the name.[10] During the late 1880s and the 1890s, Black Goose resided in his brother Lone Wolf's camp between the forks of Elk Creek, just south of present-day Hobart, in Kiowa County, Oklahoma. Black Goose died early in 1900 (Hagan 1976:248), as he does not appear on the June 1900 census (KTC 1895, 1899, 1900), and as Agent James F. Randlett nominated Apeahtone on May 7, 1900, to replace Chaddlekaungky as Judge, who was by then deceased.

The Jerome Agreement and Allotment

Throughout the mid-1800s the Kiowa homeland centered on the area of present-day western Oklahoma, western Kansas, the Texas and Oklahoma Panhandle, and the adjacent portions of New Mexico and Colorado. In 1867 the Kiowa signed the Medicine Lodge Treaty, which confined them to the KCA Reservation in the southwestern corner of Indian Territory between the present-day Washita and Red rivers from 1867 to 1901. Although the Kiowa continued to range far beyond this area, in 1875 they were forced to surrender, cease military opposition, and formally accept permanent residence within the reservation boundaries (see Map 3).

Law enforcement soon became a problem, as the Kiowa had no formal police or court system. Indians were being taken off the reservation and tried in Texas for crimes committed by or against them in Indian Territory (later Oklahoma Territory), and few if any Kiowa spoke fluent English at this time. The complex American legal system was difficult for Indians to navigate and was seen as a highly inequitable system that left Indians at the mercy of a foreign court and culture. The Court of Indian Offenses and the Indian Police were soon introduced to address this situation. Authorized by the secretary of the interior from 1883 to 1901, the Court of Indian Offenses involved a number of court systems ranging from agents acting as justices of the peace, to agent-selected judges, to elected officials. In May 1888, Special Agent E. E. White appointed Quanah Parker (Comanche), Jim Tehuacana or Towakanie Jim (Wichita), and Lone Wolf (Kiowa) judges. After the court first met that September, other Kiowa objected, as Lone Wolf was now both their tribal chief and judge. By February 1889 Black

Goose, then serving as an agency policeman, had replaced his brother Lone Wolf as judge (Hagan 1966:130).[11]

Most Anglos felt that Indians, despite being forced to give up most of their original lands and settle on small reservations, still retained too much land and were not using it "appropriately," according to middle-class Euroamerican agrarian standards. In the 1880s, pressure to acquire additional lands for Anglo settlement and to accelerate the process of assimilating Indians into the mainstream Anglo lifestyle led to new legislation to acquire their lands. For the southern Plains tribes, Article 12 of the 1867 Medicine Lodge Treaty stated that any future land cessions required the consent of at least three-fourths of the adult male Indians. In 1892 the Cherokee Commission met with the Kiowa, Comanche, and Apache to persuade them to sign the Jerome Agreement. This stipulated that all tribal members would receive a 160-acre allotment of their selection to be held in trust by the government for twenty-five years, whereupon it would be given to the individual owner as a fee simple title. All excess or nonallotted land was to be sold by the government at $1.25 per acre. The government also agreed to pay $2 million, to draw 5 percent interest annually in the U.S. Treasury.

Although the commission believed it had secured sufficient signatures to pass and implement the agreement, subject to congressional approval, by late October 1892 only 456 adult members of the total population of 2,786 members of the three tribes had signed the Jerome Agreement (Levy 2001:918). As evidence of false translation, false signatures, and illegal coercion were proved, many Kiowa began to change their minds. When Lieutenant Colonel James F. Randlett was appointed agent at the KCA Reservation in 1899, he anticipated a highly divided community but instead found a widespread united body against the Jerome Agreement, and noted that to open the reservation at that time would be a "calamity" (Clark 1994:51)

Settlers and their advocates began encouraging congressional ratification of the Jerome Agreement as early as 1892. When the agreement was presented to the U.S. Senate for ratification in 1899, the number of signatures obtained was less that the required quorum, as the secretary of the interior pointed out. Although the Kiowa and their lobbyists managed to delay the act for eight years, Congress finally ratified the Jerome Agreement in June 1900, forcing allotment upon the KCA. Soon thereafter Lone Wolf filed a bill of equity on the grounds that the Jerome Agreement, with signatures obtained through fraud and misrepresentation, had violated the articles of the 1867 Medicine Lodge Treaty. The ensuing case, *Lonewolf v. Hitchcock*, was decided by the U.S. Supreme Court in 1903, which found in favor of the U.S. government (Price 1973:425–427; Clark 1994). "The opinion of the court was that (1) the Indian had only the right of occupancy but that the fee was in the United States; (2) Indian occupancy could be interfered with or determined by the government; (3) the propriety of such action toward the Indian was not open to inquiry in the courts" (Levy 2001:918). The principle of plenary power, namely, that Congress can make and break its own treaties, laws, and decisions when it chooses to, was firmly set regarding Indian law. Consequently, *Lonewolf v. Hitchcock* is "one of the most cited cases in all of federal-Indian law" (Clark 1994:97).

Ironically, the case became moot in respect to the Kiowa protecting their land, as allotment was forced on them in August 1901, while the Supreme Court case was not decided until January 1903. Most Kiowa took their allotments in Caddo and Kiowa counties, with a few in Comanche and Grady counties. Beginning on August 6, 1901, two-thirds of the original KCA Reservation of 2,968,893 acres was opened to non-Indian settlement, resulting in 443,338 acres allotted to 2,759 members of the three tribes and a reserve of 551,680 acres as common use pasture known as the Big Pasture. By 1906 only 17 percent of the reservation lands remained in KCA control.

As two of the staunchest Kiowa opponents against the implementation of the Jerome Agreement of 1892, Lone Wolf and Black Goose sought to prevent the forcing of allotment upon the KCA Reservation. Black Goose's testimony—"We want our land [left] as it is"—succinctly reflected his and the group's stance on the issue (Clark 1994:35). As Indians continued to be asked to produce maps for Europeans and observed how they used them, they soon came to realize that maps were a powerful image and a means to define and assert place, identity, and ownership of land. Some accounts suggest that Indians may have begun to use maps as a means to try to define territory in their relations with non-Indians (Warhus 1997:4–5, 43).

The Black Goose Map

The map of the KCA Reservation drawn by Black Goose is in the Smithsonian Institution. It contains numerous rivers, mountains, camps, and noted historical and ceremonial sites labeled with pictographic drawings. These locales are numbered on the map (see Map 4) and correspond to the accompanying list. Four images have handwritten captions. An inscription on the upper right or northeast corner, positioned to be read from the east, states "Drawn by Judge Chad-dle-Kaung-Ky for R.E.L. Daniel, Anadarko, O.T. [Oklahoma Territory]." Many Plains Indian drawings and maps, including some Kiowa examples, include name glyphs, typically a small pictograph placed above a profiled head of a person and connected by a line, that serve to identify the individual (Mallery 1886, 1893). Above this inscription on Black Goose's map is the head of a long-necked bird (92), typical of Plains Indian name glyphs used as pictographic "signatures" during this time, especially in ledger art. The associated bird's head clearly identifies Black Goose. Collection data for the map (Merrill et al. 1997:42) state ". . . W. C. Shelley, Washington, D.C. presented by W. C. Shelley, June 17, 19 — . . . ." Black Goose drew the map for use by attorneys concerning the boundaries of the reservation in the case of *U.S. v. Texas,* de Corilloco jurisdiction. An old card in the collections reads De Greer [? Greer County] (Merrill et al. 1997:42). This datum indicates that the map was made for use in the case of *U.S. v. State of Texas U.S. 1 (1896).* The lawsuit had to do with a dispute over the Adams-Onís Treaty of 1819 in which both the United States and the state of Texas claimed ownership of some 1.5 million acres in what was then operating as Greer County, Texas, largely as a result of confusion over the precise locations of the 100th meridian and the two forks of the Red River. On March 16, 1896, the U.S. Supreme Court found in favor of the United States. Greer County, Texas, was then assigned to Oklahoma Territory on May 4, 1896. Following Oklahoma statehood in 1907, the county was divided to form Greer, Harmon, Jackson, and Beckham counties (Goins and Goble 2006:129).

Although Black Goose is known to have testified in the case (*U.S. v. State of Texas,* U.S. I Vol. II:652, 1896; Foreman 1937:67), why he drew the map and the context of his participation are not fully understood, as Greer County bordered but was outside the KCA Reservation. The Kiowa had no legal claim to the area of Greer County following the 1867 Medicine Lodge Treaty, and whereas *United States v. State of Texas* (1896) was over state and federal jurisdiction and boundaries, the later case of *Lonewolf v. Hitchcock* (1903) focused on treaty rights and congressional plenary power. In addition, the case files are missing from the Greer County courthouse and may have been taken for use by the lawyers. Legal scholar Blue Clark states that he knows of no maps involved in *Lonewolf v. Hitchcock* court opinions, and there is no evidence of any maps in the files of attorney William Springer, who helped appeal the case, in the Chicago Historical Society, the Library of Congress, or the National Archives.[12]

As the map was drawn for R.E.L. Daniel of Oklahoma Territory (formed on May 2, 1890), and Black Goose died in early 1900, it was inferably drawn during the 1890s. A letter from Mr. Robert Daniel to John P. Harrington in the National Anthropological Archives provides a more precise date of manufacture: "Some years ago I presented to Mr. W. C. Shelley, Attorney for the K & C [Kiowa and Comanche] about 1895–1896, a picture map of

Identification of Sites Numbered on Black Goose's Map

Site No. Modern Anglo Name Translation of Kiowa Name

Streams
1. Red River Big Sand River
2. Washita River Tipi Pole Cutting River
3. Salt Fork, Red River Star Girls Tree River
4. North Fork, Red River Sand Mountain River

5. Cache Creek (East Fork) Soldier Creek
6. Medicine Creek Medicine Bluff Creek
7. Cache Creek (West Fork) Wild Horse/ Mustang [Quahadi] Creek, a.k.a. Quanah's Creek

8. Deep Red Creek Snake Creek
9. Sweetwater Creek Maggot Creek
10. Elk Creek Elk/Pecan/ Side Dish Creek
11. Little Elk Creek Hawk Creek

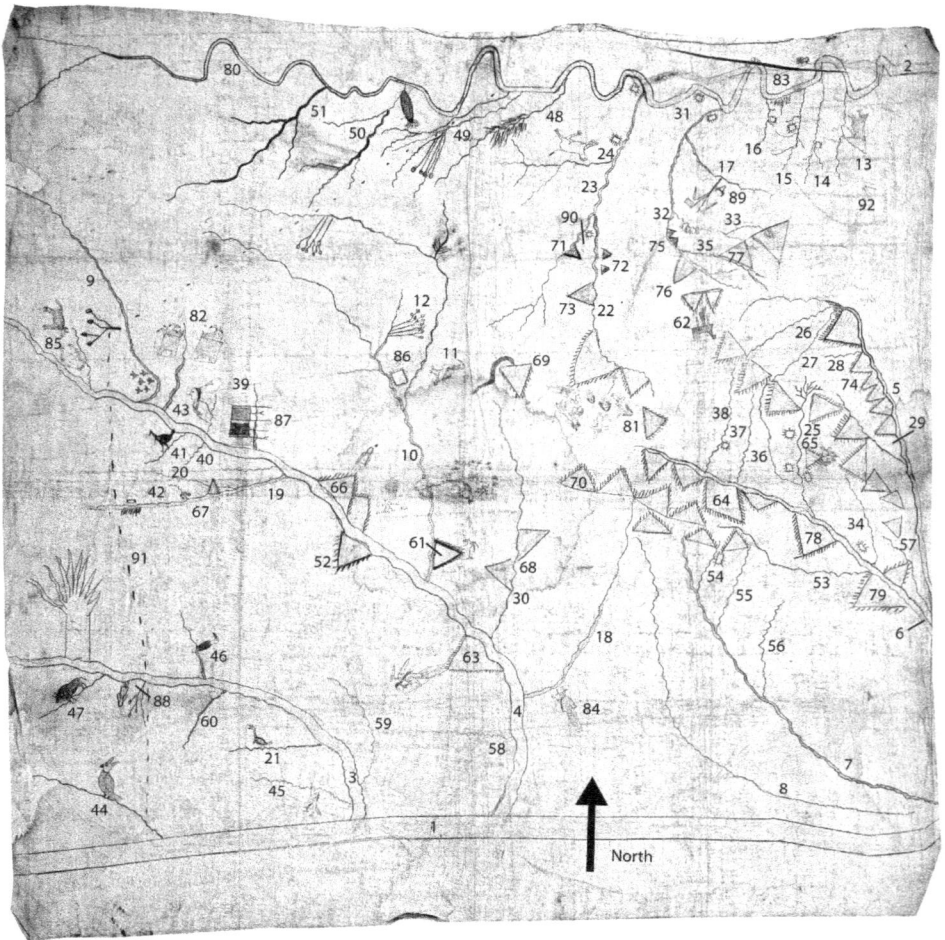

Map 4. Chaddle-Kaung-Ky Map or Black Goose's map. National Anthropological Archives, Washington, D.C. Map numbered by Jim Coombs, maps librarian, Missouri State University.

12. Trail Creek Tall Tree Creek
13. Hog Creek Hog Creek
14. Unnamed Soldier Creek
15. Gawkey (Gokey) Creek Gawkey (Ten) Creek
16. Cedar Creek Cedar Creek
17. Unnamed Unknown (East Fork, Stinking Creek)
18. Otter Creek Beaver Creek
19. Elm Fork Red River Salt River
20. Hay Stack Creek Unknown
21. Turkey Creek (Jackson Co., TX) Turkey Creek
22. Sugar Creek Pebble Creek
23. Rainy Mountain Creek Muddy/Boggy Creek
24. Little Rainy Mountain Creek Prairie Dog Eating Creek
25. Canyon Creek Timber Gap Creek
26. Tahoe Creek Unknown
27. Mission Creek Unknown
28. Chandler Creek Garden Creek
29. Lime Creek Unknown
30. Owl Creek Unknown
31. Stinking Creek Vomit Spring Creek
32. Saddle Mountain Creek Saddle Mountain Creek?
33. Unnamed Unknown
34. Jackson Creek Unknown
35. Pecan Creek Unknown
36. Tributary of Canyon Creek Unknown
37. Jimmy Creek Owl's Head/Jimmy Creek
38. Frizzie Head Creek Bushy Hair/Frizzlehead Creek
39. ? Starvation Creek Creek Where They Killed the Cheyenne
40. Sand Creek (Beckham Co., TX) Unknown
41. Turkey Creek (Beckham Co., TX) Turkey Creek
42. ? Deer Creek Unknown
43. ? Buffalo Creek Unknown
44. Buck Creek Mythical Owl Idol's Creek
45. Gypsum Creek Unknown
46. ? Bear Creek Unknown
47. ? Sand Creek (Collingsworth Co., TX) Unknown
48. Oak Creek Oak/Strong Handle Wood Creek
49. ? Cavalry Creek Unknown
50. Unknown Unknown
51. Unknown Unknown
52. Byrd Mountain Unknown
53. Medicine Creek Unknown
54. ? Post Oak Creek Unknown
55. ? West Cache Creek (head) Unknown
56. ? Pecan Creek Unknown
57. ? Ketch Creek Unknown
58. Stinking Creek (Jackson Co., OK) Unknown
59. Bitter Creek Unknown
60. ? Lake Hall [Creek] Unknown

Landforms
61. Goat Mountain Goat Mountain
62. Saddle Mountain Saddle Mountain
63. Navajo Mountain Navajo Mountain
64. Mount Sheridan Mountain That Is Looking Up/Lifting Its Chin
65. Prickly Pear Mountain Prickly Pear Mountain
66. Original Wichita Mountain Wichita Mountains
67. Haystack Mountain Part of End of the Mountains
68. Twin Mountains Unknown
69. Blue Mountain Unknown
70. Baker Peak Unknown
71. Rainy Mountain Rainy Hill/Knoll
72. Unknown Unknown
73. Unap Mountain Unap Mountain
74. Slick Hills Unknown
75. Unknown Zodaltone Mountain
76. Longhorn Mountain Longhorn Mountain
77. Unknown Bally Mountain
78. Mount Scott Big/Great Mountain
79. Mount Hinds Unknown
80. Antelope Hills Buck Antelope Hills

Datable Historical Sites and Name Glyph

81. Cutthroat Gap (1833)
82. Sun Dance Sites (1869–1870)
83. Sun Dance Where They Left the Poles Standing (1890), northeast of Carnegie, Caddo County, Oklahoma
84. Camp Radziminski (1858–1859) in Jackson and Tillman counties, Oklahoma
85. Fort Elliott (1875–1890), Wheeler County, Texas
86. Chief Lone Wolf's Camp (labeled) (1880–1920s) Kiowa County, Oklahoma
87. In The Middle's Camp (summer 1888)
88. Star Girls Tree
89. Buffalo Tree
90. Rainy Mountain School/ Boake's Trading Post, 1893
91. Texas–Oklahoma Territory line, 1890
92. Name glyph and signature of Chaddle-Kaungy-Ky, ca. 1895

that reservation, made on cloth, by Chaddle Konkey, a Kiowa Indian. Mountains and streams were designated by animals, birds, historical events, etc. instead of written words. . . ."[13] This account and an indication on the map of what appears to be Rainy Mountain School (90), built in 1893, suggest that it was made between 1893 and 1895. Although the exact date when James Mooney acquired the map is unknown—he was known for allowing some items to lie around his office for extended periods before filling out the associated acquisitions paperwork—museum records indicate that it was accessioned on December 19, 1904.

I initially suspected that the map may have also been used in the case of *Lonewolf v. Hitchcock* (Meadows 2006) as William C. Shelley, one of several Washington, D.C. lawyers representing Lone Wolf in 1901 (Clark 1994:60–61, 69), presented the map, presumably to Mooney. In addition, resistance to the Jerome Agreement was simultaneously occurring (1892–1903), the map depicts the entire reservation, the Kiowa had a larger vested interest concerning allotment than Greer County, which was outside the reservation boundary, and Lone Wolf would undoubtedly have known of his brother's map. Unfortunately the damaged accession date precludes determining whether it reached Washington, D.C., prior to the end of the Lone Wolf case, and no clear supporting data linking the use of the map in the Lone Wolf case have yet come to light.

The map consists of a square of muslin cloth measuring 90 centimeters or 35.5 inches in width, with numerous images drawn in black pencil, many of which are filled in with colored pencil. Most of the mountains are colored green. Bally Mountain (77) and the mountain to its northeast are colored tan, and a few smaller hills are colored black. The map is framed by four identifiable geographic forms: the Red River (1) to the south, the Washita River (2) to the north, the eastern edge of the Wichita Mountains to the east, and the edge of the Texas Panhandle to the west. Larger rivers (Washita, Red, the North Fork of the Red River) are colored green on the map. In between are numerous streams and mountains, many with associated pictographs for identification. These images consist of four main forms: streams, mountains and hills, residence bands or camps, and locations of notable historical events. Among the latter are religious observances, episodes of intertribal warfare, incidents involving Anglo military forces, and subsistence activities. Many of the finer details in the pictographs (human, flora and fauna, material culture) and the four handwritten labels must be viewed with magnification.

Meandering lines on the map represent streams. Primary, secondary, and tertiary streams are distinguished by the width and number of lines used to depict them: primary streams (rivers) by two parallel lines, secondary streams (creeks) by two parallel lines of a narrower width, and tertiary streams (intermittent streams and small tributaries) by single lines. Streams more than a few miles long increase in volume and size, as reflected proportionately in their length and width. Although a few smaller streams such as Long Horn Creek and Buzzard Creek appear to be absent, all major streams of the region are depicted, and there is considerable accuracy in the details of their primary forks, tributaries, and course with respect to length, width, direction, and major bends. Mountains are represented by various-sized triangles but are distinguished by the presence or absence of timber, indicated by stubble-like lines on their two upright sides. Linear rows of these triangles represent the Slick Hills (74), the main body of the Wichita Range, several individual and small clusters of mountains in the Wichita Range, and the Quartz Mountains.

The use of pictographic symbols to label locations is well established in Plains Indian cartography (Fredlund et al. 1996:10). Lone Wolf's camp (86) is identified by a small square with short radiating stubble-like lines and an associated label reading "Chief Lone Wolf's Camp." Similar symbols across the map correlate with areas where many Kiowa resided during the reservation period and later took allotments near one another. Many of these concentrations continue as contemporary Kiowa communities. Lone Wolf's camp is indicated by the largest camp symbol on the map, perhaps reflecting political influence rather than total population. Some of these glyphs correlate with sites where prominent individuals (Stumbling Bear, Ahpeahtone, Sitapatah, Lone Wolf) established their homes prior to allotment. Although these glyphs may indicate some of the first Euroamerican-style homes built for ten tribal leaders in 1877, the label "Chief Lone Wolf's Camp" suggests that they are probably intended to represent reservation bands associated with a prominent leader residing in that vicinity. Notable historical events are represented by pictographic images of people, battles, Sun Dance Lodges, and other symbols associated with specific locales. Beyond a geographically distinctive focus, these depictions refer to specific well-known events in Kiowa tribal history that date from 1833 to 1893.

Identification and Interpretation of Specific Sites

The principle of upstreaming, or the direct historical approach in archaeology, can be usefully applied to interpreting this map. I began with the most recognizable geographic and datable historical features, then used these to identify others and their related cultural and historical significance. Because the occasion for making the map and the area it represents are known, most of the map is relatively easy to interpret. Overall, the map is both extremely thorough and accurate. A total of ninety-two locations, including streams and tributary branches, fifty-three mountains and hills, fourteen camps, fourteen locales of notable historical events (some associated with the identifiable mountains, streams, or other locales), and Black Goose's name glyph and signature are depicted. At least forty-two locations are associated with pictographs and thus inferably identifiable. Four locales include handwritten labels in pencil and in English: "Navajo Mt." (63), "Goat Mt." (61) "Original Wichita Mts." (66), and "Chief Lone Wolf's Camp" (86). These locales aid in identifying others.

The "Original Wichita Mts." are also identified by the depiction of an Indian man wearing an Anglo-style jacket, an erect eagle feather, tattoos over his lower face and chin, and standing above a cluster of three mountains. The Wichita were known to have adapted Anglo clothing earlier than many of the surrounding tribes. Wichita men commonly had short lines tattooed on their chin and from the corners of their mouth, and one of the Kiowa names for them (Thố-cút-gàu or "Marked," i.e., "Tattooed Faces") comes from their predilection for facial tattoos. The Kiowa originally called only a small portion of the present-day Wichita Mountains by that name, which this map indicates as the cluster around Stewart Mountain, Soldier's Peak, and probably adjacent King Mountain.[14] The mountain on the south side of the river (52) is probably Byrd Mountain. This locale correlates with the historic Wichita Camp near Devil's Canyon visited by the U.S. dragoons and depicted by George Catlin in 1834 (Nye 1937:10). Today the entire range from Lawton, Oklahoma, westward is collectively called the Wichita Mountains. Known as "Mountain That Is Looking Up" or "Mountain That Is Lifting Its Chin" by the Kiowa, Mount Sheridan (64) is distinguished from the other mountains by its rectangular shape and a prominent uplifting point, similar to pictographs used to represent other named bluffs in Kiowa calendars (Mooney 1898:275–276).

Other locales can be identified by combining Kiowa historical sources (Mooney 1898; Nye 1937), sources on military history, U.S. Geological Survey 7.5-minute topographic maps, which provide a precise record of all existing geographic forms for comparison, and my own research in Kiowa ethnogeography. Because numerous Kiowa pictographic calendars are available for the years from 1832 to 1941, the rich Kiowa ethnographic record can be placed in chronological order. Consequently, most of the locales on the map can be identified, correlated with multiple independent sources, and in many cases linked to precisely dated historical events. Several streams and mountains with associated pictographs correlate with the exact location and name still used by the Kiowa, such as a hog for Hog Creek (13), a hawk for Hawk Creek (11), a red-colored saddle above Saddle

Mountain (62), a yellow-green prickly pear atop a mountain for Prickly Pear Mountain (65), and a prairie dog for Prairie Dog Eating Creek (24).

Noted Historical Events

Several historical events can be identified by viewing their location and associated pictographs in relation to other sites. Several of the sites demarcated on the map involve intertribal events. One image shows a headless torso, three decapitated heads, and an intact corpse strewn around a male warrior in the act of decapitating a standing Kiowa woman whom he holds by the hair (81). Blood graphically streams from the victims. This scene depicts the Osage massacre of some 150 Kiowa in 1833 at what became known as Cut Throat Mountain. The Osage man wears a roach or crest hairstyle and an erect eagle feather. The major adjacent mountains are also accurately depicted.

An Indian male wearing a quiver and holding a bow and arrow in his hand marks Navajo Mountain (63), named by the Kiowa after discovering a member of this tribe watching them from this locale. The Navajo is identified by the style of his red face paint and his red hair tie that holds his hair in a single bundle. Hairstyles are a common means of indicating tribal affiliation in Plains Indian pictography (Mallery 1886, 1893).[15] The image of an Indian man located two streams below the junction of the North Fork of the Red River and Sweetwater Creek (39) matches precisely the location of where the Kiowa killed a party of forty-eight Cheyenne Bow String Society members in 1837 (Mooney 1898:271–272, 419). This individual has braided hair, a bone whistle on a necklace, and has been shot with an arrow, indicating his demise. In the southwestern portion of the map is a man wearing a long breechclout and holding a rifle upward (45). Blue-colored smoke from the gun's barrel indicates that it is being fired into the air and may denote a warfare context.

Religious Activities

Several images depict religious activities. Images of two Sun Dance lodges (82), colored green to represent their attached foliage, correlate with the locations of the 1869 and 1870 ceremonies along the North Fork of the Red River near the junction of Sweetwater Creek (Mooney 1898:326–327). On the east-central branch of Stinking Creek is a bison skull near a tree with attached offerings (89). Although lacking a Kiowa or English name, its image and location accord with an account of a Kiowa offering site recorded by Hugh L. Scott from Iseeo in the 1890s called Buffalo Tree:

Out on the big flat east of Vomit Creek and east of Man Who Stands in the Middle is a place . . . that is a Buffalo Tree. One year the Sun Dance was made below Poor Buffalo's on the Washita in the big bend opposite the high pointed bluff and they set out to kill the buffalo for the Sun Dance and they killed the buffalo there. And some time afterwards a woman had a dream in which she saw a buffalo who told her to come out on that flat and when she saw some bones there they would be his. And when she woke up she went there where the dream told her and there was a mesquite tree growing among the bones of the Sun Dance buffalo. That is the buffalo's spirit and the Kiowa make presents to it sometimes.[16]

Under magnification a tail feather of a mature golden eagle can be seen suspended from the west side, along with a rectangular blue cloth or flag and what may be a cloth strip and an offering.

On the North Fork of the Red River is a small tributary stream associated with the image of a half-red, half-blue or -black blanket with attached decorations (87). At first glance one might think it represents the attempt by Retained His Name A Long Time (Jǎudèkáu), who took the name Bison Bull Emerging or Coming Out (Páutépjè), to bring back the bison in the summer of 1882 in the large bend on the Washita River between present-day Carnegie and Mountain View, Oklahoma, in which he used a large red blanket trimmed with appended eagle feathers (Mooney 1898:349–350; Nye 1937:263–266; Marriott 1945:142–154). The location of this image probably represents the messianic movement of Paingya (Vǎuigài or In The Middle), a former disciple and successor of Bison Bull Coming Out, who attempted to restore the land and bison and eradicate the whites. In The Middle established his camp on upper Elk Creek near Lone Wolf's camp, where he received many blankets and horses as gifts from adherents (Mooney 1898:367–357; Nye 1937:268–270).[17] As Bison Bull Coming Out's successor, In The Middle may have adopted his use of the decorated blanket in his rituals. Although not accurately reflected in this map, the distance between the North Fork of the Red River and upper Elk Creek in this area ranges from nine to twelve miles.

Just as in translating personal names, the context—the basis or reference behind a name—is essential in understanding and translating place names as well. The stream in the southwestern corner of the map is identified with a short-eared owl (44), which refers not to the bird but to a man whose medicine came from a mythical form of this animal. The Kiowa called this stream Ájéqǐjévǎu (Mythical Owl Idol's River). Ájé is a type of medicine owl in Kiowa lore, and the stream was named for a man named

Ájéqî, who carried such an idol in a shoulder pouch and who died there. This stream is present-day Buck Creek, which joins the Red River in Jackson County, Oklahoma (Mooney 1898:392).[18]

On the Salt Fork of the Red River is the image of a woman in a dress beside a small tree (88), which probably represents a Star Girls ceremony that was once held there. Mooney (1898:398) reports the stream was called Star Girls' Tree River "from a noted tree formerly there, which grew from the sprouting of a twig driven into the ground to support the 'medicine' on occasion of a ceremonial sacrifice performed by the mother of Stumbling Bear. . . . The tree was about 30 miles up the creek. . . ." This would be in the vicinity of Mangum, Oklahoma.

Several camps, among them Lone Wolf's camp (86), can be tentatively associated with known Kiowa groups. Many members of this area took their allotments just south of present-day Hobart in the forks of Elk Creek. The camp at the base of Prickly Pear Mountain (65) is most likely that of Stumbling Bear. The camp near the mouth of Jackson Creek (34) is located near the present-day Mount Scott Kiowa Church and probably represents those Kiowa who took allotments near Meers. The two camps on the west side of Canyon Creek (25) are probably those of other families associated with the Meers area. The next camp west of these is probably that of Frizzlehead, who resided along what was recently named Frizzie Head Creek (38) between Meers and Saddle Mountain. Other bands along Soldier, Gawkey, Cedar, and Rainy Mountain creeks are still reflected in the concentrations of allotments in these areas. The two camps on the east and west sides of the mouth of Stinking Creek (31) probably represent Ahpeahtone's and Afraid of Bear's camps, respectively. Two camps near the mouth of Rainy Mountain Creek (23) represent Kiowa bands in that area, one of which was probably Big Tree's camp. The camp on the south side of the mountains (near 54) probably represents Quanah Parker's camp along West Cache Creek.

ANGLO INTERACTIONS

Other images depict interactions with Anglos. An armed soldier in a blue uniform represents Camp Radziminski (84) along Otter Creek, an army camp from September 23, 1858, to December 6, 1859. It was originally located on the left bank of Otter Creek near the present-day town of Tipton, but it was moved several miles upstream in November 1858, then moved again to the east or right bank of Otter Creek in March 1859, four miles northwest of present-day Mountain Park (Frazer 1965:122–123). This image appears to represent the final camp location.

Along the western edge of the map is a vertical dotted line (91) running north to south and then turning northeast until meeting the Washita River (2). Oriented with adjacent streams and landmarks, the vertical portion of this line clearly marks the Texas–Indian Territory, later the Texas–Oklahoma Territory, border.[19] While this may appear to be the western edge of the KCA Reservation, perhaps in an attempt to claim Greer County, the locations of Mythical Owl Idol's Creek (44) and In The Middle's Camp (87) confirm this line as the Texas–Oklahoma Territory border. The diagonal extension of the line represents the top of the reservation boundary as it continues to the Washita River northwest of present-day Rainy Mountain Creek and Mountain View. In reality, the actual reservation line ran from a point on the Washita River due west until meeting the North Fork of the Red River. Altered directions are not unusual, as some native-drawn maps are extremely accurate in terms of scale and direction in some parts and less so in others, and maps are known to have been modified to include adjacent areas (Lewis 1980:15).[20] As the Washita River formed the northern border of the reservation and the map, the area to the northwest of the reservation boundary has been significantly compressed to facilitate its inclusion on the map.

Just west of the Texas–Oklahoma Territory border and north of the North Fork of the Red River is a young bison bull drawn beside a wooden corral indicated by two horizontal rows of linear rails held up by crossed vertical X-shaped posts (85). This image appears on the west side of a small tributary of the North Fork of the Red River just west of Sweetwater Creek. Located at the eastern edge of Texas, this probably represents Fort Elliott, which operated from 1875 to 1890. Commercial bison hunting in Kansas occurred from 1872 to 1881. Late in the summer of 1873 the Mooar outfit, led by J. Wright and John W. Mooar, established the first of several bison-hunting camps on the South Canadian River over the next few years. A stockaded outpost known as Adobe Walls was established as a headquarters for hunters along the Canadian. After a large force of Indians was fended off on June 27, 1874, the post was abandoned.

When the southern Plains tribes were confined to reservations in Indian Territory in 1875, Anglo bison hunters swarmed into northwest Texas, systematically slaughtering the southern herd from 1874 to 1878, until ranchers saved the last few bison. Then operating in the panhandle, General Miles recommended that an army post be established to keep Plains tribes in Indian Territory and to protect the cattle trails to Fort Dodge, Kansas. While awaiting orders from the War Department, a temporary post was established on February 3, 1875, on the north side of the North Fork of the Red River and was called "Cantonment North Fork of the Red

River." On June 5 of that year "it was moved to a point 27 miles west of Indian Territory and about thirty miles south of the Canadian River near the headwaters of Sweetwater Creek" (Crimmins 1947:5). Located on the east side of Sweetwater Creek, the area is reported to have had a large bison wallow. Although hunting parties occasionally visited the post, no Indians were permanently residing in the immediate vicinity of the post (Crimmins 1947:6–7). In 1876, Charles Rath established Rath's Trail 1.25 miles southeast of the post, along which he established Rath's Trading Post, also known by the names of Rath, Rath City, Camp Reynolds, and Hidetown, by which it was best known. It later became Mobeetie, in Wheeler County, Texas. This trail continued south and served as the route along which thousands of hides were hauled to the railhead at Dodge City (Pool 1975:118).[21] Located west of Sweetwater Creek, this pictograph may be a composite image intended to represent the original cantonment, the later Fort Elliott, and Hidetown, as the two later sites were on the east side of the creek near present-day Mobeetie. I have been unable to find any other locale that this image might represent.[22]

Other images reflect some of the negative impacts resulting from Anglo contact, especially the reduction in the bison herds. By the mid-1870s the southern Plains herds had been reduced to such an extent that some years a bison hide could not be acquired for the center pole for the Sun Dance, a situation that in turn led to two messianic movements to restore the bison and the old way of life (Mooney 1898:349–350, 356–357). The prairie dog (24) depicted on the west fork of Rainy Mountain Creek references an incident in the 1870s when a nearly starving band of Kiowa were forced to kill and eat numerous prairie dogs along this stream. Alice Marriott recorded an account of this incident in 1935 from Mrs. Tsatoke, who was born in 1867: "Prairie dogs were eaten; there is a creek named Prairie-Dog-Eating-Creek. After a heavy rain, ditches were dug and the water allowed to flood the holes and drown the dogs out. The men caught them and killed them by striking their heads against the ground."[23] On the south side of the Washita River a circle of small erect posts with a taller central pole (83) represents the "Sun Dance When They Left the Poles Standing." While building the lodge for the 1890 ceremony, news of troops dispatched from Fort Sill to stop the ceremony caused the tribal encampment to disperse, leaving the partially constructed lodge standing.[24]

OTHER LOCALES

Other identifiable images include a large tree (10) on present-day Elk Creek. This large tree probably represents a pecan, as the Kiowa call the stream Pecan Creek, and because its central and eastern branches are clearly and correctly identified as Tall Tree and Hawk Creeks by their respective associated images of a cluster of tall timber (12) and a hawk (11). The large tree on the Salt Fork of the Red River in the southwestern corner of the map may be Big Tree Creek, named for a cottonwood that formerly grew on the east bank and was so large that seven men were required to span its girth. Mooney (1898:392) reported this creek as a tributary of the Elm Fork of the Red River in Greer County, possibly Valley Creek.

Several streams on the map have pictographic labels for which no Kiowa names are known, especially on the western and southwestern portions of the present-day North Fork and Salt Fork of the Red River. These images are important because they imply that many more Kiowa place names were once known, even if only on a local band level. Through migration, confinement to a reservation, and allotment, the Kiowa have gradually lost most place names for sites outside the old reservation in southwestern Oklahoma. The association of the red-colored snake (69) with present-day Blue Mountain is unknown. One could easily assume that the creek with a black-and-white bald eagle (46) might be called Bald Eagle Creek. However, the basis of the stream's name—its cartographic purpose or context— is unknown, and the reference could be to an eagle, a behavioral habit of the species, a person's name, or something else.

Although most prominent geographic locales are shown on the map and can be identified from their associated pictographs, certain aspects are noticeably absent. Foremost, the map clearly reflects the post-Medicine Lodge Treaty reservation, located between the Washita and Red rivers and stretching from the eastern edge of the Wichita Mountains to a north-south line along the Texas state line. Other locales for which the Kiowa have place names in the adjacent parts of northwestern Oklahoma and Texas are not represented on the map. The map also emphasizes native designations, omitting many of the then largest existing non-Indian entities. As of 1898, five mission schools, three government boarding schools, a government day school, and other government buildings were all established on the reservation. Fort Sill (1869), the Kiowa Agency at Anadarko (1879), and various Christian churches and missions such as Methvin (1890) and St. Patrick's (1892) near Anadarko and Elk Creek (1893) are all absent. A rectangular image with a single line through its middle (90) on the northeastern side of Rainy Mountain (71) is probably Rainy Mountain Boarding School, or possibly Boake's Trading Post, the first incarnation of which was adjacent to the school. A faint but similarly unknown image is located on the south side of what appears to be Lime Creek (29).

As on Lean Wolf's Hidatsa map (Warhus 1997:188), Black Goose depicted many noted historical events but omitted most of the Kiowa's troubles, such as the attack on the Indian agency and their confinement at Fort Sill in 1874–1875, as well as diseases, killings, and other Anglo-induced problems. While the last attempted Sun Dance of 1890 is depicted, the two primary locations of the Kiowa Ghost Dance camps are not. Because only a few Ghost Dances (1890, 1894, 1895) had been held by the time this map was made (ca. 1895), it may not have yet been viewed as a firmly established event meriting representation on the map. The map appears to focus on presenting the Kiowa's lengthy occupation and use of the region, reinforcing a concept of Kiowa ownership and perhaps symbolically representing their preference not to have an Anglo presence in the region.

While the camps of the Kiowa, and possibly the Apache, are clearly marked, most of the area inhabited by the Comanche has no images denoting residence camps or stream names. The map also appears to emphasize those Kiowa residing in the western part of the reservation, especially Lone Wolf's camp, of which Black Goose was a member. There are more pictographic labels for streams and mountains in the western part of the reservation than in the eastern region, and several streams and sites of noted historical events in the western portion of the map are located outside the reservation boundary. Black Goose was undoubtedly more familiar with this part of the reservation than with others. Nevertheless, this map is an outstanding representation of the KCA Reservation by an individual who had spent much of his life in the area and was intimately familiar with the overall geographic, demographic, and historical makeup of the region.

ACCURACY AND STYLE

Although the Black Goose Map is fairly accurate in terms of scale and direction, some inaccuracies should be noted. Most notably, the Washita River, which bends sharply to the north-northwest at Mountain View, is presented here as continuing in a more east-west direction. Consequently, all upper tributary streams above this point are also inaccurate in terms of location and direction, probably owing to the constraints of the square piece of muslin on which the map was drawn. Although both the Washita River and the Red River have many bends, the Red River is essentially shown as following a straight course across the bottom of the map. The emphasis away from this portion of the map suggests it is a convention employed to serve as a frame for the map. Similar geographic distortions reflecting the imposition of a rectangular paper on Indian cartographers are known (Lewis 1984:97, 100, 1998:45). The area inside the reservation was clearly emphasized over the area outside it. The tributaries of Stinking Creek are presented in a more east-west direction than their true southeast-northwest courses. The absence of Kiowa communities around present-day Hog Creek (13), Saddle Mountain (62), and Stecker, Oklahoma, which were well established by 1885, may reflect an omission or occasional camp mobility prior to allotment.

The Black Goose Map differs from northern Plains Indian maps in its style of presentation. Maps drawn by Poor Wolf (Hidatsa) in 1880 or 1881 and one drawn by an Assiniboine in 1853 (Ewers 1977:36, 41) are rendered in a rather rudimentary and stick-image fashion compared with other drawings of war deeds from the same time and by the same artists and others.[25] Black Goose's map more closely resembles the southern Plains style of ledger-book imagery of the late 1860s and is similar to but more realistic and with more attention to detail than other northern Plains Indian maps such as Crazy Mule's map (Fredlund et al. 1996). This may be due to differences in each artist's drawing skills and in the purpose for drawing the map, as those previously mentioned were intended to show travel routes, whereas Black Goose's map is clearly intended to represent long-term demographic and cultural affiliation within the reservation area. Poor Wolf also provided a very detailed realistic drawing (Ewers 1977:39), and there are northern Plains Indian maps of equal skill and detail. Scholars should perhaps begin to look at different types of maps for their style and content, such as warfare accounts, travel, and demography.

Several images of Indians in distinct dress and hairstyles—Wichita (66), Navajo (63), Osage (81), Cheyenne (39)—a uniformed non-Indian soldier (84), Sun Dance Lodges (82–83), a horse saddle (62), and various animals are drawn in ledger and not stick figure fashion. Several animals are also drawn in realistic two-dimensional detail: an owl (44), goat (61), hog (13), hawk (11), bald eagle (46), snake (69), prairie dog (24), two turkeys (21, 41), and two bison (47, 85). These images exhibit great detail, such as the saddle, stirrups and belt on the saddle at Saddle Mountain, the prominent snout and curly tail on the hog at Hog Creek, the detailed plumage and ears of the long-eared owl on Mythical Owl Idol's Creek, the horns and beard on the goat on Goat Mountain, the fork-tongued and striped snake associated with Blue Mountain, the distinct profile of the prairie dog, and the distinct coat and beard on the adult bison bull, in contrast to the younger bison near the corral. Black Goose also distinguished the trees he drew: while those on Little Elk (Hawk) Creek (11) have more rounded tops, those on Trail (Tall Tree) Creek have more pointed tops (12), perhaps indicative of their species.

The form and meaning of some images are presently unrecognizable.

Clusters of possible grass or smaller flora are seen along the tributary of Little Elk Creek (11), near the head of the Elm Fork of the Red River (19), and along portions of Stinking (31), Oak (48), and other (49–50) creeks. Two locations along the Elm Fork of the Red River depict a single round object and a cluster of small oval objects, perhaps prominent rock outcrops. These images do not resemble those with attached loops depicting fortifications, breastworks, and enemy killed, as are found in other Plains Indian drawings and maps (Howard 1979:63; Fredlund et al. 1996:16). The cluster of six small four-pointed items near the mouth of Sweetwater Creek (9) resembles a formation of birds in flight. On the south side of the Washita River is a black podlike image with a green tuft on the top which has a very faint red arrow drawn through it (50). These images undoubtedly held some cultural significance, perhaps marking a resource location or the site of some noteworthy event, but their meaning is presently unknown. Although most of the images are clearly linked to locales and events known tribally, others may represent events that held importance on personal, family, or residence band levels, similar to how Kiowa pictographic calendars changed from tribal to more community-based events in the 1890s.

The map also appears to have been an ongoing labor, as there is evidence of several changes or corrections in the form of erased and in some instances moved or redrawn images. The Washita River (2) from east of Hog Creek to present-day Mountain View was originally drawn in a fairly straight line, like the Red River, then erased and redrawn to include numerous bends. In other locations clusters of flora were erased, as seen along a western tributary of the creek with the podlike object near its mouth and on the tributary of Little Elk Creek (11), where a cluster of taller objects, probably trees, was erased and replaced with a cluster of smaller items with larger leaves. Whether these "corrections" were made by Black Goose or through consultation with tribal members, they suggest an effort to ensure a more accurate depiction of the area. Finally, Black Goose appeared to be making a concession to or syncretic blend of native-style ledger art, Indian and Anglo cartographic conventions, and Euroamerican-styled bordered maps.

CONCLUSION

The Black Goose map, a rare example of a Kiowa and southern Plains Indian map, is an important contribution to a growing number of Plains and American Indian maps. In its geographic focus on the KCA Reservation in Indian and later Oklahoma Territory (1867–1901), it is a regionally important map. The combination of stylized geographic features, realistic place name glyphs, and pictographic representations of noted historical events, aided by recourse to ethnographic and historic sources on Kiowa culture, modern geological survey maps, and ongoing field research, permits a considerable amount of identification and interpretation. Although of a more recent manufacture, this map is similar to other Plains Indian maps and reflects the late-1800s style of ledger drawing. While a considerable portion of the map is fairly accurate in terms of general locations, it emphasizes topology (the representation of conceptual relationships of places to one another) rather than Euclidian topography (scale representations of distances as measured in spatial units, rather than in travel time or other criteria) (Lewis 1980, 1984; Belyea 1992; Fredlund et al. 1996:25). Other distinctly Indian characteristics include the extensive use of pictographs to identify kinds of places (camps, Sun Dance encampments, mountains) and place names (Saddle Mountain, Hog Creek), the use of more than one directional scale or orientation on a single map (Lewis 1980), and the inclusion of events as well as places (Peterson 1968, 1971; Lewis 1979:26, 1980:11; Ewers 1977; Fredlund et al. 1996:25). Although many Plains maps focus on a specific event or time, the Black Goose's map spans at least sixty years, with many images containing extraneous detail. And although the map reflects some Euroamerican influences in the use of muslin and colored pencils and in a shift from hide to ledger-book-style drawing, it retains native pictography for recording information.

As Boone (1998:118–121) demonstrates, location is generally the most important element of story in map-based historical accounts, and people, action, and dates are inserted secondarily into the locations. A defined spatial construction facilitates the recording of varied events through time and across space at different locales. The Aztec Mapa Siguenza shows events occurring over 100 years and involving two types of space, geographic and sequential. The sequential aspect of Aztec history is scattered across the map, conforming not only to space but also to time, as reflected in the lengthy wandering narratives of migration and conquest. This approach allowed the Aztecs to differentiate what was important in each half of the migration story. The first half focuses on a migration through a generally amorphous area, with the correct sequence of towns marked along the route but with little attention to exact locations. In the second half, the exact location of Tenochtitlan and towns in the Valley of Mexico and their relation to the Aztec rise to power are presented in real space. This combination is also found in other Aztec and Mixtec cartographic histories (Boone 1998:121–122). Although a degree of temporal ambiguity is common to all cartographic histories, owing to an emphasis on location over chronology, Aztec cartographic histories define identifiable territories and then place history into the territory (Boone 1998:123).

While the Mapa Siguenza is half in real space and half in sequential space, Black Goose's map appears to be all in real space. First, it does not display a sequential order, as is found in Kiowa pictographic calendars of the same period. Second, only the post-1867 reservation, a small range around its borders, and events that occurred in this area from 1833 to 1895 (that we recognize) are presented. Thus it is fixed in both real space and real time. But as Barbara Belyea (1998:141) notes, "Amerindian maps rely not on fixed positions in space but on a pattern of interconnected lines. . . . Intersection rather than spacing determines the cartographic design." As she suggests, maps become more understandable when a principle of linear coherence is sought. Through the rich record provided by Kiowa pictographic calendars, the linear coherence of many of the events depicted and their role in demonstrating a lengthy residence in the area become datable and thus recognizable.

Similar to other Plains Indian maps, this map reflects an exceptional grasp of geography, even by Western standards (Fredlund et al. 1996:25). When carefully analyzed, Black Goose's map conveys several distinct features of Kiowa life in the 1890s. First, the map has a distinct geographic and historical focus. Spatially it focuses on the post-1867 KCA Reservation area. Temporally it contains identifiable events from 1833 (Cut Throat Gap Massacre) to 1893 (Rainy Mountain Indian Boarding School). Although not every event of this period is depicted, many of the major events are, demonstrating how geography, history, and meaning are inexorably linked in Indian place-making.

Second, and more important than the identification of and cultural and historical correlation of many of the locales depicted, is the map's seemingly political purpose, to demonstrate the Kiowa's historical longevity and thus rights to their land, in this case probably to ensure that U.S. and Texas claims did not intrude into the KCA Reservation. Because all maps "embody the interests of their authors, indeed are the interests of their authors in map form," all maps are subjective to some degree (Wood 1992:71). Several works discuss the use of maps as political tools. Brody (1982) demonstrates how the Beaver Indians use maps to substantiate current land claims in Canada. Brody spent eighteen months in the 1970s helping the Beaver Indians create maps that showed their varied uses of the land. His work shows that Native American peoples have repeatedly made and asserted the legitimacy of their own maps, while contesting European maps and strategies of mapping. Wood (1992:10–11, 20–21) discusses the various intricacies, interests, and patterns of the uses of maps—that is, how maps work—including their uses in establishing political boundaries and ownership. Other scholars (Harley 1992:527–528, 533n7; Belyea 1998) provide evidence for ideological transformation in native mapmaking in Mesoamerica and Peru whereby natives began "making maps in support of their claims to land from which they had been dispossessed." John Herlihy's work at the University of Kansas provides similar examples from Central America. Goldman (1999:24–25) describes how Fort Marion ledger book art and the novel *Green Grass, Running Water* both serve as maps that challenge European modes of mapmaking. Because ledger books served as repositories for native wisdom and tradition, they not only helped to record personal and public history but were linked to native forms of defiance, self-assertion, and resistance.[26]

Like Aztec *lienzos*, large painted community maps (Boone 1998:124), the Black Goose map conveys the identity of the Kiowa community in both space and time while demonstrating that Kiowa occupation and use of this land preceded the 1867 Medicine Lodge Treaty by at least thirty-four years. Boone (1998:123–131) shows that Aztec maps or cartographic histories serve as "community charters" by presenting how land is encountered, claimed, defined, held, organized, and presented in relation to their identity. In providing a survey of the community, political affiliation, social hierarchies, and the community's economic sense of itself—who they are and where they are—these histories establish a geographic and political definition of a community. Although the 1867 Medicine Lodge Treaty provisions imposed the geographic definition of the Kiowa community by establishing a reservation, and the role of Black Goose's map as a community charter is not explicit, its role is implicit in the context of the time of its origin and in the demarcation of Kiowa from non-Kiowa lands. The map also demonstrates other aspects of Aztec *lienzos* (see Boone 1998:131). Action and location of events are emphasized over dates or participants involved, individual bands are clearly associated with different parts of the reservation, Lone Wolf's camp is depicted as larger and inferably more influential than others, and selective historical information is inserted geographically and temporally to establish ownership to this area, much as a community charter would.

Because the date and to some degree the context of the Black Goose Map are known—the context inferably to show the borders of the KCA Reservation in reference to *United States v. State of Texas* (1896), and possibly as a conscious or unconscious means to resist implementation of the Dawes Act—the map can be examined for signs indicating resistance to further American dispossession through the process of allotment. The wide range of locales and themes depicted on the map reflects a lengthy cultural and historical occupancy. This symbolic and political stance is further indicated through what has been omitted from the map. The map emphasizes a Kiowa rather than a Euroamerican presence: almost all non-Indian institutions are absent. Black Goose's testimony that "We want our land [left] as it is" (Clark 1994:35) clarifies the context of the map's making: to demonstrate the Kiowa occupancy, use of, and cultural and political attachment to the land, and existing resistance to forced allotment. As Harley (1992:527) observes for other native maps, a change in context from depicting territorial control to territorial resistance did not result in fundamental changes in the format and style of mapping.

Rundstrom (1990:166) notes that Inuit mapping represents an important form of environmental mimicry. Similar to imitating animals in hunting techniques, mapmaking "simultaneously reflected and reinforced other aspects of the culture." Mapmaking symbolized and reified the group's attachment to the land while serving as an important form of intracultural and intercultural communication with others. In drawing this map, Black Goose demonstrated his environmental, historical, and cultural knowledge and ties to the area, which are communicated both intraculturally (Kiowa efforts to prevent allotment) and interculturally (Black Goose's choice of presenting Kiowa over Euroamerican use of the land). As Rundstrom (1990:166) notes for the Inuit, "Mapping as an innately intracultural action thus became a significant means of constructing accurate map artifacts for intercultural communication."

Third, the map depicts a Kiowa viewpoint of the KCA Reservation in the 1890s. Fourth, it presents a somewhat Elk Creek-centric format. Whereas Lone Wolf's camp was actually near the western edge of the KCA Reservation, it is shown near the middle of the map, with the map clearly oriented from that point outward as a member of that camp drew it. Yet this view also conveys a degree of temporal accuracy in that this area was closest to Greer County, the focus of *United States v. State of Texas* (1896), and held much of the strongest opposition to the Jerome Commission from Lone Wolf, Black Goose, and others that led to *Lonewolf v. Hitchcock* (1903). Thus the map symbolically depicts to some degree an accurate view of not only the demographic but also the political power base and climate of the time. Fifth, this map reflects an ethnographic focus and function: even as it concentrates on the Kiowa residing along Elk Creek, it depicts other Kiowa settlements and major historical and geographic locales that held meaning for all Kiowa. Thus, although some maps are more biographical in nature, focusing on the activities of an individual, this map is more ethnographic, focusing on Kiowa culture and history in general.

As Plains Indian life changed in the late 1800s, so too did mapmaking.

Animal skin, which had become scarce, gave way to cloth, muslin, canvas, and paper, while crayons and pencils replaced paint. Several maps from the late 1800s reflect a shift in focus from traditional territories and warfare to new activities such as government scout service (Fredlund 1996), massacre sites (Moore 1987:160), travel (Peterson 1971:224; Lewis 1984:97), and even commissioned work (Thiessen et al. 1979).

Black Goose's map differs from the more numerous northern Plains maps in some aspects of how place is depicted. Although most maps cover a much larger area, such as the Iowa Non-Chi-Ning-Ga's map, the Oto Geor-Schunu-Wy-Ha's map, Miguel's Southern Plains-West Gulf Coast map (Lewis 1984:94, 99, 101), the Northern Cheyenne Crazy Mule's maps of the Upper Missouri Country and the Missouri Basin (Fredlund et al. 1996:6–7), and the Mandan Sitting Rabbit's map (Thiessen et al 1979), Black Goose's map provides more detail within a smaller area, similar to but still more detailed than Amos Bad Heart Bull's (Oglala Sioux) map (Lewis 1984:96). In terms of flora, fauna, and humans, Black Goose's map is much more realistic than the Assiniboine and Poor Wolf maps (Ewers 1977:41). With respect to artistic style, elements of Sitting Rabbit's map (Thiessen et al. 1979) and Crazy Mule's maps (Fredlund et al 1996:6–7) are similar to and sometimes surpass the quality of Black Goose's map, but those maps have less variety and fewer images overall. Finally, Black Goose's map exhibits a wider range and greater depth of cultural and historical events.

Though *United States v. State of Texas* (1896) did not affect KCA lands and the *Lonewolf v. Hitchcock* (1903) case was lost, the Black Goose Map is a rare example of a Kiowa and southern Plains Indian ledger-style map, with overall geographic and historical accuracy. This map thus is a unique example of southern Plains Indian enthnographic and pictographic art and affords a glimpse into the changing face of the KCA Reservation in the late nineteenth century just prior to forced allotment, a watershed event that changed the Kiowa, Comanche, and Apache communities forever. The very nature of the map and the changes it represents also correlate with Black Goose's life (c. 1844–1899), which spanned southern plains pre-reservation experiences in warfare and equestrian life to service as an Indian Court of Offences Judge and political advocacy during the reservation period.

The Black Goose Map uses many pictographic notations, more than many other maps studied thus far. In using single pictographs to represent narratives that would otherwise require pages of written text or lengthy oral accounts, these images compress oral traditions and the invisibility of spatial and temporal knowledge in a form that can be learned, read, associated with specific locales, and thus visualized. The Black Goose Map provides a compact and efficient means of conveying much of the Kiowa geographic and historic information of a portion of the post-1867 KCA Reservation. Finally, the map stands as a testimony and visual reference to the richness and depth of Plains Indian pictographic art. Set against a cartographic background, it depicts Kiowa cultural heritage, their demographic state, and their attempts to preserve their existing land base at the turn of the twentieth century.

CHAPTER 5

Contemporary Kiowa Ethnogeography

ALTHOUGH CONTEMPORARY KIOWA are most concentrated in Caddo, Kiowa, and Comanche counties of Oklahoma, many southern plains locales bear names originating in Kiowa names (see Map 5). While some are well known, others are scarcely known beyond their immediate community. They range from local place names in the Kiowa community of southwestern Oklahoma to more distant places whose names refer to the Kiowa, such as Kiowa County, Kansas; Kiowa Creek in the Texas and Oklahoma Panhandle; and the small towns of Kiowa in Colorado, Kansas, Oklahoma, and Alaska. While a large number of Kiowa place names are still viable, major changes have occurred in the geographic residence and focus of the Kiowa, the extent to which Kiowa place names are used, and the linguistic forms of the place names.

Although a few older Kiowa place names such as Zólṭǫ́ (Vomit Spring) are still commonly used, most are now heard in translated English, such as Saddle Mountain, Redstone, and Hog Creek. Other Kiowa place names reference locations and events of modern importance and have been composed in English, such as Chieftain Park and Luther Sahmont Bridge. Modern Kiowa place names reference a range of sites and occasions, including roads, hills, creeks, bridges, dance grounds, sites for singing '49 songs and drinking, businesses, churches, schools, and tribal government complexes. Appendix D lists all the modern Kiowa place names collected in this study.

Everyone in the Kiowa community knows that the Apache Wye is the intersection of Highway 9 with Highways 62 and 281 west of Anadarko, and that the "Indian Road" is the old Highway 9 between Fort Cobb and Carnegie through an area that has many Kiowa and Apache allotments.[1] Greg's Corner, named after Gregory Haumpy, and Moonlight Mile are both well-known '49 locations near Carnegie, Oklahoma, where people gather to sing '49 songs and drink after powwows. Other known '49 sites include Snake Pit, Hill X, and Skin Beach.

Gawky, Jimmy, Frizzie Head, and Two Hatchett creeks are all named after Kiowa men who lived nearby. Buzzard Creek, Crazy Hill, and Mopope Hill are still spoken of by Kiowa east of Fort Cobb, but are not marked. With the advent of the modern highway system, Big Tree's Crossing, once one of only two crossings on the lower portion of Rainy Mountain Creek, is unknown to many younger Kiowa. Yet Eagleheart Bridge on Cache Creek eleven miles south of Carnegie is still well-known and was the subject of a recent dispute over the impact of modifications on adjacent parcels of land.[2]

Kiowa dance grounds are often known by English names, such as Carnegie Park, Chieftain Park, Lone Bear's, and Mopope Hill, or, as found among neighboring tribes, by the current form of a tribal family name, as in Murrow's (Caddo), Mithlo's (Fort Sill Apache), Redbone's (Naishan Apache), or Whitewolf's or Looking Glass's (Comanche). Other once active dance grounds are often referred to only by their former Kiowa allottee's name; some examples are Whitehorse's, Kiowa Jim's (Tongkeamha), Kiowa Bill's (Maunhee), Frizzlehead's, and White Fox's.

Kiowa Christian churches are known by a variety of Anglo and angli-

Parker P. McKenzie Kiowa Elders' Center, Carnegie, Oklahoma.

Contemporary Kiowa Ethnogeography

Map 5. Map of contemporary Caddo, Comanche, and Kiowa counties, southwestern Oklahoma. Map by Jim Coombs, maps librarian, Missouri State University.

cized Kiowa personal and place names, such as Botone Church, Albert Horse Church (now Cache Creek United Methodist Church), Ware's Chapel, Cedar Creek, White Church, and Rainy Mountain Kiowa Indian Baptist Church. Many other Kiowa attended St. Patrick's Mission. Some rural community schools—most now long defunct—are Kiowa Flat and Samone School.

The Wichita Mountains, of great importance to the Kiowa in the pre-reservation era, have retained their geosacred and historical relevance into the modern age. In addition to the better-known places with Kiowa names, such as Mount Scott and Medicine Bluff, other locales commemorate individual Kiowa, such as Hunting Horse Hill and Quoetone Point. Large groups of descendants exist, some of whom still reside within view of these locales. Other named locations in the Wichita Mountain Wildlife Refuge reflect not only the pre-reservation residence of tribes (Kiowa, Comanche, Apache, Caddo, Wichita) but the relocation of many tribes to Indian Territory, as the place names Kiowa Lake, Caddo Lake, Apache Lake, Osage Lake, Pottawatomie Pond, and Arapaho Point indicate. Other refuge locales are named after native individuals, such as Wildhorse Creek, Geronimo Ridge, Quanah Creek, Quanah Mountain, and Quanah Parker Lake. Other locales in the Wichita Range include Little Bow Mountain, Long Horn Mountain, Unap Mountain, and Tepee Mountain. Harboring some of the last vestiges of native flora and fauna, a bison herd, and numerous cultural, historical, and religious sites, the Wichita Mountains continue as an important geographic island for the Kiowa and neighboring tribes. On the adjacent Fort Sill Army Base, the names of I-see-o Tank, Kiowa Hill, Medicine Bluffs, Medicine Creek, and Sitting Bear Creek are all derived from Kiowa names. Similarly, the names of several other sites on the post relate to place names used by neighboring tribes (Nye 1937:345–347).

Non-Indians have also adopted English translations of Kiowa place names. Rainy Mountain Ranch and Saddle Mountain Ranch are both large cattle ranching operations near the respective mountains. The names of Medicine Bluffs, Medicine Creek, and Elk Creek are all direct translations of their Kiowa forms. Anglos have also adopted translations, such as Lone Wolf, and English spellings of Kiowa personal names, as in the town names of Ahpeahtone, Gotebo, Komalty, and I-see-o Tank and Poolaw Hall at Fort Sill. With the recent assignment of street addresses for emergency service purposes, Rainy Mountain Kiowa Indian Baptist Church is now located on Aim-de-co Road, bearing the Kiowa name of former missionary Marietta J. Reeside.

Many current place names are translations of earlier Native American place names. Among the Kiowa, this is the case with places such as Saddle Mountain, Rainy Mountain, Longhorn Mountain, Red Stone, Rainy Mountain Creek, and Oak Creek. Euroamerican place names were also given that had no connection to the native name form and became the official name of a place today, as with Mount Scott in the Wichita Mountains and the Red River. Although younger Kiowa generally know only the English translation of the Kiowa name for many prominent landforms, the use of native-based ethnogeographic terms, either in Kiowa or English, remains an important part of family, community, and tribal identity. One Kiowa woman showed me Seven Sisters Creek on her great-grandmother's allotment, a name that was known largely within the Meers community, while Redstone Kiowa showed me Soldier Creek in their area. In contrast, names such as Longhorn Mountain, Saddle Mountain, Rainy Mountain, and Cutthroat Gap are known by nearly all Kiowa, even if they have never visited these locations.

This mixture of transliterated name forms from native languages, English translations, and Euroamerican-original names has resulted in seven kinds of contemporary place names used by the Kiowa today: (1) place names still pronounced in Kiowa used only by elders, such as Sépyáldá (Rainy Hill) or Táu-qòp (Saddle Mountain), but even now more often said in English than in Kiowa; (2) Kiowa names translated into English, such as Saddle Mountain and Elk Creek; (3) Anglo modifications of Kiowa pronunciations, such as Zodaltone and Gotebo; (4) modified Anglo pronunciations of Kiowa words combined with English words in the same name, such as Gawky Creek and Unap Mountain; (5) English-language names created by the Kiowa, such as Red Buffalo Hall, Feather Dance Road, Botone Church, and Odlepaugh Springs; (6) English-language names created by non-Kiowa, typically Euroamericans, such as Hobart, Carnegie, and Cache Creek; and (7) names from other Indian languages used in an anglicized pronunciation, such as Anadarko and Chickasha.

These patterns also show that except when traditional Kiowa place names are specifically sought in speech, English translations of Kiowa names (Long Horn Mountain, Buzzard Creek) or the use of modern American place names (Mount Scott, Washita River) have almost completely replaced the traditional use of place names in the Kiowa language. The most commonly used Kiowa place names are modern forms, such as Lone Bear Dance Ground, Red Buffalo Hall, Feather Dance Road, Botone Church, Chieftain Park, or Gotebo. Although the words are in English, these names are distinctly Kiowa and contribute to maintaining the Kiowa identity.

Kiowa Country: Identity, Homeland, Community

The Kiowa have always had a geographic region they considered their own, or Cáuidàumgà—Kiowa Country. This region has shifted with the migrations of the Kiowa over the centuries: from the northwestern plains, to the Black Hills, to the central and then southern plains, to the post-1867 Kiowa, Comanche, and Apache (KCA) Reservation in southwestern Indian Territory, between the Wichita Mountains and the Washita River, to a diminished and checkerboard land base of allotted tribal holdings, to, finally, individual allotments based largely on earlier reservation demography. The refiguring of Kiowa Country continues as contemporary Kiowa increasingly concentrate in urban centers outside the old reservation area owing to a reduced Indian-held land base, fractionalized land ownership, increasing population, and better access to services and economic opportunity in cities. Another factor in the rural to urban move has been a gradual decrease in the already limited Kiowa farming and stock-raising activity. Although farming and stock raising have generally been portrayed as less than successful, and most Indian families in the twentieth century increasingly leased their lands to Euroamerican farmers and ranchers, a number of Kiowa and neighboring Indians farmed and raised small herds of stock in the past.[3] Despite fewer Kiowa living in rural settings, most Kiowa still consider the rural areas of Kiowa allotments as the core or heart of Kiowa Country. Today, Carnegie, Oklahoma, with many Kiowa residents, the tribal complex, and a large core of traditionalists, is regarded by most Kiowa as the Kiowa capital.

Schnell (1994:36) notes that while the boundaries of the original allotment map could serve as a definition of the Kiowa homeland, any such boundary would be only an approximation. When Oklahoma tribes were given an opportunity prior to the 1990 census to delineate an area under their jurisdiction for statistical reporting (Tribal Jurisdictional Statistical Areas) that could not overlap with the area of any other tribe, the Kiowa, Comanche, Apache, and Fort Sill Apache chose to maintain a joint area. Schnell (1994:36) also points out that "If firm tribal boundaries cannot be drawn for simple statistical reporting purposes, their establishment between such vague mental constructs such as 'Kiowa Country' or 'Comanche Country' is an impossibility." Clearly, any definition of a homeland must be a holistic one that exceeds mere physical land under ownership and engages the life of a people in space and time. More prosaically, the definition must also accept shared, at least multiple, claims to the same land as "homeland" (Albers and Kay 1987). Thus, despite significant reductions in Kiowa land ownership, a rich body of ethnogeography, meaning, and symbolism continues that draws on all the regions the Kiowa have inhabited. Although the core of the Kiowa homeland has changed through time and has been both shared with and contested by other groups at times, an enduring sense of a homeland has instilled a sense of place, purpose, and identity in the Kiowa.

Like other parts of culture and geography, identity and ethnicity are fluid in that they change over time in content, quality, definition, and locale. As people migrate because of war or for economic reasons, they carry their identity with them and modify it in response to the next social and eco-logical environments they enter. Although some core ideologies and ethos remain basic and unaltered through these changes, others may be signifi-cantly altered or abandoned altogether in a relatively short period of time.[4]

Native Americans have redefined their identities through time in re-sponse to a number of geographic and cultural changes. The concept of a home or homeland is crucial to understanding the relationship between a people's geographic and sociocultural identity. Geographers have found that an exact definition of "home" can encompass an array of physical situa-tions—house, city, region, country, or planet (Schnell 1994:92).

One of the best ways to understand the makeup of Native American identity is to examine how native peoples talk about their own communi-ties. Kiowa frequently use the terms "home" and "home place" to refer to the Kiowa community and to their allotted land, respectively. Sometimes the two terms are used interchangeably in reference to particular portions of southwestern Oklahoma and their relationship to this region. This re-lationship is best viewed as comprising a number of interconnected ele-ments that extend far beyond any simple list of physical geography and symbolic landmarks. For any people, a sense of identity also entails an understanding of the group's composition, culture, community, and his-torical experiences. Factors counterposed to group integration, such as jealousy and factionalism, should also be understood, for they too play important roles in community structure and change. When these social, cultural, and historical constructs and their relationship to a geographic setting are understood, one is on the threshold of understanding a people's attachment to place and its imbrication in their sense of identity.

Humans often take things for granted when they are at hand and easily accessed, and individuals typically become acutely aware of the importance of a homeland and roots when they must leave that region. While living in Colorado, Anne Yeahquo described her feelings about the Mount Scott area of Oklahoma and the effects of moving away for work:

> I think Kiowas, maybe my generation and the previous one, have a
> deeper appreciation for the homeland because so many of them have
> had to leave it to make a better living. Our grandparents and great-
> grandparents lived and died there, without ever leaving. Once you
> live far from home you understand the importance. No matter where
> I live that is home for me.[5]

As Schnell (1994:92) states, "It is the existence of this sense among a people, more than any other factor, that is diagnostic of 'homeland.'" For

KIOWA ETHNOGEOGRAPHY

contemporary Kiowa, this sense of a homeland is currently centered on southwestern Oklahoma, particularly the northern half of the post-1867 reservation.

In her article "Rez Talk," Faye Lone-Knapp (2000:635) found that interviews with Hodenosaunee "revealed an underlying theme—the spatial base of the reservation. It is not only a land base, but also a historical and spiritual base upon which the majority of the interviewees described their identities." I would maintain that her article captures most of the core elements relating to contemporary Native American identity in general. Like other Native American tribes, the Kiowa also speak of identity in terms of residency, distinctions of here versus there (within or outside the reservation and tribal community), the focus of cultural ceremonies and traditions, a place to maintain cultural identity, collective references such as "our community" or "Kiowa Country," and a "home" or "home place" to return to from the outside world. These understandings also relate to the Kiowa edict, "Know where you come from."

Most Kiowa never lose their desire to return to the Kiowa community, either on vacations to visit and attend cultural activities or permanently after retirement. Deep emotional attachments are often involved that supersede other factors. From an economic standpoint, southwestern Oklahoma is not the richest environment for farming or stock raising, requiring more acres per unit of production than some other states. Today, virtually no Kiowa can afford to farm or raise stock, and thus most are forced to lease their land for smaller profits to non-Indian farmers and ranchers. Although some areas have considerable oil holdings, relatively few Kiowa receive significant income from oil royalties. Because the Kiowa community is still largely rural, economic development in this area is limited, although some benefits and services are provided through the tribe. The desire to return home speaks more to the importance of social and cultural familiarity, the security afforded by the Kiowa community, and an affinity for the landscape and the historical relation to that landscape than to an economic rationale.

The contemporary Kiowa live in two worlds, the Indian world and the non-Indian world. The percentage of time spent in each often correlates with the proximity to the native community, and the choice to live more in one world than the other varies greatly from one individual or family to another, based on many factors. Nevertheless, it is within the Kiowa community where Kiowa identity is principally defined and maintained, because it is there that the things that determine Kiowa identity, such as family, community, language, and culture, are found. These determinants also affect Kiowa outside the home area, for whenever they return, they are expected to adhere to the social norms of the home area in order to be welcomed and included. As Dennis Zotigh, who grew up out of state, then made a conscious decision to return to Oklahoma to live and become more active with his tribal culture, explained,

> The home area is also where the community contrasts Kiowa views with those of neighboring tribes and non-Indians. The tribal community is the focus of cultural and religious identity, whether it be references to powwows, society dances, and hand games, or cedarings, sweat lodges, Native American Church meetings, traditional doctoring, or Christian Church activities.[6]

Many criteria are involved in this social matrix, including the importance of tribal and self-identity, language, community participation, issues of blood quantum, and being "raised traditionally" or being "raised Kiowa." Although Kiowa enculturation is usually valued more than blood quantum, the latter can become of interest in cases of social conflict and politics.[7] Although less common today, being "raised Kiowa" in the past typically involved growing up in the home community and most often being raised by grandparents while the parents worked. Many of today's fluent speakers learned to speak Kiowa from their grandparents. Most Kiowa culture continues to be learned more through experience and observation than through formal instruction. This form of learning requires a core community to continue; however, individuals may relearn significant parts of their culture. It is also not uncommon for retirees to return to the community, become active in cultural events, and get refamiliarized with Kiowa traditions. As an example, a man who returned to Oklahoma after growing up out of state was inducted into the Kiowa Gourd Clan and began actively studying Kiowa cultural history and language. Several men have returned to the Kiowa community after military careers to become society or organizational leaders. One woman returned after living out of state for thirty-five years to become very active in a women's service organization and a church.[8]

In other cases community members that have not been interested or active in tribal culture during their youth may begin making a concerted effort to increase their knowledge and participation in Kiowa culture in their forties. Yet some Kiowa believe that the level of enculturation is qualitatively not the same as if one had grown up and been culturally active in the community all of one's life. While many members of a culture may leave the community temporarily or permanently, in all these scenarios, a core must be maintained by any culture to continue. For Kiowa, this cultural concentration is found only in southwestern Oklahoma, and although some cultural elements have been lost, others remain, to provide a continued sense of Kiowa identity.

Part of this continuity has to do with a group's value system. Although a generation gap is evident — elders are concerned about the conduct of the younger generations — some traditions are clearly fading. However, a core of values has remained, and today these cultural values form a stronger basis for Kiowa ethnicity than material culture forms or subsistence strategies; hence the focus of much recent symbolic anthropology on mental constructs and meaning over materialism. But what are these core values? My Kiowa consultants stressed respect for elders, knowing your kin, using appropriate kinship terms to address them, maintaining honor, not bringing shame to one's family, generosity and sharing (via benefits, giveaways at powwows, and feeding visitors), being active in the community, following protocol in rituals and personal actions, taking pride in one's culture, maintaining personal appearance and one's home neatly, and exercising responsibility toward one's relatives and others.[9] I have heard several Kiowa elders stress "knowing who you are" and "knowing where you come from" as core values of being Kiowa. Education is also stressed, but its importance varies, as some families emphasize modern academics while others want their children educated in Kiowa culture and traditions. One older man told me he did not want any of his sons to go to college because he "wanted them to remain Indians, Kiowas."[10]

The social status and reputation of one's immediate family are also important. In the pre-reservation period, social status was largely determined by the relationship of one's family's war record to a series of four graded social ranks (Mishkin 1940). In the reservation period, these classlike social status rankings became somewhat hereditary from one's ancestors and were condensed into two general status levels that carry with them a somewhat hereditary caste-like label or status. While a family's link to prominent ancestors, especially warriors, is still important and may frequently be recounted during public gatherings, contemporary factors are also important. In reality this is a rather vague body of knowledge, as no one really knows how many coups a particular ancestor had, and the remaining war stories are typically known and told only in abbreviated form with few details.[11] That an ancestor was a warrior, bandleader, or society chief and that he had a war record is what is stressed. Thus, families may promote an ancestor with few or many war honors.

A second factor is how one's family has conducted itself through time in regard to public behavior, cultural continuity, and achievement in both traditional and modern circles. Individual and family actions both affect and reflect on one another. Thus, the actions of either can help or hurt the other and in turn determine how an individual and the family are viewed, accepted, and interacted with by others in the community.

Family and community pride, efforts to achieve status, and limited resources and economic opportunity often lead to factionalism in nearly all areas of contemporary Kiowa life. Kiowa especially dislike any particular family or individual receiving recognition. In 1998, a dispute arose over the proposal to name a small county bridge over Stinking Creek SITAH PA TAH BRIDGE (AFRAID OF THE BEAR), after the last leader of the Ghost Dance, whose allotment and the site of the last Kiowa Ghost Dances are nearby. Most of those who argued against the naming were from other families, were not from the immediate community or descendants of Afraid-Of-Bears, and, as their own statements indicate, knew little about the man, and based their dissent in part on (incorrect) assumptions about the man's racial history (see Palmer 2003:89–91, 100–101). One individual incorrectly alleged that Sitapahtah, a full blood, had Mexican ancestry as a reason not to name the bridge after him, even as he failed to acknowledge his own varied non-Indian ancestry through both parents.[12] It is interesting to note that the adjacent road of which the bridge was a part was named Feather Dance Road, from the Kiowa name for the Ghost Dance. The name of this road was not disputed, probably because it was not family oriented in nature and thus did not bring greater status to any specific family. In the end, signs with both names were placed at the end of the road and on the bridge, respectively. When I photographed the signs in 2003, the sign marking each end of SITAH PA TAH BRIDGE had been shot several times and had bullet holes in its surface, while the Feather Dance Road sign a short distance down the same road was in mint condition and remained so until it was stolen in October 2006. Soon thereafter one of the bridge signs was also stolen. Although perhaps coincidental, it is nonetheless an interesting observation.

Although Kiowa understand the complexities of how and why many allotments have been sold and lost due to economic necessity, some elder Kiowa use the retention of one's allotted land or lack thereof as a criterion in differentiating the status of families. The fact that individuals or families no longer have their allotted land is mentioned as a negative attribute and is often accompanied by pejorative statements such as "losing their home place" or "having nowhere to go." Although it is well understood that many individuals have left the community out of economic necessity, there is also respect for those who have remained on their lands and within the community.

Failure to live up to these expectations may result in being chastised

Sitah Pa Tah Bridge and Feather Dance Road signs, Kiowa County, Oklahoma.

for "not acting like a Kiowa" or "not following the Kiowa way." In reference to the two lower social status rankings mentioned earlier, an individual or family might be referred to as káuàun (pitiful, pitiable) or dàufô (no good, worthless). More extreme, often stereotyped criticisms may be used. For example, one may be called an apple (red on the outside, white on the inside), a derogatory term for a sellout or a culturally assimilated person, often used to refer to some BIA employees. Individuals may be accused of acting like members of another tribe with which one's own tribe readily contrasts itself as a way of maintaining its own distinctiveness and identity. Even worse, one may be accused of acting white—the epitome of a greedy, materialistic, wasteful, excessive, and direction-less society that lives for the moment and has little respect for history, tradition, or aboriginal rights and lifeways—in effect, a representation of all that is not Indian.[13] Such accusations serve to nullify one's status as a Kiowa by implying the person has forgotten who he or she is and where he or she came from, two of the most important Kiowa core values. In other words, they forget their traditions.

As ideal values, how knowing who one is and where one came from are actually practiced varies greatly. Some individuals and families make great efforts to fulfill cultural expectations, others do not, and many variations and different circumstances are observable. This dichotomy is a basic difference between anthropological views of culture and society. I have always viewed culture as an ideal plan or blueprint, the template for how things should be or the ideal rules that members of a group adopt and are supposed to follow. Society, on the other hand, is how these rules are actually implemented and play out, which is never fully equal to any group's cultural expectations. Hence, norms and laws are tested, manipulated, broken, amended, rewritten, and so on. But as long as a body of cultural ideals exists, it forms a basis for constructing and changing social activities, thus allowing a developing sense of cultural tradition and continuity.

Ethnogeographic Place Names: Linguistic Comparisons

Only recently have comparative studies on American Indian place names been undertaken (see Afable and Beeler 1997; Thornton 1997), but only a comparative approach reveals the similarities and distinctions in American Indian ethnogeography. Using some of the major concepts found in Basso's (1996) work, I offer a brief comparison of Cibecue Apache and Kiowa ethnogeographic forms.

Structure and Use

Cibecue Apache place names are typically structured as highly descriptive sentences that richly describe the imagery of a location (Basso 1996). In contrast, Kiowa place names are only rarely complete sentences, taking the form rather of short phrases with descriptive content. In Basso's (1996:47) words, Apache place names are generally used in storytelling "as situating devices, as conventionalized verbal instruments for locating narrated events in the physical settings where the events occurred. Instead of describing these settings discursively, an Apache storyteller can simply employ their names, and Apache listeners, whether they have visited the sites or not, are able to imagine in some detail how they might appear." Some Kiowa place names are similar, such as Cutthroat Mountain; nearly every Kiowa knows the basics of what happened there in 1833. I have heard several Kiowa speak of what they "thought" it must have been like during the raid at Palo Duro Canyon in 1874. Because place names are thus spatially anchored to specific geographic locations, the descriptive pictures rendered in Apache place names become an indispensable element in how Apache tell stories (Basso 1996:47). Kiowa stories sometimes use place names for specificity, depending on whether a named place is close to the event being discussed.

Aside from specific locales such as individual mountains or springs, the most definitive Kiowa place names are those with the terminal suffix dé-ę̀, denoting "place at which" something happened. However, as only the oldest Kiowa regularly speak Kiowa, I rarely heard this form used during my fieldwork. Today Kiowa frequently use proper place names to ground stories, usually in reference to an area (Redstone), dance ground (Chieftain Park), school (Riverside), ball field (Indian Canyon), church (Ware's Chapel), or tribal office (the Kiowa Complex). Unless the event referred to occurred within the immediate location of a named locale such as Rainy Mountain, most simply refer to an English name of a location or the anglicized pronunciation of a family name, usually in reference to their allotment or "home place," such as "Tsoodle's," or "at Mopope's place." As the number of Kiowa speakers has declined, this pattern has gradually shifted to its English equivalent.

Emphasis in Use

With Cibecue Apache (Basso 1996) and Kiowa place names, geographic location and action are emphasized over temporal concerns of when the event happened. However, Kiowa stories are not always linked to specific locations, and this is especially true of the older stories, for which an exact location is no longer known. As the geographic specificity of such events wanes with time, the emphasis shifts to the content of the story. Elders often do not state where such an event occurred, focusing instead on action and the lesson (moral or cultural practice) featured in the story. When I asked elders where a story took place and they did not know, they tended to give general references, such as somewhere out on the plains, "before this part of the country opened up," or they simply expressed little concern for where it actually occurred.

Basso's (1996:12–13) consultants describe geographic place names as painting a picture of the location. As Charles Henry said, "Now they could speak about it and remember it clearly and well. Now they had a picture they could carry in their minds. You can see for yourself. It looks like its name." Reflecting on Henry's insights, Basso continues, "they make and bestow a place-name, a name describing the place itself, just as it looked a long time ago, just as it looks today . . . much is contained in Apache place-names, preserving as they do both the words of his ancestors and their graphic impressions of an unfamiliar land."

According to Basso (1996), Apaches tell stories in a way that leaves a fair amount of detail unspoken, allowing the listener to imagine the event and the characters involved, and often to draw their own conclusions. Depictions serve as bases on which to build, and those in Apache stories function to open up one's thinking, allowing listeners to travel in their own mind. Kiowa stories are similar in that key elements of the story are emphasized over temporal, and sometimes other, details, and the listeners are often left to imagine part of the account and to draw their own interpretations and conclusions from it.

Water-based place names are one of the most common forms. Because many place names are based on existing geographic features, they are often an indicator of environmental change, especially concerning water sources. Many Kiowa place names are not as descriptive as those Basso describes for the Cibecue Apache, because they are generally phrases, while Apache place names are complete sentences. However, some Kiowa place names provide highly descriptive forms as phrases or sentences that convey rich descriptive imagery of a location.

Mountain That Is Looking Up (Qópótàbǫ̀) or Mountain That Is Lifting Its Chin (Qópótàgàu) is a highly descriptive name that paints a picture in one's mind. Creek Where White Bear Brought The White Women Back (Sét-tháidètháukàuimáimàufâcâundèvàu) vividly describes White Bear's return of several Anglo female captives taken in Texas to army troops in Kansas. Sôldàum (Onion Ground) aptly describes the low-lying area north of the Wichita Mountains in Kiowa County, Oklahoma, that once boasted large quantities of wild onions, mesquite, and antelope. Although much of this area is now cultivated, remaining areas still reflect the traditional landscape that the Kiowa named it for. Other place names that paint vivid pictures in the imagination include Dǫ́igàuváudáudéę̀ (Place Where a River Is Positioned Deep Below It), Dáuálkǫ̀gàiéhòldèę̀ (Place Where Black Kettle Was Killed), Xǫ́jôigáthàdàudéę̀ (Rock House in Which They Were Contained), and Sáqàutjàuáàutàundèvãu (Creek Where the Cheyenne Were Annihilated). Even Táuqòp (Saddle Mountain) conveys the image of a mountain shaped like a saddle. As with any place name, context or cultural familiarity is essential to making the location come alive to the fullest extent in the listener's mind.

As Basso (1996:89) writes, "The capacity of Western Apache place-names to situate people's minds in historical time and space is clearly apparent when names are used to anchor traditional narratives that depict ancestral life and illustrate aspects of 'ancestral knowledge.'" He also states (1996:89), "For as persons imagine themselves standing in front of a named site, they may imagine that they are standing in their 'ancestor's tracks.'" Remembering and respecting elders, their efforts to maintain tribal culture, and what they stood for is a major part of what "being Kiowa" consists of. Reservation-based place names lead many Kiowa to think of the families residing in the immediate area and thus associated with that locale. Recent literature on the Kiowa (see Meadows 1995, 1999; Lassiter 1998; Ellis 2002; Lassiter et al. 2002) is full of oral accounts and reflections of Kiowa referencing the act of remembering their elders during discussions of allotments and a wide array of activities.

Kiowa place a great deal of emphasis on song and dance, remembering elders, and continuing the traditions they provided at the same locales. As Harry Lee Tofpi related to Clyde Ellis (2003:177) concerning dance grounds,

> God gave us these ways. He gave us lots of ways to express ourselves, to keep our ways. One of them is these dances. When I go to them, whatever they are—powwow, Gourd Dance, Black Legs, whatever— I'm right where those old people were. Singing those songs, dancing where they danced. And my children and grandchildren, they've learned these ways too, because it's good, it's powerful.

OPTIMAL VIEWING

Cibecue Apache place names are also often structured around concepts of explicitly identifying optimal positions for viewing. It is from these points of reference that a location can be viewed clearly and unmistakably in terms of what its name depicts. "To picture a site from its name, then, requires that one imagine it as if standing or sitting at a particular spot, and it is to these privileged positions, Apaches say, that the images evoked by place-names cause them to travel in their minds" (Basso 1996:89). Like mountains or cave formations, distinct features are often recognizable only from certain angles. If an individual moves a short distance in another direction, the feature is no longer recognizable. Such is the case with Buddha Mountain on the Lijiang River in Guangxi Province in southern China. As travelers ascend the river by boat, the Buddha is recognizable for only about fifteen seconds.

I have seen various geographic, animal, human, and other images pointed out on trips with Anglo-Americans, Native Americans, and in Japan and China. Cultures clearly possess relatively similar aesthetic standards when viewing such formations. The concept of optimal viewing also applies to several Kiowa sites. Medicine Bluffs and parts of Red Stone can only be seen from certain angles. Saddle Mountain most clearly reflects its name when viewed from the northwest or southeast. To look at it directly from the northeast or southwest would result in one end of the mountain obscuring the rest of the saddle. Double Mountain in Texas is recognizable only at certain angles, and from another angle appears to have three points, not two. Two Buttes in Colorado is also "limited" in recognition by the angle at which it is viewed. Mount Sheridan in the Wichita Mountains provides an excellent example of optimal viewing. The Kiowa refer to it as Mountain With Its Throat Stuck Out or Mountain That is Looking Up, which resembles a man with his face looking upward, as if lying on his back. This image is recognizable only from the east and west. The Wichita named the mountain Buffalo Bull's Face from what they perceived from another angle.[14]

From these criteria it becomes apparent that although there are major structural differences between Western Apache and Kiowa place names and in the manner and degree to which they are used, there are also several basic similarities. In terms of use, the Kiowa share a number of patterns with the Apache, including using place names in the following manner: (1) as situating devices in oral history, (2) to emphasize geographic location and action over temporal location, (3) to allow listeners to imagine the event but draw their own conclusions, (4) to anchor traditional narratives that depict ancestral life and illustrate aspects of ancestral knowledge, (5) to lead individuals to reflect on ancestors with fondness and respect, and (6) to identify locations for optimal viewing.[15]

Native American Religious Sites, Access, and Commercial Development

For centuries, sacred sites across America have been under siege from lumbering, mining, and recreation concerns, development, and more recently sociospiritual or religious activities, in particular New Age practitioners.

One of the most common contemporary problems concerns conflict between Native American religious practitioners and land-managing federal agencies, specifically issues of Indian access to and protection of traditional sacred sites for religious practices on public lands that are now owned and managed by state and federal governments (Moore 1991; Walker 1991; Forbes-Boyte 1999; Burton 2002). The definition of what constitutes a sacred site is found in Executive Order 13007, which was signed into law by President Clinton on May 24, 1996.

> "Sacred sites" means any specific, discrete, narrowly delineated location on Federal land that is identified by an Indian tribe or Indian individual determined to be an appropriately authoritative representative of an Indian religion, as sacred by virtue of its established religious significance to, or ceremonial use by, an Indian religion; provided that the tribe or appropriately authoritative representative of an Indian religion has informed the agency of the existence of such a site.

This executive order requires federal land managers to "accommodate access to and ceremonial use of Indian sacred sites by Indian religious practitioners, where such accommodation is not clearly inconsistent with law or essential agency functions," and requires managers to prevent adverse effects to the physical integrity of such sites, "subject to some caveats." This order was intended as a supplement to strengthen existing protections in the 1993 Religious Freedom Restoration Act and in the 1994 American Indian Religious Freedom Act Amendments. Although this definition and Executive Order 13007 were intended to increase protection and native access to such sites, it is based on a Euroamerican legal tradition. As such, it is inconsistent with many traditional Indian religious concepts and values associated with both belief and space, native beliefs about how sacred power is animated and exists in a landscape, and beliefs about how sacred sites are integrated, boundless, and interactive with their surrounding landscapes. Most land management agendas and decisions either ignore native land use issues and religion or give them a low priority.

Recently, there have been both positive and detrimental results in cases involving access to and development of Indian sacred sites. Some groups have been able to regain or protect certain sacred areas, such as Blue Lake (Taos Pueblo) and Mount Adams (Yakima); others have not. Because Bear Butte is a state park, the balance between multiple use policies focusing on access for public use and Native Americans' need for adequate access and privacy to engage in religious practices remains difficult for land managers.

In turn, a conflict based on differences between legal and social definitions of ownership has arisen (Forbes-Boyte 1999). Through the efforts of the University of Arizona, the Vatican, and other institutions, Mount Graham, the tallest peak in the Pinaleño Mountains, now has an astrological observatory built on it southeast of Phoenix, Arizona. Mount Graham is considered by some San Carlos Apache to be sacred (Bordewich 1996:205–239). Several other legal battles to protect sacred sites are ongoing.

Many sacred sites have been completely destroyed or altered to the point that they can no longer facilitate native religious practices. Other sites are on the threshold of those changes. A number of well-known sites, such as Devil's Tower, the Black Hills, Bear Butte, the Sweetgrass Hills, Valley of the Chiefs, and Badger–Two Medicine Area, have been the focus of political and economic changes. Often seen as symbolic artifacts of Euroamerican appropriation, they remain important religious locales to many Indian tribes, resulting in major ideological and legal battles that have in turn attracted major publicity. Many other sites remain less well known. As native peoples continue to try to reassert their religious rights, they enter a complex and highly bureaucratic system of due process that involves state and federal statutes and administrative policies.

One of the most contested grounds is access to and protection of religious sites in national parks (Keller and Turek 1998). Campbell and Foor (2004:163) have examined the case of the Big Horn Medicine Wheel, where, as in many such cases, a central issue became "weighing a value system based on inextricably associating a spiritual world and physical geography against a system that inherently separates the two." The reassertion of Indian religious rights and the accompanying need to have access and control of sacred sites often conflicts with the socioeconomic interests and cultural meanings assigned by Euroamericans to such sites. As Campbell and Foor (2004:177) note, "Sacred sites, by Euroamerican standards, are either cultural artifacts or hold a socioeconomic benefit." Because the religious observances of most Europeans and Euroamericans take place in built structures—churches, synagogues, cemeteries—there is some difficulty grasping the concept of the sacred existing in natural landscapes. They may admire a natural site for its beauty and what it can offer by way of solace or as a retreat, but they usually do not view such sites as sacred in the way they view the settings and structures in which they conduct their own religious practices.

In America, abandoned churches are often made into houses and barns or razed to make room for other buildings. Cemeteries are abandoned, lost, and even relocated to make room for highways and lakes. Indian rituals and ceremonies performed at sacred sites and aimed at promoting harmony, balance, and world order are generally outside the Euroamerican experience. In turn, when government-mandated rights for native peoples to use specific locales for religious purposes are implemented, Euroamericans, especially local non-Indians, may perceive such actions as threatening and disorienting. "Native American perceptions of the environment as a 'living entity,' with certain locations possessing a 'sacred' nature, are viewed as anti-progress and anti-capitalist. Thus the idea of a 'sacred geography' remains an alien construct for most Euroamericans. How could a natural area or site be a culturally recognized wellspring of spiritual knowledge?" (Campbell and Foor 2004:177–178). After all, you can pray anywhere, right? But, as many a developer has undoubtedly thought, "This would be the perfect place for a new strip mall!"

Euroamericans also often fail to understand that geosacred sites need significant buffer zones to ensure that practices can be held in an undisturbed or pristine area. Each culture has a concept of the appropriate circumstances for religious observances. Christian churches have designated special or sacred zones, which may be the land the church sits on or only specific parts of the building or grounds. Even though Christian churches might close their doors to limit distractions from outside, they would not try to limit access or permit highly disruptive activities. Imagine a man trying to fast and pray atop Bear Butte with dirt bikes, four-wheelers, hikers, and campers intruding on his position. Now imagine people camping out on the steps of a church, playing music, hiking through the church as they please, and revving their motorcycles in the parking lot. Churches would claim rights of private property, disturbance of the peace, and freedom of religion to stop such encroachments. Why are native peoples not extended the same rights and protections?

Outdoor services require a different set of practical considerations. Like many Shinto and Polynesian rites, religious practices held out-of-doors require a quiet and peaceful atmosphere for practice and efficacy. As Campbell and Foor (2004:178) describe for northwestern Plains groups,

> sacred landscapes, whether natural or human-made, require
> continual dialogue. Human action and speech are essential to
> communicate with the sacred beings. Through prayer, song, and oral
> evocation, those seeking "medicines" activate and connect with the
> spiritual world. The importance of religious praxis as a vehicle for
> spiritual revelation is characteristic of the majority of tribes who use
> these sacred arenas. Contemporary northwestern Plains religious
> authorities recognize these sacred sites as places of pilgrimage,
> prayer, vision questing, ritual, and ceremony to carry out that

dialogue. It is a dialogue that requires, if not demands, an animate, pure unspoiled ecology with a degree of solitude.

Non-Indians often fail to recognize that although a specific site may be the final destination for a religious practitioner, the site is not limited to the area in which activities are conducted but encompasses the surrounding landscape in what is a reciprocal and inseparable context.

BIG HORN MEDICINE WHEEL

As described by Campbell and Foor (2004), the Big Horn Medicine Wheel exemplifies the kind of conflict that can arise concerning access to and protection of Indian sacred sites now on public use land. Their findings on this subject provide a background for looking at Kiowa and other native georeligious sites.

Of 135 known medicine wheels across the plains, the Big Horn Medicine Wheel is the best known. Although Euroamericans became aware of the site in the 1880s, no archaeological investigations were undertaken until the late 1950s, when members of the Wyoming Archaeological Society discovered the presence of both prehistoric and historic remains. These included a fire hearth, chipped stone tools, leather, bone, wood, a brass bead, a perforated shell bead, various glass trade beads, and a potsherd, many of which came from within the excavated cairns. Later investigations revealed the structure was begun during the late prehistoric period and that it is a composite structure with the radials younger than the central cairn. Structural alterations through time suggest that many groups used this site for religious purposes (Campbell and Foor 2004:170–172).

Although the site cannot be directly linked to any particular tribal group, striking cultural continuities in the form of structure and ideology are found that transcend the contributions and use of different ethnic groups through time. Of architectural importance are the similarity of the wheel to social conceptions of the sacred, and the fact that many (if not all) groups that encountered it contributed in some way to the site's structure through ritual use, deposition of materials, or additions or alterations to its structure. Ethnographic data and oral history accounts from several northern Plains tribes attest to the sacred nature and importance of the site and make it clear that similar medicine wheels "served as vision quest sites, memorials to prominent leaders and events, navigational aids, ethnic boundary markers, a means of clocking astronomically important religious observances, a place to receive spiritual healing, as well as possible Sun Dance and Thirst Dance structures" (Campbell and Foor 2004:170–175).

These data demonstrate that indigenous societies not only used sites built by previous groups, they also recognized such locales and their surroundings as sacred, as sources of power, and contributed to them while incorporating these structures into their own distinct cultural traditions. In turn, as Campbell and Foor (2004:174) write, "Sacred sites like the Big Horn Medicine Wheel connect contemporary peoples with their persistent, long-standing religious traditions." In reviewing some 300 sacred sites, Walker (1988:262) noted that "all groups tend to hold sacred the boundaries between cultural life and geological zones" and that "all groups possess a body of beliefs concerning the appropriate sacred times and rituals to be performed at such sites. It has also become apparent to me that sacred sites serve to identify fundamental symbols and patterns of American Indian cultures."

Following Euroamerican discovery, the Big Horn Medicine Wheel remained a site of curiosity with little or no economic or cultural value. Although cattle ranching, logging, hunting, fishing, and other outdoor developments increased in the region, only one snowmobile route passed near the site. Not until tourism developed in the 1900s did non-Indians begin to view the site as having potential economic and cultural significance. With the Big Horn Mountains providing a scenic route to the more influential Yellowstone National Park, local communities began efforts to develop tourism. Once the unique nature of the medicine wheel was recognized, efforts to have the site designated as a national landmark began as early as 1915. Landmark status, focusing on its archeological value, was achieved in 1970 under the 1966 National Historic Preservation Act. However, only the landmark itself was protected; the surrounding area was left open to multiple forms of public use. As plans to develop modern park facilities to facilitate visitors directly around the site emerged, the context for conflict with native religious views was set. These plans remained dormant until 1989, when plans emerged to timber the nearby Elk Draw and Tillet's Hole areas. Tourism and timber sales would effectively destroy the medicine wheel as a sacred site and for native religious purposes (Campbell and Foor 2004:169–170).

Controversy focused on indigenous concerns of the sacred versus multiple-use land management policies on public lands began in 1991, when the U.S. Forest Service began identifying Traditional Cultural Property under section 106 of the National Historic Preservation Act. For six years, various federal and state agencies worked with the Medicine Wheel Coalition and the Medicine Wheel Alliance to resolve rising Indian concerns about the site and Medicine Wheel Mountain. When an agreement in the form of the Medicine Wheel Historic Preservation Plan was completed in 1996, it allowed for a 23,000-acre "area of consultation" around the site. This plan was intended to permit traditional cultural use at specified times of the year, restrict timber and grazing use, prohibit vehicular traffic to the site, develop a system to monitor adverse site impact, and extend the National Historic Landmark boundaries around it. Following the removal of the Wyoming State Historic Preservation Office from the section 106 process, owing to the termination of its Native American Affairs Program, the Mountain States Legal Foundation filed a lawsuit on February 16, 1999, on behalf of Wyoming Sawmills, Inc. Claiming that (1) protection of American Indian sacred sites violated the First Amendment clause, (2) the Medicine Wheel Historic Preservation Plan signed by the U.S. Forest Service unconstitutionally required the Forest Service "to establish and promote Native American religious practices," (3) the closing of the Horse Creek timber sales was "for the sole purpose of furthering Native American religions," and four other claims, the foundation supported the timber company's desire to harvest timber in the Medicine Wheel area (Campbell and Foor 2004:175).

The proposed protection area, amounting to more than a million acres, of which only 40 percent had harvestable timber, represented only 1 percent of the total Bighorn National Forest acreage, and only 60 percent of the proposed 1 percent to be protected had harvestable timber. The suit nevertheless continued, questioning the preservation act on several federal statutes having to do with failure to follow the "establishment clause," whereby "Congress shall make no law respecting an establishment of religion." Despite a local court upholding the Forest Service, Wyoming Sawmills Inc. appealed the decision. The ongoing case illustrates the larger picture of the continued challenge to indigenous religious concerns by non-Indian economic interests, but with indigenous resistance (Campbell and Foor 2004:176).

Events surrounding the Big Horn Medicine Wheel, the Badger–Two Medicine Area, and other sacred sites demonstrate that as long as definitions of the sacred are drawn up by government agencies, "any site deemed sacred can fall prey to religious oppression" (Campbell and Foor 2004:178). Thus, governmental power and legalities and public support can severely inhibit religious meanings and access to specific locales. As Campbell and Foor (2004:179) conclude,

> A close examination of the Big Horn Medicine Wheel issues suggests that the disputes today seldom revolve around the reality of indigenous traditional concerns or use. In reality, they center on two issues: competing land uses by different stakeholder groups, and the

question of how to establish boundaries that acknowledge traditional Native American values. Landscapes are designated to recognize that events tied to the use of the specific features are connected. These controversies point to the problems involved in weighing a value system based on inextricably associating a spiritual world and physical geography against a system that inherently separates the two.

Although Anglo appropriation of much of North America has severed tribal contacts with many sacred sites, tribes have maintained contact with some older sites while developing other, newer locales of a sacred nature. Mainstream Euroamerica clearly views land primarily as an economic commodity to be used in a productive manner according to its value system (Campbell and Foor 2004:176). That which is set aside and preserved in parks and other areas is usually of recreational, aesthetic, historical, or environmental value, but not on a sacred basis. Thus it is done so from a Euroamerican rather than a Native American value system. However, despite major differences in economics and values, we must be careful not to lose site of history, as past Native Americans clearly recognized the value of land and resources, as reflected in numerous instances of migrations, warfare, and both offensive and defensive demographic movements related to efforts at controlling valued territories for horse acquisition, bison hunting, trade routes, riverine farming areas, and other interests. Much of plains history focuses on shifting symbiosis, merger, and war related to these very resources (Albers 1993), factors which can be demonstrated in other regions as well. As Campbell and Foor (2004:177) note, "Despite the establishment of legal mandates to incorporate indigenous concerns and perspectives into public-land policy management, Euroamerica continues to interpret and view Native American religious beliefs and practices either with a degree of scorn and derision or with avid, romantic curiosity." Both views are not only misplaced and inaccurate, they miss the larger issue, that of two different views of religion, land, and their interrelationship.

Kiowa Religious Sites

Because Kiowa religious practices underwent some changes, issues of preservation and access to geographic sites for religious observances are not as problematic for the Kiowa as they are for some other tribes. Kiowa mythology is rarely tied to any specific geographic locale, and usually involves the northern plains. Most stories of origins and the Kiowa culture-hero-trickster Séndé (Saynday) fall into this form. Although the Kiowa acknowledge Devil's Tower in their history and small groups periodically visit the site, its distant location makes the issue more pressing for northern plains tribes. Although the site does hold spiritual and religious qualities for some, most Kiowa I have spoken with have indicated that their reason for visiting the site was more historical or out of curiosity than religious. With the Kiowa Sun Dance defunct and vision quests no longer being undertaken, access to many sites is no longer needed. The return of the bison into the north side of Mount Scott is one of the few mythological-historical accounts tied to a specific geographic locale that I have found.

Today, most Kiowa religious practices fall into one of six categories: (1) Native American Church meetings, (2) Christian Church services, (3) visiting tribal medicine bundles to pray and leave offerings, (4) sweat lodges, (5) individual prayer, and (6) for a few individual Kiowa, Sun Dances. Because most existing Kiowa religious practices are held on private allotments under trust status or on land protected by group organizations (Christian churches), access and protection are not a problem. And because it is largely "invisible" to the public, individual prayer also does not represent a problem as there are many places in southwestern Oklahoma that still offer solitude and a fairly pristine locale. The non-Indian owners of Longhorn Mountain accommodate Indian requests to harvest cedar, pray, and leave offerings at the site and thus represent no real impediment. Rainy Mountain remains as trust status land and can be visited by any Kiowa. Although few Kiowa live around Saddle Mountain and it is no longer used as a vision quest site, the proximity of the highway makes it easy to view, and its social and historical significance continues. With most of the Wichita Mountains in the Wichita Mountains Wildlife Reserve, public access to much of the area is available. Mount Scott has a paved road to the top, and although many Kiowa still visit it and other areas in the Wichita Mountains, I have heard no complaints regarding access.

The few Kiowa who do Sun Dance typically participate in Crow, Cheyenne, and Lakota ceremonies in their respective tribal communities and are thus beyond the scope of Kiowa tribal law. In 1997 the family of Vanessa Jennings was preparing to receive the gift of a Crow Big Lodge Ceremony or Sun Dance from members of the Crow Tribe in Montana and to hold the dance on their family allotment that July. Stiff resistance from a handful of influential Kiowa men culminated in their filing a suit against Jennings in a CFR (Code of Federal Regulations) or CIO (Court of Indian Offenses) court. Judge Phil Lujan eventually placed a restraining order against Mrs. Jennings to prevent her holding a Sun Dance on her private trust status land or contributing to any future dance in "Kiowa Country." Many Kiowa feel that Judge Lujan's decision directly contradicted the freedom of religion and personal property clauses in both the Kiowa Tribal Constitution, which is subject to Congressional approval, and the U.S. Constitution, which tribal constitutions are required to uphold. Furthermore, when a Kiowa male began holding a Sun Dance on his trust status land less than a mile from Jennings' home, no interference followed, which points to what many people feel was widespread bias associated with the case.[16]

Endangered and Potentially Endangered Kiowa Sites

Currently five Kiowa sites of historical and/or religious importance are in immediate danger of destruction, or almost gone. The first is Unap Mountain, which is currently being commercially mined for stone. At present, two-thirds of the mountain's south side is gone. The second is the kíájôi or defensive earthworks near the mouth of Rainy Mountain Creek, which is almost unrecognizable from ongoing farming. Third, the Momaday family house and arbor just east of Mountain View, which figure so prominently in the writings of N. Scott Momaday, is in stable but declining condition. This is perhaps the last intact Kiowa arbor dating to the 1930s. Momaday plans to restore the structures and develop them into a heritage center, but has been delayed by obtaining consent from all heirs to the property.

The fourth site encompasses much of the Wichita Mountains, and the associated problems are of much greater size and significance. Numerous large metal wind turbines for the production of electric power have been installed at the newly developed Blue Canyon II Wind Farm fifteen miles north of Lawton. In 2004, eighty-four 1.8 megawatt wind turbines from Vestas Wind Systems were installed by Zilkha Renewable Energy of Houston Texas, on a 3,800-acre parcel along the crest of the Slick Hills adjacent to the Wichita Mountains. Public Service Company of Oklahoma (PSO) has signed a ten-year contract to purchase power from the wind farm, which is capable of producing 151.2 megawatts of power for more than 31,000 homes. More turbines have since been installed. Today these turbines extend along the Slick Hills from Highway 58 northeast of Meers to Saddle Mountain. With towers ranging from 60 to 78 meters in height and rotor diameters of 80 meters, each turbine sweeps an area of 5,027 meters squared.[17]

Most Indians and non-Indians agree that they are ugly, and that they obstruct the view of much of the north side of the Wichita Mountains for miles. Portions of the turbines are visible even in the northern-most edges of the Kiowa community. Park rangers in the nearby Wichita Mountains Wildlife Refuge indicate the turbines are altering the migration paths of whooping cranes.[18] Comments from Kiowa in 2006 varied from "I think they're ugly," "I wish they'd cut them down," and "I don't care what they do as long as they remove them" to "Oh, aren't they pretty," to the remark of one lady near Meers who, drawing a triangle with her hands, stated, "I see them as sort of a feng shui thing. I have Mount Scott and Mount Sheridan to the south of my home and the turbines to the north along the Slick Hills. It's like everything is in its place."[19] While most Kiowa dislike their presence, no organized opposition has arisen. Although this portion of the Slick Hills is not associated with the locale of any specific pan-Kiowa religious rituals, the presence of the turbines clearly interferes with the concept of a pristine buffer zone, associated with other native religious sites. At present, almost any activity on the north side of the mountains involves seeing at least a portion of the wind turbines. The turbines now obscure the once pristine view of the hills north of the Saddle Mountain Church and Cemetery.[20] Because the turbines are largely on non-Indian land and are designed to supply power to the city of Lawton, Indian people in the surrounding area do not see them as an economic benefit. On the other hand, many Kiowa and members of others tribes live in Lawton.

The fifth site is Jimmy Creek Spring. As an alternative to rising water prices from the city of Lawton, Oklahoma, Comanche County Water District No. 1 turned to the Hillary family, which owns the Meers-Saddle Mountain Ranch near Medicine Park, Oklahoma. Currently serving 1,100 customers, the water from the Hillary family lands is more than the district requires. The district would pay 75 percent of the rate charged by the city of Lawton, which is reported to have increased 215 percent over the last three years. The ranch has requested the state water board for three groundwater extraction permits on three sections of land they own totaling 4,186 acre-feet per year, and one stream-water permit to extract 464 acre-feet per year from Jimmy Creek. An acre-foot is 325,850 gallons. According to one estimate this represents 95 percent of all water produced by Jimmy Creek Spring.

However, the spring-fed creek that runs through the Hillary family's ranch originates from a spring located on the 160-acre Jimmy Quoetone allotment, which is now part of the Hillarys' property. Seventy-five people, including dozens of Quoetone's descendants, other nearby Indian and non-Indian landowners, and representatives of the U.S. attorney's office and the Interior Department, appeared at an Oklahoma Water Resources Board's monthly meeting to stop the project. Opponents fear that the permits, if granted, would result in the depletion of Jimmy Creek, a major tributary of Medicine Creek and a main source of water for Lake Lawtonka, the water supply for Lawton. They hope to stop the Hillarys' efforts to sell up to 1.5 billion gallons of water per year.

Because the federal government has reserved water rights for tribes and individual Indians, federal intervention is possible. Two issues are being investigated. The first is whether awarding states water rights would infringe upon federal water rights reserved for Indian families in the affected area. The federal government's position is that water that belongs to Indian families who have a reserved water right under federal law cannot be appropriated, and anything that affects the stream is part of the reserved water rights. The second issue is whether an exclusionary zone can be established around the Jimmy Creek Spring to ensure that any water wells drilled in the vicinity do not penetrate the subterranean cavern where it originates.

While legal battles over definitions of sacred land are common on the northern plains, this case may represent the first such instance on the southern plains, as some Kiowa tribal members have declared the site sacred. Daisy Quoetone Mammedaty stated that she frequently accompanied her grandfather Jimmy Quoetone to a site along the creek where he conducted daily prayers. "To me, it's as holy as any church," she said. She also described it as "special, precious, sacred." Addressing "the spiritual aspect" of Jimmy Creek, Minister Deborah Quoetone stated that she uses water from the creek for baptizing infants. The Hillary family offered to abandon seeking the surface water permit if the three underground permits were granted. The Oklahoma Water Resource Board voted 7-2 to table issuing the four permits until the November 2006 meeting. Some local non-Indian residents continue to support the proposal.[21] This case may establish precedence for future legal cases as development on the southern plains Indian Country continues to affect sites of historical, cultural, and religious importance.

Concerning potentially endangered sites, Cutthroat Mountain and Long Horn Mountain should also be considered. Jack Haley is exploring the possibility of leaving the Cutthroat Mountain site to the Kiowa Tribe for their management and protection. While Long Horn Mountain is presently used for cattle grazing, the Sloan family, which is reported to be sensitive to the Kiowa's use of the mountain and one member of which is married to a Kiowa, have rejected offers to install wind turbines. Of all remaining Kiowa sites, the historical importance of Cutthroat Mountain and the cedar from Long Horn Mountain make these two of the most important named Kiowa sites in terms of spiritual significance. Because landmarks are places that are easily identifiable and whose meaning can easily be conveyed to others, they are ideal subjects for cultural protection and management. As American Indian cultural resources involve the surrounding area and not solely isolated parts of these locales, they are better protected as cultural landscapes than as traditional cultural properties (Stoffle et al. 1997:238).[22]

Invisible Sites

It is often easier to remember and locate a site that has been formally named. However, a geographic location does not have to be formally named to have cultural significance, whether in the form of history, power, symbolism, or humor. There are clearly far more unnamed locales than there are named locales, and many "invisible" sites exist that hold a great deal of cultural, historical, and spiritual significance for individuals, Kiowa families, and the Kiowa in general.[23] As is true of most Kiowa culture, these locales are typically learned of through stories about events that occurred there. A sample of stories, all associated with places in or adjacent to the old KCA reservation and the allotments taken by individual Kiowa, illustrate this point. Although none of these sites is formally marked or named, all serve as examples of the depth and variety of unnamed and often unrecorded geographic locales in the Kiowa community.

As a child, Pe-a-to-mah (who later married Hunting Horse) was camped with her family at the east end of Longhorn Mountain when a spider bit her. A woman doctored her, but was unsuccessful. The family sent a rider for the noted doctor Tónáuqàut, who came to the camp and successfully ministered to her.[24] At the 1874 Sun Dance, White Bear gave away his famous zébàut, or fletched arrow, to White Cowbird, a brother of Sun Boy. This occurred near Qópáutkáun (End of the Mountains), now called Walsh Mountain (Mooney 1898:338), just northwest of Granite, Oklahoma.

As tribes tried to cope with confinement to a reservation and the ensuing dramatic changes in their lives, numerous prophetic movements arose during the 1880s and 1890s. In 1882, Jáudèkáu (Retained His Name A Long Time) assumed the name Páutépjè (Bison Bull Coming Out) and announced that he would bring back the bison. He erected a tipi on a high bank in the bend of the Washita River between present-day Carnegie and Mountain View, and many Kiowa gathered. After ten days and nights of rituals, he failed to produce the bison, and his following dispersed. This event appears to have been held on or near the same peninsula where the Ghost Dance would later be held from 1894 to 1917. Shortly thereafter, Bóttàlyî—(Stomach Boy, also known as Íltàuhę̀, or He Wouldn't Listen) attempted a demonstration of his alleged powers. Setting up his lodge on the cap rock between present-day Gotebo and Komalty, the same vicinity in which White Bear undertook a vision quest in 1873, he proclaimed he would bring the sun down out of the sky. When he failed, his followers dispersed (Mooney 1898:349–350; Nye 1937:263–266).

Claiming to be Bison Bull Emerging's successor and to possess more power, Vą́uigài (In The Middle) tried to revive his mentor's prophecy in

1888. In The Middle predicted that a great whirlwind would blow away all of the whites and any Indians living among them, followed by a four-day fire that would burn any establishments they had made in the country. Then the bison would be brought back. He also failed. This attempt was made at a camp near Lone Wolf's camp on Upper Elk Creek (Mooney 1898:356–357). While these sites probably had names, such as Place Where Bison Bull Emerging Tried To Bring Back The Bison and Place Where He Wouldn't Listen Tried To Bring Down The Sun, they have not survived. Nevertheless, these invisible sites remain important historical and geographic locales to the contemporary Kiowa community.

On January 9, 1891, three Kiowa boys, one of whom had been whipped by Mr. Wherrit at the government Indian school at Anadarko, ran away. Attempting to reach a Kiowa camp, they were overtaken by a blizzard that evening, and, after nearly reaching the camp, froze to death. The boys were found a few days later near the base of a mountain by a search party. Mooney (1898:360–361) reported that they were attempting to reach their homes at a Kiowa camp some thirty miles from the school. Nye (1937) stated this was the camp on Stinking Creek, which Corwin (1958:111) indicated was "near Zodal-tone Springs on Stinking Creek." Other Kiowa have reported the boys were attempting to reach the Kiowa camp on Upper Cache Creek, probably Eagle Heart's near present-day Chieftain Park. These two locations are a short distance apart. Miscalculating which hill the camp was located near, they continued on too far southwest, where they succumbed to the storm. Nye (1937:275) reported the boys were found at a hill southwest of Zodeltone Springs, which places them close to the Cache Creek site. One individual stated they were found near the northeast slope of the hill, just west of the intersection of Highway 58 and County Road 1410, about 2.2 miles southwest of Alden and just a little over this distance northwest of the Cache Creek camp. In 1874, Little Chief was killed by cavalry troops along Stinking Creek. In the summer of 1891, Polant (Fólą́jè or Coming Snake) was shot across from the mouth of Elk Creek in present-day Greer County (Nye 1937:275–276).

There have also been many uplifting and humorous incidents. The first Kiowa to accept Christianity were baptized in the Washita River between present-day Randlett Park and Riverside Indian School on January 22, 1893. One elder pointed out a site along Highway 9 west of Stinking Creek where Jim Todome and Harry Hall "obtained" a beef for a meal they were having. The men knew an Anglo farmer with cattle. Whenever a cow died, he always allowed the Kiowa to have the hide and any meat that was edible. Needing beef, the men contemplated how to kill a cow so that after they reported it to the farmer and he found no suspicious cause, he would give it to them. After Todome devised a plan, they approached one of the cows, inserted a rifle into its rear end and shot it. As they "just happened" to be going by on their way to Carnegie, they saw the cow and reported it to the farmer, who, though perplexed at its sudden demise, gladly gave it to them.[25] I cannot drive by this stretch of the road without smiling to myself when I think of this story.

A similar incident featured an Anglo farmer who leased a Kiowa man's allotment. The Kiowa and his grandson came by wagon to cut a load of wood one day. After loading their wagon with firewood they departed, stopping to thank the farmer as they drove out, who told them to come back again. Little did he know the Kiowa had killed one of his calves by hitting it over the head with an axe, loaded it into the wagon, and covered it with firewood.[26]

Parker McKenzie told me of an event he saw at a Fourth of July picnic around 1907, about a half-mile south of the junction of Highways 9 and 58, on the west side of the highway and just southeast of present-day Mountain View. With the town renamed Mountain View and the railroad completed, a large group of whites had gathered. Several Kiowa had been invited to attend the gathering, with some performing exhibitions of horse riding and other activities. The event committee put Big Tree, Gotebo, and Saingko in charge of butchering four steers for the occasion. After the first steer was killed, the three men were gathered around the beef butchering it with large knives. As most of the whites had never seen Indians, let alone Indians butchering a beef, they began to crowd around the group, finally becoming so close the men were having trouble continuing their work. McKenzie overheard Big Tree grumbling to Gotebo about the whites being so close that he did not have enough room to work. Gotebo commented that they needed to do something to make them back up. One of the men had cut into the stomach lining and exposed all of the entrails. Seeing this, Big Tree told the others to watch him and that he would clear them all out. Big Tree cut a piece of the bloody liver out and squirted some gall onto it for flavoring. Then he bit into the organ, and with the blood running down his chin he gave a loud war-whoop and, rising up from the ground, proceeded to wave his butcher knife and continued to whoop and holler. Taking his cue, Gotebo followed suit, producing an even louder war cry and making similar motions with his blood-stained knife. McKenzie admitted that even though he knew what they were going to do, their actions scared him. When he turned around to see what effect it had on the crowd, only Indians remained. All of the non-Indians had run back towards town and were out of sight. The Indians resumed their butchering.[27]

A few years prior to allotment, Parker McKenzie's father, General

McKenzie, was making his way on horseback to a dinner at the camp of several friends. Stopping at Buzzard Creek, he bathed, put on a fresh set of clothes, and tied his breechclout and dirty clothes in a bundle behind his saddle. Arriving at the camp he joined the other men inside a lodge, and after some visitation the meal was served. At this time, food was often passed around in large bowls or pots, from which individuals took out a portion they desired. As the men ate, their hands became greasy from the meat. The host called to his wife to get a cloth or a towel to wipe their hands and mouths with. The wife in turn instructed one of the small children, "Cáui bé bàu" (Bring a cloth/wrag). The child returned with a large cloth. Each man in turn wiped his hands and mouth on a portion of it then passed it to the next. Being one of the last to arrive McKenzie had been seated on the northeast side of the lodge and so was one of the last to be served and to receive the cloth. As it was handed to him, he looked at it and suddenly proclaimed with surprise, "Hégàu nàu jáuigòp" or "Oh my, my breech- clout!" The other men immediately began to spit and wipe their mouths with their sleeves![28]

An elderly Kiowa woman told me of her childhood days at St. Patrick's Mission in Anadarko. Once, while taking Communion, she got the host stuck in the back of her throat. Despite her efforts she could neither swal- low it nor get it to come forward in her mouth. Adhering to the strict tradition taught by the school, she could neither chew the sacrament nor use her hands to remove it. Unable to talk and periodically gagging, she remained in this predicament for some time, all the while sure that she had Jesus Christ stuck in her throat and that she was going to go to hell for her actions.[29]

A Kiowa woman made a bank deposit at Cooperton, Oklahoma, and was hurrying to return to Anadarko. As she sped north from Cooperton, she passed a state trooper. Knowing that she was well over the speed limit and that he would pursue her, she pulled off the highway and waited for the officer to catch up. As he pulled in behind her with his lights flashing, she stepped from her truck and began to walk down the side of it toward the patrol car. The officer likewise stepped out and began to approach her. Just as she passed the tailgate of her truck, her hosiery, which had snagged on an exposed spring on her truck seat, broke, and was so stretched that it fell into two clumps around her ankles. As she approached the squad car she stepped in a pothole and lost her balance. Picking herself up and with her hair and dress disheveled, she tried to compose herself and face the offi- cer. No longer able to maintain his composure, the officer began to laugh uncontrollably at the events that had just unfolded before him. Feeling she had suffered enough, he stated that after what she had been through he couldn't give her a ticket, and gave her a warning and asked her to drive slower.[30]

Although these events did not result in the formation of place names, or represent places for which their associated names have not survived, they suggest some of the range of events that make up Kiowa history and, more important, the places and events that individuals remember and tell stories about. Thus, even without formal place names, they are still geographically important. These include celebrations of Sun Dances, successful raids and battles, tragic accounts of Cutthroat Mountain and Palo Duro Canyon, and others that induce side-splitting humor when told around dinner tables in contemporary Kiowa homes. Stories of these types are too numerous to count, let alone fully record, and although some are always being lost, many remain and continue to be told in family and community circles. Many Kiowa view the land as a living entity, with history happening all around them in a continuing flow of human activities. The survival of this knowledge for any culture depends on whether individuals take the time to successfully transmit and pass it down. Oral history, whether in the form of stories, songs, or place names, is important to maintaining ethnicity and community for any human group, including that in Kiowa Country.

This Is Still Kiowa Country

The Kiowa have made three major migrations in recorded history. The first migration was onto the northern plains from the headwaters of the Yellowstone River and the Bitterroot Mountain area of Montana in the late 1600s to early 1700s. The second was a move to the southern plains in the mid- to late 1700s, probably from the attraction of horses to the south and military pressure from tribes such as the Lakota and Cheyenne, who forced them out of the Black Hills. The third move involved their physical confinement within the KCA Reservation in Indian Territory in 1875.

For native peoples, reassignment to a fraction of their previous homeland or to an entirely new region reduced their land base and mobility to a greater degree than ever before, and proved very difficult. Important sacred or historical sites, including burial grounds, had to be left behind and in time often became lost to the respective tribes. Even the availability to gather certain flora and fauna changed. Although such movements occurred in the past, whether voluntarily or from warfare or other pressures, they were initiated by Indians. The later, non-Indian-induced removals continue to be viewed by native peoples as qualitatively different.

As demonstrated by the small number of Kiowa names for northern plains locales, one result of migrations is the disassociation and reconfiguration in the number, spatial range, and knowledge of place names associated with a former homeland. The process was repeated with confinement to a reservation in 1875. Since that time, many Kiowa place names outside southwestern Oklahoma that James Mooney (1898) recorded are no longer known even by the oldest Kiowa. Another result has been the geographic extent of the homeland recognized by contemporary Kiowa. The Kiowa sometimes had the same name for up to four different places, primarily for mountains and streams (see Appendices 2 and 3). Duplicate names for several locales suggests either that different sites of a similar nature resulted in an identical name being bestowed by different Kiowa groups, or that existing place names were transplanted to new locales of a similar nature as the Kiowa migrated south, or that a combination of these two scenarios obtained.

Because portions of a landscape hold different meanings and different attachments for individuals, some variation in the concept of a homeland is to be expected. For some, the Kiowa homeland entails all known lands the Kiowa have traversed, from Devil's Tower and the Kiowa Mountains in the north to parts of Mexico. For others it is primarily those areas with remaining concentrations of Kiowa people, namely, the southern plains; and for still others, it is the allotted lands in southwestern Oklahoma where Kiowa are concentrated.[31]

I asked one elder Kiowa woman to define how far Kiowa Country extended from present-day Carnegie, Oklahoma. Her response:

> Well, probably just around [here], you know it's different communities. It's not just like Carnegie and Meers and maybe Red Stone, and Hobart. But over there [Hobart] they are more in town. There's no one out, just one or two families lives out, so that one doesn't qualify.

Her answer implies that living on trust status land is a principal defining element in whether a community is still Kiowa Country or not. Even though trust status land is still owned in some areas, many Kiowa have moved into towns and no longer reside on rural allotments. We continued with the following exchange:

> "What about the northland, like Devil's Tower, do you think about that as Kiowa Country? Is it still Kiowa Country to you?"
> "Well no, not really. You know 'cause other people claim it, but it's in our stories. It's part of us as far as our stories go, but . . . I don't consider it like I do where I live, and Red Stone, and you know all those other places, Meers. I don't, not in that context, 'cause I'm too

far removed. But I enjoy visiting you know. I feel the connection that way. And like I said, it's a privilege to have been there under the circumstances that I was."[32]

In any population, the definition of, depth of attachment to, and degree of importance people attribute to geography vary. Just as modern wars continue to reconfigure international boundaries, plains territories frequently shifted, and the concept of what composed a tribe's territory often exceeded what the tribe actually resided in or controlled. That the Kiowa still recognize a homeland is more important than agreeing on its precise parameters. A similar range of variation in what constitutes a homeland and how people relate to that area is observable in other peoples both in America and abroad.[33]

Despite different definitions of a homeland, an attachment to specific geographic locales is a major part of American Indian identity.[34] During hearings before the Alaska Native Claims Settlement Act of 1971, many Inuit found themselves struggling to maintain "their desire to continue to use and occupy specific lands and their determination to realize continuity in cultural integrity." As Iverson (1998:156) points out, one village chief spoke of a different kind of ownership, one won "through battles and that was by tradition . . . the inheritance we received from our ancestors." Anthropologist Ann Fienup-Riordan noted this was a "relational" concept of ownership, one "where a man has a right to, and in fact an obligation to, use a site because of his relationship to previous generations of people who had a definite relationship to the species taken at the same place" (Iverson 1998:156). I would maintain that the Kiowa similarly regard much of southwestern Oklahoma. In Euroamerican society, such feelings of obligation do exist, on family farms, for example, and in urban stores or businesses, but they generally give way to the ultimate questions of legal ownership and economic vitality. The Nelson Island Inuit believe that "when a person lives like his grandparents from the land and the sea, he feels that those grandparents are still alive in him" (Iverson 1998:156). In similar fashion, Vanessa Jennings believes that she must live on her grandmother's allotment in order to continue the way of life her grandparents provided for her and to continue her grandmother's artistic work at the same locale.[35]

The Kiowa home area is the focus of what is considered most traditional, most conservative, and above all most basic to tribal identity and knowledge. For many Indians, the local community also represents support in an ongoing struggle against the outside, particularly the non-Indian world. In turn, a large body of oral history references both general and particular experiences. Although the home community often offers only limited economic opportunities and options, it remains a geographic and cultural safe haven, both for those who remain there and for those who leave for jobs but frequently return to visit or live for periods of time. The home community is where individuals feel connected to their families, friends, culture, and tribal identity. Several Kiowa have stated that they come home to visit, attend tribal cultural events, and to "recharge their batteries." For many tribes, a relatively small group size, extended kinship, and a shared culture are important elements of community. These factors in turn often manifest in a people's sense of being distinct (Lone-Knapp 2000:636–638).

Delores Harragarra lives on her mother Richenda Toyebo's allotment west of Carnegie. When I asked her what places were important to her in the area, she responded,

> Well, where I live cause it's all, for the most part, Kiowa still own it. You know I go there its Kiowa country and all around, all that land-base is still Kiowa. I don't think there are too many places that can say that.

When I asked Mrs. Harragarra what she thought about when she thought of her home place, she referred to extended kinship, a land base, a bandlike sense of community, and roots and a sense of belonging:

> You know, it's all Kiowa country. I'm there and those are my roots. And I'm fortunate to be there, 'cause there's a lot of people that, Kiowas, they don't know where they belong. When they come to Kiowa country they don't have the foggiest [idea] of where their family's allotment was 'cause it's gone and so they're just lost. And I just feel fortunate that I'm still there. And it's still a part of, you know, my family. I'm not looking at it in terms of monetary [value] or anything. I'm looking at it in terms of, for the most part my family is still around me and that's the way it was in the old days you know they were all together in villages or bands or whatever. So I consider us just a band that's still there. Of course not everyone was together, the bands were at different locations at different times.[36]

For many Kiowa, place names like Xòaî (Rock That Grew Upwards), Qółtàqòp (Cutthroat Mountain), Sépyáldá (Rainy Hill, i.e., Rainy Mountain), Gǘcįnyį́qòp (Long Horn Mountain), and Xóhót (Canyon, i.e., Palo Duro Canyon) do what Basso (1988:121) says of Western Apache place names: they accomplish multiple important social actions simultaneously. Whether spoken in Kiowa or in their modern English forms, the names of these sites can produce a mental image of the particular geographic locale, evoke or reference prior stories or historical accounts, and affirm the value and validity of ancestral wisdom and lifeways. The number of functions a place name has depends on the extent of an individual's knowledge of and relationship with a particular site. Better-known sites are almost universal in having some degree of familiarity and meaning for most Kiowa, while less well-known local sites tend to be of more significance at a local level. Kelly and Francis (1994:47) show that among the Navajo, the types of places mentioned and the nature of the relationship people have with geographic locales often vary from one generation to the next.

As Lone-Knapp (2000:636) observes of the Hodenosaunee (Iroquois), "It was a sense of kinship or relatedness to the community that was the basis for their more specific descriptions of their place or role in communities. Social, political, economic, and spiritual aspects of their lives were linked to this relationship to their communities." Recognition of the multidimensional quality of ethnic identity in general and of an ongoing commitment to the social, political, economic, historical, and spiritual life of the community is essential to understanding the ethnogeography and ethnic identity of contemporary Indian communities. That such an identity will continue for the Kiowa is not in doubt. How it will evolve and in what contexts remains to be seen.

In May 2003, I attended the Toyebo family reunion at Rainy Mountain Kiowa Indian Baptist Church. After the noon meal and visiting, "Games, History, Stories, Door Prizes, and More Toyebo Family Trivia" were held. A large part of the afternoon program consisted of the elders of each lineage addressing the gathering. They emphasized the need to recognize kin, know one another, and maintain their family history, including Kiowa names. Each elder named the members of their direct family, asked them to stand up, and recounted where they lived, their activities, work or school status, and accomplishments. For those who had Kiowa names, their elders announced them, often with their translations, and sometimes explaining the origin of the name and past owners of the name. Many of the elders spoke of prominent geographic locations in the Rainy Mountain area and of their experiences at these locales during their lifetime.[37] Like naming ceremonies, this is a good example of how much Kiowa family, community, and tribal oral history is handed down—through stories and in public contexts for all to witness.

For any culture to continue as a functioning, distinct entity, some geographic base or homeland is required. Even though the Kiowa homeland has been reduced in size and checkerboarded by the legacy of allotment, this residual land base remains vital to sustaining a distinct Kiowa community. Individual sites continue to be of importance historically, socially, and sacrally. For those willing to embrace it, these sites continue to offer knowledge and lessons in the form of morals and historical events from the lives of both past and present Kiowa in southwestern Oklahoma.

Bernadine Rhoades spoke of the sense of history and community that ties Kiowa people to their homeland in southwestern Oklahoma:

> I believe that as a Kiowa, I have invested in this land, my people who have invested blood. You have a feeling that this land covered with all the highways and everything else is where my ancestors walked. Most people that have come here, they left the land that their ancestors were, where they were, and walked the land.[38]

Although the Kiowa retain legal ownership of only a small amount of land, the allotted land and the surrounding region that made up the former reservation remain the basis for the Kiowa sense of a homeland. This core area and Kiowa sites in the surrounding area are where Kiowa ethnic identity, culture, and community focus continue.[39] That the Kiowa have been on the southern plains for only a little more than two centuries and essentially left behind the northwestern plains where their ancestors walked does not diminish the validity of their bond to their present homeland.

Conclusion

What do the Kiowa data offer for other studies of Native American place names and ethnogeography? First, they provide a model for an area in which little geographic research has been undertaken. Second, they underwrite a strong case for the relationship between sense of place and ethnic identity. Third, they help to expand geographic concepts such as disassociation, geosacred, and invisible sites for studies of this type. The Kiowa data also support Thornton's (1997:221–222) summary of the major analytical discoveries thus far made in anthropological studies of Native American place names. Using his criteria, I will link these theoretical concepts to Kiowa ethnogeography with examples of place names and their practices, while expanding on other concepts.

1. Place names are important cultural and linguistic domains of human knowledge that are worthy of study, individually and in relation to other aspects of human culture and behavior. Kiowa

place names recall not only the geography, history, and flora and fauna of their area but also signal the cultural emphasis on these resources, as well as what the Kiowa perceive as significant in the geographic and cultural landscape around them.

2. Like other Native American peoples, the Kiowa cherish the land and have a rich appreciation of their own geography, toponyms, and how they relate to place names as an important part of their ethnic identity and sense of being. The continued use of Kiowa and English translations of Kiowa place names, modern community names such as Rainy Mountain and Redstone, and the multifaceted nature of the people, cultural forms, and history associated with these names is especially rich. Sometimes it may also take on new uses and connotations. Dan Gelo reports a Kiowa and Comanche gospel band in the late 1970s and early 1980s called The Zodaltones, a name he describes as "a very clever allusion to both Kiowa place and stereotypical non-Indian band naming."[40]

3. Place names function as durable artifacts that provide important clues to the historical and cultural geography of a region. Kiowa place names reflect the visual nature of their environment, the use of mountains and hills as navigation aids, the emphasis of particular resources to particular areas, and the association of specific historical events to their locations. Place names also serve to chronicle Euroamerican-induced changes from military, settlement, religious, and educational influences.

4. Place names are determined in part by what is of cultural interest to a particular population, such as subsistence needs and navigation, but they are also constrained by the physical nature of the environment and the limits of human cognition. Kiowa seem not to have created names for specific sites where bison were procured, but, reflecting the importance of a martial ethos to their culture, did create names to commemorate the site and outcome of specific battles. Kiowa did not create names for Anglo homes and ranches but did name trading posts, military forts, and major settlements, such as El Paso, Texas. Communal religious events such as Sun Dances, and inferably their sites, were formally named, while the locales of more individually oriented practices such as vision quests were not. The physical environment affected the construction of Kiowa place names by requiring the Kiowa to link names to the closest nearby landmark of significance and recognition, such as a stream, hill, or mountain, or to use a generic suffix denoting "Place At Which (Something Occurred)." Kiowa

recognized oceans as unique but lacked knowledge of land beyond these bodies of water or even of the entire range of the continent they resided on.

5. As in other cultures, Kiowa linguistic structures and capabilities influenced how places were defined and named. However, these native terms also show great adaptability to new forms, such as expanding use of the word for trail to Anglo roads and use of the words for mountain and stream crossings to staircases. As well, the Kiowa terms are readily translated and adopted by non-Indians.

6. An individual's inventory of place names is limited in comparison with that of his or her culture but typically includes familiarity with names beyond the realm of personal experience. Just as many Anglos have never visited noted biblical sites, many Kiowa from the 1800s to today have never been to Devil's Tower or Cutthroat Mountain, yet they know of their importance in Kiowa history.

The structure and hierarchy of individual place name inventories are generally related to patterns of social differentiation. This is reflected in how some names are known only to the Kiowa of particular communities. Just as individuals in the same state today may have different knowledge concerning important locales near their home areas, undoubtedly in the preservation era southern Kiowa divisions had names for places that were largely unknown among the more northern divisions.

A strong correlation exists between population and place name densities. This is reflected in how contemporary Kiowa know more place names on the southern plains than on the northern plains, more place names in the post-1867 KCA Reservation than in adjacent parts of the southern plains, and more place names in the area of the reservation where Kiowa communities developed than in the less populated parts, as shown by the number of names for locales north of the Wichita Mountains compared to the south.

7. Place names function as powerful linguistic symbols that evoke a wide array of mental and physical associations, many of which are especially poignant and emotionally and spiritually moving. These symbols serve as important tools in narrative, story, song, personal names, formal speeches, and poetry, as well as on signs, churches, flags, and other items bearing the Kiowa tribal seal. Place names such as Devil's Tower, Cutthroat Gap, Hueco Tanks, Palo Duro Canyon, and Rainy Mountain have produced a myriad of images from the early history of the Kiowa to their contemporary culture. Several Kiowa have personal names based on specific named places

or that describe events that occurred at a particular geographic locale. Following Jacobs's (1934) idea of geographic text and Kendall's (1980) idea of personal names as texts, I would add that place names, like personal names, are best understood as texts, in that each is generally associated with a wide array of cultural and historical knowledge. As such, they are an important means of understanding and recording indigenous geography, worldview, language, community and tribal history, and ethnography.

For some groups, the fundamental ethnographic tasks of recording, mapping, transcribing, and interpreting place names to ensure their preservation remain. However, as Thornton (1997:222) suggests, further research awaits concerning four primary issues. The first is the need to recognize geographic landscapes as cultural landscapes, with place names and the places they name cultural resources worthy of protection. One purpose in writing this book was to identify and inventory these sites to preserve knowledge of them and to aid in future protection. Second, the relationship between place and place names in social life is not fully understood. In my fieldwork I uncovered considerable geographic knowledge among the Kiowa, and many ways in which this knowledge was used. Third, Native American concepts of place and being and their essential inseparability await sensitive inquiry, to which I hope I have contributed with this book. And fourth, collaborative projects with native peoples should be undertaken that will not only produce more thorough research but will also provide them with a means to contribute in representing their own geographies. Numerous tribal place name and mapping projects have recently been undertaken (see Brody 1982; Warhus 1997:208–299). Many of these projects involve not only the documentation of place names but the development of associated tribal maps. These efforts are but one aspect of the larger movement in cultural revival and the reestablishment of tribal rights. Black Goose's map and the maps in this book may be of future use in these areas. Maps of this genre are not only important for cultural preservation, they represent tribal efforts to assert their identity and their connection to the land even as they establish their place in modern society.

To these approaches, I would add three other important concepts: (1) For most sites to continue to be important for a culture, they must be accessible to the group. (2) Greater recognition of presently unnamed or "invisible" sites is needed to ensure their protection. (3) Disassociated sites should be inventoried before they are lost, especially among groups with few remaining native speakers.

In listening to members of northern plains tribes speak of their ongoing connection to named places, I was struck by the wide range of locales that members of these tribes still visit for historical and religious purposes. In contrast, few places outside southwestern Oklahoma are visited by significant numbers of Kiowa other than Devil's Tower, Palo Duro Canyon, Medicine Lodge, and Hueco Tanks, the latter three of which are all of more historical importance. One contributing factor may be the difference in land ownership between the northern and southern plains groups. Although many of the prominent northern plains locales are still located on public lands as national and state forests and parks or as Bureau of Land Management lands, most southern plains sites are in private hands. A greater number of northern sites have also been identified and developed as historic sites. Although there are recorded instances of Kiowa revisiting such sites (Nye 1937: photographs following p. 234; Medicine Lodge 1994), these were through the requests and arrangements of non-Indian military personnel and historians. In many instances Kiowa who had firsthand experience with many of the historical and religious sites on the southern plains were prevented from visiting those sites for many years after they entered the reservation in 1875. With the loss of firsthand contact—disassociation—the cultural connection to many named places outside southwestern Oklahoma was lost with the passing of the last pre-reservation generation.

The importance of invisible or unnamed places needs greater recognition and inquiry as they often outnumber named places. Just as there are no people without history, the same could be said about land, which does not have to be named to be important. These approaches should help preserve tribal bodies of knowledge while also increasing understanding of Native American views of and interaction with the land.

As Dudley Patterson, a Cibecue Apache, told Keith Basso (1996), "Wisdom sits in places." "When one comes to know the cultural significance of a particular place, one begins a long journey toward wisdom, a quality that helps sustain life, that is, above all, 'an instrument of survival'" (Iverson 1998:181). Many Kiowa place names were left behind when the Kiowa entered the reservation in 1875. This body of knowledge could easily have been several times the number of place names recorded in this book. At present, no Kiowa names are known for Fort Arbuckle II (1850), Fort Supply (1868), the Kichai Hills, Red Rock Canyon, and Rock Mary, a well-known landmark along the California Trail in Caddo County, Oklahoma—all prominent places that would have been known to earlier Kiowa. Names for other, more distant places, such as the Glass Mountains in Major County, Oklahoma, and Carlsbad Caverns, are also presently unknown. Yet a considerable body of Kiowa place names is still extant, much of which would have been lost if not for the efforts of James Mooney (1898). It is important to recognize that place names are a fragile cultural and linguistic resource that can be lost within a generation. The current decline of the Kiowa language threatens to hasten this loss.

This book represents an initial attempt to preserve and explore this body of Kiowa knowledge and wisdom. That road has been both long and interesting, but it has also given me a much deeper appreciation for various parts of the plains, southwestern Oklahoma, and for the Kiowa who continue to call this region home. The Kiowa have left a distinct mark on the southern plains landscape, both visible and invisible. Where I once traveled through Kiowa Country seeing only the most visible and obvious physical geographic sites, I now see more of the invisible landscape. I see an area that is alive with history and action, similar to what my grandparents conveyed to me in southern Indiana. In learning how Kiowa relate to and make sense of their homeland I became more aware of the ideas, oral history, and the intangible yet meaningful symbolic attachments. This allowed me to know more about what it means for the Kiowa, which in turn facilitated a dialectic exchange between visible and invisible landscape. I have also gained a better understanding of the concept and the importance of a homeland as a physical and psychological anchor for ethnic identity, both for the Kiowa and for myself. Geographers continue to describe the centrality of land and place in Indian identity (Rundstrom et al. 2000:98), and many Kiowa retain a strong sense of place and belonging in southwestern Oklahoma. As long as the Kiowa continue to be linked to and interact with the physical landscape around them, as long as elders continue to pass on oral traditions such as geographic and personal place names, the distinct cultural association of the Kiowa with the land will continue as a vital part of Kiowa cultural and spiritual traditions. As friends and relatives regularly point out, "This is still Kiowa Country."

Kiowa Geography and Weather Terms

á-àu-tàun—a clearing in the timber.

á-bàul-hàu—forested knoll or hill (verbal adj.).

á-jǒ-byǫi—a circular opening in the timber.

á-kǫ̀-dàu—timber so thick it shades the side darkening the area.

àu-jáu-gà—an island.

áu-sě—(s/d) any stream smaller than a creek, which may be wet or dry, áu-sě-gàu(t).

bį́-dàu—foggy ("moist-aired").

bį́-sòt-dàu—light, continual, or lengthy rain.

bǫ́i-bá-hét-cá or bǫ́i-bá-hép-cá—(s/d/t) lightning.

dàum—Earth, land, ground, or a region of land.

dàum-áun-tǫ̀—ocean.

fǎ-dá—flat, grassy prairie.

fě-dàum—sandy land.

hîl-dàu—a valley, lit. formed as a valley (verbal adj.).

jâun—any narrow mountain pass or gap.

jě-gà-kàun-hòt—(s/d/t) ice cycle.

jò-hǎu—a concavity in a cliff, bluff, tree, and so on. Commonly mistranslated as bluff.

káui-káu-hót-gà—cave (verbal adj., seldom used as a noun).

kį́-á-jôi—man-made earthworks, commonly erected for defense against an attack in plains warfare.

pán—the firmament, heavens, clouds, and such.

pį́-gáu—a hill, hillock, rise in the ground, or elongated hill.

pį́-hót—area within a bend in a river or creek.

pį́-yâu—"at the summit" of a hill or ridge.

qál-sép-dàu—very wet or heavy rain.

qǎu-gáu—a bank, bluff, cliff, or precipice.

qóp—a mountain.

sán-gá—any escarpment.

sḗ-chó—a pond.

sḗ-chó-èl—a lake.

sép—rain.

thến—(s/d/t) hail.

thến-káut-cà—hailstones or a piece of hail.

thól—snow.

thól-pắ-gà—granulated (i.e., powdery) snow.

thól-qál-sép-dằu—wet snow.

tǫ́-tèp or tǫ́-tèp-gà—(s/d/t) (lit. water/emerging) any spring of water.

tót—a crossing or point to ascend, as at a river, mountain, or staircase.

vắu—a watercourse (a creek or river of any size).

vắu-sót—(s/d/t) thunder.

xṓ-chél-dè (s/d), xṓ-sául-dè (t)—any conspicuous standing rock
   formation.

xó-hót—lit. "rocks crowding in," a canyon.

xṓ-tót (rock crossing)—a rock-bottomed stream crossing.

yắ-dá—a small knoll, mound, or hill.

Kiowa Land-Based Place Names

Mountains

Áu-kàui-qòp—Honeycomb Tripe Mountain, lit. Wrinkled Mountain).
One of four mountains in the Bear Lodge Story formed when fleeing
children threw a series of four bison intestinal organs backward to
impede the pursuing bear. Each organ in turn became a form of terrain similar to its composition (Harrington 1939:168).

Àu-sǫ́-qòp—Gray Mountain. Location unknown.

Bím-sàl-qòp—Tripe Hair Mountain. One of the four mountains in the
Bear Lodge Story (Harrington 1939:168). *See* Áukàuiqòp.

Cáui-qòp—Kiowa Mountains. The high peaks north and west of the
Yellowstone area of Wyoming, at the head of the Yellowstone and
Missouri rivers. Named for the Kiowa living there.

Chól-fá-káui-qòp—Brain Sack Mountain. One of the four mountains in
the Bear Lodge Story (Harrington 1939:168). *See* Áukàuiqòp. Also
known as Qágòpbímkàuiqòp.

Dǎu-jó-hâu-qòp—Medicine Bluff Concavity Mountain. Described as
"T'at'ohak'o(p)—One Hill-Medicine Mountain," just west of Mountain
View, Oklahoma (Sangko to Marriott, August 21, 1935, AMP-WHC).
Probably the mesa butte at Kiowa Flat, Sect. 5-8, T7N, R15W, Gotebo
East Quad, Kiowa County, Oklahoma. Possibly the nearby hill in Sect.
11, T7N, R16W.

È-àun-hâ-fàui-qòp—Trailing the Enemy Mountain, Unap Mountain,
1,812 feet in elevation, in Kiowa County, Oklahoma. Named after
Éàunhâfàui (Trailing The Enemy or Unap), whose allotment was one
mile northwest.

Fài-qóp—Sun Mountain. Guadalupe Peak, located three miles west of
Pine Springs in northwest Culberson County, Texas. The highest point

in Texas (8,751 feet in elevation). Forming the southernmost tip of the Guadalupes, the sheer-cliffed and rugged El Capitan juts out prominently to the south of the taller mountains. Named for the sun's rays, which produce a shining glow from the mountain's surface that can be seen for miles, Sun Mountain is part of the Guadalupe Mountains, running more than 100 miles along this region of the Texas–New Mexico border. The mountain offers an unobstructed view for almost 100 miles of the Delaware Basin to the east and the Salt Basin to the west. With several springs and a perennial stream, which are rare in this arid part of west Texas, and an unusual oasis-like plant community containing biotic associations otherwise unknown in western Texas and southern New Mexico (Fabry 1988:1–11), it was a favorite base camp for Kiowa raiding into Mexico. The peak towers over nearby Guadalupe Pass, and nineteenth-century travelers, including John Russell Bartlett, were often deceived by the peak's great height, reported seeing the peak a full week before they reached it, and consistently underestimated their distance from it (Conkling and Conkling 1947; Bartlett 1965; Tennant 1980). The Guadalupe Mountain Range "is an uplifted segment of the Capitan reef, a limestone barrier reef that formed some 280 million years ago from algae in a shallow inland sea. The geological information revealed in the sheer escarpments and deeply incised canyons of the Guadalupe have made this exposed portion of the Capitan reef one of the world's best known and most studied fossil reefs" (Fabry 1988:1–3). Guadalupe Peak (also known as Signal Peak) is now a part of Guadalupe Mountains National Park, which has numerous caves. Guadalupe Peak is unique in being a huge fossilized prehistoric ocean reef. Along with Denali, Mount Ranier, and Clingman's Dome, Guadalupe Peak and its surrounding environs are so spectacular that it is one of only four state highpoints designated a National Park.

Gų̀-cį́-nyî-qòp—Long Horn Mountain. A small mountain, 1,952 feet in elevation, on the north side of the Wichita Mountains in Kiowa County, Oklahoma. Named after Gų̀cį́nyî (Long Horns or Elk), whose allotment was one mile west of the mountain.

Gúl-qóp—Red Mountain. (1) A small mountain near Eagle Heart's camp along Upper Rainy Mountain Creek on the Kiowa reservation. Probably one of the mountains northwest of Cooperton, in Kiowa County, Oklahoma. (2) An unspecified mountain described as being located a short distance above the river at Colorado Springs and on an extreme northern head branch of the Arkansas (possibly another name for Pike's Peak per Mooney 1898:403), and possibly Red Mountain south

of the Arkansas River and southwest of Pueblo. (3) Sierra Blanca
Mountain in central Mexico.

Í-jà-qóp—Ute Mountains. The central Rocky Mountains of Colorado and
New Mexico, named for the Ute Indians of that region.

Jɛ́-bè-qòp—Mountain Sheep Mountain. (1) The Big Horn Mountains of
north-central Wyoming. (2) Little Bow Mountain ten miles south of
Hobart, on the east side of the North Fork of Red River, just below Elk
Creek in Kiowa County, Oklahoma (Mooney 1898:425). Named for
the Jɛ́bèyòi or Jɛ́bègàu (a.k.a. Áljóyîgàu) or Mountain Sheep Society,
which used to dance at a spring located there near the river, sometimes incorrectly called C'á-bòl-î-qòp (Domestic Sheep or Goat
Mountain).

Jɛ́-gà-kɔ̀-qòp—Black Ice Mountain. Located near the southern edge of
the Staked Plains and named for the appearance of frozen ice on the
trees after a rain while a Kiowa war party camped there in the winter
of 1834–1835 (Mooney 1898:269). Possibly Davis Mountain in Davis
Mountains State Park near Fort Davis, Jeff Davis County, Texas.

Jó-hį̀-qòp—Tipi Mountain. Tepee Mountain in southwestern Kiowa
County, Oklahoma, named for being shaped like a tipi.

Jót-ką́ui-qòp—Oak Bark Mountain. The Santa Rosa Mountains of northern Coahuila, Mexico.

Ką́ui-tą́u-qòp—Love Making Mountain. A mountain between the Elm
Fork and the North Fork of the Red River in Greer County, Oklahoma;
named for the nearby spring of the same name. Probably Quartz
Mountain in present-day Quartz Mountain State Park, 1,887 feet in
elevation.

Qá-gòp-bím-kàui-qòp—Brain Sack Mountain. One of the four mountains
in the Bear Lodge Story (Harrington 1939:168). Also known as
Chólfákáuiqòp. See Áukàuiqòp.

Qól-tà-qòp—Neck Cutting (lit. Throat/Neck Cutting/Severing [i.e., Be-
heading] Mountain) or Beheading Mountain. Cutthroat Mountain.
A hill on the north side of the Wichita Mountains on a branch of Glen
Creek, one mile northwest of Baker Peak in Comanche County, Oklahoma. The site is just east of the To-Gei-Ah allotment, in the south-
central part of Sect. 7, T4N, R15W, Cooperton Quad, and is now part
of the Jack Haley Ranch. Named for the Osage attack and massacre of
a Kiowa camp there in 1833. Although the Kiowa name means Cutthroat Mountain, many people refer to the area as Cutthroat Gap,
which would be Qól-tà-jâun.

Qóp-áut-káun or Qóp-áut-káun-gà—End of the Mountains or Last Mountain (lit. mountain/last). Mount Walsh, now called Walsh Mountain,

2,464 feet in elevation, in Greer County, Oklahoma. Named for marking the western end of the Wichita Range in southwestern Oklahoma. The suffix -gà makes it an adverbial form denoting "at." Kiowa elders in the Hobart area state that this included the entire set of mountains in this area, from Lugert to Granite, Oklahoma, the area from Soldier Peak and Teepee Mountain to Walsh, Brown, and Granite mountains. This area was the winter camp of Kiowa living along Elk Creek. Also known as Xóautkáungà.

Qóp-ét-jàu — Great or Big Mountain/s. (1) The Sierra Madre Range of the southern Rocky Mountains in New Mexico, Chihuahua, and Sonora. (2) Mount Scott in Comanche County, Oklahoma. Commonly called Qóp-êl (Big Mountain) by younger Kiowa, the personal name of Homer Buffalo.

Qóp-gà — At or Towards the Mountains. The Fort Sill area on the old Kiowa reservation, Comanche County, Oklahoma.

Qóp-ó-tà-gàu — Mountain With Its Throat Stuck Out (i.e., That Is Lifting Its Chin) or Qóp-ó-tà-bò — Mountain That Is Looking Up. Mount Sheridan, Comanche County, Oklahoma. Named for the resemblance to a human chin and throat thrust out as one looks upward.

Qóp-thái-màu — White Mountain. A mountain west of the head of the Pecos River in New Mexico. Probably Santa Fe Baldy Peak (12,622 feet in elevation) or a nearby member of the Santa Fe Mountains.

Sál-kâui-qòp — Reticulum or Leaf Tripe (Honeycomb Stomach) Mountains. "Manifold Mountain" in the Black Hills of South Dakota, per Mooney (1898:160, 419). Harrington (1939:168) also inplies that this name may refer to the Badlands of South Dakota. Probably named for its resemblance to the rolling leaf tripe or second stomach of a bison.

Sę́-à-lầu-qòp — Prickly Pear Mountain. A low rocky hill 1,620 feet in elevation near Stumbling Bear's old camp on the old road to Fort Sill, along present-day Canyon Creek and Highway 58 and just northeast of the state historical marker on the east side of the highway, T:4N, R:13W, Sect. 24, northeast of Meers, Comanche County, Oklahoma. Named for the prevalence of prickly pears growing on it.

Tám-chế-qòp — Burial Mountain. Buzzard Mountain southwest of Hobart, Oklahoma, where many Kiowa were interred. Kiowa County, Oklahoma. Burials are also reported in the northeastern member of the Muleshoe Mountains nearby.

Tàu-gûi-qòp — Apache Mountains (lit. Sitting/Outside/Mountains), named for the Naishan or Kiowa Apache. The present-day Wichita Mountains east of the break at present-day Cooperton, Kiowa County, Oklahoma.

Táu-qòp—Saddle Mountain (lit. Mountain That Can Be Sat On). Saddle Mountain, elevation 2,118 feet, in northwest Comanche County, Oklahoma.

Thái-qòp—White Mountain. Pikes Peak near Colorado Springs, Colorado. Named for its snowy white peak.

Thô-cút-qòp—Wichita Mountains (lit. Face/Mark or Tattoo Mountain). The western range of the present Wichita Mountains in southwestern Oklahoma. This portion includes the part between Elm Creek and the North Fork of Red River. According to Parker McKenzie. his generation associated this term with the mountains west of the break at present-day Cooperton, Oklahoma. Named for the Wichita, who still resided there in 1834.

Tǫ-hè-qòp—Waterless Mountains. Located near the head of Otter Creek in Kiowa or Comanche County, Oklahoma (FSA-HLS 1:213).

Xó-áut-káun-gà—End of the Stones (i.e., Mountains). Mount Walsh, now called Walsh Mountain, in Greer County, Oklahoma. Named for marking the western end of the Wichita Mountains. Also known as Qópáutkáun.

Xǫ́-kǫ́-qòp—Black Rocks Mountains. The Black Hills of South Dakota.

Yí-qòp—Two Mountains. Double Mountain, a pair of separate 600-foot-high hills located just north of the headwaters of Count Creek, thirteen miles southwest of Aspermont and eight miles south of Peacock, in southwestern Stonewall County, Texas. A well-known Indian landmark recorded by Randolph B. Marcy in 1849.

Hills and Ridges

Á-yàl-dà—Timber Hill ("At Timber Hill"), a hill near the state line in southern Kansas, on Medicine Lodge Creek. Probably in Barber County.

Ául-káui-pì-gàu—(Crazy Ridge). The site was named for an incident in which Big Bow, angry over the interest of another man in his wife, chased him around this ridge and killed him. Finney (1976:25–26) gives several versions behind the site's name. Kiowa today state that this is the flat-topped and steep-sided small hill about three-quarters of a mile east of present-day Fort Cobb, in Caddo County, Oklahoma. Following Battey's (1876) and Nye's (1937:179) description of "Murder Mountain," located approximately three miles south of the Fort Cobb post site, and a campsite of Kickingbird's band in the winter of 1872–1873, which Finney (1976:26) confirms. James Twohatchett was told that this site was a popular campsite for local Indians, traders, and cattle drivers. Although Finney (1976:26) recorded the term for the site as a "Pay'-yah (Hill)," a pí-gáu, an elongated hill, of which this site is. Some Kiowa state that the original Crazy Hill was a short distance farther south of present-day Fort Cobb on the hill east of Henry Tanedooah's allotment; however, this is the site where Many Wives was beaten by the Cáuitémgòp Society for disobeying a closed hunt law. No place name for this locale is known. Crazy Hill would be Ául-káui-yàl-dà.

Câi-yàl-dà—Comanche Knoll. A hill at the head of Deer Creek, a southern tributary of the South Canadian River in D-County, Oklahoma, probably Sugar Loaf Mound in Custer County, 2.1 miles southeast of Thomas, Oklahoma. *See* Câiyàldàvàu.

Chá-dàu-yàl-dà—Prairie Dog Hill. A prominent mountain or bluff twenty miles west of Vernon, Texas, between the Pease and Red rivers. Medicine Mounds, a cluster of four hills containing Big Mound, which is shaped like a prairie dog hill, the northwesternmost and most prominent feature, is located in Hardeman County, Texas, and was a Comanche vision quest site.

Fí-bò-yàl-dà—American Horse Hill. A hill near the head of Fíbòvàu, possibly a head branch of the Pease River in northwestern Texas. Named for a fight in which the Kiowa captured several horses, the largest they had ever seen, from Texans in the winter of 1841–1842. Also known as Tǫzótcótvàu.

Kǫ-yàl-dà—Dark Hill. Located between the Smoky Hill and Háuxòvàu (? Solomon) rivers in Kansas. Probably part of the Blue Hills in Mitchell County.

Pí-yâu-jó-chél-dè—House Upon the Hill Summit (lit. Hill-Atop-House-Positioned or Located; pí-yâu denotes "at the summit"). Signal Mountain at Fort Sill, Comanche County, Oklahoma. Named for the stone house built on it in 1871 for conducting communication signals.

Sáut-qàun-yàl-dà—Manure (Buffalo Chip) Hill. A hill near Duck Creek on the Salt or White River Fork of the Brazos River in Dickens and Kent counties, Texas. Note: sáut-qàun is manure that comes out already firm, sáu-gà is wet feces. Quitaque (Dung Hills) to the northwest in Floyd County is similarly named.

Sép-yál-da—Rainy Hill. Rainy Mountain located six miles south-southeast of Gotebo, Kiowa County, Oklahoma. Named for always raining whenever the Kiowa camped near this vicinity.

Tàn-yál-dá—Bare/Bald Hill. Las Mores Mountain near Fort Clark, northeast of Brackettville, Kinney County, Texas.

Thái-yàl-dà—White Hill. (1) A hill or hills near the head of White River, a tributary of the Brazos River in Texas. (2) A hill between Sedan and Mountain View in Kiowa County, Oklahoma. (3) A knoll on the south side of Highway 9, 5.3 miles west of the junction of Highways 9 and 54 at Gotebo, Kiowa County, Oklahoma. The hill is part of a long southwest-northeast escarpment or cap rock and is reported to have been a vision quest site of White Bear following his release from prison on October 8, 1873.

Thầu-gú-yàl-dà—Buck Antelope Antler's Hill. The Antelope Hills, six prominent peaks on a large peninsula on the south side of the South Canadian River, in Sect. 32, T16–17N, R25W of the Antelope Hills Quad, in northwest Roger Mills County, Oklahoma. The hill was a former marker of the U.S.-Mexican border and a later landmark for pioneers on the California Trail.

Bluffs, Concavities, and Escarpments

Àu-hį̃-jó-hàu—Cedar Bluff/Concavity. A bluff on the north side of the Smoky Hill River, roughly opposite the mouth of Timber Creek, near Fort Hays, Kansas. Probably the bluff in Sect. 26-27, T15S, R18W in Liebenthal Quad, Ellis County.

Āul-káui-jó-hâu—Crazy Bluff/Concavity. A bluff on the south side of Bear Creek near its head, between the Cimarron and Arkansas rivers, near the western Kansas Line. Named for an exuberant scalp dance held there in celebration of a Caddo scalp in the winter of 1860–1861.

Dáu-jó-hâu—Medicine Bluff Concavity. Mount Rochester on the Upper South Canadian River in the Texas Panhandle. Hugh L. Scott (HLS-FSA 1:105–106) records a site called Medicine Butte as a high pointed butte on the north side of the Canadian that "looms up high above the other—like a mountain with cut side" that can be seen from the top of the Antelope Hills [of Oklahoma] and "has strong medicine." The 1884 Indian Territory map depicts "Mt. Rochester" on the Roberts-Hemphill County Border, just north of the South Canadian River. Although not labeled on the modern Barton Creek Quad U.S.G.S. map, it is probably one of several hills of elevation ca. 2,800 feet in this area.

Fá-sán-gá—Plains escarpment. The west bluff edge or escarpment of the Llano Estacado or Staked Plains just east of the Texas–New Mexico border. Mooney recorded Bluff or Mesa Prairie, pa-gya—prairie, san-ga—bluff edge (JMKFN 11:148).

Gúl-jó-hâu—Red Bluff Concavity. (1) A bluff on the north side of the Canadian River above the mouth of Mustang Creek and a few miles above Adobe Walls in Hutchinson and Roberts counties in the Texas Panhandle. The site of William Bent's trading post in 1843–1844 and Kit Carson's fight with the Kiowa in 1864. (2) A prominent red bluff on the west side of Highway 270/281 near Greenfield, Blaine County, Oklahoma. Cheyenne Sun Dances were held on the east side of this bluff.

Kó̜-jó̜-hâu — Dark Cove/Bluff Concavity. A bluff near the head of the Cimarron River in southeastern Colorado or northeastern New Mexico. Probably Black Mesa in Cimarron County, Oklahoma, near the Oklahoma, Colorado, and New Mexico state lines.

Sá-qàul-gùl-jó̜-hâu — Cheyenne Red Bluff Recess. The Red Hills on the North Canadian River above Fort Reno, near Canadian County, Oklahoma.

Thái̜-jó̜-hâu — White Cliff/Bluff. (1) A bluff on the upper South Canadian River near the New Mexico line, probably in Quay County, New Mexico, or Oldham County, Texas. (2) A bluff at or beyond the head of Páuvàu in southeastern Colorado in 1840–1841, probably in Baca or Las Animas county.

Xó̜-gúl (Xó̜-gúl-jò̜-hâu) — Red Stone. The red sandstone bluffs and concavities along the south side of the Washita River just south and west of Washita in Caddo County, Oklahoma.

Xó̜-gà-dó̜-gà — Below/Beneath The Rocks. The extreme northwestern end of Zodletone Mountain and the adjacent small hill to the northwest and across Saddle Mountain Creek, T:6N, R:14W, Sect. 8 on the Stinking Creek Quad in Kiowa County, Oklahoma. Saddle Mountain Creek flows between the sheer cliffs of these two hills and has a unique microenvironment noticeably different from the surrounding landscape and similar to areas along Medicine Bluff Creek in the Wichita Mountains.

Xó̜-qáu-dáu-há — Rock Bluff/Cliff Medicine (lit. Bluff-Medicine-Very). Medicine Bluff in the Wichita Mountains of Oklahoma. Located today on the Fort Sill Military Range in Comanche County, Oklahoma. Named for its frequent use as a fasting and vision quest site. A large underwater monster is reported to live in the pool below.

Other Landforms

Á-jâun (gà) — Timber Gap. The pass through the Wichita Mountains, now Highway 58, northeast of Meers, Comanche County, Oklahoma.

Á-kàul-è̜ — "Timber Together," or Timber Grove. Verden in Grady County, Oklahoma. Named for the large timber grove located there under which several early Indian-Indian and Indian-Anglo councils were held. A smoke shop on the west side of Verden bears this name.

Á-kọ̀-vằu-sò-lẹ̀-gàu or Á-kọ̀-vằu-yáp-fá-hê-gàu—Dark Timber River Soldier Place. Fort Larned, built in 1859 on the south bank of the Pawnee Fork, approximately eight miles above its junction with the Arkansas River, Pawnee County, Kansas. *See* Màunkàugúldévằu.

Á-thàu-kàui-dàum-bè or Á-thàu-kàui-dàum-gà—Within or Along Timber or Forested Mexican Country. The forested region of northern Mexico along the Rio Grande, including Nuevo Leon, Tamaulipas, and southeastern Texas.

Áu-tạ́-thại-gà-qùl-dé-ẹ̀—Salt Place or Bed (lit. Place Where Salt Is). The salt beds on the upper South Canadian River at the New Mexico state line, probably east of Logan, New Mexico, in Oldham County, Texas, and Quay County, New Mexico.

Ául-tháu-dáu—Head Wound (lit. Lanced, Punctured, or Caused To Issue Forth From the Head). The salt plains in Alfalfa County, Oklahoma, now part of Salt Plains National Wildlife Refuge. Named for a Kiowa man who was shot and killed (resulting in his brains issuing forth from the wound) there while getting salt when the Kiowa raided a wagon train. A major source of salt in this region of the plains, the area attracted many animals and was a major crossroads of Indian activity.

Cáui-dàum-gà—Kiowa Country. The collective term for the Kiowa homeland, now usually used in reference to southwestern Oklahoma.

Câi-qùl—Comanche Cache. The vicinity of a spring in the mountains of northern Coahuila, Mexico, one day's journey south of the Rio Grande. Probably named from being a base camp for Comanche raids into northeastern Mexico.

Chèn-vằum-pì-hót—Boggy Creek Peninsula. The peninsula just west of the mouth of Rainy Mountain Creek and the Washita River northeast of Mountain View, Kiowa County, Oklahoma. The site of the first Kiowa Ghost Dance in 1890.

Dáu-ál-kọ̀-gài-é-hòl-dè-ẹ̀—Place Where Black Kettle Was Killed. The Washita Battlefield near Cheyenne, in Roger Mills County, Oklahoma. Named for the attack on Black Kettle's camp there on November 27, 1868.

Dọ́i-gàu-vằu-dấu-dé-ẹ̀ or Dọ́i-gàu-vằu-qầu-dé-ẹ̀—Place Where a River Is Positioned Deep Below It or Place Where a River Lies Deep Below It (lit. Deeply River Positioned/Lies Place At Which). Cataract and Colorado canyons in Havasupai country in Arizona.

Fá-gà̀—Prairie or Open Field. The Staked Plains of Texas.

Góm-gá-jâun—Wind Pass/Canyon. A canyon pass at the extreme head of the Double Mountain Fork of the Brazos River in Texas, located above Cáujàuvàu (Trading Creek). Probably near Canyon in Lubbock County, Texas. Possibly Yellow House Canyon.

Gú-à-nà-dè-tháu-hò̃—Where Quanah Led His Confederates, or Quanah's Battleground. Adobe Walls in east-central Hutchinson County, Texas. Named for the fight there on June 27, 1874 (Mooney 1898:203, 404).

Gúl-qáu-fà—Red or Paint Bank. A rocky bank east of Stumbling Bear's camp on Ájâunvàu near Meers, Comanche County, Oklahoma. Named for being a source of red paint mineral.

Hó-áun-thàu-kâui—White Man's Road. The California Road. The main emigrant road to California in southwestern Texas (Mooney 1898:319).

Î-ó-gû-è̱-vàu-só-lè̱-gàu—Fort Elliott (lit. Maggot Creek Soldiers), built in 1875. Located along the east side of Sweetwater Creek, one mile northwest of Mobeetie on Highway 152 in Wheeler County, Texas. Also known as Káutó̱dè̱ạ̀vàusólè̱gàu.

Káu-tó̱-dè-ạ̱-vàu-só-lè̱-gàu—Fort Elliott (lit. Creek Where a Robe Was Left Soldiers) in Wheeler County, Texas. Also known as Î̱ógûè̱vàusólè̱gàu.

Màun-kàu-gúl-dé-vàu-gà Yàp-fà-hê Cíl-dé-è̱—Where Soldiers Are Stationed At/On Red Sleeve Creek. Fort Larned, built in 1859, on the Pawnee River in Pawnee County, Kansas. Named for the Comanche Red Sleeve killed there in 1847. A three-part adverbial expression used as a place name.

Pí-hót—Peninsula, Bend in the River. (1) A well-known Sun Dance (1839, 1885, 1890) locale on the south side of the Washita River northeast of Carnegie, Kiowa County, Oklahoma. (2) A bend in the Washita River near the mouth of Stinking Creek and the second Kiowa Ghost Dance site, just west of Carnegie, Kiowa County, Oklahoma.

Qáu-dàl-hòp-gá-thà̱-dàu-è̱—Where They Surrounded the Wagon Freighters. The Lyman Wagon Train Battlefield on the north side of the Washita River, northeast of Fort Elliott in Hemphill County, Texas. Named for the fight there on September 9–13, 1874.

Qóp-tái-dè-jó-chél-dè—Mountain Top Structure or Building (lit. Mountain-Atop-House-Positioned-On). Signal Mountain on Fort Sill Military Base, Comanche County, Oklahoma. Named for the military lookout and signal tower built there in 1871.

Qóp-tháu-káui-dàum-bè—Within the Mexican Country (lit. Mountain Mexican Country). An adverb used as a place name for New Mexico.

Sé-sè-vàu-hò̱-àun—Arrowpoint River Trail. The Santa Fe Trail along the Arkansas River in Kansas. Named for the Kiowa name of that river.

Sôl-dàum—Onion Flat (lit. Onion Ground). The area between the Wichita Mountains, Rainy Mountain, and Hobart in Kiowa County, Oklahoma. A low-lying, occasionally flat and marshy area that was thickly covered with mesquite trees and noted for deer and antelope hunting but not for residence, hence the lack of allotments chosen in this area.

Tàn-yál-dá-yáp-fà-hê-cà—At Bare/Bald Hill Soldier Place (lit. Bare/Bald Hill Soldiers). Fort Clark, near Brackettville, Kinney County, Texas. Built in 1852, Fort Clark was located at a spring forming the head of Los Moras (The Mulberries) Creek, a well-known base camp used by southern Plains tribes raiding into Mexico.

Tǫ́-sál-dàu—Heated Water. The Yellowstone Park area of Wyoming. Named for the hot water geysers of the area. See Nabokov and Loendorf (2004:67, 71–75): "Tung Sa'u Dah—'hot water' or 'the place of hot water.'"

Vǎu-êl-thàu-kàui-gà—Great Rio Grande River Settlement (lit. River Great White Man's Place). Fort McIntosh, built in 1849, on the lower Rio Grande, on the east side of present-day Laredo, Webb County, Texas. Now the site of Laredo Community College. Mooney (1898) reports that the Kiowa seldom went south or east of this vicinity.

Xó-áut-káun-gà—At the End of the Bluff (lit. Stone's End At). Mooney (1898:338) describes it as on the south side of the North Fork of the Red River, above the junction of Elm Fork, in Greer County, Oklahoma. It is probably Mount Walsh, elevation 2,303 feet. Named for its marking the western end of the Wichita Mountain Range in southwestern Oklahoma. *See* Qópáutkáun. One Kiowa elder near Hobart, Oklahoma, calls the area between Quartz Mountain and Mount Walsh by this name.

Xǒ-chél-dé-è̩—Where Standing or Positioned Rock Is (singular). A ten-foot-high formation on the west bank of the Elk River, five miles southeast of Elk City, Beckham County, Oklahoma. Harrington (1939:170) notes that this name would probably also be applied to Pawnee Rock, fifteen miles west of Great Bend, Kansas, and north of the Arkansas River. The triplural (three or more) form is Xǒ-sául-dé.

Xó-hót—Canyon. Palo Duro Canyon, south of Canyon, Randall County, Texas.

Xò-aî—Rock That Grew Upwards. Sometimes translated as Tree Rock (Mooney 1898:428) or Up a Rock. Because Kiowa place names generally do not contain diphthongs, as in personal names, the diphthong (ai) implies the rock moving upward, in reference to its origins. (1) Devil's Tower National Monument in Crook County, Wyoming.

Named for the noted Kiowa story in which seven children were saved from a pursuing bear when a stone they stood on grew, raising them to safety. (2) An upright standing rock column on the Salt Fork of the Arkansas River in Kansas.

Xó-jôi-gá-thà-dàu-dé-ę̀—Rock House in Which They Were Contained (lit. Stone-House-Confine-It Is/At Which). Hueco Tanks, located thirty-two miles northeast of El Paso, in El Paso County, Texas, now Hueco Tanks State Historical Park. The site is a 400-foot-high granite formation containing numerous huecos or rock basins that trap rainwater and has served as a source of water in the region for a millennium. The most reliable cistern is present-day Comanche Cave. Named for a battle in 1839 in which a Kiowa raiding party was trapped for several days in one of the rock basins before escaping.

Xó-pá-jó́—Adobe House (lit. Rock Dust House). Bent's Fort on the north bank of the Arkansas River in Otero County, Colorado, approximately 15 miles above the junction with the Purgatoire River and abandoned in 1849. The same name was used for Fort Lyon built in 1860 near the same site, until it was relocated farther upstream in 1867.

Xó-qáu-dáu-há-gà—At Medicine Bluff, the name of Fort Sill, Comanche County, Oklahoma. An abbreviation of Xó-qáu-dáu-há-gà-yáp-fà-hę̀-gàu-qúl-dé-ę̀ or Where the Soldiers Stay At Medicine Bluff (lit. Rock Cliff Medicine At Soldiers Collective They Are).

Xó-sáu or Xó-sául-dè—Standing/Positioned Rocks (triplural). (1) A location in the Yellowstone region, possibly the Yellowstone or Upper Missouri River. (2) The Mississippi River, named for frozen erect blocks of ice, according to D. K. Lonewolf (Harrington 1939:167).

Xó-thàu-kàui-dàum-bè—Along Rock Mexicans Country (lit. Stone Mexicans Country Along). The Mexican country around Silver City, New Mexico, from which the Kiowa traded for silver ornaments.

Xól-hę̀-dè-vàu-gà-yàp-fà-hę̀-gà-qúl-dé-ę̀—At No Arm's Creek Where the Soldiers Are Stationed. Fort Zarah, built in 1864, near present-day Great Bend, Barton County, Kansas. Formerly on the north bank of Upper Walnut Creek, two miles above its junction with the Arkansas and just above Allison's Trading Post.

Yáp-fá-hê-qùl-dé-ę̀—(Place At Which the Soldiers Are). A shortened form of the previous name.

More Recent Anglo Locales

Á-ná-dá-kò—the Kiowa pronunciation of Anadarko, Oklahoma.
Cí-pòt-cà—the Kiowa pronunciation of Cooperton, Oklahoma.

É-zèn-cà—Inside the Agency. A Kiowa pronunciation of "agency." The Indian Agency at Anadarko, Oklahoma.

É-zè-yàu—In the Agency Area. A Kiowa pronunciation of "agency." The Indian Agency at Anadarko, Oklahoma.

Gǘ-sé-jàn—The Kiowa pronunciation of Washington, D.C.

Jò-áui-dè—Many Tipis/Houses. The twentieth-century Kiowa name of Oklahoma City, Oklahoma.

Láwt-cá—"At Lawton," the Kiowa pronunciation of Lawton, Oklahoma.

Ó-cóm-sé-lè—The Kiowa pronunciation of Oklahoma City, Oklahoma.

Kiowa Water-Based Place Names and Astrological Place Names

Streams

Ằ-càui-vâu — Hawk Creek. (1) Little Elk Creek, the east fork of present-day Elk Creek, near Hobart, Kiowa County, Oklahoma. (2) An upper branch of White River, a tributary of the Brazos River in Texas.

Ắ-cǐ-nyì-vàu — Tall Tree Creek. The middle fork of Elk Creek, Kiowa County, Oklahoma. Named for a very large tree that once stood on it (Mooney 1898:393). Probably Trail Creek in Washita County, Oklahoma.

Ắ-còt-à-vàu — Chinaberry Tree Creek (lit. Hard Wood Creek). Palo Duro Creek in the northern Texas Panhandle.

Ắ-dàui-ét-jé-vàu — Big Tree Creek. Possibly Valley Creek, a northern tributary of the Elm Fork in Greer County, Oklahoma. Named for a large cottonwood that formerly grew on its east bank. Also known as Chẽjánvàu.

Ắ-fàt-dàu-vàu or Ắp-àt-dàu-vàu — River With Low Spreading Branches. The Cimarron River in Oklahoma, also known as Jòhâudèhêmdèvàu.

Ắ-gùn-tà-vàu — Tipi Pole Cutting River. The Washita River of west-central Oklahoma. Named for the cutting of cottonwood tipi poles along this stream.

Ắ-jâun-vàu — Timber Gap or Pass Creek. Present-day Canyon Creek, which flows along the former road to Fort Sill, now Highway 58. A tributary stream of Medicine Bluff Creek located north of Mount Scott and east of Meers, Comanche County, Oklahoma. Named for the timber gap that allowed travel. Scott (HLS-FSA 1:210–211) also records the name of Yamparika Creek for this stream.

Ắ-jé-qǐ-jé-vàu — Ájéqǐ's River (Mythical Owl Idol's River). Buck or Clear Creek, in Collingsworth and Childress counties, Texas, that joins the

Red River in Jackson County, Oklahoma. Named for Ájéqî, a man who carried an Á-jé (a medicine owl in Kiowa lore) idol in a shoulder pouch and died there.

Á̱-jò-à̱-vàu—Timber Enclosure or Windbreak Creek. Mule Creek, a tributary of the Salt Fork of the Arkansas River in Kiowa, Comanche, and Barber counties, Kansas. Named for a circular opening in the timber resembling a wind break, and/or from the Pawnee, who often built such enclosures around their camps (Mooney 1898:392).

Á̱-kò̱-chèn-vàu—Dark Timbered Muddy Creek. Lebos Creek in Greer County, Oklahoma. Sometimes called Á̱kò̱vàu.

Á̱-kò̱-vàu—Dark Timber River. (1) The Pawnee Fork of the Arkansas River, Pawnee County, Kansas, also known as Màunkàugúldévàu. (2) An abbreviation of Á̱kò̱chènvàu in Greer County, Oklahoma. (3) Boggy Creek, a tributary of the South Canadian on the Wichita Reservation. Sometimes called "Gi ata Pada ti" (Backbone or Ridge Creek) for the high ridge separating it from the South Canadian River. Named for the dark shade created by heavy timber. Present-day Buggy Creek near Minco, in Caddo County, Oklahoma.

Á̱-sè̱-sè-vàu or Á̱-sè-sè-vàu—Wooden Arrowpoint or Lance Point River. The Brazos River of Texas. The Comanche use the same translation for the stream. Note: sé̱-sè (triplural for arrow points) is sometimes used for "lances" (d/t fì-tàu).

Á-thàu-hâui-gá-càun-dè-àu-sè̱—Stream Branch Where They Brought Back the Bonnet. The fourth creek entering the North Fork of the Red River from the north below Sweetwater Creek. Named for a Kiowa war party that returned with a captured Ute war bonnet in the summer of 1869. Designated an intermittent stream and not a creek or river, this appears to be the second intermittent branch in Sect. 1, T9N, R26W, of the Mayfield Quad in Beckham County, Oklahoma.

Á̱-yàl-dà-vàu—Timber Hill River. Medicine Lodge Creek, a tributary of the Salt Fork of the Arkansas in Kiowa and Barber counties, Kansas, and Grant County, Oklahoma. Named for Á̱-yàl-dà (Timber Hill), along the stream near the Kansas-Oklahoma border. The site of several Sun Dances and the 1867 Medicine Lodge Treaty.

Á̱-zót-vàu—Driftwood Creek (lit. Logs-Floating-Creek). A southern tributary of the Arkansas southeast of Bent's Fort in Las Animas, Baca, and Prowers counties, Colorado, near a "double mountain" (probably Two Buttes). Probably Two Butte Creek. Named for large quantities of driftwood from small tributaries along its lower course.

A̱u-cù-vàu—Sidedish Creek. (1) Elk Creek near present-day Hobart, Kiowa County, Oklahoma. Also known as Qócáuivàu and Jónáèvàu.

(2) A river in Chihuahua from which a trail led across to the Pecos. Possibly the North Concho River. Both streams are named for the high density of pecan trees along their courses, which the Kiowa ate as a side dish (ặu-cù) in meals.

Ãu-hį́-vàu — Cedar Creek. (1) Duck Creek, a branch of the Salt or White Fork of the Brazos River in Texas. Also known as Sáutqàunyàldàvàu. (2) Cedar Creek southeast of Carnegie, Oklahoma. Named for the high density of cedar trees along this stream.

Ãu-tą́-tháį-vàu — Salt River. (1) The Salt Fork of the Arkansas River in north-central Oklahoma. (2) The Elm Fork of the Red River in Greer County, Oklahoma (GWH-OHS). (3) A southern branch of the South Canadian River in the Texas Panhandle near the New Mexico line and near where the Ute captured the Taime in 1868. Named for a nearby deposit from which Indians procured salt.

Ául-pép-vàu — Frizzle Head Creek (lit. Bushy Hair Creek). Frizzie Head Creek, a small tributary of Medicine Bluff Creek between Meers and Saddle Mountain just before the road turns north toward Saddle Mountain, Comanche County, Oklahoma. Named for Ãulpépjè (Frizzle Head 1824–1907), who resided near there (Corwin 1958:143; Toncacut 2000:91).

Ãul-têm-ét-kúi-càun-dé-ę̀-vàu — Head Dragging Creek (lit. Where They Dragged the Head At Creek). A small tributary of the Clear Fork of the Brazos River in Texas. Named for an Arapaho killed by Comanches, who was beheaded and the head brought back to a Kiowa camp on the end of a reata (riata) in the winter of 1837–1838.

Bó-sén-vàu — Buzzard Creek. A small tributary of the Washita River 2.5 miles west of the Apache Wye (the intersection of Highways 9 and 281) and just west of Mopope Hill, Caddo County, Oklahoma. Named for the preponderance of buzzards in the vicinity, which remain today. No relation to the Bosin (Buzzard) family, who lived near Anadarko.

Câi-yàl-dà-vàu — Comanche Knoll River. Deer Creek, a southern tributary of the South Canadian in D-County (later Dewey County), south of Taloga, Thomas, and Hydro, in Custer and Dewey counties, Oklahoma. *See* Câiyàldà.

Cặu-jàu-vàu — Trading Creek. The Double Mountain or North Fork of the Brazos River in Texas. Possibly named from a prominent trail along this stream leading to the Staked Plains and New Mexico.

Cáu-kį̀-dè-vàu — Ten Creek. Present-day Gokey (Gawky) Creek, a southern tributary of the Washita River between Carnegie and Fort Cobb, Caddo County, Oklahoma. Named for Cáukį̀gàcùt (lit. Ten Battle Marks), a Kiowa man who lived along its course (GWH-OHS).

Chá-dàu-yàl-dà-fę̀-vầu—Prairie Dog Hill Sandy Creek. The Pease River, an upper branch of the Red River in Texas. Named for Prairie Dog Hill, a prominent hill or low mountain between the Pease and Red rivers twenty miles west of Vernon, Texas. Probably near Medicine Mounds in Hardeman County. *See* Chádàuyàldà.

Chá-fį̀-vầu—Prairie Dog Eating Creek. A western fork of Rainy Mountain Creek (Mooney 1898:427). Parker McKenzie described this stream as a small stream running north of Gotebo, Kiowa County, Oklahoma, and toward Cordell, Oklahoma. Black Goose's map places it as the larger western branch of Rainy Mountain Creek originating north of Gotebo, crossing Highway 9 one mile east of Gotebo and joining Rainy Mountain Creek just south of Mountain View, Oklahoma. Hicks (GWH-OHS) listed it as "Little Rainy Mountain Creek," which confirms this. Two versions of the origin of the name are known and may be related. In one version, it was named for a heavy rain around 1873 while the Kiowa were camped there in which a large number of prairie dogs were drowned out, killed, and eaten by the Kiowa. In the second version, provided by Parker McKenzie, the stream was named in the 1870s when Kiowa hunting for bison found numerous bison slaughtered by Anglo hunters, who had skinned them for their hides, leaving the carcasses to decompose. Nearly starving, a Kiowa band, including his maternal grandparents, were forced to kill and eat numerous prairie dogs along this stream (Parker McKenzie to the author, August 19, 2004).

Chę̀-ján-vầu—Horse's Headdresses Creek. Possibly Valley Creek, a northern tributary of the Elm Fork in Greer County, Oklahoma. Named for the Chę̀-ján-màu or Horse's Headdresses Military Society. Also known as Ádàuiétjévầu (Mooney 1898:392).

Chèn-vấu—Boggy/Muddy Creek. (1) Lower Rainy Mountain Creek near Mountain View, Kiowa County, Oklahoma, the entire East Fork of Rainy Mountain Creek according to some. Named for the lower portion of the stream being deep-sided, muddy, and having only two crossing locations prior to modern development (GWH-OHS). (2) The Little Wichita River near Henrietta, Clay County, Texas.

Cú-jò-ì-vầu—Baby Bird Creek. An unknown stream southwest of Double Mountain in Stonewall County, Texas, near the old California Trail.

Cûi-qà-vầu—Pawnee River. Probably the Kansas (Kaw) River or a tributary branch (Smoky Hill, Saline, Solomon, Republican) in Kansas. Described as situated between the Arkansas and Platte, but tributary to neither. Mooney (1898:297) lists it as Smoky Hill.

Cûi-qòl-jé-vầu—Wolf Neck's River. A branch of White River running into

the Brazos River in Texas. Named for a Comanche known to the Kiowa
as Wolf Neck. The full name may have been Cûi-qòl-pà-jé-vàu (Wolf
Necklace's River).

Cûi-vàu — Wolf Creek. Present-day Wolf Creek, a tributary of the North
Canadian River at Fort Supply, Woodward County, Oklahoma.

É-qú-vàu — Garden Creek (lit. Crops-Planted-Creek). Chandler Creek in
northern Comanche County, Oklahoma, that drains into Lake Ells-
worth. Named for either (1) the Chandler family, the first known
Anglo family to plant crops along this creek, or (b) the Apache, who
had their principal corn fields along this creek (Mooney 1898:401).

Fâ-bò-vàu — American Horse River. An upper branch of the Pease River
in Texas, described as midway between the Red River and the Staked
Plains where they are one day's journey apart. Named from a fight in
which the Kiowa captured several horses, the largest they had ever
seen, from Texans in the winter of 1841–1842. Also known as
Tǫzótcótvàu and Fíbòvàu.

Fé-vàu — Sandy River. The Smoky Hill River of Kansas. Named for the
prevalence of sand in this stream.

Fê-vàu — Turkey Creek. (1) A small southwestern tributary of Elk Creek
on the North Fork of Red River in H County (Washita County), Oklahoma. Probably one of the tributaries just east of Retrop, Oklahoma.
(2) Little Turkey or Turkey Creek, a southern tributary of the North
Fork of Red River beyond Mount Walsh. Previously in Greer and now
in northwest Beckham County, Oklahoma.

Fé-vàu-èl — Big or Great Sand River. The Red River between Oklahoma
and Texas, so called both above and below the North Fork. Named for
the prevalence of sand in the stream. Modern Kiowa sometimes call
the river Gúlváu, a translation of the English name "Red River."

Fén-hà-vàu — Sugar Creek. (1) Sugar Creek on the Wichita Reservation
north of Anadarko, Caddo County, Oklahoma. Sometimes called
Thócútvàu, which was probably the earlier name for the stream. (2)
The later name of Xò-dôm-vàu (Pebble Creek), a tributary of Rainy
Mountain Creek southwest of Mountain View, in Kiowa County, Okla-
homa. Mooney (1898:428) lists the later stream as "Stone Mortar
Creek." The streambed is full of pebble-sized stones, reflecting the
origin of the name. In both cases, the name Sugar Creek may be of
Euroamerican influence.

Fí-bò-vàu — American Horse River. A head branch of the Pease River in
Texas, also known as Tǫzótcótvàu and Fâbòvàu.

Fó-vàu — Beaver River/Creek. (1) The North Canadian River and its upper
branch (Beaver Creek) in northwestern Oklahoma and the Oklahoma

Panhandle. (2) Otter Creek, a branch of the North Fork of the Red River in Kiowa, Comanche, and Tillman counties, Oklahoma. (3) Beaver Creek, east of Fort Sill, Comanche and Cotton counties, Oklahoma.

Fŏ-vău-sân—Little Beaver Creek. Little Beaver Creek, east of Fort Sill in Grady, Stephens, and Cotton counties, Oklahoma.

Gú-à-nà-dè-vàu—Quanah's Creek. West Cache Creek in Comanche County, Oklahoma. The Kiowa pronunciation of Quanah (Parker), named for his residing along the creek. Also known as Gúhàlèváu.

Gú-hà-lè-vàu—Wild Horse/Mustang Creek or Kwahadi Creek. West Cache Creek, Comanche County, Oklahoma. Named for the Kwahadi Comanche living in this area of the reservation. While Ko-be is the Comanche term for wild horses or mustangs and appears in several personal names, Gú-hà-lè-gàu, the Kiowa name for the Kwahadi Comanche of the Staked Plains associated with wild horse herds of this region, is based on the Kiowa term for mustangs, but incidentally also resembles the Kiowa pronunciation of Kwahadi. Also known as Gúànàdèváu.

Gúl-qúl-dé-ę̀-vàu—Creek Where There Is Paint. Clay Creek, a southern tributary of the Arkansas in Prowers County, Colorado. Named for a prevalent supply of clay for paint. Also known as Yáldávàu.

Gúl-váu—Red River. (1) The South Canadian River in Oklahoma. With a valley of up to 40 miles in width in places, this river separates the northern and southern high plains. Named for its red color, produced from its flow over the "red-bed" strata of the area. (2) The Big Wichita River near Wichita Falls, Texas.

Hą̀u-pài-vàu—Gun Powder River. The Powder River in Montana and Wyoming.

Hą̀u-xò-vàu—Cannonball River (lit. Iron Stone River). A tributary of the Kansas River, probably the Solomon or perhaps the Republican. Named for abundant iron nodules in the vicinity. The description of Kóyàldà suggests the Solomon.

Hîl-gà-ą̀-jé-vàu—Coming Down a Valley's River (lit. At a Point In the Valley Going Along River). The Devil's or San Pedro River, which joins the Rio Grande below the Pecos in Val Verde County, Texas. Described as flowing with a noisy current and having very large fish. Dan Gelo (personal communication, 2006) reports that this remains an accurate description of the river. A war trail into Mexico crossed nearby.

Ì-ó-gû-ę̀-vàu—Maggot Creek. Traitor and Sweetwater Creeks in Wheeler County, Texas. Named after a Kiowa hunting party that had to throw away a quantity of fly-blown meat there. Battey's (1873:166) Ì-ó-vàu (Rice Creek) correlates with this site.

Já-kàu-gà-váu or Já-kàu-qì-váu—Eye Triumph Creek. A small branch of
Apache Creek, an upper branch of Cache Creek in southern Caddo
County, Oklahoma. Probably Tahoe or Mission Creek or a tributary of
one of these. Named for a Navajo eye brought home as a war trophy in
the winter of 1879–1880 (see Mooney 1898:345–346).

Jà-má-tàun-à-váu—Star Girls Tree River. The Salt Fork of the Red River in
Greer County, Oklahoma. Named for a noted tree that grew from a
twig driven into the ground to support the "medicine" during the Star
Girls Ceremony, a ritual invocation and sacrifice periodically performed in tribute to the Star Girls by mothers on behalf of their sick
children, but now defunct. Stumbling Bear's mother led this ceremony (Mooney 1898:398).

Jái-fè-è̦-vàu—Skunkberry Creek. "A southern tributary of the South
Canadian, about opposite Lathrop. White Deer Creek (?)" (Mooney
1898:424). Lathrop was a small settlement on the south side of the
Canadian River in north-central Oldham County, Texas. The head of
White Deer Creek is due east of Lathrop in southwest Hutchinson
County, Texas. Several southern tributaries of the Canadian in this
area intersect with this line.

Jé-à-vàu—All Kinds of Trees Creek. A stream near Fort Dodge, Kansas.
Possibly Buckner Creek in Hodgeman County.

Jò-hâu-dè-hêm-dè-vàu—River Where Jòhâusàn Died. A byname for the
Cimarron River, where at the juncture of North or Kiowa Creek, near
where the Arkansas River crosses into Oklahoma, he died in 1866
(HLS-FSA:1:78). Also known as Áfàtdàuvàu.

Jó-vàu or Jó-hi̦-vàu—Tipi/Tepee Creek. A tributary of the North Fork of
the Red River near Tepee Mountain, southeast of Lugert, Kiowa
County, Oklahoma (GWH-OHS). The last Ghost Dances near Hobart
were held here.

Jón-á-è-vàu—Pecan Creek. (1) Present-day Elk Creek near Hobart, Kiowa
County, Oklahoma. Named for dense pecan groves in this vicinity.
Also known as À̦ucùvàu. Formerly called Qócáuivàu from the presence of elk in the Wichita Mountains (Mooney 1898:400). (2) The
Nueces River of Texas (also called Pecan River by the Comanche).
(3) The southernmost tributary of Sé̦vàu, probably the Sabinas Hidalgo
branch of the Lower Salado River in Neuvo Leon, Mexico.

Jón-váu—Fat River. The South Platte River of Colorado. Named for the
abundance of bison there. Also known as Fat, Greasy, and sometimes
Goose River to many tribes of the region.

Jót-qáut-à-vàu—Oak or Postoak Creek (lit. Tool-Handle Wood Stream). A
small southern tributary of the Washita River in Kiowa County, Okla-

homa. Later named Kàujŏlàvàu after the death of Jótqáutằ (Oak Trees) in 1893.

Káu-hòl-vàu—Mescal Bean Creek. A river somewhere southwest of Double Mountain, Texas, near the old California emigrant trail. Named for mescal bean bushes growing on it. Káu-hòl is Kiowa for both the mescal bean and mescal bean bandoleers.

Kàu-jŏl-à-vàu—Easily Debarked Tree Creek. Oak Creek, a small southern tributary of the Washita River, just above Rainy Mountain Creek, between Mountain View and Gotebo, Kiowa County, Oklahoma. Named for the characteristic oak trees along its course. Also known as Jótqáutằvàu.

Kắu-tŏ-dè-ạ̀-vàu—Creek Where a Robe Was Left. Battery Creek. The upper branch of Sweetwater Creek near Fort Elliott in Wheeler County, Texas. Probably the uppermost branch flowing north and west past New Mobeetie.

Káui-qò-vàu—Flint Creek. A northern tributary of the South Canadian River about ten miles above Adobe Walls. Big Clear or Mustang Creek per Mooney (1898:409). This distance suggests it is Pats Creek in west-central Roberts County, Texas. Named for the abundance of flint along its course.

Kǫ́-yàl-dà-vàu—Dark Hill River. Named for nearby Dark Hill, located between the Smoky Hill and Hặuxòvàu rivers. Probably Salt Creek near the Blue Hills in Mitchell County, Kansas.

Máu-qûi-vàu—Turning Around or Behind Creek. East Cache Creek in Caddo, Comanche, and Cotton counties, Oklahoma. Named for its course, which winds back towards itself. Also known as Sólèvàu.

Màun-kàu-gúl-dé-vàu—Red Sleeve's Creek. The Pawnee River or Pawnee Fork of the Arkansas River in Kansas. Named after the Comanche leader killed there in the summer of 1847 during an attack on traders at the crossing of the Sante Fe Trail and the Pawnee Fork, below later Fort Larned. Also known as Ãkòvàu.

Pài-jó-vàu—Sod House River (lit. Earth or Dirt House River). A stream southwest of Double Mountain, Texas, named for an adobe house built beside it. The term pài-jó was later used for wooden frame houses.

Páu-vàu—Bison Bull River. (1) Buffalo Creek, a southern tributary of the Cimarron River in Oklahoma. Possibly Buffalo Creek in Harper and Woodward counties. (2) Possibly Bear or Two Butte Creek in southeastern Colorado, described as a small, timberless, northern and possible tributary of the Cimarron River, probably in Baca or Las Animas County of Colorado. Note: Present-day Buffalo Creek in northern Baca

County joins Bear Creek. Plains tribes commonly knew the Cimmaron River as the "Buffalo Bull River" (Clark 1885:424).

Pàul-kầu-jè-vầu—Wooly Leggings' Creek. Paulaka Creek (Dick 1959:31), near the foot of the mountain beside Saddle Mountain Mission and near the south edge of Kiowa County, Oklahoma. Probably the first of two small tributaries in the SW1/4 of the SE1/4 of Sect. 28, T5N, R14W of the Saddle Mountain Quad. Named for Pàul-kầu-jè or Pàul-kâu (Wooly Leggings, Paudle-kaut 1901:42), whose allotment was one mile southeast of Saddle Mountain. A local name among Saddle Mountain Kiowa.

Pò-hón-ầ-vầu—Walnut Creek. Scott Creek, an upper branch of the North Fork of the Red River, south of Fort Elliott. With only two major tributary streams in this area of Texas, this is probably Cantonment Creek in Gray County, Texas.

Qầ-hị̂-fị̀-vầu—Tonkawa (lit. Man Eaters) Creek. Tonkawa Creek, a small tributary just south and east of Anadarko, Oklahoma, that flows northeastward into the Washita River. The branch draining the steep valley on the south side of present-day Indian City campground was the site of an intertribal attack resulting in the massacre of nearly half the Tonkawa on October 24, 1862.

Qáp-jầu-jái-dè-vầu—Brave Old Man's Creek. The name of "Cash" (Cache) Creek, probably East Cache Creek, recorded by Rev. George W. Hicks in the 1890s (GWH-OHS). The name refers to Qápjầujáidè (Brave Old Man), who probably had his camp near the headwaters of this stream, the vicinity where Hicks did much of his missionary work.

Qàun-chè-hâ-jé-vầu—Short Man's Creek. The extreme head of East Cache Creek near Eagle Heart's camp on the Kiowa reservation. Named after Short Man, who lived near the head of the stream. Near the Caddo-Kiowa county line south of Carnegie, Oklahoma.

Qầu-jó-vầu—Sun Dance Creek. A southern tributary of the North Canadian River at the 100th meridian in Oklahoma. Kiowa Creek in Lipscomb County, Texas, and Beaver County, Oklahoma. Named for frequent Sun Dances held along its course because of the abundance of suitable timber. Not to be confused with Kiowa Creek in Kiowa and Comanche counties, Kansas, or Medicine Lodge Creek in Barber County, Kansas.

Qầul-vầu—Arikara River (lit. Biter River). The Ree or Grand River in South Dakota. Named for the corn-eating Arikara who lived along it (Mooney 1898:408).

Qó-cáui-vầu—Elk Creek. (1) The former name of Jónáèvầu, now Elk

Creek, near Hobart, Kiowa County, Oklahoma. Named for elk in the nearby Wichita Mountains. Apparently a very old name, as Parker McKenzie reported that the Kiowa never referred to the creek by the name of Gúc̣ínyívàu (Elk Creek, lit. Long Horn Creek, the old term for elk) in his youth. Also known as Ą̊ucùvàu. (2) Red Deer Creek, a southern tributary of the South Canadian in Roberts and Hemphill counties, Texas.

Qól-ì-tò̜-vàu—Necklace Shell Water (Gorget) River. The North Platte River in Nebraska and Wyoming. Also known as Qólĩvàu and Qólpàvàu. Sometimes mistakenly called Qól-pà̜-qà-vàu (Sioux River) from its proximity to that tribe and the similarity of their name (Qól-pà̜-gàu—Necklace People). Named for profuse mussel shells that were collected and fashioned into gorgets and necklace pieces for personal adornment.

Qól-ì-vàu—Necklace Shell (Gorget) River. (1) The Musselshell River of Montana. (2) The North Platte River. Also known as Qólpàvàu (Necklace River, not to be confused with Sioux River, from the coincidental proximity of the Lakota). Both named for the high density of mussel shells in the river, which were collected and fashioned into gorgets and necklace pieces for personal adornment.

Qól-pà̜-vàu or Qól-pà̜-qá-vàu—Necklace or Necklace People (i.e., Sioux) River. (1) The North Platte River, named for the profuse mussel shells, which were used as ornaments. *See* Qólĩvàu. (2) The lower Missouri River, named for the Qólpà̜qágàu or Lakota.

Qóp-á-vàu—Mountain Timber Creek (lit. Mountain Timber Creek). (1) San Francisco Creek, a small tributary of the North Canadian, between Palo Duro and Beaver creeks, probably in Texas County, Oklahoma. (2) Present-day Frisco Creek in Sherman and Hansford counties, Texas. So named because the principal timber varieties growing on it generally occur only in the mountains.

Qóp-fé-vàu—Sand Mountain River (lit. Mountain Sand River). The North Fork of the Red River in Texas and southwestern Oklahoma. Hicks (GWH-OHS) confirms this name and location. Said to be called the Nueces by Mexicans (Mooney 1998:411); however, the Nueces is farther southeast in Texas.

Qóp-tháu-káui-vau—Mexican Creek. Delaware Creek east of Anadarko, Caddo County, Oklahoma. Named for a group of Mexicans who resided along the stream for a time.

Sá-nè-vàu—Snake Creek. Deep Creek. Probably Deep Red Creek, which joins West Cache Creek, south of Fort Sill near Lawton, in Tillman and Cotton counties, Oklahoma. A small tributary named Snake Creek joins Cache Creek northwest of Walters above the confluence of Deep Red Creek and Cache Creek.

Sá-qàut-jàu-á-àu-tàun-dè-vầu — Creek Where the Cheyenne Were Annihilated. Named for the fight between forty-eight Cheyenne Bow String Society members and a large camp of Kiowa, Apache, and Comanche in 1837. Mooney (1898:271–272, 419) provides three accounts. The first indicates the KCA camp was on "a small tributary of Scott creek [also known as Walnut Creek] . . . an upper branch of the North fork of Red river, southward from the present Ft. Elliott." After engaging the enemy outside their camp, the KCA followed the Cheyenne, "continuing along the trail down the north side of the creek to a short distance below its junction with Sweetwater. They came upon the main camp of Cheyenne, who dug holes in the sand." From this description, the Kiowa camp appears to have been somewhere south of present-day Mobeetie, in Wheeler County, Texas. Mooney (1898:419) later states, "a northern tributary of North fork of the Red river, the second below Sweetwater Creek, in F-County, Oklahoma." This is in western Beckham County. From examining USGS 7.5 toptographic maps of the Mayfield and Prentiss Quads of Oklahoma, streams downstream from the confluence of Sweetwater Creek with the North Fork of the Red River include three small, unnamed tributary streams, Buffalo Creek, six small tributary streams, Cat Creek, two small tributary streams, then Starvation Creek. Starvation Creek is much larger than Cat Creek. From Mooney's (1898:419) description and that the unnamed drainages in this area are small intermittent streams, and likely to have been viewed by the Kiowa as intermittent streams (vau), the fight may have occurred at the mouth of Catt Creek or possibly Starvation Creek. The Black Goose map (Meadows 2007:267, Fig. 1, no. 43) supports these designations, placing the event on the north side of the North Fork Red River, two streams below its confluence with Sweetwater Creek.

Still later, Mooney (1907:377 n.2) states, "The encounter took place on the head of a small southern tributary of the Washita, on the Red River divide, about 12 miles south of present Cheyenne, Oklahoma." This account, which may have been from the Cheyenne, suggests the head of a branch of Croton Creek near Dempsey. Although still in the general area, I am inclined to believe the former designations supported by the Black Goose map.

Sàu-pól-àul-tọ̀-vầu — Owls Head Creek. Jimmy Creek, the western branch of Ấjâunvầu near Meers, Comanche County, Oklahoma. Named for either a tree that contained knots resembling two owl heads or two such figures carved into a tree. One family member reported that the name was derived from the large number of owls that lived along the stream in the past. Named for Jimmy Quoetone, who lived near a prominent spring that feeds the steam.

Sáut-qàun-yàl-dà-vàu — Manure Hill Creek. Duck Creek, a small branch of the Salt Fork or White River Fork of the Brazos River in Texas. Also known as Åuhįvàu. Named for a nearby hill of the same name. Sáut-qàun is manure that comes out already firm; sáu-gà is wet feces.

Sẹ̀-à-làu-vàu — Prickly Pear Creek. A tributary of the Arkansas River approximately ten miles below Bent's Fort in Colorado, possibly Caddo or Rate Creek. Named for the preponderance of ripe prickly pears encountered there during a Sun Dance in the late fall of 1856. Probably near the Otero-Bent county line.

Sẹ̀-à-vàu — Willow Bush Creek (lit. Smell Wood Creek; ài-vį́ is willow tree). (1) A northern tributary of the Washita River in Oklahoma about four miles below Sugar Creek. (2) The Sabinas River, a tributary of the Salado River in Nuevo Leon, Mexico. (3) A northern tributary of Beaver Creek, just above the junction of Palo Duro Creek in Texas County, Oklahoma. (4) Box Elder Creek, south of Stecker, Caddo County, Oklahoma.

Sé-cáun-vàu — Dogwood Creek (Mooney 1898:420) (lit. Water Scum River). A small southern tributary of the South Canadian River in the Texas Panhandle, a short distance below Adobe Walls, possibly present-day Chicken Creek. Probably named for slow-moving water-scum-filled portions of the stream. Several short streams on the south side of the South Canadian River exist in this region.

Sé-sè-váu — Arrowhead River. The Arkansas River of Colorado through Oklahoma. Named for numerous prehistoric camps along its route where projectile points were collected and reused. Many Plains tribes used the same name for this river. By the mid-1800s the Arkansas served as a northern boundary of the normal Kiowa range.

Sẹ̀-vàu — Cactus River. The Salado River in Nuevo Leon, Mexico. Named for the prominent, tall cacti (*Cereus giganteus*) along its course.

Sém-hát-vàu — Apache Creek (lit. Thieve's Creek). An upper branch of East Cache Creek that joins Chandler Creek southwest of Apache, Oklahoma. Named for the Naishan Apache who resided on it during the reservation period, probably one of two small tributaries joining Chandler Creek proper in northern Comanche County, Oklahoma.

Sén-fól-é-vàu — Water Lillies Creek. Pond Creek, a northern tributary of the Washita, north of present-day Anadarko, Caddo County, Oklahoma. Sugar Creek is the only major stream fitting this description.

Sép-yál-dá-vầu—Rainy Hill Creek. The fork of Rainy Mountain Creek that joins Sugar Creek about one mile southeast of Rainy Mountain Kiowa Indian Baptist Church near Mountain View, Kiowa County, Oklahoma. Reported to be a post-reservation Kiowa translation of the English name by some elders.

Sét-ché-yồ-vầu—Domestic Hog Creek. Hog Creek, west of Anadarko, Caddo County, Oklahoma. Named for domestic hogs that escaped from the Caddo north of the Washita River, started roaming in this vicinity, and became wild. From Sét (bear), ché-yồ (pet or domestic) and vấu (stream).

Sét-thái-dè-tháu-kàui-mái-màu-fầ-câun-dè-vầu—Creek Where White Bear Brought the White Women (lit. White Bear-Anglo-Women-to-Bring-His-Creek). North or Kiowa Creek, a northern tributary of the Cimarron River, Comanche County, Kansas. Named for White Bear bringing and ransoming captive white women and children captured in Texas at Fort Dodge in 1866.

Só-lè-vầu—Soldier Creek. (1) East Cache Creek in Comanche and Cotton counties, Oklahoma. Named for the soldiers at Fort Sill. Also known as Xồqáudấuhásólèvầu and Máuqûivầu. (2) A small stream five-eighths of a mile west of the intersection of Highways 9 and 281 on Highway 9 that flows through the Redstone bluffs into the Washita River. A local name among the Redstone Kiowa. (3) Otter Creek west of Lawton, Oklahoma. Named for troops at Camp Radziminski in 1858–1859 (HLS-FSA:1:214). Also known as word. (4) The byname for the North Fork of the Red River. Named for an incident in which a group of U.S. cavalry camped near the stream; a flood came and the soldiers could not escape for two days and nights (Kauley 1975:12). A local name among Hobart Kiowa.

Són-thái-vầu or Són-thấ-vầu—White Grass Creek (possibly Són-thá-vầu, Bison Grass Creek). A branch of the White River and tributary of the Brazos River in Floyd, Crosby, Garza, and Kent counties, Texas.

Tál-kòp-vầu—Smallpox Creek. Mule Creek, a tributary of Medicine Lodge Creek near its juncture with the Salt Fork of the Arkansas, Alfalfa County, Oklahoma. Named for the first Sun Dance held there after the 1861–1862 smallpox epidemic.

Tán-vầu—Wild Turnip River. Possibly Harrington's (1939:170) Baking River or Paint Baking River, inferably in the Wyoming–South Dakota region. Sundstrom (2005) believes it may refer to the Belle Fourche River.

Tàn-yál-dá-vầu—Bare/Bald Hill River. Possibly Las Moras Creek near

Fort Clark and Brackettville, Kinney County, Texas. Named for a
nearby hill (Las Mores Mountain) of the same name.

Tấu-qòp-vầu—Saddle Mountain Creek. A small tributary of Stinking
Creek, north and east of Saddle Mountain, from which it derives its
name, in Kiowa County, Oklahoma.

Thái-vầu—White River. (1) An extreme northern tributary of the South
Canadian River, one day's journey below the salt beds at the New
Mexico line and approximately halfway to Gúljóhâu. Possibly Major
Long's Creek in the northwestern portion of the Texas Panhandle.
(2) The main stream of the Brazos River in Texas; also White River,
alias Catfish Creek near its head. This is clearly the White River Fork
of the Brazos and probably Crawfish Creek in Floyd and Crosby counties southeast of Plainview, Teas. Gelo (2000:290, personal communication 2006) states that the Comanche name for White River, the
White Fork of the Brazos, is based on the presence of caliche strata
along the stream's canyon walls.

Thầu-zòt-á-vầu—Buck Antelope Corral Creek (lit. Male or Buck Antelope
Driftwood or Corral Creek). Bear Creek between the Cimarron and
Arkansas rivers on the border of Baca County, Colorado, and Stanton
County, Kansas. Note: one tributary stream of Bear Creek in Baca
County, Colorado, is present-day Antelope Creek.

Thố-cút-vầu—Wichita Creek (lit. Faced Marked [Tattooed] Creek). A by-
name for Sugar Creek north of Anadarko, Caddo County, Oklahoma.
Named for the Wichita who were placed on a reservation there. More
commonly known as Fénhầvầu.

Tố-hè-vầu—Waterless or Dry Creek (lit. Water Without Creek). Sand
Creek, a northern tributary of the Arkansas River in Cheyenne, Kiowa,
and Lincoln counties, Colorado, and the stream on which the Sand
Creek Massacre occurred in 1864.

Tố-kố-vầu—Black Water Creek. A southern tributary of the Washita
River, approximately five miles below the Washita Battlefield site.
Probably the unnamed stream that enters the Washita 0.40 miles
above its intersection with county road E0940 between Cheyenne and
Strong City, Oklahoma; T14N, R23W, Sect. 28, Cheyenne Quad.

Tố-sáui-hyế-vầu—Blue Water Creek. The Colorado River of Texas. Also
known as Blue Water or River to the Comanche.

Tố-tép-èl-vầu—Big Spring Creek (lit. Water or Spring Big Creek). De-
scribed as southward from Double Mountain near the emigrant road.
Probably Giraud Creek of the Red Fork of the Colorado River in Texas.
The town of Big Spring and Big Spring State Park are located in

Howard County, Texas. This seems to be present-day Beals Creek, which flows east from Big Spring into the Colorado River.

Tǫ́-tép-vàu — Spring Creek. Fontaine qui Bouille (Boiling Water) Creek in Colorado. Sundstrom (2005) believes this is Manitou Springs in Colorado. *See* Tǫ́bíndádàu.

Tǫ́-xém-gá-vàu — Winding Creek. Crooked Creek in Gray and Meade counties, Kansas, and Beaver County, Oklahoma.

Tǫ́-zót-cót-vàu — Swift Water River/Creek. A head branch of the Pease River in Texas, described as midway between the Red River and the Staked Plains where they are one day's journey apart. Probably named for the stream's swift current. Later renamed Fâbòvàu and Fíbòvàu. While the estimate of a day's travel is not specified, it would seem to refer to that of a war party rather than a camp. The number of tributary streams feeding into the Pease River at this point between the Red River and the Staked Plains are few. This stream is probably Kent Creek in southeast Briscoe County, Texas, or a nearby tributary.

Váu-êl — Big or Great River. (1) The Rio Grande of New Mexico and Texas. (2) A great river beyond Qópétjàu (southern Rocky Mountains), probably the Colorado. (3) The Missouri River, according to Boyd (1983:1), but I was unable to confirm this with elders I interviewed.

Váu-êl-sàn — Little Big River (lit. River Big Little). The Pecos River in New Mexico and Texas, frequently crossed on raids into Mexico.

Váu-kó-èl--Broad Creek. A by-name used by some Kiowa for Medicine Bluff Creek in Comanche County, Oklahoma. More commonly known as Xǫ́qáudáuhávàu.

Váup-fá-hâl — River Confluence. The Pecos-Rio Grande River confluence in Val Verde County, Texas. A large set of white bluffs rise above the floodplain between the two streams at their juncture. An important site for Kiowa raids in northern Mexico.

Xò-dôm-vàu — Pebble Creek. The original Kiowa name of Sugar Creek (Fénhặvàu), a major tributary of Rainy Mountain Creek, in Kiowa County, Oklahoma. Named for the stream's stone-littered streambed (Mooney 1898:436; GWH-OHS).

Xǫ́-qáu-dáu-há-vàu — Medicine Bluff Creek. Medicine Bluff Creek, a tributary of East Cache Creek running through Ft. Sill in Comanche County, Oklahoma. Named for the prominent bluff of the same name. See next entry, also known as Váukóèl.

Xǫ́-qáu-dáu-há-só-lè-vàu — Medicine Bluff Soldier Creek. A by-name for East Cache Creek (which Medicine Bluff Creek joins) in Comanche and Cotton counties, Oklahoma. Named for nearby Medicine Bluff and the soldiers stationed at Fort Sill after 1869. Also known as Sólèvàu.

Xó-sáu-vầu or Xó-sáu-jòl-vầu—(Pipestone River). The Yellowstone and Upper Missouri River ('Tso'sa'Pa'), per Mooney (1898:153, 429), although the etymology is uncertain. See Harrington (1939:167–168). Xó-sául-dè-vầu (Standing/Positioned Rocks River) is another possible name.

Xó-thái-vầu—White Rock River. A southern tributary of the North Fork of Red River above Doan's Store in Greer County, Oklahoma, possibly Wanderer Creek.

Xó-vầu—Rock River. (1) The Purgatoire or Las Animas River, a southern tributary of the Arkansas River in Colorado. (2) The San Saba River, a southern tributary of the Colorado River of Texas, also called Rock River by the Comanche.

Xól-hé̱-dè-vầu—No Arm's Creek. Upper Walnut Creek, named for William Allison, who ran a trading post on the Upper Arkansas just below the junction of Upper Walnut Creek in Kansas, ca. 1850–1865. Probably east of Great Bend in Barton County, Kansas.

Yál-dá-vầu—Hill Creek. Clay Creek, a southern tributary of the Arkansas River in Prowers County, Colorado. Named for its flowing northeastward above nearby Two Buttes Hill in Baca County, Colorado. Also known as Gúlqúldéè̱vầu. It is possible that Two Buttes, the major landmark in this area of Colorado, was called Yál-dà (Hill) or Yí-yál-dà (Two Hills).

Yí-qòp-vầu—Two Mountains River. The Double Mountain Fork of the Brazos, near Double Mountain in Stonewall County, Texas.

Yí-vầu-dầu-dè—At the Two Creeks or Forks. The forks of the Washita River, where Gageby Creek (in Wheeler County, Texas) joins the main stream, near the western edge of Roger Mills County, Oklahoma.

Zól-tò-vầu—Vomit Creek. Stinking Creek, west of Carnegie, in Kiowa County, Oklahoma; the portion of the stream below Zól-tò (Vomit Spring) was once called Walnut Creek (Mooney 1898:430). Kiowa elders state that the creek was simply called Zóltó̱, for the spring farther upstream.

Springs, Ponds, and Lakes

Ầu-hí-tò̱—Cedar Spring. A water hole on the Staked Plains of Texas or New Mexico. Possibly Laguna Sabinas in northeastern Gaines County, Texas, the largest of the salt (alkali) lakes in the region, approximately six miles long and four miles wide. It was named for the stubby twisted cedars that grew along its edge. *Juniperas sabina* includes the Eurasian juniper and the American red cedar, hence Red Cedar Lake.

The lake is brackish but potable and is fed by several freshwater springs at the north end, some of which were once sizable perennial streams, as well as by several wells on the south end, some of which were dug by Indians. Laguna Sabinas was an important water source along a route through the southern Llano Estacado, along a trail that led up the Colorado River to Tobacco Creek, along that stream until it ceased flowing, then west to Cedar Lake, to Seminole Wells, to Monument Spring, and finally westward to the Pecos River (Brune 1981; Fenton 1981; Gelo 2000). *See* Xôgàzę́mà.

Bón-tǫ̀ — Stinking Spring. A water hole on the Staked Plains, probably named for its high sulfur or alkali content. Probably Sulphur Springs, eight miles north of Lenorah, in Martin County, Texas, along present-day Sulphur Spring Draw at the head of the Colorado River. Brune (1975:53–54) notes that these springs were on the old Comanche Trail from New Mexico to Mexico and had several pure freshwater springs, one of which was slightly sulfurous.

Fài-qòp-tǫ́-tèp — Sun Mountain Spring. Located at Guadalupe Peak, east of present-day El Paso, Culberson County, Texas. A favorite base camp with several springs commonly used by Kiowa, Comanche, and Apache raiding parties traveling into Mexico. Probably Pine and Smith Springs at Pine Springs, New Mexico (Brune 1975:40).

Fài-tǫ́ — Sun Spring. An eastwardly flowing well-spring on the Staked Plain of Texas, approximately 1.5 days' journey southwest from Double Mountain. Named for a round hole in the stone from which the spring rises. Probably Big Spring, two miles south of Big Springs in Howard County, Texas. Marcy (1849) described it as a "fine spring flowing from deep chasms in the limestone rock into an immense reservoir of some 50 feet in depth." The site was a favorite Indian campground (Brune 1975:46).

Fé-tǫ̀ (-tèp) — Sand Spring. A water hole on the Staked Plains of Texas or New Mexico, possibly Sand Springs in Howard County, Texas. The name is an abbreviated form.

Kyáu-tǫ́ — Love Making Spring. A spring in a bend along the south side of the North Fork of the Red River, near Mount Walsh in Greer County, Oklahoma. Probably near Granite, Oklahoma. Named because Kiowa and Cheyenne men camping on the opposite sides of the stream used to follow women going to the spring to gather water to court them.

Qáun-kį́-tǫ̀ — Turtle Spring. A water hole on the Staked Plains of western Texas.

Sé-chó-êl — Big Pond. A large lake in Coahuila or Chihuahua, Mexico, reportedly containing an island with a Mexican fort.

Sén-fól-é-sé-chó—Water Lily Pond. Swan Lake on the old Wichita reservation north of Anadarko, Caddo County, Oklahoma.

Sén-fól-é—Water Lillies. Fort Cobb, Caddo County, Oklahoma. Named for the high density of water lilies along the Washita River in this vicinity.

Tél-tò or Tél-tò-tèp—White Clay Spring. A water hole on the Staked Plains of Texas named for the white clay there. Possibly Tierra Blanca or Ojo Blanco in Texas and New Mexico. Tierra Blanca Creek runs through Curry County, New Mexico, and Deaf Smith County, Texas.

Tó-bín-dá-dàu—Boiling Water. Colorado Springs, Colorado. Named for the natural springs located there. Sundstrom (2005) believes it is Manitou Springs in Colorado where two springs a few yards apart at the head of the stream emit boiling vaporous water with a hissing noise. One spring emits sulfur, the other soda hot enough to cook meat. The Arapaho called it Medicine Fountain and made offerings at the site (Sage 1846:169–170). *See* Tótépvàu.

Tó-dáu-hâ—Medicine or Mysterious Lake. A large and deep natural rock-lined well near the head of Scout Creek in the Texas Panhandle (Mooney 1898:426). I was unable to identify this creek.

Tó-dáui-hâ or Tó-dáui-hyâ—Medicine or Mysterious Water. A lake in the mountains of the far north near which the Naishan Apache place one of their most important early stories. The Apache hunted near the vicinity of Castizil (Bear Hill) and obtained the Four Quartz Rocks Bundle, one of their original three tribal medicine bundles, from a lake known as *Kutijje* (Medicine Water) (McAllister 1935:6–7, 1965:215). "Medicine Water . . . is thought to be located in the Black Hills of South Dakota in a region known as Bear Mountain or Black Rock" (McAllister (1965:215). These are undoubtedly Bear Butte, and probably, Bear Butte Lake. The Medicine Water may be Bear Butte Lake or another nearby lake. Although no Kiowa name for Bear Butte is recorded, the above description in a region known as Bear Mountain, and its importance to nearly all tribes around the Black Hills, suggest the Kiowa knew of Bear Butte, which would be Sét-qòp.

Tó-kó—Black Water Pond/Lake. A pond on the edge of the Staked Plains, approximately three days' journey west of Double Mountain, Texas. Possibly Agua Negra or Blackwater Draw near the western Texas line at about 34 degrees, in Bailey County, Texas, northwest of Double Mountain (Mooney 1898:426).

Xó-gà-zé-mà—Shifting Stones. A lake on the Staked Plains of Texas. Named because the stones there shift about, probably from wave action along the shore. Possibly Laguna Sabinas (Cedar Lake) in northeastern Gaines County, Texas. (Mooney 1898:428; Brune 1981; Fenton 1981; Gelo 2000). *See* Å̀uhį̀tò̜.

X̄ó-tái-tó̜-dáu-dè—Spring Where There Is a Rock Above (lit. Rock Above-Spring It Is). Cedar Spring, about four miles south of Anadarko in Caddo County, Oklahoma, on the old road to Fort Sill.

Zól-tó̜—Vomit Spring. Zodaltone Springs. Named for Zóltó̜ (Vomit Spring). A set of four springs (three round and about 20 inches in diameter and one larger square-shaped spring about 2.5 feet in diameter) near the middle of the stream that contain concentrated sulfurous water. Reportedly the first Kiowa to drink from the spring vomited. Some elders state the water is still sulfurous but potable now. Several springs exist along the creek, the central sulfur springs on the northwestern side of Zodaltone Mountain, just below (north) of the confluence of Saddle Mountain and Pecan Creeks, in Sect. 8, T6N, R14W in Kiowa County. The springs were used as a spa and health resort to sit, soak, and use mud packs in the early 1900s, and are still used by some Kiowa for treating arthritis.

Stream Crossings

Tót—Crossing. The term used for Big Tree's Crossing on Rainy Mountain Creek, east of Rainy Mountain Church, Kiowa County, Oklahoma.

Astrological Place Names

Cûi-cà-jà̜—Pawnee Star. The North Star, used as a travel aid, which led to the Pawnee territory in Kansas and Nebraska. Their camps are said to have been directly underneath it (HLS-FSA 1:59).

Já̜-êl—Big Star. Venus, or the Morning Star.

Jà̜-góm-tò̜—Backbone of the Stars (lit. Star Backbone), the Milky Way. Caused by a race between a wild horse and an antelope in which their feet raised dust (HLS-FSA 1:60).

Já̜-má-tà̜u-dàu—Star Girls. The Pleiades constellation, named for the Star Girls Story. When the Pleiades are on the meridian in winter it is the middle of the night, and when they have almost set it will soon be morning. The Kiowa did not recognize the Big Dipper as a constellation (HLS-FSA 1:59), which indicates that the Pleiades is the correct constellation associated with the story.

Já̜-qòm (Old Star)—Scott notes, "There is a circle of stars, July 10, '97 [1897] about 9:00 P.M. tonight in the west high up—the handle of the dipper is a part of it. And another star in the center, which is called "Old Star" because it is like an old man with a fire in the center of a council. Has no knowledge of the dipper" (HLS-FSA 1:59).

Qóm–sáu–gàu (Jackrabbit)—the Big Dipper. The handle is his arched back, the pointers are the tips of his ears (HLS-FSA 1:59).

The Duck—"Standing in front of the dipper ready to shoot him are two stars that come up with a turning movement like the motion of a duck's wing we call the duck" (HLS-FSA 1:60).

Modern Place Names Related to the Kiowa

(by State)

Alaska

Kiowa, Anchorage County (Bright 2004:224)

Colorado

Kiowa, Elbert County
Kiowa County
Kiowa Creek, Elbert County
Satank, Garfield County (Bright 2004:422)
Satanta, Grand County (Bright 2004:422)

Iowa

Kiowa Marsh, Sac County

Kansas

Big Bow, Stanton County
Kiowa Airport, Barber County
Kiowa Creek, Kiowa, Comanche, and Clark counties
Kiowa, Barber County
Kiowa State Fishing Lake, Kiowa County
Kiowa Township, Kiowa County
Satanta, Haskell County (Bright 2004:422)

Oklahoma

Big Kiowa Creek — Southeastern Roger Mills County
Cut Throat Gap — Comanche County. Named for the 1833 Cutthroat
    Massacre.

Cut Throat Lake—Comanche County. Sect. 17, T4N, R15W, Cooperton Quad. As above.

Cut Throat Mountain—Comanche County. As above.

Frizzie Head Creek—The modern name of Áulpépvàu.

Hunting Horse Hill—Wichita Mountains, Comanche County.

Jimmy Creek—Near Meers, Comanche County. Named for Jimmy Quoe-tone, who lived near the spring feeding this stream. Also known as Sàupólàultòvàu.

Kiowa—A small town in Pittsburgh County. A post office was established there May 6, 1881. Named for nearby Kiowa Hill.

Kiowa Hill—A 946-foot-high hill in Pittsburgh County.

Kiowa County—In southwestern Oklahoma.

Kiowa Lake—Located in the Wichita Mountains, Comanche County,

Kokoom Pool—A baptism pool for the Saddle Mountain Kiowa Indian Church on the head of Saddle Mountain Creek. Named for Kokoom, a church deacon, who lived nearby.

Little Bow Mountain—Located east of the junction of Elk Creek and the North Fork of the Red River, ten miles south of Hobart, Kiowa County. Named for Little Bow (Ke-in-kau or Qą́híqǫ̀yì: Yearling Male Bison, born 1853), son of chief Big Bow, who camped there in the 1890s (Nye 1937:275). Also known as Ję́bèqòp.

Little Kiowa Creek—In southeastern Roger Mills County.

Long Horn Creek—An eastern tributary of present-day Sugar Creek just south and west of Long Horn Mountain in Kiowa County. Named for Long Horn, who lived on the creek near the western end of the mountain.

Medicine Bluffs—Fort Sill Army Base, Comanche County. Also known as Xôqàudàuhá.

Navajo Mountain—A pair of mountains in the Wichita Mountain Range 9.5 miles northeast of Altus in Jackson County. Although I have never heard the mountain called by its Kiowa name, it would be Á-bà-hô-qòp. The Kiowa reportedly once pursued and caught a Navajo hiding on the mountain to scout the surrounding area.

Odlepaugh Springs—A cluster of springs at a foothill on the An-an-dau-a allotment in the Southwest 1/4 of Sect. 28, T5N, R14W, in Kiowa County. The spring is about three-quarters of a mile northwest of the Saddle Mountain Cemetery, forms the head of Saddle Mountain Creek, and was the second baptism site for Saddle Mountain Kiowa Indian Church. Named for Odlepaugh, husband of An-an-dau-a (see Dick 1959).

Quetone Point—Wichita Mountains, Comanche County, named for that
Kiowa family.
Rainy Mountain—Kiowa County, a translation of the Kiowa name.
Saddle Mountain—Comanche County, a translation of the Kiowa
name.
Seven Sisters Creek—A small tributary of Medicine Bluff Creek that
crosses County Road E1540 1.1 miles east of Meers in Comanche
County. Named for the seven sisters of Kiowa mythology.
Stinking Creek—A southern tributary of the Washita River, 2.5 miles
west of Carnegie on Highway 9, Kiowa County. *See* Zóltǫ́.
Tarbone Mountain—A corruption of the name Tah-bone-mah (Sees The
Morning Star), also known as Iseeo, and named for him. Formerly
known as Mount Tarno, and I-See-O Mountain (Morgan 1973:239).
Wichita Mountains, Comanche County.
Tepee Mountain—Located 3.75 miles southeast of Lugert in southwest-
ern Kiowa County. Rev. George Hicks (GWH-OHS) lists "Do-paw
Tepee Creek," which is probably modern-day Tepee Creek, beside
Tepee Mountain. Tepee Mountain may once have had a Kiowa name,
which would be Jóqòp. Named for the mountain's shape, which re-
sembles a tipi.
Time O-Day Spring—Sect. 17, T4N, R15W, Cooperton Quad. Named for
the Tą́imé captured during the 1833 Cutthroat Massacre.
Two Hatchett Creek—A modern name for the small creek that crosses
Highway 9 about 2.2 miles east of present-day Fort Cobb, Caddo
County. Named for the family that resided along the creek. The Kiowa
name would be Yí-hàu-tò-vàu.
Unap Mountain—Kiowa County, a translation of the Kiowa name.
Zodletone Mountain—An isolated mountain along Zoddletone Spring,
2.5 miles east and 6.5 miles south of Mountain View in Kiowa County,
Oklahoma. The Kiowa name would be Zól-tǫ́-qòp (Vomit Water
Mountain).

Dance Grounds

Red Buffalo's—On his allotment, now the Kiowa Tribal Complex and Red
Buffalo Hall at Carnegie, Caddo County.
Chieftain Park—On the A-sane-hiddle allotment two miles northeast of
Highway 58 and County Road E1440, along East Cache Creek. Two
miles north of where Highway 58 turns east toward Apache, Caddo
County.
Cornbread Tanedooah's—William Tenedooah's allotment east of Carne-

gie, Caddo County, in the southwestern corner of County Roads E1320 and N2500.

Amy Dongade's—On her allotment southwest of Anadarko.

Eagleheart's—On East Cache Creek, approximately eleven miles south and one-quarter mile east of Carnegie.

Edgar Keahbone's—On his allotment near Red Stone, Caddo County.

Frank Bosin's—His allotment, now the Anadarko airport, Caddo County.

Frizzlehead's—His allotment southeast of Alden on the south side of East Cache Creek and just west of the intersection of Cache Creek and County Road N2480 in Caddo County.

Jack Bointy's—On his allotment, two miles west of Carnegie on the south side of Highway 9, between County Road N2440 and Stinking Creek.

Jack Sankadota's—On his allotment northwest of Stecker, Caddo County.

Kiowa Bill's—His allotment four miles south of Hobart, Kiowa County, and west along Elk Creek.

Kiowa Jim's—Jim Tonkeamha's allotment thirteen miles south of Carnegie, Caddo County, south of present-day Highway 58.

Lone Bear's—His allotment just southeast of Carnegie, in Caddo County, approximately three-quarters of a mile west-southwest of White Church and northwest of the junction of County Roads N2480 and E1340.

Mopope's—The hill one-half mile northeast of the junction of Highway 9 and County Road N2580, 2.25 miles west of the Apache Wye, Caddo County.

Ned Brace's—At his home southeast of Carnegie.

Sheep Mountain—Present-day Little Bow Mountain, where Little Bow or Kei-in-kau had his camp, ten miles south of Hobart, Kiowa County.

Silverhorn's—At his home west of Stecker, Caddo County.

Tia-Piah Park—East of Love's Store and I-44 in Comanche County.

Tsoodles—George and Henry Tsoodle's allotments along Stinking Creek southwest of Carnegie, Kiowa County.

White Buffalos's—His allotment one mile south of present-day Washita on top of the Red Stone Bluffs along County Road N2600, Caddo County.

White Fox's—The home of White Fox on the east side and near the end of County Road N2440 just south of the Washita River, northwest of Carnegie, Caddo County.

White Horse's—The home of Charley Whitehorse on the southwestern corner of the junction of County Roads E1350 and N2590, west of the Apache Wye, Caddo County.

'49 Sites

Greg's Corner — A popular '49 site southeast of Carnegie, Caddo County.

Hill X — The hill east of Riverside Indian School, north of Anadarko, Caddo County.

Moonlight Mile — County Road N2450, between County Roads E1340 and E1350, two miles south, one mile west, then south on N2450 from Carnegie, Caddo County, on the border of Sects. 24 and 19, the Caddo-Kiowa county line.

Skin Beach — A sandbar on the Washita River just upstream from Randlett Park, in Anadarko, Caddo County.

Snake Pit — An area along the Washita River northwest of the present-day Wal-Mart, Anadarko, Caddo County.

Hand Game Sites

The Astrodome — A domelike structure in Boone, Caddo County, where the Plains Apache hosted many games.

Billy Goat Hill — A small hill on the property of Thurman Kadayso near Boone, Caddo County.

Bruce Haumpy's — Near Carnegie.

Carnegie Park — The county fair buildings in Carnegie, Caddo County.

Julia Daingkau's — East of Carnegie.

Shady Front — A former house of Ace and Ina Paddlety Chalepah remodeled to facilitate hand games on the corner southeast of the junction of County Roads N2580 and E1360, 2.5 miles west of the Apache Wye on Highway 9, and one-quarter mile south, Caddo County. Named for a row of cedar trees shading the house front.

White Fox's — *See* White Fox's, above.

Schools

Fort Sill Indian School — Located just east of I-44 near the Indian Health Service Hospital in Lawton, Comanche County.

Kiowa Flats — A community school three miles west of Mountain View and 1.5 miles north of Highway 9 on County Road N2350, Kiowa County.

Rainey Valley School — A former community school located two miles south and one mile west of Rainy Mountain Church Cemetery, in Kiowa County.

Rainy Mountain Indian School — On the east side adjacent to Rainy Mountain, Kiowa County.

Riverside Indian School—Just north of Anadarko and the Washita River, on Highway 281, and west of the BIA Area Office, Caddo County.

Samone School—A former community school located along Stinking Creek, just south of Highway 9 on County Road N2430, three miles west of Carnegie, Kiowa County.

Kiowa Churches

Albert Horse Church, south of Alden, Caddo County. Now known as Cache Creek United Methodist Church.

Cedar Creek Church, southeast of Carnegie, Caddo County, 1911.

Cottonwood Grove Methodist Church, Verden, Grady County.

Elk Creek Mission, south of Hobart, Kiowa County, 1893.

Hog Creek, West of Anadarko, Caddo County, 1913.

J. J. Methvin Memorial United Methodist Church, Anadarko, Caddo County.

Little Red Church, southwest of Carnegie, Caddo County.

Methvin Methodist Institute, Anadarko, Caddo County, 1890.

Mount Scott Kiowa Methodist Church, east of Meers, Comanche County.

Rainy Mountain Kiowa Indian Baptist Church, southwest of Mountain View, Kiowa County, 1893.

Redstone Mission, Redstone, Caddo County.

Saddle Mountain Mission, Saddle Mountain, Kiowa County, 1903–1963.

Sahmone Methodist Church, two miles west of Carnegie, Kiowa County.

Saint Patrick's Catholic Mission, Anadarko, Caddo County, 1892.

Stecker Methodist Church, west of Stecker, Caddo County.

Ware's Chapel Methodist Church, Hog Creek, Caddo County.

White Church, southeast of Carnegie, Caddo County.

Cemeteries

Anquoe Family Cemetery, between Carnegie and Mountain View in Kiowa County.

Carnegie Cemetery, southeast of Carnegie, Caddo County.

Cedar Creek Cemetery, southeast of Carnegie, Caddo County.

Elk Creek Cemetery, south of Hobart, Kiowa County.

Gotebo Cemetery, Gotebo, Kiowa County.

Mount Scott Kiowa Methodist Church Cemetery, east of Meers, Comanche County.

Rainy Mountain Kiowa Indian Baptist Church Cemetery, southwest of Mountain View, Kiowa County.

Redstone Church Cemetery, Redstone, Caddo County.

Saddle Mountain Church Cemetery, Saddle Mountain, Kiowa County.

Sahmone Cemetery, two miles west of Carnegie, Kiowa County.

Satepauhoodle Family Cemetery, one-half mile east of Carnegie on Highway 9, Caddo County.

Stecker Methodist Church, west of Stecker, Caddo County.

Tanedooah Family Cemetery, east of Carnegie on old Highway 9, Caddo County.

Tanehaddle Family Cemetery, northeast of Carnegie, Caddo County.

Togamote Family Cemetery, northeast of Carnegie, Caddo County

Two Hatchet Family Cemetery, east of Fort Cobb, Caddo County.

Ware's Chapel, three-quarters of a mile west of Hog Creek on Highway 9, east of Caddo County.

Trading Posts — Stores

Ahtone's Trading Post — An Indian store in Fort Cobb in the 1980s–1990s.

Boake's Store — (1) A store northeast of Rainy Mountain School on the south side of County Road E1390, Kiowa County, Oklahoma. (2) A second store one mile due east of Rainy Mountain, also on the south side of County Road E1390, the remains of which are still standing.

Snoopy's — An Indian store of the Davilla Family in Anadarko, Caddo County, in the 1980s and early 1990s.

Areas

Arkansas Bend — The area of the bend in the Washita River just west of Carnegie and at the end of Feather Dance Road or County Road N2440 on the south side of the Washita River.

Dirty Shame — Intersection of County Road E1380 and Highway 58, six miles south of Carnegie.

Crazy Hill — The modern name of Áulkáuipìgàu (Crazy Ridge), *see above.*

Indian Canyon — A red sandstone canyon one-half mile east of Fort Cobb where many baseball games were held in the 1950s–1970s.

Kiowa Country — The popular Anglo term applied to the Kiowa, Comanche, and Apache Reservation prior to allotment in 1901. This area comprised Kiowa, Comanche, Tillman, Cotton, and portions of Caddo, Grady, Stephens, and Jefferson counties (Gould 1933:124).

Mopope Hill — The home of Steve and Jeanette Mopope, two miles west of the Apache Wye on Highway 9 and one-half mile north. Many dances and hand games were held there in the 1950s–1970s.

Square Top—Intersection 2.5 miles west of Anadarko on Country Road E1340, Caddo County. Today a store and several Indian homes are located from this intersection north, now known as Square Top Road.

Windmill Corner—An intersection three-quarters of a mile east of Redstone Baptist Church where County Roads E1340 and N 2620 meet. Named for a dilapidated windmill that still stands there.

Small Towns—Post Offices

Ahpeatone—A small hamlet in western Cotton County, twelve miles west of Walters. A post office existed there from July 22, 1907, to June 30, 1916 (Shirk 1965:5). Named for the Kiowa leader Ahpeahtone.

Gotebo—A small town six miles west of Mountain View, in Kiowa County. Following the rescue of a local Anglo rancher from a flood-swollen stream by Gotebo, the small town formerly named Harrison, Indian Territory, changed its name to Gotebo in 1904 to commemorate the event. A post office was opened in Harrison on August 17, 1901, and changed to Gotebo on February 25, 1904 (Shirk 1965:90, 98).

Kiogree or Kiogre—A post office from May 3, 1902, to March 15, 1904, located three miles northeast of Headrick in southwestern Kiowa County, near the Greer County line. The name was coined from the names Kiowa and Greer County (Gould 1933:91–92; Shirk 1965:118).

Komalty—A small hamlet along the railroad line five miles northeast of Hobart, Kiowa County, Oklahoma. Named for Komalty, the chief of a minor band of Kiowa, who lived nearby. A post office operated there from December 6, 1901, to March 31, 1938. Now listed as Komalty Siding.

Lone Wolf—A small town southwest of Hobart, in Kiowa County. A post office was established January 29, 1901. Named for the later Lone Wolf (formerly Mam-a-day-te), who lived south of Hobart.

Navajoe—A post office from September 1, 1887, to May 15, 1905, located three miles northwest of Headrick in Jackson County. Named for nearby Navajoe Mountain. Shirk (1965:147) reports that the battle at the mountain was between a group of Navajo and Comanche. *See* Navajo Mountain.

Rainy—A post office from April 28, 1894, to May 15, 1905, located in southern Washita County, six miles east of Rocky. Named for nearby Rainy Mountain Indian Church and Mission (Shirk 1965:174).

Randlett—A post office established May 3, 1907. Named for Indian agent James F. Randlett.

Saddle Mountain—A small hamlet in southeastern Kiowa County, fifteen miles south of Mountain View. A post office operated there from January 22, 1902, to May 31, 1955. Named for nearby Saddle Mountain and the Saddle Mountain Indian Mission.

Stecker—A small town nine miles southwest of Anadarko, in Caddo County. A post office operated there from April 2, 1909, to September 30, 1954. Named for Indian agent Lieutenant Ernest Stecker.

Tokio—A post office from September 27, 1901, to January 31, 1905, located six miles southeast of Gotebo, in Kiowa County. Named after the Kiowa word towkyowy (jócyôi), or "long building," which the Kiowa used to describe the 125-foot-long building, which was a store that housed the post office (Shirk 1965:207).

Buildings and Casinos

Gotebo Hall—The reception hall-kitchen at Rainy Mountain Kiowa Indian Baptist Church, Kiowa County. Named after Gotebo (1847–1927), the first reservation-era Kiowa male baptized into Christianity in 1893 and later a deacon at the church.

Kiowa Casino Red River—The Kiowa casino in southern Cotton County.

Kiowa Tribal Complex—Carnegie, Caddo County.

Parker McKenzie Elder Center—The Kiowa elder's center at Carnegie, Caddo County. Named for tribal member Parker P. McKenzie (1897–1999).

Red Buffalo Hall—The gymnasium at the Kiowa Tribal Complex in Carnegie, Caddo County, named for Red Buffalo, on whose allotment the complex now stands.

Saynday's Bar—A former name of a bar on the east side of Carnegie on Highway 9, Caddo County.

Roads and Intersections

Apache Wye—The intersection of Highways 9 and 281, west of Anadarko, that turns south toward Apache, Caddo County.

Feather Dance Road—County road N2440 running north of Highway 9, two miles west of Carnegie, Caddo County. Named for the Kiowa Ghost Dance site.

Indian Road—The old Highway 9 between Fort Cobb and Carnegie, now County Road E1330, which passes through an area of many Kiowa and Kiowa-Apache allotments in Caddo County.

Parker McKenzie Drive—The street east from Highways 8 and 281 on the north side of Anadarko to the Kiowa Agency, Caddo County.

Bridges and Stream Crossings

Big Tree Crossing—A crossing point on Rainy Mountain Creek on Big Tree's allotment, one mile northeast of Rainy Mountain Church, Kiowa County. Site of the first baptisms at Rainy Mountain Church.

Eagle Heart Bridge—A bridge crossing East Cache Creek on County Road E1430, eleven miles south and one-quarter mile east of Carnegie, off Highway 58, Caddo County. Named for being near Eagle Heart's camp. Rebuilt in 2006.

Luther Samount Bridge—The bridge across Canyon Creek on County Road E1530 three miles northeast of Meers in Comanche County. Named for Luther Samount or Sahmaunt, who lived nearby.

Sitapah Tah (Afraid of the Bear) Bridge—The bridge over Stinking Creek on County Road N2440, one-quarter mile north of Highway 9, west of Carnegie, Caddo County. Named for the Ghost Dance leader Sitapahtah, who lived nearby.

Montana

Kiowa—Glacier County. Reportedly named after the Blackfeet name for bear, kya-Yo, but also located near the Kiowa Mountains.

New Mexico

Kiawa Mountain or Kiowa Mountain—Elevation 9,735 feet, three miles southwest of Tusas, Rio Arriba County, named for a forgotten association with the Kiowa (Pearce 1965:79; Julyan 1998:185; Bright 2004:217).

Kiowa Canyon—A canyon just south of Kiowa Mountain, Rio Arriba County.

Kiowa—Colfax County, fifteen miles southwest of Capulin. Formerly called Kiowa Camp, then Kiowa District for a campsite the Kiowa often used. A post office operated there in 1877–1880, 1890–1892, and 1901–1904. The Fort Union Road passed just northwest of the town (Julyan 1998:185).

Kiowa Flats—A prairie just northeast of Kiowa Spring, Colfax County (Julyan 1998:185).

Kiowa Lake—A lake just south of Kiowa Mountain, Rio Arriba County.

Kiowa Mesa—A mesa just southeast of Kiowa, Colfax County (Julyan 1998:185).

Kiowa National Grasslands—In the northeastern part of the state (Julyan 1998:185).

Kiowa Spring—A spring on the northeast side of Kiowa Mesa, Colfax County (Julyan 1998:185).

Texas

Kiowa Peak—A hill, 1,862 feet in elevation, twenty miles northeast of Aspermont and 2.5 miles northwest of a bend in the Double Mountain Fork of the Brazos River, Stonewall County.

South Dakota

Fort Kiowa—An American Fur Company trading post (1822–1825) near Oacoma.

Other Miscellaneous Places

Adobe Mounds—A cluster of defensive earthworks (kį́ájôi) erected in 1833 approximately one-third to one-half mile north of the home of the late Parker McKenzie, in the bend of the Washita River on the west side of Rainy Mountain Creek, northeast of Mountain View, Kiowa County. The earthworks were built after the Kiowa discovered Osage in the area. When no attack came, the group broke camp the following day and moved toward the Wichita Mountains.

Bear Butte—South Dakota. See Tǫ́dáuihyâ.

Buffalo Tree—A site on the east-central branch of Stinking Creek where Poor Buffalo killed a bison to obtain the hide for the Sun Dance center pole on the nearby Washita River. A woman later dreamed the bison came to her and told her to come to the flat, and when she saw some bison bones they would be his. After awaking she went to the area and found a mesquite tree growing among the bones of the buffalo. Regarded as the buffalo's spirit, the Kiowa began periodically making presents to it. Although no Kiowa name for the site is known it may have been Páu-á-dàu (Bison Tree) or Páu-á-dàu-dé-ę̀ (Place At Which The Bison Tree Is). The location of this event on Black Goose's map and Iseeo's description (HLS-FSA 1:172–173) suggests it was located near the Little Red Church, Sect. 25, T7N, R14W, Stinking Creek Quad in Kiowa County.

Ice Sticking Down River—The Missouri River (lit. Water Hard-Stick Down River or Rough Ice River). Named for blocks of ice that stuck down under the water in the spring thaws when the river broke up. Jếqáunvàu (Hard Ice River) is a possible name.

Medicine Wheel—Although no Kiowa name for the Big Horn Medicine Wheel of Wyoming is known, elders report that it would be Dáui-qàu-dàl (Medicine Wheel) or Xô-qàu-dàl (Stone Wheel).

Spear Lake—A lake in Wyoming that one of the two Kiowa culture heroes or Half-Boys walked into in early Kiowa history. No Kiowa name for the lake is known. Sundstrom (2005) believes it to be Lake DeSmet.

Upper Albian Kiowa Formation—A geological formation stretching from western Iowa to western Kansas.

Names of Kiowa Calendar Entries 1833–1892

From Mooney (1898) *Calendar History of the Kiowa Indians*

Translations by William C. Meadows and Parker P. McKenzie

1832–1833 Winter. Áulhą́ugàágòbàudèsài (Winter That They Captured the Money).

1833 Summer. Ém qóltàdèfài (Summer That They Cut Off Their Heads).

1833–1834 Winter. Ją́vátcádèsài (Winter That the Stars Fell).

1834 Summer. No official name. No Sun Dance held.

1834–1835 Winter. Páutònéhòldèsài (Winter That Bull Tail Was Killed).

1835 Summer. Jónpą̀qą̀ujò (Cattail Rush Sun Dance).

1835–1836 Winter. Thòêléhòldèsài (Winter Big Face Was Killed).

1836 Summer. Cûivàuqàujò (Wolf River Sun Dance).

1836–1837 Winter. Qą́hî̜jèéhòldèsài (Winter That Man Was Killed).

1837 Summer. Sáqàutjàuáàutàundèfài (Summer That the Cheyennes Were Annihilated). Also called Áutqą́unjófài (Wailing Sun Dance Summer).

1837–1838 Winter. Áultémétkúicâundèsài (Winter That They Dragged the Head).

1838 Summer. Cûivàugàsáqáutjàuèmjòhâfàudèfài (Summer the Cheyenne Attacked the Camp on Wolf River).

1838–1839 Winter. No official name.

1839 Summer. Píhótqą́ujó (Peninsula Sun Dance).

1839–1840 Winter. Tálkòpsài (Smallpox Winter).

1840 Summer. Gúljòhâuqą̀ujò (Red Bluff [concavity] Sun Dance).

1840–1841 Winter. Káuisáubídàumsài (Hide Quiver War Expedition).

1841 Summer. No official name. No Sun Dance held.

1841–1842 Winter. Áulháubáqî́éhòldèsài (In the Winter They Killed Áulháubáqî̀, or Right-Sided Short Cut Hair).

1842 Summer. Áldàqáujò (Repeated Sun Dance).

1842–1843 Winter. Cą̀uqóljèhêmdèsài (In the Winter Goose Neck Died).

1843 Summer. Ánchènqúldèqàujò (Nest-building Sun Dance).

1843–1844 Winter. No official name.

1844 Summer. Qólpą̀qî̀qàujò (Dakota Sun Dance).

1844–1845 Winter. Ãthàuhâuiqî̀éhòldèsài (Winter That They Killed War Bonnet).

1845 Summer. Xő̀qólqàujò (Stone Necklace Sun Dance).

1845–1846 Winter. No official name.

1846 Summer. Páugù̀hę́jèáð̀pą̀idèqàujò (Sundance When Hornless-Bull Was Made a Koitsenko.

1846–1847 Winter. Sénpàugàéttáutcàudèsài (Winter in Which They Shot the Mustache).

1847 Summer. Màunkàugúléhòldèfài (Summer in Which They Killed Red Sleeve).

1847–1848 Winter. No official name.

1848 Summer. Ő̀pą̀qàujò (Choking Rope Sun Dance), in reference to the Qóichę́gàu Society ropes.

1848–1849 Winter. No official name.

1849 Summer. Máuî̀càqàujò (Cramps or Cholera Sun Dance).

1849–1850 Winter. No official name.

1850 Summer. Ã̀còtà̀qàujò (Chinaberry Trees Sun Dance).

1850–1851 Winter. Táuncî̀páuhòldèsài (Winter in Which They Killed Tangiapa).

1851 Summer. Pà̀iqáujó (Dusty Sun Dance).

1851–1852 Winter. Mà̀yî̀thő̀gàhàundèsài (Winter in Which the Woman Was Frozen).

1852 Summer. Qâuthǫ̀gàéhòldèfài or Hą́uthǫ̀gàqî̀éhòldèfài (Summer That They Killed Touch-The-Clouds [Knife Shirt or Iron-Shirt Man]).

1852–1853 Winter. No official name.

1853 Summer. Bî̀sòtqàujò (Showery Sun Dance).

1853–1854 Winter. No official name.

1854 Summer. Áyàldàvà̀uqàujò (Timber Hill Creek Sun Dance).

1854–1855 Winter. No official name. May be Câigù̀á́ǰjèéhòldèsài (Winter in Which They Killed Likes the Enemy).

1855 Summer. Tǫ́gű̀yáfàidà (Summer of Sitting With Legs Crossed and Extended).

1855–1856 Winter. No official name.

1856 Summer. Sę̀àlà̀uqàujò (Prickly Pear Sun Dance).

1856–1857 Winter. Jő̀gàqúldèsài (Winter in Which They Left Their Tipis Behind).

1857 Summer. Ápồjàuèqíádåudèqåujò (Sun Dance in Which the Forked Stick Sprouted).

1857–1858 Winter. No official name.

1858 Summer. Ájồbyồiqåujò (Timber-Circle Sun Dance).

1858–1859 Winter. Cûiqáujèéhòldèsài (Winter in Which They Killed Wolf Lying Down).

1859 Summer. Åuhį́jòhåuqåujò (Cedar-Bluff [concavity] Sun Dance).

1859–1860 Winter. No official name. May be Cìkáuijèhémdèsài (Winter in Which Back-Hide Died).

1860 Summer. No official name. No Sun Dance held. Possibly Thẹ̀nébáudàiéhòldèfài (Summer in Which They Killed Bird Appearing).

1860–1861 Winter. Áulkáuijóhâusài (Crazy Bluff [concavity] Winter).

1861 Summer. Thôicùtápạ̀xèpdèqåujò (Sun Dance at Which They Left the Spotted Horse Tied).

1861–1862 Winter. Tálqòpsài (Smallpox Winter).

1862 Summer. Tálqòpkàkàunqåujò (Sun Dance After the Smallpox), also sometimes known as Tálqòpqåujò (Small Pox Sun Dance).

1862–1863 Winter. Ápfáchàtsài (Treetop Winter) or Chệgàusáupáné- fàutjàusài (Winter in Which the Horses Ate Ashes).

1863 Summer. Xólhệ̀jèdévåuqåujò (No Arm's River Sun Dance).

1863–1864 Winter. Åultòêlhémdèsài (Winter in Which Big Head Died).

1864 Summer. Ásàuhệ̀qåujò or Ásàuihyệ̀qåujò (Ragweed Sun Dance).

1864–1865 Winter. Chènhốsài (Muddy Traveling Winter).

1865 Summer. Píhótqåujó (Peninsula Sun Dance).

1865–1866 Winter. No official name. Possibly Jánkốgàiéhòldèsài (Winter in Which They Killed Black Bonnet Brow).

1866 Summer. Hą́ukàupèlqåujò (Flat Metal [i.e., German Silver] Sun Dance).

1866–1867 Winter. Áfàmáuljèéhòldèsài (Winter in Which They Killed Struck His Head Against a Tree).

1867 Summer. Tháukố́àsèmxèpdèqåujò (Sun Dance at Which Black Ear Was Stolen). Also known as Qóichệ́gàuétốpàidèqåujò (Sun Dance at Which the Koitsenko [Qóichệ́gàu] Were Initiated).

1867–1868 Winter. Áyàldàsài (Timbered Hill Winter). Also known as Tháubóléhóldésài (Winter in Which They Killed Spoiled Ear).

1868 Summer. Į́jàgàudáuhóldèqåujò (Sun Dance When the Utes Killed Us) or Áyàldàvåuqåujò (Timbered Hill River Sun Dance).

1868–1869 Winter. Jángúléhòldèsài (Winter in Which They Killed Red Bonnet Brow).

1869 Summer. Àthàuhâuigácàundèqàujò (Sun Dance at Which They Brought the War Bonnet).

1869–1870 Winter. Jǫ́báutétfẽ́dèsài (Winter in Which They Were Frightened by the Bugle).

1870 Summer. Èqúgàqíádầudèqầujò (Plant Growing Sun Dance). Also known as Ka-do Painyonhade (Dusty Sun Dance), Qáujófàiǫ̀hâdè.

1870–1871 Winter. Sétầgàiátǫ̀ặcàundèsài (Winter in Which They Brought Sitting Bear's Bones).

1871 Summer. No official name. No Sun Dance held.

1871–1872 Winter. No official name.

1872 Summer. No official name. No Sun Dance held.

1872–1873 Winter. Jégừgàuchándèsài (Winter in Which the Pueblos Came).

1873 Summer. Ìógûẹ̀vầuqầujò (Maggot Creek Sun Dance).

1873–1874 Winter. Séthấidèchándèsài (Winter in Which White Bear Returned).

1874 Summer. Xóqáukặunâudèqầujò (Sun Dance at the End of the Bluff or Last Mountain).

1874–1875 Winter. Cíèléhòldèsài (Winter in Which They Killed Big Meat).

1875 Summer. Qyầutóqầujò (Love Making Spring Sun Dance).

1875–1876 Winter. No official name.

1876 Summer. Ìógûvàupfàhàlqầujò (Sun Dance at the Forks of Maggot [Sweetwater] Creek).

1876–1877 Winter. No official name.

1877 Summer. Jặmátàunầvầuqầujò (Star Girls Tree River Sun Dance). Also known as A gat-hodal Ka-do (? Ágàthòlqầujò) or Measles Sun Dance. Possibly Gúlhólgáqầujò (Measles Sun Dance), as gúlhôlgà and gúlhôlqî are the standard Kiowa terms for the measles.

1877–1878 Winter. Qóptáidèjǒchéldèsài (Signal Mountain Winter).

1878 Summer. Áldàqầujò (Repeated Sun Dance).

1878–1879 Winter. No official name. Possibly Áttóthầiéhòldèsài (Winter in Which They Killed White Cow Bird).

1879 Summer. Chẹ̀fị̀qầujò (Horse Eating Sun Dance).

1879–1880 Winter. Jákầuqàsài (Eye Triumph Winter).

1880 Summer. No official name. No Sun Dance held.

1880–1881 Winter. No official name.

1881 Summer. Qáujósálhádè (Hot Sun Dance) or Jógúlsáuòmhầfèdèqầujò (Sun Dance at Which Blood Came Up from the Young Man).

1881–1882 Winter. Èmdáujòaúdèsài (Winter in Which They Played the Tipi Game [Hand Game]).

1882 Summer. No official name. No Sun Dance held.

1882–1883 Winter. No official name. Bótèljèhêmdèsài (Winter in Which Big Stomach Died).

1883 Summer. Àulqàujôiqàujò (Nez Perce Sun Dance).

1883–1884 Winter. No official name.

1884 Summer. No official name. No Sun Dance held.

1884–1885 Winter. No official name.

1885 Summer. Píhótqá̖ujósàn (Little Peninsula Sun Dance).

1885–1885 Winter. No official name.

1886 Summer. No official name. No Sun Dance held.

1886–1887 Winter. No official name.

1887 Summer. Kà̖ujólàvǎuqà̖ujò (Oak Creek Sun Dance).

1887–1888 Winter. No official name.

1888 Summer. No official name. No Sun Dance held.

1888–1889 Winter. No official name.

1889 Summer. No official name. No Sun Dance held.

1889–1890 Winter. No official name.

1890 Summer. Ápȯjàuéttódáudèqà̖ujò (Sun Dance When the Forked Poles Were Left Standing).

1890–1891 Winter. Pá̖uá̖gàichándèsài (Winter in Which Sitting Bull Came).

1891 Summer. No official name. No Sun Dance held. Possibly Fólá̖jèéhòldèsài (Summer in Which They Killed Approaching Snake).

1891–1892 Winter. No official name.

1892 Summer. No official name. No Sun Dance held.

Statistical Analysis of Kiowa Place Names

(Based on Categorization of Geographic Forms)

Land Forms

Mountains	No. of Sites
Color (ice 1)	9
Fauna (organs 5)	7
Tribal territory	4
Size	2
Location	3
Shape	3
Individual residence	2
Flora	1
Burial site	1
Dual formation	1
Warfare event	1
Courting locale	1
Military Society	1
Lack of water	1
Religion	1
Tribal name	1
Faunal feces	1
Weather trait	1
Flora	1
Civil conflict	1
Total: 12 names, 14 sites	

Bluffs/Concavities	No. of Sites
Color	6
Religion	2
Position	1
Group-color	1
Warfare event	1
Flora	1
Shape (escarpment)	1
Total: 11 names, 13 sites	

Total: 34 names, 38 sites

Hills, Ridges, Escarpments	No. of Sites
Color	4
Fauna	2
Fauna (warfare)	1
Surface	1
Dwelling	1

Other Land Names	No. of Sites
Military posts	9
Geological form	5
Warfare event	5
Flora	4
Resource location	2
Shape	2
Non-Indian territory	2

Travel route (stream)	2	Trading post	1
Stream	1	Dwelling	1
Mythological event	1	Position	1
Tribal name	1	Location	1
Weather (wind)	1	Wetness	1
Geysers	1	**Total: 39 names, 42 sites**	
Tribal territory	1		

More Recent Place Names of Anglo Locales

Anglo Locales	**No. of Sites**	Group residence (town)	1
Kiowa pronunciations of Anglo place names	7 (towns 5, Indian Agency 2)	**Total: 8 names, 8 places**	

Astrological Place Names

Astrological Bodies	**No. of Sites**	Myth (animal)	1
Stars (Tribal Name)	1	Human attribute	1
Planets (Size)	1	Animal attribute	2
Constellations		**Total: 7 names, 7 places**	
Myth (humans)	1		

Water Forms

Streams	**No. of Streams**	Water taste	3
Flora	26	Springs	2
Fauna	26	Stream confluence	2
Resource location	16	Death locale (individual)	2
Mineral (stone 2, soil 6)	8	Stream current	2
Color	7	Direction	2
Warfare events	6	Shape	2
Personal name or residence	6	Tribal territory	2
Military post	5	Tribal (name)	1
Size	5	Disease	1
Geological characteristic	4	Weather	1
Misc. activities or events	4	Dwelling	1
Religious or ceremonial site	3	Faunal residue	1
Tribal residence (reservation)	3	Lack of water	1
Material culture	3	Mountain	1

Military Society	1	Resources	1
Natural phenomena	1	Position	1
Personal name	1	Shape	1
Non-Indian territory	1	Size	1
Trading post owner	1	Soil	1
Total: 126 names, 151 streams		Smell	1
		Courting locale	1
Springs, Ponds, Lakes	**No. of Sites**	Taste	1
Flora	3	**Total: 18 names, 18 places**	
Motion	2		
Religion	2	**Crossings**	**No. of Sites**
Color	2	Stream crossings	1
Fauna	1	**Total: 1 name, 1 place**	

Notes

INTRODUCTION

1. Although Kiowa elders use the term American Indian more often than Native American, both are used by the Kiowa and many other native groups. In this book I use the two terms interchangeably.

CHAPTER 1

1. These include academic (Gill 1990; Moore 1991; Walker 1991; Harkin 2000) and popular (Milne 1994, 1999) works.
2. Parker McKenzie to the author, March 18 and 26, 1994.
3. Geographer Yi-Fu Tuan (1975) developed the term *geopiety* to describe the deep connection between a people and place based on religious concepts and a love of the land. Geopiety entails a worship of heaven and earth with reverence toward a homeland that is manifested in "local-level religion." Groups expressing geopiety tend to have strong ties to areas deemed sacred in their region (see Forbes-Boyte 1999:26).
4. Some Indians seem observant of such areas even when there are no visible cultural indicators, perhaps because of a different level of awareness or a similar approach to and use of such places.
5. See also Forbes-Boyte (1999:26–27).
6. Saltanaviciute (2000) surveys issues related to the protection of Native American sacred sites.
7. To my knowledge, what contemporary American Indians do with household waste is largely undocumented. While some Kiowa make great efforts to keep their homes and surrounding land free of trash and debris, others do not. Ironically, one elder who was asked to speak on American Indian respect for the land uses a large arroyo-like ditch beside his house as a dump for appliances, tires, and domestic trash. Of the few Kiowa homes I am familiar with, only a small percentage actively recycle.

CHAPTER 2

1. Saioma to Marriott, July 3, 1936, AMP-WHC. Marriott recorded Aiyadldabep'a as the South Canadian, which the Kiowa call Gúl-váu or Red River, but that is a mis-

take by her, her Kiowa consultant, or her translator. Áyàldàvàu (Timber Hill River) is Medicine Lodge Creek in Kansas and Oklahoma.

2. "Paint Mines," HLS-FSA 1:210–211.

3. Gelo (2000:275n4) provides a similar list of land- and water forms for the Comanche.

4. Parker McKenzie to the author, 1992.

5. Scott (HLS-FSA 1:213) noted in the 1890s that the Kiowa Mountains were near where the Gros Ventre then lived and were very tall mountains. From the Fort Belknap Reservation, this would suggest the Rocky Mountains in northwestern Montana.

6. RSC.

7. HLS-FSA 1:105–106.

8. See Grinnell (1906:16–17) for a similar Cheyenne example.

9. See Mooney (1898:309).

10. Saioma to Marriott, July 3, 1936, AMP-WHC.

11. The discussion in this section is based on research on a sample of more than 2,000 Kiowa personal names (Meadows n.d.-b).

12. These are only a sample of Kiowa personal names.

13. Candace Greene to the author, e-mail, 2005.

14. Meadows (n.d.-b).

15. This individual had never visited or had knowledge of these locations to influence their views. Their perception of these locales as spiritually important may reflect that some individuals are more in touch with intuitive thought.

16. The following description of the geography and archaeology of Hueco Tanks is taken from Davis and Toness (1974), Sutherland (1991, 1995), and Kegley (1980); the *Houston Chronicle,* August 6, 2000; Archaeological Institute of America, *Online News,* February 25, 1997; *Handbook of Texas Online,* April 12, 2005; *Texas Parks and Wildlife Newsstand,* September 13, 1999; Side Canyon Travel; Petroglyph Paintings From Hueco Tanks—Texas (2008); and Hueco Tanks State Historical Park—Desert USA 1996-2008).

17. HLS-FSA 1:78–81. Although the date Scott (HLS-FSA 1:78–81) lists (pre-1833) does not agree with other accounts, the rest of the account is similar.

18. Although Martineau (1973:69–83) interprets the panel of drawings at Comanche Cave as depictions of the Kiowa's ordeal at Hueco Tanks in 1839, several factors do not support this conclusion. First, he assumes that pictographs use the same imagery as historic Plains Indian sign language. Second, many of the depictions resemble prehistoric more than documented historic forms of nineteenth-century Plains Indian pictographic art. Martineau's interpretation of kilts (1973:80–81) as feathered fans used in doctoring is highly unlikely. Because the Kiowa wore buckskin kilts only during the Sun Dance, and these kilts do not show the characteristic Kiowa Sun Dance paint styles; they are likely of southwestern derivation, possibly Apache kilts worn in ceremonial *Gan* and *Naie*'s dances. Third, Martineau's analogies are random and his interpretations of complex emotions and actions do not seem supportable. He sometimes seems to grasp at interpretations, such as that figures with upraised hands (1973:72, see Figures 18 and 19) symbolize the sign language symbol for Kiowa and a headless man (Figure 6) is a marker of thirst, although the figure is shaped and dressed more like a woman than a man. Martineau (1973:74) interprets an upside-down man as symbolizing a dead man; however, Kiowa calendars with

entries denoting death from this same decade use entirely different symbols. His interpretations (1973:74–83) of small animals as Mexicans in hiding (Figures 2 and 5), furry tails as limp and thus ready to die (Figure 18), a large Mexican as indicating the Mexicans were more numerous than the Kiowa (Figure 27), a Mexican with a long coat (which seems to be simply a duster or long coat) as indicating the wearer was afraid to show himself (Figure 28), and other sorts of metaphors border on the ridiculous. A few pages later (1973:83) Martineau asserts that the author did not intend the symbols to be read in any particular order, which leads one to ask how he knew in what order they were intended to be read. Further, although carbon dating of rock art was not standard practice at the time Martineau published his study, he assumes that all the drawings were made at the same time, which may or may not be true. Martineau seems to disregard Kirkland and Newcomb's (1967) research altogether. His self-promotion as an Indian expert on the dust jacket and the publisher of the text also suggest that it was not a peer-reviewed scholarly work.

19. "Piece of Kiowas' Past Found in Park." *LC*, November 11, 1997.

20. Ibid. This article states, "They left behind two warriors—one dead, and the other badly wounded—and 32 pictographs to tell the world what had happened to them in that place." Mooney (1898) records that only one warrior, Dagoi, was left behind at the site.

21. Brune (1975:46) records two such sites in Hudspeth County, Texas. The first involved the annihilation of a band of Apache in 1881 at Apache Spring, the second at Eagle Spring or Ojo del Aguila: "Because the Apache Indians as well as the white men relied on this spring for water, several skirmishes took place here." Likewise, fighting is recorded between the Texas militia and Kickapoo at Dove Creek Spring in Irion County, between Apaches and Texans at Barrila or Jug Spring in Jeff Davis County, and between Indians at Big Spring in Howard County: "When other Spaniards arrived in 1768, the Comanche and Pawnee Indians were fighting for possession of the spring."

22. HLS-FSA 1:172–173.

23. Parker McKenzie to the author, November 17, 1990.

24. Parker McKenzie (n.d.-c, n.d.-d).

25. Parker McKenzie to the author, December 12, 1993.

26. EK, "The Family Names," 13.

27. HLS-FSA 1:103, 173–174; Kintadl to Jane Richardson VI-2, 1935, SFN 786–788.

28. Although Sundstrom (2003:264) suggests that the latter may refer to the discovery of mammoth tusks in the vicinity, the accounts imply that the objects were smaller.

29. See Force (1997) for a taphonomic reanalysis of the site.

30. While such a name would probably be Xódáuhą́qàudàl (Stone Medicine Circle/Wheel), or Xóqàudàl (Stone Circle/Wheel) in shortened form, no such name is known.

31. Scott (HLS-FSA 1:105) reports a similar Blackfoot Sioux custom of marking vision quest sites at Bear Butte and elsewhere.

32. Biatonma or Mrs. Hunting Horse and Ioleta MacElhaney to Alice Marriott, III-35–39, July 11, 1935, AMP-WHC.

33. Atah to Marriott, February 1, 1936, AMP-WHC.

34. Frank Given to Marriott, August 9, 1935, AMP-WHC.

35. Sangko to Marriott, August 21, 1935, AMP-WHC.

36. HLS-FSA 1:39–42.

37. Author's field notes, March 20, 2006.

38. Parker McKenzie to the author, February 19, 1998.

39. Chaddle-Kaungy-Ky map (ca. 1895).

40. HLS-FSA 1:171.

41. HLS-FSA 1:192.

42. Author's field notes, 2005.

43. Author's field notes, 2004. In 1990 I was shown a Cheyenne site with similar offerings of money, feathers, cloth strips and bundles, tobacco, and other items in a cedar grove near Canton, Oklahoma.

44. Mooney (1898:257–269); HLS-FSA 1:162–170.

45. Atwater Onco (Rowell 2004). Although a major tragedy for the Kiowa, large-scale massacres are not unheard of in intertribal warfare. Some 486 people were killed at the Crow Creek Site in South Dakota in the 1300s A.D. (Willey 1990), while a party of nearly 1,000 Oglala and Brule Lakota killed almost 100 Pawnee in August 1873 during their summer bison hunt in western Nebraska, at a place now known as Massacre Canyon (Parks 2001:521).

46. Silverhorn to James Mooney, JMKFN MS 2531 6:165; Mrs. Hokeah to Collier, IV-24, July 18, 1935, SFN 554; Weiser Tongkeamha to the author, 1990.

47. Parker McKenzie to the author, 1991.

48. McKenzie (n.d.-a.). "Rainy Mountain Kiowa Indian Baptist Church Membership List," 1893–1928.

49. Although photography of the murals is not allowed, they have been published in *Southwest Art* (Denton and Maudlin 1987).

50. Members of a Comanche family related how their ancestor, born in the stone-walled confinement during the winter of 1874–1875, received the name Teppekahni or Stone House, now known as Tippeconnie.

CHAPTER 3

1. Author's field notes, February 27, 2003.

2. Although some tribes use the name for the cottonwood as a generic term for trees, Kiowa tend to specify species.

3. Scott (HLS-FSA II:69–70) recorded the story as a Saynday story entitled, "How the Kiowas Got Their Country." Parsons (1929:15) called it "How the Kiowa Became Paramount." The version of Nabokov and Lowendorf's (2004) informant, titled "Close to the Heart of God: Kiowa Yellowstone Origins Narration," focused on God instead of the Kiowa trickster.

4. Momaday (1969:8) reports seven sisters and one brother, who turned into the bear. Mooney (1898:239) associates the Star Girls Story with the Pleiades. In the 1890s, Scott (HLS-FSA 1:60) reported versions with six boys and a girl, (1:99) "children," and an account from Taybodle (1:173) mentioning eight girls. Parsons (1929:9, FN3) reported the Kiowa story with the Pleiades but the Crow story with the Big Dipper. Iseeo reported seven girls, while Victor Paddlety reported six brothers and two sisters, one of the sisters becoming the bear (Stone 1982:4–6).

5. Marry Buffalo to Alice Marriott, October 20, 1935, AMP-WHC.

6. George Poolaw to Alice Marriott, May 28, 1936, AMP-WHC.

7. Benefit dances are held to raise funds for these trips (see *ADN*, October 4, 2001).

8. Iseeo to Hugh L. Scott, "What the Old Kiowa Say About the Crow," HLS-NAA. Mooney (1898:153, 429) gave the name of the Yellowstone or Upper Missouri as Xôsáuvàu (Rocks Standing [River]). Delos K. Lonewolf gave a similar description and translation (Harrington 1939:167) based on blocks of ice thawing and refreezing in the Mississippi River. However, the Kiowa word for ice is jé̖-gà, and the form would be Jé̖sáuvàu (Ice Standing River).

9. Mooney (1898:405) reported that "Gwa'hale'go (Kwahadi) was another name for the Thóqą̀hyò̖p and was the Kiowa corruption of the Comanche Kwahadi (Antelopes). Whether Gúhàlè̖ is a further corruption of the Comanche or not, it is not the Kiowa word for antelopes (tháp, s/d/t; and kái-cùn s/d, or kái-cù-dàu t) (McKenzie n.d.-d) and was associated with the wild horse herds of that region. The Comanche term for wild horses (kobe) occurs as a loan word in other Kiowa personal and place names and does not seem to apply to this usage.

10. Parker McKenzie to the author, April 17, 1994.

11. Ibid. The name Samone needs clarification. At allotment in 1901, there are two individuals in different communities with similar names. Luther Sah-maunt (KFR 1901:266) near Mount Scott, and Sa-maun-ty (KFR 1901:104), the husband of Kah-gem, west of Carnegie. For Sa-maun-ty, Mooney (MS 2331:6:175) notes, "345 Semonti (Mexican captive—same origin as Luther's name, but different pronunciation." Sa-maun-ty is listed with his wife Gyazemti or Tsogyazema (Shifting Rocks). Luther Sah-maunt was the son of Ti-ke-itty and a captive Mexican mother named Sate-ko-mah. Sa-maun-ti or Sa-maun-ty was a Mexican captive taken as a child. Corwin (1958:105) states that when Luther Samaunt was born he was named Ramon by his mother, and his name was recorded as Sahmaunt on agency rolls. Kiowa elders state that Luther Sah-maunt's name is usually given as Sé̖-mâun, which can also mean cocklebur, while Sa-maun-ti's name is usually given as Sà-máun.

Sé̖-mâun is probably the Kiowa pronunciation of Ramon as Kiowa contains no "r" sound. The 1881 census (KTC 1881:26) lists Sa-mau-ty (Cockle Burr). Sa-maun-ti and his wife took their allotments due north of Sit-a-pah-tah's allotment, on which present-day Samone Cemetery is located. Kahgem (1846–1913) is buried in Rainy Mountain Cemetery. I have not been able to locate where Sa-maun-ti is buried. Luther Sahmant is buried in Mount Scott Cemetery. Whether both names are derived from Ramon or Sa-maun-ty's name is derived from cocklebur is unclear. This information suggests that Sa-maun-ti's name may have been anglicized to Samone and became the name of the cemetery and school near his home.

12. Several Kiowa elders interviewed between 1989 and 2006 confirmed these community names.

13. Parker McKenzie to the author, October 15, 1997.

14. Author's field notes, February 27, 2003.

15. Author's field notes.

16. Atwater Onco to the author, October 28, 1997.

17. Dorothy Whitehorse DeLaune to the author, July 9, 2004.

18. Ina Aunko Miller to the author, July 27, 2005.

19. An Amish community was started near my hometown in 1994 and affords an excellent opportunity to observe their impact on future ethnogeography.

20. Ernestine Kauahquo Kauley to the author, March 25, 2005.

21. *ADN*, July 3, 2002.

22. Schnell (2000:171) reports cases of individuals gaining psychological renewal from revisiting their family's home place, even if it involves sleeping in dilapidated houses or a car and bathing in nearby creeks. This is a part of what Kiowa describe as "charging their batteries" by returning home to visit.

23. Anne Yeahquo to the author, February 28, 2003.

24. Anne Yeahquo to the author, February 28, 2003.

25. Vanessa Jennings to the author, October 19, 2000.

26. Parker McKenzie to the author, September 18, 1992.

27. "Early day history told of Redstone Baptist Church," *ADN*, January 5–6, 2002.

28. For the most comprehensive works on Kiowa religion, see Kracht (1989, 1992, 1997, in press) and Lassiter et al. (2002).

29. Ibid.

30. Delores Toyebo Harragarra to the author, March 19, 2003.

31. Odlepaugh Springs is about one-half mile west of where the Saddle Mountain Church stood. The baptism site was a few feet north of the actual bubbling spring (Toncacut 2000:181).

32. "The Passing of A (Former) Kiowa Tribal Committeeman: Randlett L. (Zotigh) Hall," *ADN*, October 26, 2001.

33. One elder told me that based on inconsistencies with family history and accounts of individuals (William Cizik via his son-in-law Oscar Tsoodle) who used to care for Big Bow's grave, there is suggestive evidence that the right burial may not have been recovered. Author's field notes, September 18, 1992. I can neither confirm nor negate these accounts.

34. Author's field notes, 2004.

35. For a discussion of the Kiowa Ghost Dance, see Kracht (1992).

36. A man-made swimming hole with diving boards, Dietrich's Lake was a well-known landmark for many years. Ben Kracht, personal communication, June 2006.

37. Labeled an "Indian Ceremonial Grounds" on the Fort Cobb 7.5 USGS topographic map, the Redbone (Naishan Apache) Dance Ground is one of the few modern Indian geocultural sites on contemporary topographic maps.

38. Atwater Onco to the author, October 15, 1997.

39. Schnell (1992, 2000:172) provides similar responses.

40. Oscar Tsoodle to the author, October 13, 1990.

41. Vanessa Jennings to the author, October 11, 1997.

42. Asau Jack Yellowhair to the author, May 22, 1998.

43. See also Schnell (1994:31).

44. Healy's synopsis (1997:74–75) of the Kiowa "Koitsenko" Society contains many mistakes and is highly unreliable. For the most thorough accounts, see SFN and JMKFN.

45. *KIN*, May 2006, 32(6), 6.

46. *KIN*, June 2006, 32(7), 7.

47. Author's field notes, June 29, 2004. Although some Kiowa deny that the Redstone area and the Redstone Church are haunted, others, including some community members, maintain that it is.

48. The dedication for "The Historical Marker For the Site of the Cutthroat Gap

Massacre of 1833" was held by the Kiowa Historical Society and the Oklahoma State Historical Society on January 20, 1995.

49. Lester Harragarra, Oklahoma Department of Transportation, to the author, March 27 and August 12, 2005.

50. Recently the Comanche were successful in having Squaw Creek in Lawton, Oklahoma, renamed with the proper Comanche name for the stream. However, the sign has not yet been replaced. "Squaw Creek Changes to Numu Creek," *CNN* January 2006, 5(1), 1.

CHAPTER 4

1. See Petersen (1971), Harris (1989), Warhus (1997:197–207), Viola (1998), and Greene (2001) for the variety of flora and landforms shown in Kiowa and Cheyenne ledger art and calendars, some of which are linked to specific named streams, hills, and other locales. While at Fort Marion, Howling Wolf and others depicted landscapes far removed from their home area.

2. For summaries of the current understanding of indigenous North American cartography and discussions of the breadth of works in this area, see Brody (1982), Harley (1992), Winchell et al. (1994), Warhus (1997), Lewis (1980, 1984a, 1984b, 1998), Rundstrom et al. (2000), and Sutton (2002). Of these, Lewis (1998) is the most comprehensive work to date.

3. See Mallery (1886, 1893), Lewis in De Vorsey (1978:75, 78n18), Ewers (1977, 1997a, 1997b), Lewis (1984a; 1984b), Andrews et al. (1995), and Warhus (1997:169–207).

4. For a list of native drawn maps, see Andrews et al. (1995) and Fredlund et al. (1996:25–27). George Bent (Cheyenne) produced maps of the aboriginal territory of the Cheyenne and of the Sand Creek Massacre (Moore 1987:160). Howling Wolf (Cheyenne) drew a map of his voyage from Fort Marion, Florida, which he gave to his father, Minimic. The map was drawn while at sea after leaving Savannah (Peterson 1971:224).

5. Although Lewis (Lewis ed. 1998:50 n.21) states that a Kiowa drew a map in the sand for Whipple (1855, 1856) during his survey, the associated data demonstrate that they were actually Tigua and not Kiowa. As Whipple (1855:Ch. 3) recorded, "They are Tiguex; or according to their own language, "Ki-o-wum-mi," which by referring to the vocabulary, is found to denote two." Other data indicate that they were Tigua from San Domingo Pueblo, were associated with southern origins, and were then living at San Domingo. The similarity of "Ki-o-wum-mi" to Kiowa seems to have led Lewis to make this interpretation.

6. Rundstrom (1990:156–157) shows that Inuit maps are not only highly accurate but also reflect cultural values in the form of highly developed levels of observation and memory in Inuit behavior and thought. That is, "values embodied in other institutions are implicit in cartographic artifacts."

7. Lewis (1980:110) uses the term "cartographic device," as varied forms of this type of artifact were not drawn to scale, not constructed according to particular projections, and were not consistent in representing all phenomena in a given class above a given threshold size. However, as Belyea (1992) points out, Lewis, like most scholars of Indian maps, view their composition through a comparison and expectation of European and not native cartographic patterns.

8. Lewis (1980:15, 1984:92) and Rundstrom (1990) provide similar observations.

9. Extensive geographic knowledge over large areas is recorded for the plains, Great Basin, Subarctic, and Arctic, where men were commonly intimately familiar with areas spanning hundreds of square miles. Maps were clearly useful. Although qualitatively different, Pawnee astronomy maps encompass even larger units of space and distance.

10. The Kiowa terms for the wild and domestic goose are cấu (s/d) and cấu-gáu. The Canadian goose is known as châl-thài (s/d) and châl-thài-màu (t) (lit. white-belted). The crane or great blue heron is known by the term pì-qóp-jè (s/d) and pì-qóp-cáut (t). Note that s/d/t stand for single, dual, and triplural forms in Kiowa (McKenzie n.d.). Based on these terms, Black Goose appears to be the correct name form for Chaddle-Kaungy-Ky. Tsadalkonzha, Tsadalkonkya, and Tsadalkongya are varied spellings of Black Goose's name (Merrill et al. 1997:42, 428). Black Goose was also the name Kiowa linguist Parker McKenzie knew him by.

11. CIA-KCF W. D. Myers to the Commission of Indian Affairs, February 18, 1889, Kiowa Court File (Hagan 1966:130).

12. Blue Clark to the author, e-mail, February 12, 2007.

13. Robert Daniels to John P. Harrington, August 19, 1936, JPHP. Courtesy of Candace Greene.

14. Parker McKenzie stated that older Kiowa distinguished the mountains west of the pass at Cooperton, Oklahoma, as the Wichita Mountains and those east of the pass as the Apache Mountains, from the Apache's preference for camping around them. This identification affirms this distinction in regard to the earlier description of the Wichita Mountains. Parker McKenzie to the author, February 19, 1998.

15. Navajo containing similar hairstyles are common in Kiowa ledger art (see McCoy 1987:Plates 4, 12).

16. HLS-FSA 1:172–173.

17. Vấui-gài is probably the short name form of Kố-vàui-gài, denoting Right In The Center/Middle. He was born in 1843.

18. Kiowa men and women had personal names based on this creature.

19. The only trail to cross the KCA Reservation, the Western Cattle Trail crossed at Doan's Store on the south side of the Red River and west of the mouth of the North Fork of the Red River, whence it ran to Fort Supply and on to Dodge City (Morris et al. 1986:Map 46). Thus this line represents the Texas–Indian Territory line and not the Western Cattle Trail.

20. As Lewis (1980:15) notes, "There the cacique reached the edge of the deerskin and swung what would seem to be the Red and Arkansas rivers clockwise through almost ninety degrees in order to accommodate them."

21. Crimmins (1947:5) suggests that Hidetown was established prior to Fort Elliott's construction: "The natural place to select was one used by buffalo hunters and called 'Hide town,' with a wagon road on the Jones-Plummer Trail to Ft. Dodge."

22. To hold their last Sun Dance, in 1887, the Kiowa were forced to buy a bison from Charles Goodnight, who then had a small herd of captive bison in northern Texas. His ranch holdings were along Palo Duro Canyon far west into Texas (in present-day Armstrong, Briscoe, Donley, Hall, and Swisher counties) and are not the intended identification of this locale (Mooney 1898:355; Crimmins 1947:7, 10–11). I have been unable to identify any rancher in this area during the 1890s with bison.

23. Po-e-to-mah (Mrs. Tsatoke) and Ioleta Hunt MacElhaney to Alice Marriott, July 10, 1935, AMP-WHC.

24. The easternmost mountain southeast of the Buffalo Tree has a series of small linear marks at the center of its base. Despite magnification, it is unclear what these marks represent. Although it may possibly represent a stand of timber, it is also in the immediate vicinity where the three Kiowa boys froze to death on January 9, 1891, and may refer to that incident (Mooney 1898:360–361).

25. The Poor Wolf Map is reported to have been drawn in either 1880, when he visited Washington, D.C., or 1881, when W. J. Hoffman visited Fort Berthold. Candace Greene, personal communication to the author, September 21, 2005.

26. Brotherson (1992) stresses the importance of viewing native maps and literary texts as closely related equally legitimate modes of representation.

CHAPTER 5

1. Although most Kiowa refer to it as the Apache-Y, it is recorded on maps as the Apache-Wye.

2. *ADN*, September 8–9, 2001.

3. For in-depth accounts of Indian agriculture, see Stahl (1978) and Lynn-Sherow (2004). I have interviewed several Kiowa and Plains Apache who once farmed, a few well into the 1950s. Presently I know of only two Kiowa men who actively farm and ranch.

4. Japan's change from a pre-Second World War militaristic nation, which required an oath to and recognition of the emperor as a descendant of the sun, to the postwar modern, highly peaceful society, despite its military scope having been limited by treaty provisions, is an example.

5. Anne Yeahquo to the author, February 28, 2003.

6. Dennis Zotigh to the author, e-mail, August 14, 2002.

7. I disagree with Schnell (1994:95) on this point. Having studied Kiowa social and political conflict, racial discrimination in the form of the "race card" (i.e., "I'm a higher degree of blood quantum than you" and "I'm Indian, you're not") is commonly used against others, Indian or non-Indian.

8. Author's field notes, 1990–1998.

9. One of Schnell's (1994:97) informants listed "Trust, loyalties, commitments, convictions, stubbornness, persistence, perseverance, these are the important things to us."

10. Author's field notes, May 1998.

11. This conclusion is based on interviews with several elders, who were unable to answer most follow-up questions concerning details of family accounts of war deeds performed by their ancestors. I believe this mirrors how many of the smaller details in oral history become omitted and vague while the gist of the story remains intact enough to permit a general level of continuance as it is handed down.

12. The fiscal year 1900 Kiowa Census lists Sit-ah-pa-tah (no. 223), born in 1844, as a full-blooded Kiowa.

13. Schnell (1994) records the same basic appellations.

14. HLS-FSA 1:57.

15. I suspect some of these differences are due to the fact that Basso's work, conducted from 1979 to 1984 (Basso 1996:xv), preceded my own work (1989–2007)

by several years, and he obtained information from a great number of elder fluent speakers.

16. Author's field notes, 1995–2006.

17. Public Service Company of Oklahoma (2005). In 2003 the Rosebud Lakota became the first American Indian tribe to install commercial scale wind turbines for energy production. Since then dozens of tribes have considered wind as a source of energy that is economically viable and that fits with native values. Honor The Earth (2005) has implemented projects to install wind turbines on Pine Ridge Reservation and solar panels on the Western Shoshone Reservation in Nevada.

18. Ben Kracht, letter to the author, June 2006.

19. These are a few of the comments I collected from Kiowa tribal members in July 2006.

20. Author's field notes, 2006.

21. "Water request spurs neighbor's objections," *TO*, September 13, 2006, 13A; "Jimmy Creek debate—State board considers future use of billions of gallons of water in county," *LC*, September 13, 2006, 1C; "Despite Opposition, some support Hillary water request," *LC*, September 24, 2006, 3A–4A.

22. For problems in preserving Native American landmarks versus cultural landscapes, see Stoffle et al. (1997:234–238).

23. Schnell (1994:82–84) first described this feature under the term "invisible landscape."

24. Poetomah to Alice Marriott, 1935, AMF-WHC.

25. Parker McKenzie to the author, August 9, 1994.

26. Author's field notes, 1998.

27. Parker McKenzie to the author, April 17, 1992. Echols (1978) provides a similar version (with Poor Buffalo instead of Saingko) of the incident he recorded from McKenzie.

28. Parker McKenzie to the author, January 16, 1994.

29. Author's field notes, 2004.

30. Author's field notes, 2004.

31. Schnell's (2000:170) findings concerning the area of Kiowa allotments are similar to what contemporary Kiowa consider Kiowa Country.

32. Delores Toyebo Harragarra to the author, March 19, 2003.

33. Schnell (2000:170) provides an accurate and succinct description of the Kiowa view of their homeland.

34. Schnell (2000:155) notes an interesting contrast between Arrell Gibson's characterization of Oklahoma in reference to non-Indians as the "Land of the Drifter" from a sense of a lack of rootedness due to economic insecurity and the strong sense of homeland among Oklahoma Indians, which provides an important part of their sense of identity.

35. Vanessa Jennings to the author, October 19, 2000.

36. Delores Toyebo Harragarra to the author, March 19, 2003. Author's field notes.

37. Toyebo Family Reunion. Author's field notes, Rainy Mountain Kiowa Indian Baptist Church, May 17, 2003.

38. Bernadine Herwana Toyebo Rhoades (Rowell 2004).

39. Schnell (2000:173) is similar: "For the Kiowa, at least, the importance of their core area, as well as certain places outside that area is difficult to overstate. It is an

anchor for their identity, and it has endured despite the disappearance of the tribe's territorial integrity, for the existence of a homeland is not simply a matter of real estate."

40. Daniel J. Gelo, personal communication to the author, February 16 and July 9, 2006.

Bibliography

Unpublished Sources

Maps

Chaddle-Kaungy-Ky. ca. 1895. Map (Black Goose's map). Washington,
  DC: National Anthropological Archives, Kiowa Collections, Ethnology
  233091 (cat. no. 43633).

Archival Sources

AA — Anadarko Agency.
AMP-WHC Alice Marriott, Kiowa Field Notes, 1934–1936. Western
  History Collections, University of Oklahoma, Norman.
EK — Ernestine Kauley, "The Family Names." Unpublished document,
  author's copy.
HLS-FSA — Hugh L[ennox] Scott Ledgerbooks (ca. 1892–1897). 4 vols.
  Fort Sill Museum Archives, Fort Sill, OK.
HLS-NAA — Hugh Lennox Scott, National Anthropological Archives, MS
  4525, Kiowa Files. Smithsonian Institution, Washington, DC.
Index Family Record Sheet, 1929. Department of the Interior, Office of
  Indian Affairs. Copy in author's possession.
GWH-OHS — Rev. George Washington Hicks Diaries, 1887–1906.
  Oklahoma Historical Society, Oklahoma City, OK.
JMKFN — James Mooney, Kiowa Field Notes. MS 2531, vols. 1, 2, 3, 6, 7,
  11, 12; MS 2538, Box 2, Folder 1, National Anthropological Archives.
  Smithsonian Institution, Washington, DC.
JPHP — John P. Harrington Papers, National Anthropological Archives.
  Smithsonian Institution, Washington, DC.

JQF—*Jimmy Quoetone Family Reunion.* Privately published, 1986.
    Courtesy of Anne L. Yeahquo.
KFR—Kiowa Family Record, Fiscal Year 1901. Prepared by Parker P.
    McKenzie. Copy in author's possession.
KTC—Kiowa Tribal Censuses, 1880, 1881, 1889, 1895, 1899, 1900.
    Copies in author's possession.
RSC—Roberts Silverhorn Calendar. Sam Noble Museum of Natural
    History, University of Oklahoma, Norman.
SFN—Santa Fe Laboratory of Anthropology 1935 Kiowa Field Notes,
    National Anthropological Archives. Smithsonian Institution,
    Washington, DC.

NEWSPAPERS

ADN—Anadarko Daily News, Anadarko, OK.
CNN—Comanche Nation News, Comanche Nation, Lawton, OK.
KIN—Kiowa Indian News, Kiowa Tribe of Oklahoma, Carnegie, OK.
TO—The Oklahoman, Oklahoma City, OK.
LC—Lawton Constitution, Lawton, OK.

Published Sources

Afable, Patricia O., and Madison S. Beeler. 1997. "Place-Names." In
    Handbook of North American Indians. Vol. 17, *Languages,* ed. Ives
    Goddard, 185–199. Washington, DC: Smithsonian Institution.
Albers, Patricia C. 1993. "Symbiosis, Merger, and War: Contrasting
    Forms of Intertribal Relationships Among Historic Plains Indians." In
    The Political Economy of North American Indians, ed. John H. Moore,
    94–132. Norman: University of Oklahoma Press.
Albers, Patricia, and Jeanne Kay. 1987. "Sharing the Land: A Study in
    American Indian Territoriality." In *A Cultural Geography of North
    American Indians,* ed. Thomas E. Ross and Tyrel G. Moore, 47–91.
    Boulder, CO: Westview Press.
Andrews, Sona, David Tilton, and Mark Warhus. 1995. *Archive of North
    American Indian Maps on CD-ROM.* Archival database. Department of
    Geography, University of Wisconsin–Milwaukee.
Barrett, Samuel A. 1908. "The Ethno-geography of the Pomo and
    Neighboring Indians." *University of California Publications in American
    Archaeology and Ethnology* 6(1):1–332.
Bartlett, John Russell. 1854. *Personal Narrative of Explorations and
    Incidents in Texas, New Mexico, California, Sonora, and Chihuahua.*

2 vols. New York: United States–Mexican Boundary Commission, 1850–1853.

Basso, Keith H. 1987. "Speaking with Names: Language and Landscape among the Western Apache." *Cultural Anthropology* 3(2):99–130.

———. 1996. *Wisdom Sits in Places: Landscape and Language Among the Western Apache.* Albuquerque, NM: University of New Mexico Press.

Belyea, Barbara. 1992. "Amerindian Maps: The Explorer as Translator." *Journal of Historical Geography* 18:267–277.

———. 1998. "Inland Journeys, Native Maps." In *Cartographic Encounters: Perspectives on Native American Mapmaking and Map Use,* ed. G. Malcolm Lewis, 135–156. Chicago: University of Chicago Press.

Berlandier, Jean Louis. 1980. *Journey to Mexico During the Years 1826 to 1834.* 2 vols. Translated and edited by Sheila M. Ohlendorf, Josette M. Bigelow, and Mary M. Standifer. Austin: Texas State Historical Association.

Berlo, Janet C., and Ruth B. Phillips. 1998. *Native North American Art.* Oxford History of Art. New York: Oxford University Press.

Boas, Franz. 1887. "The Study of Geography." *Science* 9(210):137–141.

———. 1901–1907. *The Eskimo of Baffin Land and Hudson Bay; from Notes Collected by Capt. George Comer, Capt. James S. Mutch and Rev. E. J. Peck.* 2 vols. Bulletin of the American Museum of Natural History 15. Reprint, New York: AMS Press, 1975.

———. 1934. *Geographical Names of the Kwakiutl Indian.* Columbia University Contributions to Anthropology, vol. 20. New York: Columbia University Press.

———. 1966. *Kwakiutl Ethnogeography,* ed. Helen Codere. Chicago: University of Chicago Press.

Boone, Elizabeth Hill. 1998. "Maps of Territory, History, and Community in Aztec Mexico." In *Cartographic Encounters: Perspectives on Native American Mapmaking and Map Use,* ed. G. Malcolm Lewis, 111–134. Chicago: University of Chicago Press.

Bordewich, Fergus M. 1996. *Killing The White Man's Indian: Reinventing Native Americans at the End of the Twentieth Century.* New York: Doubleday.

Boyd, Maurice. 1981. *Kiowa Voices.* Vol. 1, *Ceremonial Dance, Ritual, and Song.* Fort Worth: Texas Christian University Press.

———. 1983. *Kiowa Voices.* Vol. 2, *Myths, Legends and Folktales.* Fort Worth: Texas Christian University Press.

Bright, William. 1958. "Karok Names." *Names* 6(3):172–179.

———. 2004. *Native American Placenames of the United States.* Norman: University of Oklahoma Press.

Brody, Hugh. 1982. *Maps and Dreams*. New York: Pantheon Books.

Brotherson, George. 1992. *Book of the Fourth World*. Cambridge: Cambridge University Press.

Brune, Gunnar. 1975. *Springs of Texas*. Fort Worth, TX: Branch-Smith.

Burton, Lloyd. 2002. *Worship and Wilderness: Culture, Religion, and Law in Public Lands Management*. Madison: University of Wisconsin Press.

Campbell, Greg, and Thomas A. Foor. 2004. "Entering Sacred Landscapes: Cultural Expectations Versus Legal Realities in the Northwestern Plains." *Great Plains Quarterly* 24(3):163–183.

Campbell, T. N., and William T. Field. 1968. "Identification of Comanche Raiding Trails in Trans-Pecos Texas." *West Texas Historical Association Year Book* 44:128–144.

Carlson, Alvar W. 1990. *The Spanish-American Homeland: Four Centuries in New Mexico's Río Arriba*. Baltimore, MD: Johns Hopkins University Press.

Carroll, Charles H. 1983. *Ute Mountain Land Exchange Ethnographic Study*. Albuquerque: Public Service Company of New Mexico.

Carroll, John B., ed. 1956. *Language, Thought, and Reality: Selected Writings of Benjamin Lee Whorf*. Cambridge, MA: MIT Press.

Clark, Blue. 1994. *Lone Wolf v. Hitchcock: Treaty Rights & Indian Law at the End of the Nineteenth Century*. Lincoln: University of Nebraska Press.

Clark, William P. 1885. *The Indian Sign Language*. Philadelphia: L. R. Hamersley. Reprint, Lincoln: University of Nebraska Press, 1982.

Conkling, Roscoe P., and Margaret B. Conkling. 1947. *The Butterfield Overland Mail, 1857–1869*. 3 vols. Glendale, CA: Clark.

Corwin, Hugh D. 1958. *The Kiowa Indians: Their History and Life Stories*. Lawton, OK: Privately published.

Corwin, Hugh D., ed. 1975. "The A-nanthy Odle-Paugh Kiowa Calendar. By A-nanthy Odle-paugh." *Prairie Lore* January 154–163.

Crawford, Isabel Alice Hartley. 1915. *Kiowa: The History of a Blanket Indian Mission*. New York: Fleming H. Revell.

————. 1998. *Kiowa: A Woman Missionary in Indian Territory*. Lincoln: University of Nebraska Press.

Crimmins, Col. M. L. 1947. "Fort Elliott, Texas." *West Texas Historical Association Year Book* 23:3–12.

Cruikshank, Julie. 1981. "Legend and Landscape: Convergence of Oral and Scientific Traditions in the Yukon Territory." *Artic Anthropology* 18(2):67–93.

————. 1990a. "Getting the Words Right: Perspectives on Naming and Places in Athapaskan Oral History." *Artic Anthropology* 27(1):52–65.

————. 1990b. *Life Lived Like a Story: Life Stories of Three Yukon Native Elders.* Lincoln: University of Nebraska Press.

Davis, John V., and K. Sutherland Toness. 1974. *A Rock Art Inventory at Hueco Tanks State Park.* Special Report 12. El Paso, TX: El Paso Archaeological Society.

de Laguna, Frederica. 1972. *Under Mount St. Elias: The History and Culture of the Yakutat Tlingit.* 3 pts. Smithsonian Contributions to Anthropology 7. Washington, DC: Smithsonian Institution Press.

Deloria, Vine, Jr., and Clifford M. Lytle. 1983. *American Indian, American Justice.* Austin: University of Texas Press.

De Vorsey, Louis. 1978. "Amerindian Contributions to the Mapping of North America: A Preliminary View," *Imago Mundi* 30:71–78.

DeLorme Inc. 1998a. *Oklahoma Atlas & Gazetteer.* Yarmouth, ME: DeLorme.

————. 1998b. *Kansas Atlas & Gazetteer.* Yarmouth, ME: DeLorme.

————. 1998c. *Colorado Atlas & Gazetteer.* Yarmouth, ME: DeLorme.

————. 1998d. *Texas Atlas & Gazetteer.* Yarmouth, ME: DeLorme.

DeMallie, Raymond J., and John C. Ewers. 2001. "History of Ethnological and Ethnohistorical Research." In *Handbook of North American Indians.* Vol. 13, *Plains,* 23–43. Washington, DC: Smithsonian Institution Press.

Denig, Edwin T. 1930. "Indian Tribes of the Upper Missouri." Edited with Notes and Biographical Sketch by J. N. B. Hewitt. In *Forty-sixth Annual Report of the Bureau of American Ethnology,* 1928–1929, pp. 375–628. Washington, DC: Smithsonian Institution, Government Printing Office.

Denton, Joan Frederick, and Sanford L. Maudlin Jr. 1987. Kiowa Murals, "Behold I Stand in Good Relation to All Things," *Southwest Art,* July 68–75.

Dick, Claribel F. 1959. *The Song Goes On: The Story of Ioleta Hunt MacElhaney.* Philadelphia: Judson Press.

Dodge, Col. Richard Irving. 1877. *The Hunting Grounds of the Great West.* London: Chatto & Windus.

————. 1882. *Our Wild Indians.* Hartford, CT.

Du Bois, Cora. 1935. "Wintu Ethnogeography." *University of California Publications in American Archaeology and Ethnology* 36(1):1–139.

Echols, Lee E. 1978. "The Kiowa Raiders of Rainy Mountain." *True West,* March–April: 6–13, 41–45.

Ellis, Clyde. 1996. *To Change Them Forever: Indian Education at the Rainy Mountain Boarding School, 1893–1920.* Norman: University of Oklahoma Press.

————. 2002. "The Jesus Road at the Kiowa-Comanche-Apache
   Reservation." In Luke Eric Lassiter, Clyde Ellis, and Ralph Kotay, *The
   Jesus Road: Kiowas, Christianity, and Indian Hymns*, 17–70. Lincoln:
   University of Nebraska Press.
————. 2003. *A Dancing People: Powwow Culture on the Southern Plains*.
   Lawrence: University of Kansas Press.
Ellison, Rosemary. 1973. *Painted Tipis by Contemporary Indian Artists*.
   Anadarko, OK: Indian Arts and Crafts Board, Oklahoma Arts and
   Crafts Cooperative.
Erwin, Ed. 2000. "Pictographs at Hueco Tanks Park." *Houston Chronicle*,
   August 6.
Ewers, John C. 1977. "The Making and Uses of Maps by Plains Indian
   Warriors." *By Valor and Arms* 3(1):36–43.
————. 1997a. "The Use of Artifacts and Pictures in the Study of
Plains Indian History, Art, and Religion." In *Plains Indian History and
   Culture: Essays on Continuity and Change*, ed. John C. Ewers, 61–81.
   Norman: University of Oklahoma Press.
————. 1997b "The Making and Use of Maps by Plains Warriors." In
   Plains Indian History and Culture: Essays on Continuity and Change,
   ed. John C. Ewers, 180–190. Norman: University of Oklahoma
   Press.
Fabry, Judith K. 1989. *Guadalupe Mountains National Park: An
   Administrative History*. Professional Papers no. 19. Santa Fe, NM:
   National Park Service, Department of the Interior, Division of History,
   Southwest Cultural Resources Center Southwest Region.
Feest, Christian F. 1992. *Native Arts of North America*, updated version.
   New York: Thames and Hudson.
Fenton, James I. 1981. "Cedar Lake: Mirror of Staked Plains History,"
   Permian Historical Annual, 21:33–48.
Finney, Whitham D. 1976. *Along The Banks of the Washita: The Story of a
   Town*. Fort Cobb, OK: privately published.
Fixico, Donald L. 2000. *The Urban Indian Experience in America*.
   Albuquerque: University of New Mexico Press.
Forbes-Boyte, Kari. 1999. "Litigation, Mitigation, and the American
   Indian Religious Freedom Act: The Bear Butte Example." *Great Plains
   Quarterly* 19 (Winter):23–34.
Force, Frank. 1997. "The Domebo Site: A Taphonomic Reanalysis."
   Master's thesis, Department of Anthropology, University of
   Oklahoma, Norman.
Foreman, Grant, ed. 1937. *Adventure on the Red River: Report of the
   Exploration of the Headwaters of the Red River by Captain Randolph B.*

Marcy and Captain G. B. McClellan. Norman: University of Oklahoma Press.

Fort Sill Museum. 2004. Faces of Fort Sill. Program brochure, Fort Sill National Historic Landmark, July 24. Fort Sill, OK.

Foster, James Monroe. 1960. "Fort Bascom, New Mexico." *New Mexico Historical Quarterly,* 35.

Frazer, Robert W. 1965. *Forts of the West: Military Forts and Presidios and Posts Commonly Called Forts West of the Mississippi River.* Norman: University of Oklahoma Press.

Fredlund, Glen, Linea Sundstrom, and Rebecca Armstrong. 1996. "Crazy Mule's Maps of the Upper Missouri, 1877–1880." *Plains Anthropologist* 41(155):5–27.

French, David H., and Katherine S. French. 1997. "Personal Names" In *Handbook of North American Indians.* Vol. 17, *Languages,* ed. Ives Goddard, 200–221. Washington, DC: Smithsonian Institution.

Galley of Art (Anadarko). 2003. Promotional flier. Anadarko, OK: Gallery of Art.

Gelo, Daniel J. 1986. "Comanche Belief and Ritual." Ph.D. diss., Department of Anthropology, Rutgers University, New Brunswick, NJ.

———. 2002. "Comanche Land & Ever Has Been: A Native Geography of the Nineteenth-Century Comanchería." *Southern Historical Quarterly* 103(3):272–307.

Gill, Sam D. 1990. *The Sacred Geography of the American Mound Builders.* Lewiston, NY: Mellen Press.

Goins, Charles R., and Danney Goble. 2006. *Historical Atlas of Oklahoma,* 4th ed. Norman: University of Oklahoma Press.

Goldman, Marlene. 1999. "Mapping and Dreaming: Native Resistance in *Green Grass, Running Water.*" *Canadian Literature* 161–162:18–41.

Gould, Charles N. 1933. *Oklahoma Place Names.* Norman: University of Oklahoma Press.

Greene, Candace. 2001. *Silver Horn: Master Illustrator of the Kiowas.* Norman: University of Oklahoma Press.

Grinnell, George B. 1906. Cheyenne Stream Names. *American Anthropologist* 8:15–22.

———. 1922. "The Big Horn Medicine Wheel." *American Anthropologist* 24:299–310.

Grobsmith, Elizabeth A. 2001. *Lakota of the Rosebud: A Contemporary Ethnography.* Belmont, CA: Wadsworth.

Gulliford, Andrew. 2000. *Sacred Objects and Sacred Places.* Boulder: University Press of Colorado.

Hagan, William T. 1966. *Indian Police and Judges*. Lincoln: University of Nebraska Press.

———. 1976. *United States-Comanche Relations*. Norman: University of Oklahoma Press.

Hail, Barbara, ed. 2000. *Gifts of Pride and Love: Kiowa and Comanche Cradles*. Bristol, RI: Haffenreffer Museum of Anthropology, Brown University.

Hale, Duane K. 1981. "Gold in Oklahoma: The Last Great Gold Excitement in the Trans-Mississippi West 1889–1918." *Chronicles of Oklahoma* 59:304–319.

Hallowell, A. Irving. 1955. *Culture and Experience*. New York: Schocken Books.

Harkin, Michael E. 2000. "Sacred Places, Scarred Spaces." *Wicazo Sa Review* 15(1):49–70.

Harley, J. Brian. 1992. "Rereading the Maps of the Columbian Encounter." *Annals of the Association of American Geographers* 82(3):522–542.

Harrington, John P. 1916. "The Ethnography of the Tewa Indians." In *29th Annual Report of the Bureau of American Ethnology for 1907–1908*, 29–618. Washington, DC: Smithsonian Institution, Government Printing House.

———. 1939. "Kiowa Memories of the Northland." In *So Live the Works of Men*, ed. Donald D. Brand and Fred E. Harvey, 162–176. Albuquerque: University of New Mexico Press.

Harris, Moira F. 1989. *Between Two Cultures: Kiowa Art from Fort Marion*. St. Paul, MN: Pogo Press.

Haynes, Gary. 2002. *The Early Settlement of North America: The Clovis Era*. Cambridge: Cambridge University Press.

Healy, Donald T. 1997. Flags of the Native Peoples of the United States. Raven. *A Journal of Vexillology. North American Vexillological Association*, vols. 3–4, 1996–1997.

Hickerson, Nancy P. 1994. *The Jumanos: Hunters and Traders of the South Plains*. Austin: University of Texas Press.

Hoffman, Jack L. 1998. "Domebo." In *Archaeology of Prehistoric Native America: An Encyclopedia*, ed. Guy Gibbon, 214–215. New York: Garland.

Honor The Earth. 2005. *Energy Justice Initiative*. Pamphlet. Minneapolis, MN: Author. Available: http://Honorearth@earthlink.net.

Howard, James H. 1972. "Notes on the Ethnogeography of the Yankton Dakota." *Plains Anthropologist* 17:281–307.

————. 1979. "The British Museum Winter Count." *British Museum Occasional Paper* 4, London.

Hoxie, Frederick E. 1979. "From Prison to Homeland: The Cheyenne River Indian Reservation Before World War I." *South Dakota History* 10(1):1–24.

Hunn, Eugene S. 1990. *Nch'I-Wána: "The Big River." Mid-Columbia Indians and Their Land*. Seattle: University of Washington Press.

————. 1994. "Place-Names, Population Density, and the Magic Number 500." *Current Anthropology* 35(1):81–85.

————. 1996. "Columbia Plateau Indian Place Names: What Can They Teach Us?" *Journal of Linguistic Anthropology* 6(1):3–26.

Hyde, George E. 1968. *Life of George Bent*. Norman: University of Oklahoma Press.

Iverson, Peter. 1998. *"We Are Still Here": American Indians in the Twentieth Century*. Wheeling, IL: Harlan Davidson.

Jackson, A. T. 1938. *Picture-Writing of Texas Indians*. Austin: University of Texas Press.

Jacobs, Melville. 1934. *Northwest Sahaptin Texts. Part 1*. Columbia University Contributions to Anthropology, 19. New York: Columbia University Press.

James, Edwin. 1822–1823. *Account of an Expedition from Pittsburgh to the Rocky Mountains*. 2 vols. Philadelphia: Carey and Lea.

Jennings, Vanessa. 2003. "The Tradition of the Kiowa Battle Dress and Aw-Day-Tah-Lee in My Family." *Whispering Wind* 32(3):8–16.

Jett, Stephen C. 2001. "The Navajo Homeland." In *Homelands: A Geography of Culture and Place in America*, ed. Richard E. Estaville, 168–183. Baltimore, MD: Johns Hopkins University Press.

John, Elizabeth A. H. 1985. "An Earlier Chapter of Kiowa History." *New Mexico Historical Review* 60:379–397.

Julyan, Robert. 1998. *The Place Names of New Mexico*. Albuquerque: University of New Mexico Press.

Kauley, Ernestine Kauahquo. 1975. "Kiowas, Children of the Sun." In *Pioneering in Kiowa County*, 9–18. Hobart, OK: Kiowa County Historical Society.

Kegley, George. 1980. *Archeological Investigations at Hueco Tanks State Park*. Austin: Texas Parks and Wildlife Department.

Keller, Robert H., and Michael Turek. 1996. *American Indians and National Parks*. Tucson: University of Arizona Press.

Kelley, Klara Bonsack, and Harris Francis. 1994. *Navajo Sacred Places*. Bloomington: Indiana University Press.

Kelley, Klara B., Harris Francis, and Peggy F. Scott. 1990. "Navajo Sacred Places on Hopi Partitioned Lands." Confidential MS on file, Navajo-Hopi Land Commission and Navajo Nation Historic Preservation Department, Window Rock, AZ.

Kendall, Bonnie. 1980. "Exegesis and Translation: Northern Yuman Names as Texts." *Journal of Anthropological Research* 36(3):261–273.

Keyser, James D. 2004. *Art of the Warriors: Rock Art of the American Plains*. Salt Lake City: University of Utah Press.

Keyser, James D., and Michael A. Klassen. 2001. *Plains Indian Rock Art*. Seattle: University of Washington Press.

Kiowa County Historical Society (KCHS). 1976. *Pioneering in Kiowa County*. Hobart, OK: Author.

Kirkland, Forrest, and W. W. Newcomb, Jr. 1967. *The Rock Art of Texas Indians*. Austin: University of Texas Press.

Kracht, Benjamin R. 1989. "Kiowa Religion: An Ethnohistorical Analysis of Ritual Symbolism, 1832–1987." Ph.D. diss., Southern Methodist University, Dallas, TX.

———. 1992. "The Kiowa Ghost Dance, 1894–1916: An Unheralded Revitalization Movement." *Ethnohistory* 39(4):452–477.

———. 1997. "Kiowa Religion in Historical Perspective." *American Indian Quarterly* 21(1):15–33.

———. In press. *Kiowa Belief and Ritual, 1832–2005*. Lincoln: University of Nebraska Press.

Kroeber, Alfred E. 1916. "California Place Names of Indian Origin." *University of California Publications in American Archaeology and Ethnology* 12:31–69.

Lane, Belden C. 1988. *Landscapes of the Sacred: Geography and Narrative in American Spirituality*. New York: Paulist Press.

Lassiter, Luke E. 1998. *The Power of Kiowa Song*. Tucson: University of Arizona Press.

Lassiter, Luke E., Clyde Ellis, and Ralph Kotay. 2002. *The Jesus Road: Kiowas, Christianity, and Indian Hymns*. Lincoln: University of Nebraska Press.

Leonhardy, Frank C. 1966. Domebo: A Paleo-Indian Mammoth Kill in the Prairie-Plains. *Contributions of the Museum of the Great Plains*, no. 1. Lawton, OK.

Levy, Jerrold E. 1959. "After Custer: Kiowa Political and Social Organization from the Reservation Period to the Present." Ph.D. dissertation, Department of Anthropology, University of Chicago, Chicago.

———. 2001. "Kiowa." In *Handbook of North American Indians*. Vol. 13,

Plains, 907–925. Raymond J. DeMallie, vol. ed. Washington, DC: Smithsonian Institution Press.

Lewis, G. Malcolm. 1981. "Indian Maps." In *Old Trails and New Directions: Papers of the Third North American Fur Trade Conference*, ed. C. M. Judd and A. J. Ray, 9–23. Toronto: University of Toronto Press.

———. 1979. "The Indigenous Maps and Mapping of North American Indians." *The Map Collector* 9:25–32.

———. 1984. "Indian Maps: Their Place in the History of Plains Cartography." *Great Plains Quarterly* 4:91–108.

———. 1998. "Maps, Mapmaking, and Map Use by Native North Americans." In *The History of Cartography*, vol. 2, book 3, *Cartography in the Traditional African, American, Arctic, Australian, and Pacific Societies*, ed. David Woodward and G. Malcolm Lewis, 51–182. Chicago: University of Chicago Press.

Lewis, G. Malcolm, ed. 1998. *Cartographic Encounters: Perspectives on Native American Mapmaking and Map Use*. Chicago: University of Chicago Press.

Linford, Lawrence D. 2000. *Navajo Places: History, Legend, Landscape*. Salt Lake City: University of Utah Press.

Lone-Knapp, Faye. 2000. "Rez Talk: How Reservation Residents Describe Themselves." *American Indian Quarterly* 24(4):635–640.

Lounsbury, Floyd G. 1961. "Iroquois Place Names in the Champlain Valley." In *Report of the New York-Vermont Interstate Commission on the Lake Champlain Basin*, pp. 21–66. New York Legislative Document no. 9, Albany, NY.

Lynn-Sherow, Bonnie. 2004. *Red Earth: Race and Agriculture in Oklahoma Territory*. Lawrence: University of Kansas Press.

Mallory, Garrick. 1886. "Pictographs of the North American Indians: A Preliminary Paper." In *4th Annual Report of the Bureau of American Ethnology*. Washington, DC: Smithsonian Institution.

———. 1893. "Picture-Writing of the American Indians." In *10th Annual Report of the Bureau of American Ethnology*. Washington, DC: Smithsonian Institution.

Marcy, Randolph B. 1849. *Report of Capt. R. B. Marcy's Route from Fort Smith to Santa Fe*. 31st Cong., 1st Sess., Sen. Exec. Doc. 64, 169–227.

Marriott, Alice. 1945. *The Ten Grandmothers*. Norman: University of Oklahoma Press.

———. 1968. *Kiowa Years: A Study in Culture Impact*. New York: Macmillan.

Marriott, Alice, and Carol Rachlin. 1968. *American Indian Mythology*. New York: Thomas Crowell.

Martineau, LaVan. 1973. *The Rocks Begin to Speak*. Las Vegas, NV: KC Publications.

Matthiessen, Peter. 1979. *Indian Country*. New York: Penguin Books.

Mayor, Adrienne. 2005. *Fossil Legends of the First Americans*. Princeton, NJ: Princeton University Press.

McAllister, J. Gilbert. 1935. "Kiowa-Apache Social Organization." Ph.D. dissertation, Department of Anthropology, University of Chicago, Chicago.

———. 1965. "The Four Quartz Rocks Medicine Bundle of the Kiowa-Apache." *Ethnology* 4(2):210–224.

McCoy, Ronald. 1987. *Kiowa Memories: Images from Indian Territory, 1880*. Morning Star Gallery, Santa Fe, NM.

McKenzie, Parker P. n.d.-a. *Rainy Mountain Kiowa Indian Baptist Church Membership Roster, 1/22/1893–4/8/1928*. Author's copy.

———. n.d.-b. *Kiowa Names of Indian Tribes*. Author's copy.

———. n.d.-c. *Kiowa Names of Birds and Reptiles*. Author's copy.

———. n.d.-d. *Kiowa Names of Mammals*. Author's copy.

Meadows, William C. 1995. "Remaining Veterans: A Symbolic and Comparative Ethnohistory of Southern Plains Indian Military Societies." Ph.D. diss., University of Oklahoma, Norman.

———. 1999. *Kiowa, Apache and Comanche Military Societies: Enduring Veterans, 1800 to the Present*. Austin: University of Texas Press.

———. 2006. "Black Goose's Map of the Kiowa-Comanche-Apache Reservation in Oklahoma Territory." *Great Plains Quarterly* 26(4):265–282.

———. In press. *Kiowa Military Societies: Ethnohistory and Ritual*.

———. n.d.-a. "New Linguistic Data on Kiowa Origins." Unpublished manuscript.

———. n.d.-b. "Kiowa Naming Practices and Personal Names." Unpublished manuscript

Meadows, William C., and Kenny Harragarra. 2007. "The Kiowa Drawings of Gotebo (1847–1927): A Self-Portrait of Cultural and Religious Transition." *Plains Anthropologist* 52(202):229–244.

Meadows, William C., and Parker P. McKenzie. 2001. "The Parker P. McKenzie Kiowa Orthography: How Written Kiowa Came Into Being." *Plains Anthropologist* 46(177):233–248.

Merrill, William L., Marian Kaulaity Hansson, Candace Greene, and Frederick J. Reuss. 1997. *A Guide to the Kiowa Collections at the Smithsonian Institution*. Smithsonian Contributions to Anthropology, no. 40. Washington, DC: Smithsonian Institution Press.

Milne, Courtney. 1994. *Spirit of the Land: Sacred Places in Native North America*. New York: Viking Books.

———. 1999. *Sacred Places in North America: A Journey into the Medicine Wheel*. New York: Stewart, Tabori, and Chang.

Mishkin, Bernard. 1940. *Rank and Warfare among the Plains Indians*. American Ethnological Society Monograph 3. New York: J. J. Augustin.

Momaday, N. Scott. 1969. *The Way to Rainy Mountain*. Albuquerque: University of New Mexico Press.

———. 1976a. "A First American Views His Land." *National Geographic* 150(1):13–18.

———. 1976b. *The Names: A Memoir*. New York: Harper and Row.

Mooney, James. 1896. "The Ghost Dance Religion and the Sioux Outbreak of 1890." Part 2. In *Fourteenth Annual Report of the Bureau of American Ethnology, 1892–93*, 641–1110. Washington, DC: Smithsonian Institution Press.

———. 1898. "Calendar History of the Kiowa Indians." In *Seventeenth Annual Report of the Bureau of American Ethnology*. Washington, DC: Smithsonian Institution Press.

———. 1907. *The Cheyenne Indians. American Anthropological Association, Memoirs* I. (Reprint, New York: Krauss Reprint Corporation, 1964.)

———. 1911. "In Kiowa Camps." *Proceedings of the Mississippi Valley Historical Association* 3:43–57.

Moore, John H. 1987. *The Cheyenne Nation: A Social and Demograhic History*. Lincoln: University of Nebraska Press.

Moore, Steven C. 1991. "Sacred Sites and Public Lands." In *Handbook of American Indian Religious Freedom*, ed. Christopher Vecsey, 81–99. New York: Crossroad Publishing.

Morgan, E. Buford. 1973. *The Wichita Mountains: Ancient Oasis of the Prairies*. Waco, TX: Texian Press.

Morris, John W., Charles R. Goins, and Edwin C. McReynolds. 1986. *Historical Atlas of Oklahoma*, 3rd ed., updated from the 1980 Census. Norman: University of Oklahoma Press.

Nabokov, Peter. 2006. *Where the Lightning Strikes: The Lives of American Indian Sacred Places*. New York: Viking Press.

Nabokov, Peter, and Lawrence Loendorf. 2004. *Restoring a Presence: American Indians and Yellowstone National Park*. Norman: University of Oklahoma Press.

Nostrand, Richard L. 1980. "The Hispano Homeland in 1900." *Annals, Association of American Geographers* 70(3):382–396.

———. 1992. *The Hispano Homeland*. Norman: University of Oklahoma Press.

———. 1993. "The New-Mexico-Centered Hispano Homeland." *Journal of Cultural Geography* 13(2):47–60.

Nostrand, Richard L., and Lawrence E. Estaville, Jr. 1993. "Introduction: The Homeland Concept." *Journal of Cultural Geography* 13(2):1–4.

Nye, Colonel Wilber S. 1937. *Carbine and Lance: The Story of Old Fort Sill.* Norman: University of Oklahoma Press.

———. 1962. *Bad Medicine and Good: Tales of the Kiowas.* Norman: University of Oklahoma Press.

Oklahoma Department of Tourism and Recreation (ODTR). 1991. *Oklahoma Great Plains Country Adventure Guide.* Oklahoma City, OK: Author.

Palmer, Gus, Jr. 2003. *Telling Stories the Kiowa Way.* Tucson: University of Arizona Press.

Palo Duro Canyon. 2004. Palo Duro Canyon State Park Interpretive Guide. Austin: Texas Parks and Wildlife Foundation.

Parks, Douglas R. 2001. "Pawnee." In *Handbook of North American Indians.* Vol. 13, *Plains,* 515–547. Raymond J. DeMallie, vol. ed. Washington, DC: Smithsonian Institution, Government Printing Office.

Parks, Douglas R., and Waldo R. Wedel. 1985. "Pawnee Geography: Historical and Sacred." *Great Plains Quarterly* 5(3):143–176.

Parsons, Elsie Clews. 1929. *Kiowa Tales.* Memoirs of the American Folk-Lore Society 22. New York.

Pearce, T. M., ed. 1965. *New Mexico Place Names: A Geographical Dictionary.* Albuquerque: University of New Mexico Press.

Peterson, Karen Daniels. 1968. *Howling Wolf: A Cheyenne Warrior's Graphic Interpretation of His People.* Palo Alto, CA: American West.

———. 1971. *Plains Indian Art from Fort Marion.* Norman: University of Oklahoma Press.

Pool, William C. 1975. *A Historical Atlas of Texas.* Austin, TX: Encino Press.

Pope, John. 1855. *Report of Exploration of a Route for the Pacific Railroad from the Red River to the Rio Grande,* 33rd Congress, 2nd Sess., House Executive Document No. 91, pp. 53–54. Washington, DC: Government Printing Office.

Price, Monroe E. 1973. *Law and the American Indians: Readings, Notes, and Cases.* Indianapolis: Bobbs-Merrill. Reprint, Charlottesville, NC: Mitchie Co., 1983.

Rainy Mountain Kiowa Indian Baptist Church (RMKIBC). 1992. *Rainy*

Mountain Kiowa Indian Baptist Church Centennial Booklet. Mountain
View, OK: Author.

Richardson, Jane. 1940. *Law and Status among the Kiowa Indians.*
American Ethnological Society Monograph 1. New York: J. J. Augustin.

Ronda, James P. 1987. "A Chart in His Way: Indian Cartography and the
Lewis and Clark Expedition." In *Mapping the North American Plains,*
ed. Frederick C. Luebke, Frances W. Kaye, and Gary E. Moulton.
Norman: University of Oklahoma Press.

Roemer, Kenneth M., ed. 1988. *Approaches to Teaching Momaday's "The
Way to Rainy Mountain."* New York: MLA.

Ross, Norman A., ed. 1973. *Index to the Decisions of the Indian Claims
Commission.* New York: Clearwater Press.

Ross, Thomas E., and Tyrel G. Moore, eds. *A Cultural Geography of North
American Indians.* Boulder, CO: Westview Press.

Rundstrom, Robert A. 1990. "A Cultural Interpretation of Inuit Map
Accuracy." *The Geographical Review* 80(2):155–168.

Rundstrom, Robert A., Douglas Duer, Kate Berry, and Dick Winchell.
2000. "Recent Geographical Research on Indians and Inuit in the
United States and Canada." *American Indian Culture and Research
Journal* 24(2):85–110.

Rydjord, John. 1968. *Indian Place-Names: Their Origin, Evolution, and
Meanings, Collected in Kansas from the Siouan, Algonquian, Shoshonean,
Caddoan, Iroquoian, and Other Tongues.* Norman: University of
Oklahoma Press.

Sage, Rufus B. 1846. *Scenes in the Rocky Mountains, and in Oregon,
California, New Mexico, Texas, and the Great Prairies; or Notes by the
Way, During an Expedition of Three Years, with a Description of the
Countries Passed Through, Including Their Geography, Geology, Resources,
Present Condition, and the Different Nations Inhabiting Them, by a New
Englander.* Boston: Wentworth. Reprint as *Rocky Mountain Life,*
Lincoln: University of Nebraska Press, 1982.

Saltanaviciute, Jurgita. 2000. "Native American Sacred Sites: Battle for
Protection." Master's thesis, University of Wyoming, Laramie.

Salzmann, Zdenek. 1998. *Language Culture & Society: An Introduction to
Linguistic Anthropology,* 2nd ed. Boulder, CO: Westview Press.

Sanmann, Kent. 1992. "Kiowa Place Names and Geographical Terms."
Geography 5990 seminar paper. University of Oklahoma. Copy in the
author's possession.

Sapir, Edward. 1912. "Language and Environment." *American
Anthropologist* 14(2):226–242.

Scarberry-Garcia, Susan. 1996. "N(avarre) Scott Momaday." In *Handbook of Native American Literature,* ed. Andrew Wiget, 463–477. Garland Reference Library of the Humanities, vol. 1815. New York: Garland Publishing.

Schama, Simon. 1995. *Landscape and Memory.* New York: Alfred A. Knopf.

Schnell, Steven M. 1993. "The Kiowa Homeland in Oklahoma." Master's thesis, Department of Geography, University of Kansas, Lawrence.

———. 2000. "The Kiowa Homeland in Oklahoma." *The Geographical Review* 90(2):155–176.

———. 2001. "The Kiowa Homeland in Oklahoma." In *Homelands: A Geography of Culture and Place across America,* ed. Richard L. Nostrand and Lawrence E. Estaville, 139–154. Baltimore, MD: Johns Hopkins University Press.

Schoolcraft, Henry R. 1844. "Aboriginal Names and Geographic Territory of the State of New York." *Proceedings of the New York State Historical Society.*

Schubnell, Mattias. 1985. *N. Scott Momaday: The Cultural and Literary Background.* Norman: University of Oklahoma Press.

Shanley, Kathryn, W. 1998. "'Writing Indian': American Indian Literature and the Future of Native American Studies." In *Studying Native America: Problems and Prospects,* ed. Russell Thornton, 130–151. Madison: University of Wisconsin Press.

Sharp, Jay W. 1987. "A Hueco Tanks Engagement: The Apache Battle That Wasn't." *The Artifact* 25(1):81–93.

Shirk, George H. 1965. *Oklahoma Place Names.* Norman: University of Oklahoma Press.

Sonnichsen, Charles L. 1958. *The Mescalero Apaches.* Norman: University of Oklahoma Press.

Stahl, Robert J. 1978. "Farming Among the Kiowa, Comanche, Kiowa Apache, and Wichita." Ph.D. diss., Department of Anthropology, University of Oklahoma, Norman.

Stoffle, Richard W., David B. Halmo, and Diane E. Austin. 1997. "Cultural Landscapes and Traditional Cultural Properties: A Southern Paiute View of the Grand Canyon and Colorado River." *American Indian Quarterly* 21(2):229–249.

Stone, Richard. 1982. *First Encounters: Indian Legends of Devils Tower.* Belle Fourche, SD: Sand Creek Printing.

Sundstrom, Linea. 2003. "Sacred Islands: An Exploration of Religion and Landscape in the Northern Great Plains." In *Islands on the Plains: Ecological, Social, and Ritual Use of Landscapes,* ed. Marcel Kornfeld and Alan J. Osborn, 258–300. Provo: University of Utah Press.

———. 2004. *Storied Stone: Indian Rock Art in the Black Hills Country.* Norman: University of Oklahoma Press.

———. 2005. Kiowa Place Names, from L. Sundstrom's Database of Northern Plains Indian Place Names. Courtesy of L. Sundstrom.

Sundstrom, Linea, Linda Olson, and Lawrence Loendorf. 2001. "Hulett South Site 48CK1544." *Wyoming Department of Transportation. State project #:PREB-S-061-00—038.* Loendorf and Associates.

Sutherland, Kay. 1991. *Rock Paintings at Hueco Tanks State Historical Park.* Austin: Texas Parks and Wildlife Department.

———. 1995. *Rock Paintings at Hueco Tanks State Historical Park.* Austin: Texas Parks and Wildlife Department.

Sutton, Imre. 1975. *Indian Land Tenure: Bibliographical Essays and a Guide to the Literature.* New York: Clearwater.

———. 2002. "Cartographic Review of Indian Land Tenure and Territoriality: A Schematic Approach." *American Indian Culture and Research Journal* 26(2):63–114.

Sutton, Imre, ed. 1985. *Irredeemable America: The Indians' Estate and Land Claims.* Albuquerque: University of New Mexico Press. Published in cooperation with the Institute for Native American Studies, University of New Mexico, Albuquerque.

Tennant, Alan. 1980. *The Guadalupe Mountains of Texas.* Austin: University of Texas Press.

Thiessen, Thomas D., W. Raymond Wood, and A. Wesley Jones. 1979. "The Sitting Rabbit 1907 Map of the Missouri River in North Dakota." *Plains Anthropologist* 24(Pt. 1):145–167.

Thomas, Alfred B., trans.-ed. 1941. *Theodoro de Croix and the Northern Frontier of New Spain, 1776–1783.* From the original documents in the Archives of the Indies, Seville. Norman: University of Oklahoma Press.

Thornton, Thomas F. 1995a. "Place and Being among the Tlingit." Ph.D. diss., Department of Anthropology, University of Washington, Seattle.

———. 1995b. "Tlingit and Euro-American Toponymies in Glacier Bay." In *Proceedings of the Third Glacier Bay Science Symposium, 1993,* 294–301. Anchorage, AK: National Park Service.

———. 1997. "Anthropological Studies of Native American Place Naming." *American Indian Quarterly* 21:209–228.

Toll, Oliver W. 1962. *Arapaho Names and Trails: A Report of a 1914 Pack Trip.* Privately published.

Tokacut (a.k.a. Hall, Harlan). 1995. *Remember We Are Kiowas: 101 Indian Stories.* 1st Books Library. Dallas, TX: Writers Write.

———. 2002. *A Kothondo: 101 Kiowa Indian Poems.* 1st Books Library. Dallas, TX: Writers Write.

Townsend-Gault, Charlotte. 1994. "Northwest Coast Art: The Culture of Land Claims." *American Indian Quarterly* 18:445–467.

Trimble, Martha Scott. 1973. *N. Scott Momaday*. Boise State College Western Writers Series, No. 9. Boise, ID.

Tuan, Yi-Fu. 1975. "Geopiety: A Theme in Man's Attachment to Nature and to Place." In *Geographies of the Mind: Essays in Historical Geosophy in Honor of John Kirtland Wright*, ed. David Lowenthal and Martyn J. Bowden, 11–40. New York: Oxford University Press.

Vannette, Walter M., and Reed Tso. 1988. *Navajo Religious Use of the 1934 Reservation Area*. Expert Witness Report, Brown and Bain, P.A., Phoenix, and the Navajo Nation Department of Justice, Window Rock, AZ.

Velie, Alan R., ed. 1991. *American Indian Literature: An Anthology*, rev. ed. Norman: University of Oklahoma Press.

Viola, Herman J. 1998. *Warrior Artists: Historic Cheyenne and Kiowa Indian Ledger Art Drawn by Making Medicine and Zotom*. Washington, DC: National Geographic Society.

Walker, Deward E., Jr. 1988. "American Indian Sacred Geography." In *American Indian Religious Freedom, Special Supplement*. New York: Association on American Indian Affairs.

———. 1991. "Protection of American Indian Sacred Geography." In *Handbook of American Indian Religious Freedom*, ed. Christopher Vecsey, 100–115. New York: Crossroad.

Warhus, Mark. 1997. *Another America: Native American Maps and the History of Our Land*. New York: St. Martin's Press.

Waterman, Thomas T. 1920. "Yurok Geography." *University of California Publications in American Archaeology and Ethnology* 16:177–314.

———. 1922. "The Geographic Names Used by the Indians of the Pacific Coast." *Geographic Review* 12(2):175–194.

———. n.d. [Untitled MS on place naming.] Ms on file, Anthropology Archives, Berkeley, Bancroft Library, University of California, Berkeley.

Watson, Editha L. 1964. *Navajo Sacred Places*. Window Rock, AZ: Navajo Tribal Museum.

Webb, Walter Prescott. 1931. *The Great Plains*. Boston: Ginn and Co.

Whipple, Lieut. Amiel Weeks. 1855. *Report of Explorations for a Railway: Near the Thirty-Fifth Parallel of Latitude, from the Mississippi River to the Pacific*, vol. 1. Washington, DC: U.S. Army Corps of Topographical Engineers.

———. 1856. *Report of Explorations for a Railway: Near the Thirty-Fifth*

Parallel of Latitude, from the Mississippi River to the Pacific, vol. 2.
Washington, DC: U.S. Army Corps of Topographical Engineers.

Wilkins, David E. 2002. *American Indian Politics and the American
Political System.* Lanham, MD: Rowman and Littlefield.

Willey, P. 1990. *Prehistoric Warfare on the Great Plains: Skeletal Analysis of
the Crow Creek Massacre Victims.* New York: Garland.

Wilson, George R. 1919. *Early Indiana Trails and Surveys.* Indianapolis:
Indiana Historical Society. Reprinted 1986.

Winchell, Dick, James Goodman, Stephen Jett, and Martha Henderson.
1994. "Geographic Research on Native Americans." In *Geography in
America,* ed. G. Gaile and C. Willmott. Colmbus, OH: Merrill Press.

Wichita Mountains Wildlife Refuge. 1997. *Wichita Mountains Wildlife
Refuge.* Albuquerque, NM: Southwest Natural and Cultural Heritage
Association.

Wood, Denis, with John Fels. 1992. *The Power of Maps.* New York:
Guilford Press.

Woodard, Charles L. 1989. *Ancestral Voice: Conversations with N. Scott
Momaday.* Lincoln: University of Nebraska Press.

Films

Earth Island Institute. 2001. *In The Light of Reverence.* Sacred Land Film
Project of Earth Island Institute. Christopher McLeod, producer.

Idaho Power. 2001. *The River Has Many Stories: A Native Perspective of
Cultural Resources in Hells Canyon.* Boise: Idaho Power; Portland, OR:
Hare in the Gate Productions.

Rowell, Donna M. 2004. *Vanishing Link: My Spiritual Return to the Kiowa
Way.* A Film by Donna M. Rowell. DigiGlyphs Inc.

Internet Sources

Archaeological Institute of America, *Online News,* February 25, 1997
(www.archaeology.org/online/news/hueco.html).

Handbook of Texas Online,
January 19, 2008 (www.tsha.utexas.edu/handbook).

Hueco Tanks State Historical Park—Desert USA (www.desertusa.com/
magoo/may/stories/hueco.html). Texas Park and Wildlife Newsstand,
"Computer-Enhanced Photos Uncover Hueco." Tanks Rock Art,
1996–2008 (www.tpwd.state.tx.us/news).

Medicine Lodge, 1994. Peace Treaty, Medicine Lodge, Kansas. Dede

Morgan-Vick, "Peace Treaty: The Product of a Town Working Together" (222.cyberlodg.com/mlcity/peacetreaty.html).

Onlymp.com, "Petroglyph Paintings From Hueco Tanks—Texas," 2008 (www.onlymp.com/gallery/petro/texas/hueco).

Public Service Company of Oklahoma, news release, March 2 and 8, 2005, Blue Canyon II Project Summary, Wind Power For PSO Customers (www.psoklahoma.com/news).

Sharp, Jay, "Konate's Staff," 2005 (www.desertusa.com/mag05/jun/konate.html).

Index